THE POLITICS OF NON-STATE
SOCIAL WELFARE

D1557028

THE POLITICS OF NON-STATE SOCIAL WELFARE

EDITED BY MELANI CAMMETT AND LAUREN M. MACLEAN

Cornell University Press
Ithaca and London

First published 2014 by Cornell University Press
First printing, Cornell Paperbacks, 2014

Printed in the United States of America

Library of Congress Cataloging-in-Publication Data

The politics of non-state social welfare / edited by Melani Cammett and Lauren M. MacLean.
    pages cm
Includes bibliographical references and index.
ISBN 978-0-8014-5264-2 (cloth : alk. paper)—
ISBN 978-0-8014-7928-1 (pbk. : alk. paper)
1. Charities—Political aspects. 2. Non-governmental organizations—Political aspects. 3. Human services—Political aspects. 4. Public welfare—Political aspects. I. Cammett, Melani Claire, 1969– editor of compilation. II. MacLean, Lauren M., editor of compilation. III. Gough, Ian. Mapping social welfare regimes beyond the OECD. Contains (work):
    HV70.P65   2014
    361.7—dc23   2013043157

Cornell University Press strives to use environmentally responsible suppliers and materials to the fullest extent possible in the publishing of its books. Such materials include vegetable-based, low-VOC inks and acid-free papers that are recycled, totally chlorine-free, or partly composed of nonwood fibers. For further information, visit our website at www.cornellpress.cornell.edu.

Cloth printing   10 9 8 7 6 5 4 3 2 1
Paperback printing   10 9 8 7 6 5 4 3 2 1

Contents

Acknowledgments

This collaboration was inspired early on by the recognition of our mutual interests during and after graduate school at the University of California, Berkeley. After many provocative conversations comparing what was the same or different about the politics of social welfare in different corners of Africa and the Middle East, we seized the opportunity provided by the Harvard Academy, where Melani Cammett was a fellow, to organize an international workshop, "The Politics of Non-state Social Welfare." The conference was held at Harvard and included about thirty scholars working in this emerging research area from a wide range of diverse disciplinary backgrounds and empirical contexts. The intellectually charged discussion at the workshop pushed us to focus the book on the range of non-state provision in the developing world. We are excited to further the dialogue among scholars working in this area and hope that our collective thinking in this volume spurs the development of future research.

Some of the book's contributors have acknowledged separately the scholars, colleagues, and communities that helped them to collect data, interpret, and write their chapters, but here we thank the many colleagues who have provided crucial support and encouragement for the overall book project. To begin, we would like to thank the Harvard Academy for its generous support of the "Politics of Non-state Social Welfare" conference. In particular, we are grateful for the intellectual engagement of Jorge Dominguez and the indispensible programmatic and logistical support of Larry Winnie and Kathleen Hoover. We would also like to acknowledge the passionate and critical engagement of all of our conference presenters and discussants, particularly

Bob Kaufman, who helped us to synthesize some of the core insights of the papers. Since the conference, many colleagues have read and critiqued various chapters and drafts of the manuscript. Special thanks go to Danielle Carter, Julia Lynch, Jim McGuire, Joan Nelson, and Hillel Soifer, as well as the two anonymous reviewers of and the contributors to a 2010 special issue of *Studies in Comparative International Development*, in which we presented some initial ideas on non-state welfare provision. We are also grateful for the suggestions we received at meetings of the American Political Science Association, the Midwest Political Science Association, and other conferences and workshops, as well as the feedback of the contributors to this volume. The process of working with Roger Haydon and the outstanding external reviewers at Cornell University Press helped us to develop the analytical framework and strengthen the overall coherence of the volume. Along the way, several students provided terrific research assistance by investigating relevant literature as well as digging up elusive statistics, including Andrea Dillon, Isaac Jabola, Sophia Manuel, and Isaac Schlecht. We are grateful for the support of the Office of the Vice Provost for Research at Indiana University, which provided funds to assist in the publication of this book.

As always, we could not do any of this work without the love, support, and happy distractions provided by our families, Jason, Jasper, Skylar, and Benjamin MacLean, and Angelo, Alex, Lena, and Nikos Manioudakis.

THE POLITICS OF NON-STATE
SOCIAL WELFARE

Introduction

Melani Cammett and Lauren M. MacLean

Non-state actors supply basic social services to ordinary people even more extensively than states in many countries around the world. Non-state providers (NSPs) often have deep historical roots in their respective polities and, in some cases, predate the establishment of modern states by centuries. Although the role of non-state actors in social welfare provision is not new, their numbers, diversity, and importance have grown tremendously over the past several decades. In sub-Saharan Africa, individuals now appeal to both extended family members and friends to help pay hospital fees, and a rapidly increasing number of nongovernmental organizations (NGOs) launch welfare initiatives as states around the continent cut subsidies and reform social programs. Likewise, in parts of Latin America, and indeed in most other developing regions, international and domestic NGOs, and, increasingly, private firms are key suppliers of social welfare[1] in both urban and rural communities. In the Middle East, North Africa, and South and Southeast Asia, in particular, Islamist and other sectarian and religious organizations play a crucial role in providing social services, which many observers highlight to explain their popularity. Even in the United States, where the welfare state is far more developed, secular NGOs and faith-based organizations are critical components of social safety nets.

The importance of NSPs in social welfare regimes contradicts expectations about the ever-expanding role of the state in shaping the livelihoods and social

---

1. In this volume, we use the term "social welfare" to refer to health, education, and support for the poor and disadvantaged groups. We define social welfare in more detail below.

security of citizens. Ever since Otto von Bismarck instituted social welfare programs in Prussia in the 1880s, and perhaps even earlier, Western governments have provided an expanding number of social services to their citizens. Many assumed that with industrialization and economic growth, developing countries would eventually follow suit.

But, now, at the beginning of the twenty-first century, it seems that we are living in a new world. Just as states are no longer fighting all the wars (e.g., 9/11 and Israel's war with Hezbollah in Lebanon), states no longer—or, in some cases, never did—provide many social welfare services. For the past three decades, the World Bank, the International Monetary Fund, and other donors have advocated economic reforms that require states to reduce their roles while NGOs, private companies, community groups, and other non-state actors increasingly provide public goods and basic welfare. Meanwhile, many developing countries have also liberalized their authoritarian political regimes over the past several decades. Thus, neoliberal globalization and democratic openings have combined to create new spaces for non-state actors to emerge, operate, and grow.

The justifications for expanding non-state welfare provision generally emphasize technical advantages or efficiency gains. We show in this book, however, that the shift towards non-state social welfare provision is deeply political. The relationship between states and citizens is fundamentally transformed as social service delivery migrates away from governments to a host of other non-state providers, including churches, international relief agencies, and ethnic or sectarian groups, or as non-state actors consolidate and expand their existing welfare activities. Non-state provision is not merely a neutral, technocratic solution to a policy problem; it can have profound effects on political life.

This book thus places the *politics* of non-state social welfare front and center: What are the *political consequences* of non-state social welfare? Specifically, we highlight the potential ramifications of non-state provision for three important outcomes, including equitable and sustainable access to welfare, accountability for citizens, and state capacity. This book demonstrates a wide range of variation in all three of these outcomes.

First, equitable and sustainable access to welfare is an important outcome with highly tangible implications for citizens. Policymakers the world over claim that they prioritize the improvement of general well-being by ensuring that all citizens are able to meet their basic needs and pursue economic and social advancement. From a normative standpoint, a rich tradition of scholarship in political theory debates the "common good," highlighting the centrality of equitable access to social services and the ability of citizens to achieve minimum living standards (Aquinas 1265–74; Barnes 1984; Rawls 1971). Thus, the equity of access to basic services is an important policy goal, but non-state provision has diverse effects on this outcome. As chapter 2 elaborates, few non-state providers have either the resources or the mandate to provide broad, equitable access to their services. Even with the best of intentions on the part of staff members and administrators, many NSPs lack the material resources and capabilities to serve broadly or sustainably (Wood 1997). Furthermore, some NSPs include restrictive eligibility criteria, whether in their formal rules or informal practices, ensuring that their pools of beneficiaries do not include all needy households in their catchment areas.

Of course, the limitations of NSPs should not suggest that the welfare state automatically ensures fully equitable access to services. State-run programs are frequently mismanaged or rife with clientelism, thereby restricting access to public benefits. In theory, however, the state is the only institution that can be mandated to provide universal access to services whether through its own agencies or third-party providers.

A growing body of research points to the importance of our second outcome of interest, accountability for citizens (Cornwall, Lucas, and Pasteur 2000; Gaventa and Cornwall 2000; Kilby 2006). Development agencies and international donors, too, increasingly recognize the value of accountability mechanisms in protecting the rights and obligations of democratic citizenship (Department for International Development 2000; World Bank 2007). How does non-state provision affect the avenues that citizens use to seek accountability for adequate social welfare services? Several of the book's chapters reveal how accountability may be very difficult when citizens face a fragmented scene of multiple non-state providers. The politics of accountability may hence become more intensely charged and complex for citizens to navigate on a day-to-day basis.

Finally, we contend that the political consequences of non-state provision can affect state capacity, which is increasingly linked to a variety of important political and economic outcomes such as democratic stability and quality as well as economic growth and development (Acemoglu 2005; Evans 1995; Kohli 2004; Mahoney 2010; Soifer 2013). Non-state social welfare can have both positive and negative effects on the development of capable states. With effective non-state partners, the state is able to free up resources to devote to other policy concerns and faces fewer challenges to its role as the "steward" of well-functioning welfare regimes. States with higher levels of regulatory capacity in the first place are more likely to ensure that NSPs play a constructive and effective role in welfare regimes.[2] For less capable states, however, the increase in the short-term resources for social development afforded by non-state provision may be outweighed by a decline in the longer-term capacity of the state to provide or regulate social welfare.

NSPs are highly variegated, with radically different consequences for citizens and states in the polities where they operate. What explains this variation

---

2. For example, it is well established that public stewardship is essential for health care systems that promote public health and provide efficient and equitable care (World Health Organization 2000). This claim also accords with research on the importance of state capacity for economic development (Acemoglu 2005; Chaudhry 1993; Mahoney 2010).

in the political consequences of non-state provision? We argue that two main sets of factors condition the political effects: (1) the type of non-state provider (NSP); and (2) its relationship to the state. In chapter 2, we highlight the four most relevant aspects of NSP form: the level of formalization; the locus of operation; the extent of profit orientation; and the nature of eligibility criteria. We then theorize how varying levels of NSP and state capacity create four different modes of NSP-state relations, ranging from appropriation (low NSP and low state capacity) and substitution (high NSP and low state capacity) to state domination (low NSP capacity and high state capacity) and coproduction or delegation (high NSP and state capacity). Based on these conceptualizations of NSP type and state-NSP relations, in chapter 2 we present several propositions about the political consequences of non-state welfare provision, which are examined in the following empirical chapters and then assessed in the conclusion. The propositions suggest how specific characteristics of NSPs combine with distinct modes of NSP-state relations to produce more positive or negative outcomes for citizen access, accountability, and, ultimately, long-term state capacity.

To assess these propositions, the contributors to this volume focus on a range of distinct types of NSPs with different relationships to the state. Each chapter addresses how non-state welfare by specific types of NSPs affects access to services, accountability for citizens, or state capacity, or all three, in the countries that they cover. Although we do not theorize these three key outcomes as contiguous links in a causal chain, several of the chapters reveal the complex interactions between the outcomes. Thus, when NSPs work in collaboration with public actors, and when they aim for *inclusive access* to their services, NSPs can actually serve to increase the *capacity of the state*. In answering these core questions about political consequences, the chapters also address prior questions: When and why does non-state welfare provision emerge and become consolidated? Many of the chapters highlight how the history and dynamics of non-state provision over time are critical for understanding contemporary politics.

To date, most research on the welfare state focuses almost exclusively on the advanced industrialized economies (Esping-Andersen 1990; Skocpol 1992; Pierson 1994; Iversen 2005; Lynch 2006). But these studies have limited applicability to the developing world, where democracies are less consolidated, state institutions are weaker, and informal, rural labor markets predominate (Gough et al., 2004). Some recent studies analyze welfare regimes in the developing world, but focus mainly on state policies and public rather than non-state actors (Kaufman and Segura-Ubiergo 2001; Rudra 2002, 2007; Mares 2003; Kaufman and Nelson 2004a; Haggard and Kaufman 2008; Brooks 2009; Seekings 2009; Mares and Carnes 2009). Although Gough et al. (2004) emphasize that "informal security" outside of the state is an important aspect of welfare regimes in much of the developing world, their approach clusters together highly heterogeneous countries into the same categories and does not unpack the role of non-state actors in service provision. This leaves important questions unanswered about the distinct consequences of various welfare regimes across the developing world. More policy-oriented work on development highlights the importance of non-state actors in social protection. However, much of this literature focuses narrowly on the role of NGOs (Fox and Brown 1998; Brown and Kalegaonkar 2002; Mercer 2003; Brinkerhoff 2007; Teamey 2007; Brinkerhoff 2008; Heins 2008) rather than the full array of organizations and institutions with which ordinary people interact to meet their basic needs. The analytical framework and collective contributions of this volume move beyond NGOs to interrogate the politics of non-state provision by a wider range of non-state providers.[3]

To capture the most prevalent welfare systems in the developing world—including Asia, Africa, Latin America, and the Middle East—we focus on a large, middle-range set of countries where public welfare programs are limited and non-state and informal providers dominate.[4] We intentionally exclude the most highly institutionalized welfare state regimes such as South Korea or Tunisia (Ben Romdhane 2006), which have received the most extensive attention (Haggard and Kaufman 2008). We also exclude weak and collapsing states in Africa, Asia, and Latin America, such as Somalia, Afghanistan, Palestine, or Haiti, from the analysis. Within this predominant middle category of cases, we find important sources of variation, particularly regarding the types of NSPs that provide or shape access to social welfare. To highlight parallels between welfare regimes in developing and more industrialized countries, the book assesses the political consequences of non-state social service provision in the United States and Russia. Our analysis aims to capture the similarities and differences in non-state provision in the vast majority of developing countries and even in more developed contexts. This book assembles original comparative research on Africa, Central Asia, East Asia, South Asia, Latin America, the Middle East, Russia, and the United States.

In this day and age, when international donors, policymakers, and parts of the aid community increasingly promote and fund non-state welfare, it is critical to know more about the political ramifications of such non-state provision. The next section of this chapter presents working definitions of NSPs and the types of social welfare activities addressed in this volume. To contextualize the rise of NSPs in the late twentieth and early twenty-first centuries, we then

---

3. Von Benda-Beckmann and Kirsch's (1999) conceptualization of "social security systems" also includes a more comprehensive range of actors beyond state agencies, including churches, NGOs, family, and neighbors. Their work draws on scholarship in legal anthropology that highlights dichotomies between formal and informal or traditional and modern providers whereas we emphasize the distinction between state and non-state providers as pivotal. See also von Benda-Beckmann et al. (1988).

4. This category of countries corresponds to what Gough et al. (2004) refer to as "informal security regimes."

provide some overall estimates of the growing importance of and background on NSPs as key actors in development.

What Are NSPs?

Non-state providers refer to all providers outside of the public sector, including charitable and for-profit institutions, as well as domestic and international actors (Moran and Batley 2004). Of course, as we highlight in more detail here and in the subsequent chapters, the boundaries between the state and non-state providers are frequently blurred. Non-state providers may receive significant levels of state financing or even deliver services from state-owned offices and buildings.[5] Sometimes state civil servants are officially seconded to work for NSPs or, at other times, civil servants wear two hats, and have actually founded or work as active employees of local NGOs or faith-based organizations (FBOs) (Tripp 2001). In addition, states increasingly establish contracts with the private sector to provide services (Prager 1994). Despite these kinds of overlaps, NSPs nevertheless have their organizational origins and bases significantly outside of the state.

This volume focuses on the non-state provision of *social welfare*—and not "public goods provision" more generically. Social welfare may be viewed as one subtype of the broader category of public goods. As a result, we do not include here the provision of such public goods as roads and other transportation infrastructure, electricity, telecommunication networks, markets, police, and military security. In this book, we define social welfare provision as the direct delivery or indirect facilitation of services and programs that promote well-being and social security.[6] Essentially, this includes health, education, and support for vulnerable populations such as the elderly, disabled, and the poor. Notably, we conceptualize health broadly to include sanitation and water— which are often placed in the larger category of public goods—because these services have direct ramifications for health outcomes. Outbreaks of cholera, endemic in many developing countries and often in the wake of destructive conflict or natural disasters, illustrate unmistakably the salience of sanitation and water to public health and overall social welfare (Moran and Batley 2004). In many developing countries, the state's direct provision of social welfare is limited primarily to health and education services. In some countries, states may provide a modest range of pension, retirement, unemployment, and

---

5. Salamon and Sokolowski (1999) find that nonprofits in twenty-six countries around the world receive nearly 39% of their total revenues from public sector payments.

6. Whereas some scholars have promoted the concept of "well-being" (Gough et al. 2004) and others (Hirtz 1995; von Benda Beckmann et al. 1988) have advocated the concept of "social security," we maintain the concept of "social welfare" in order to facilitate a dialogue with other scholars working on the welfare state and to clarify that we are addressing social services beyond the income support for the aged also known as Social Security in the United States.

income or antipoverty programs for vulnerable populations, but this is more the exception than the rule. Given the relatively limited direct and even indirect roles of the state in welfare regimes in the developing world, the book examines holistically the origins, dynamics, and consequences of the non-state provision of social welfare.

The Rise and Resurgence of NSPs over Time

Since at least the 1980s, non-state providers have assumed an increasingly important role in the financing and direct provision of social welfare around the world. This trend toward increased NSP activity is in part related to a shift in the development policy prescriptions of major donor organizations such as the World Bank during an era of neoliberal globalization (World Bank 1997, 2004b; Klein and Hadjimichael 2003; Organization for Economic Cooperation and Development 2005).

Quantitative data on the levels of various types of NSPs over time are difficult to obtain and evaluate. Of all NSP types, international NGOs (INGOs) are most likely to be monitored on a global scale. The data on the numbers, geographic location, and funding of international non-governmental organizations reveal the expansion of this type of NSP activity around the globe.

First, the quantity of INGOs has grown exponentially over time, declining only slightly during the economic retraction of the Great Depression in the 1930s (Davies 2008; Sikkink and Smith 2002). Not only have the numbers of INGOs increased dramatically, from approximately one thousand in 1945 to over sixty thousand in 2007 (Davies 2008), but the geographic locations of these INGO headquarters have spread particularly rapidly outside of Europe. Finally, the activities of INGOs have expanded as they were reported to receive over $10 billion in funding from multilateral and bilateral donors in 2007 (Davies 2008).

Country-level data also suggests that *domestic* NGOs are also growing in numbers and spreading outside of capital cities. (See table I.1.)

In this volume, Jennifer N. Brass (chapter 5) points to the rapid increase in the numbers and activities of local NGOs in Kenya. In India, it is estimated that over 1.2 million NGOs now operate, with more than half based in rural areas (Society for Participatory Research in India 2002). Many of these organizations in India are not legally registered or incorporated as NGOs and would be better characterized as smaller, informal community based organizations (CBOs). Again, it is difficult to find comparable quantitative data on NGOs from earlier time periods but the available evidence suggests a significant expansion of NGOs and CBOs around the world.[7]

---

7. For example, Salamon and Sokolowski (1999) found that NGO employment grew by 24% in the early 1990s in the eight countries of their study where time series data was available. Notably, this rate of growth is three times faster than overall employment growth.

TABLE I.1.
Increase in NGOs in selected countries covered in empirical chapters, 1980–2010

	1980	1990	2000	2010
Argentina				15,800 (2012)
Azerbaijan			300	2,700–3,700 (2011)
Ghana	80	700	1,300	4,772
India		20,000–30,000 (1989)		3.3 million (2008)
Kazakhstan			6,000	36,815 (2011)
Kenya		250–400	4,000	6,000
Russia		30–40 (1987)	275,000	450,000–600,000 (2005)
Tanzania	25	137	3,000 (2001)	5,300

Sources:
    For Argentina: Centro Nacional de Organizaciones de la Comunidad (CENOC), "Listado de Organizaciones Inscriptas en nuestra Base de Datos," http://www.cenoc.gov.ar/busqueda.html, accessed July 31, 2012; Salamon 1994.
    For Azerbaijan: International Center for Not-for-Profit Law 2012; United States Agency for International Development 2000, 2011.
    For Ghana: Atingdui 1995; United States Agency for International Development 2011.
    For India: "Nongovernmental organizations," http://www.anand.to/india/ngo.html; http://www.slideshare.net/BrownBag/kumaran-on-ngos-in-india-presentation; Government of India 2009.
    For Kazakhstan: United States Agency for International Development 2000, 2011.
    For Kenya: Liston 2008; NGO Regulation Network, www.ngoregnet.org/Library/SUMMARY_OF_REGULATORY_SYSTEM_FOR_NGOS_IN_KENYA.doc.
    For Russia: Flounders 2006; Gvosdev 2005; United States Agency for International Development 2000, 2011.
    For Tanzania: International Center for Not-for-Profit Law, http://www.icnl.org/knowledge/ijnl/vol9iss1/art_7.htm; International Council on Social Welfare, http://www.icsw.org/doc/0011_2e_Barut_Eng.ppt; United Republic of Tanzania 2001; United States Agency for International Development 2010.

The role of for-profit firms as providers of social welfare also appears to have increased over the past several decades. Many studies indicate a marked expansion in the number of for-profit health clinics and schools. For example, a UNESCO background paper (Aga Khan Foundation 2007) shows that non-state primary school enrollments increased by 58% between 1991 and 2003 while public sector enrollments increased by only 10%. Notably, the percentage increase of private primary enrollments during the 1990s exceeded 100% in sub-Saharan Africa and what is termed the "Arab states." World Bank data indicates that private primary enrollments have increased at a remarkably accelerated rate across all world regions (except Organization for Economic Co-operation and Development members) between 2000 and 2010. This volume reveals that the role of for-profit firms in social welfare is not always neatly distinguished from the state and extends well beyond the health and education sectors. In chapter 10, Alejandra Mizala and Ben Ross Schneider show the political consequences when the central state allocates funding for public and private providers in a national school voucher system in Chile. In chapter 4, Alison Post highlights how the private sector management of water and sanitation systems has significant effects for the social welfare regime in Argentina.

For-profit firms have also increased their role through corporate social responsibility (CSR) initiatives (Contreras 2004; Hess, Rogovsky, and Dunfee 2002; Nwankwo, Phillips, and Tracey 2007). Data on the extent of social welfare expenditures through corporate social responsibility efforts was surprisingly unavailable at the country, regional, or global levels. Instead, most CSR reporting is submitted annually by individual firms. Elkington (2003) does find, however, that the number of firms engaged in reporting of their CSR activities is increasing over time (Center for Corporate Citizenship 2011). Based on a comparative analysis of foreign oil companies in Central Asia, Pauline Jones Luong's chapter presents a nuanced view of the role of multinational firms in welfare regimes (chapter 3).

The increasing role of ethnic and sectarian organizations has been heralded in case studies of diverse countries in Asia, Africa, and the Middle East (Cammett 2014; Cockburn 2008; Flanigan 2008; Hefner 2005; Shadid 2002; Thachil 2014), but little quantitative data exists that documents the provision of social welfare by such groups across developing countries or regions around the world. Melani Cammett's chapter on Lebanon in this volume (chapter 7) is based on one of the first nationally representative survey data sets that points to the significant role of sectarian parties and organizations in providing social welfare services.

The trends with less formal types of NSPs are even more difficult to evaluate quantitatively. The chapter by Anirudh Krishna (chapter 9) is based on an original survey that was one of the first systematic attempts to gather quantitative data on the role of informal brokers of government services in several states in India. Lauren M. MacLean's chapter (chapter 8) also draws from a unique primary data set to compare patterns in informal family and friendship networks of reciprocity in Ghana and Côte d'Ivoire. Other scholars (Abu Sharkh and Gough 2010) have used World Bank data on international remittances to serve as a proxy for the extent of international family and friendship networks cross-nationally around the world. Table I.2 shows the available data on remittances over time from several of the countries highlighted in the book.

These data reveal the growing importance of international flows of remittances, but they are limited in two important ways. First, it is unclear from the data to what extent remittance receipts were used to finance social welfare provision. And, second, the data miss entirely the internal flows of family and friendship support that occur within and between communities inside the borders of any one country.

TABLE I.2.
Increase in worker's remittances received in selected countries covered in empirical chapters, 1980-2008 (current $US)

	1980	1990	2000	2008
Argentina		41,700,000 (1993)	50,000,000	605,920,000
Azerbaijan			57,132,000	1,416,054,000
Ghana	500,000	6,000,000	32,400,000	126,104,960
India	2,755,694,909	2,351,865,793	12,738,252,470	49,143,759,987
Kazakhstan			63,872,440	120,150,116
Kenya		71,364,121 (1994)	584,854,297 (1999)	667,317,334
Lebanon			2,544,440,000 (2002)	5,774,482,500
Russia			362,700,000	801,910,000
Tanzania			5,300,000 (2001)	9,322,369

Source: World Bank Development Indicators (2010), http://databank.worldbank.org.

Overall, we conclude that the role of diverse non-state providers in the provision of social welfare is becoming increasingly important over time throughout the developing world. The rise of non-state provision, however, should not suggest that the state is absent or declining in all dimensions of welfare regimes. The reduction in public welfare *provision* over recent decades in many developing countries has been accompanied by a net increase in public social expenditures in some regions (Economic Commission for Latin America and the Caribbean 2010). State social expenditures on health and education in developing countries have frequently increased even as international donors have called for non-state actors to take on more of the burden of supplying basic services and infrastructure. For example, public health spending has increased as a percentage of GDP across all developing regions in the past decade, a trend that is mirrored in the wealthier OECD countries. Similarly, the pattern generally holds for public spending on education, although government expenditures dipped below 1980 levels in Africa during the 1990s before rebounding to a higher level in the late 2000s (Kaiser Family Foundation 2011; World Development Indicators 2013).

Yet, as the literature on the welfare state has shown (Esping-Andersen 1990; Mares 2003), data on expenditures provide only a limited view of the actual operation of welfare systems and may even present a misleading view. Just because aggregate public expenditures have increased does not mean that the additional funds were spent effectively or equitably (Kaufman and Nelson 2004a; Paes de Barros et al. 2009). Furthermore, strong state regulatory capacity or "stewardship" (Saltman and Ferroussier-Davis 2000; World Health Organization 2000) is essential to ensure that state and non-state providers offer high *quality* services in an efficient, impartial, and accountable fashion.

The Origins of Non-state Social Welfare

How can we understand the origins of non-state social welfare? Why is there so much attention to the role of non-state providers in developing countries now at the beginning of the twenty-first century? The dominant explanation in much of the economics literature is that non-state provision of social welfare emerges from *market failure* (Deaton 1992; Stiglitz 2005; Dercon 2002; Alderman and Paxson 1992). Essentially, in many developing countries markets do not exist for the provision of social services such as education and health. Private sector companies have little profit motive to provide services in areas with such endemic poverty. Not only is the supporting infrastructure of roads and electricity very poor in many developing countries but individual and household incomes are frequently low and highly variable, reducing the ability of individuals and families to pay fees for private services. According to this literature, widespread market failure results in the emergence of non-state actors such as domestic and international religious organizations, NGOs, CBOs, families, and friends stepping in to deliver and finance needed social services.

What these explanations miss, however, is politics. An economistic emphasis on the individual response to price signals in the contemporary time period obscures the influences of the structures of state and societal power and the hierarchies of inequality within these societies. This book's more multidisciplinary group of contributors highlight instead that the emergence of NSPs is not necessarily as fluid or automatic as an approach based on market failure implies.

The core issue is not simply the failure of markets, but rather, as an alternative perspective holds, *the failure of the state*. The tacit assumption shared by many of the scholars who point to market failure is that the state is equally incapable of providing social services, and, hence, state failure is an implicit component of the explanation for the origins of non-state provision (Kamat 2003; Gough et al. 2004). Indeed, some important new scholarship has emphasized the role of non-state providers in contexts of absolute state failure, such as in the eastern region of the Democratic Republic of the Congo (Seay forthcoming), Afghanistan (Jalali 2006; Rubin 2002), and Colombia (Koonings and Kruijt 2004). Although state failure may seize headlines and certainly portend grave human consequences worthy of sustained academic attention, state failure is actually rather rare in developing countries. Far more common than state failure is the persistence of state weakness (Jackson and Rosberg 1982; Rotberg 2003b; Rice and Patrick 2008). For this reason, we exclude failed or collapsed states from our empirical cases and focus instead on disaggregating the spectrum of weakness that predominates across Africa, Asia, Latin America, and the Middle East.

Some scholars have conceptualized state strength or weakness in terms of the state's level of macroeconomic development (Rice and Patrick 2008).[8] Hence, a particular state's poverty or lack of financial resources indicates weakness in its inability to finance or deliver extensive services for social welfare. And yet the empirical cases covered in this book suggest that non-state provision has originated in states that are both relatively rich and poor. We argue that the level of economic development is useful in understanding the relative scarcity of public provision in developing countries when compared to advanced in-dustrialized cases, but it does not illuminate effectively the significant variation between developing countries. Our collective analysis of mostly lower income countries reveals that state weakness goes well beyond the limitations of finan-cial resources. Instead, we highlight the relative strength or weakness of the state's regulatory capacity.

From a distinct vantage point, other scholars also emphasize the regulatory reach of the state by arguing that the adoption of neoliberal reforms by most developing countries since the early 1980s explains the origins of non-state provision of social welfare. Here, the literature emphasizes that the problem was not market or state failure, or even an overly weak state, but rather an excessively interventionist state that prevented free markets from operating efficiently (Bates 1981; World Bank 1981; Collier and Gunning 1999). The ini-tial solution advocated by the World Bank, the IMF, and other donors was to reduce the role of the state across the board (World Bank 1981). For the provision of social welfare, neoliberal reforms initially meant the elimination or drastic reduction of previous state subsidies for social services in the 1980s and 1990s and the introduction of user fees. By the beginning of the twenty-first century, many states had softened their earlier austerity policies by mak-ing basic health and education either free or more affordable to all (MacLean 2011b).This literature suggests that the overall reduction of the state's role in the provision of social welfare opened up a new space for non-state actors (Tripp 1997).

We agree that neoliberalism[9] as an ideology and set of policies has likely stimulated the growth of non-state provision over time. Ideological trends—especially in the early years of the 1980s and 1990s—called for state retrench-ment and replacement by private providers. The combination of these trends

8. While Susan Rice and Stewart Patrick's index combines indicators from four areas of state effectiveness (economic, political, security, and social welfare), they conclude that poverty is highly correlated with state weakness (Rice and Patrick 2008).

9. As Boaz and Gans-Morse (2009) point out, neoliberalism is a contested and vaguely de-fined term. In this volume, we use the term to mean a promarket ideology associated with policies to promote economic liberalization, privatization, deregulation of markets, and, most broadly, the promotion of private actors in the economy and society.

and conditionality imposed by international financial institutions helps to explain the rise and resurgence of NSPs in diverse regions of the developing world. But there are two problems with this argument. First, as noted above, public social spending actually *increased* on aggregate in many developing countries over the past few decades. In part this is due to domestic pressures and policies and in part to shifts over time in the policies of the international financial institutions (IFIs), especially the World Bank, which began to emphasize the importance of social safety nets in its lending policies from the 1990s onward (World Bank 1997, 2001/2002), Thus, as states were called on to reduce their engagement in direct service provision, state spending on social programs and related policies appears to have increased in some countries and regions. Second, the claim that promarket reforms explain the rise of NSPs does not explain variation across different country cases. For example, MacLean shows that even social welfare provision by families looks quite different on the ground in rural villages of Ghana and Côte d'Ivoire where the World Bank pushed the adoption of similar economic reform packages starting in the 1980s. She finds that Ghanaians reported more willingness to support extended family networks than their Ivoirian counterparts. Thus, the actual landscape of NSPs varies across different countries, depending on historical legacies of state and non-state provision in prior historical moments. As we discuss in chapter 2, these distinct configurations of NSPs have different consequences for the lives of ordinary citizens.

A related theoretical explanation for the origins of non-state provision might be the push for *decentralization* around the world from the 1980s and continuing until today (Bardhan and Mookherjee 2006; Crook and Manor 1998; Falleti 2010; Grindle 2007). Decentralization was frequently an essential component of neoliberal reform packages. When the state's role could not be eliminated entirely, state authority was shifted away from the center and delegated to a more local level (Grindle 2007; Ayee 1994). Like neoliberalism more generally, the decentralization of governance may increase the opportunity for non-state actors to play significant roles in the provision of social welfare. Where the literature on neoliberalism highlights an increased role for private businesses and international nongovernmental organizations in social provision, the scholarship on decentralization points to expanded social service financing and delivery at the local level by domestic NGOs, CBOs, and more informal social networks.[10] Hence, it is not simply the total failure of markets, or the absence of the state, which has stimulated the origination of

---

10. The decentralization trend also provides incentives to "contract out" social services to private firms and other NSPs. When responsibilities for certain sectors are decentralized without sufficient resources either from the national government or at the local level, local governments must find alternative, affordable arrangements for providing services. Contracting out shifts cost burdens away from local governments and has the added "benefit" of allowing them to avoid paying higher union wages for public employees. We thank Alison Post for this observation.

non-state provision of social welfare but, rather, the administrative reorganization of public welfare delivery at *multiple* levels that explains development outcomes. But here again this set of arguments has limits. Decentralization was commonly shared across all of the cases after the early 1980s, and yet significant variation exists in the patterns of non-state provision among different developing countries.

In contrast to all of these explanations for the relatively recent rise of NSPs, we note that non-state provision is *not* new. Many NSPs were established long ago and have extensive institutional legacies. For example, Michael Jennings (chapter 6) shows how faith-based organizations have been operating in Tanzania since at least the colonial era, and Cammett traces the origins of religious providers in Lebanon to the Ottoman and French Mandate periods. Thus explanations for the origins of NSPs cannot be located exclusively in market failure, state failure, recent promarket policies, or decentralization reforms beginning in the 1980s, even if deeply historically rooted provider types have evolved and adapted themselves in the twentieth and twenty-first centuries. The policy reforms of the past three decades may explain why non-state actors have gained in prominence more recently, but it is the particular historical context of state administrative power that explains variation in non-state social welfare in many developing countries. The book's contributors understand the origins of non-state provision to have occurred much earlier than the onset of the recent wave of globalization and thus emphasize how the specific histories of state formation have shaped the origins of NSPs around the world.

Overview of the Book

The next chapter supplements this brief survey by conceptualizing the variety of welfare regimes in sixty-five non-OECD countries, indicating the distinct roles of NSPs in each type. In chapter 2, we complement Ian Gough's survey of welfare regimes (chapter 1) by creating a detailed typology of NSPs that operate in the different welfare systems that he delineates. We spell out each type's potential degree of inclusiveness in allocating social benefits and conceptualize distinct patterns of state-NSP relations, ranging from collaborative to more competitive. We build on these analytical foundations to develop baseline hypotheses about the consequences of non-state provision for access to services, citizenship experiences of accountability, and state capacity. In brief, we emphasize that the degree of NSP inclusiveness and the nature of state-NSP relations are the primary determinants of the consequences of non-state provision.

In part I, each of the case studies is situated within our typology of NSPs. The chapters show how distinct types of NSPs stimulate divergent consequences for equitable and sustainable access to services, accountability, and state capacity.

Part II tests the limits of our argument by examining three cases that might not be expected to fit. In the chapters on Chile (chapter 10), Russia (chapter 11), and poor, urban neighborhoods in the United States (chapter 12), Alejandra Mizala and Ben Ross Schneider, Linda Cook, and Scott Allard, respectively, show how similar pockets of non-state provision exist even in places with relatively established welfare-state bureaucracies. On the one hand, these chapters reveal how segments of the population are forced to meet their basic needs through informal and insecure arrangements even in more developed welfare states. On the other hand, they highlight the importance of NSP-state relations and particularly the state's capacity to regulate non-state providers in order to enhance accountability to citizens and the quality of service provision.

In the concluding chapter of the book we integrate the theoretical and empirical material by assessing the degree to which the propositions presented in chapter 2 are borne out by the empirical case studies of distinct NSP types in the chapters in parts I and II. The conclusion explores the specific conditions under which non-state providers may *enhance* access to welfare, mechanisms of accountability, and state capacity by mediating between state agencies and communities to help implement development projects and welfare programs. Conversely, the chapter also builds on the empirical evidence presented in the chapters to show how non-state social welfare provision can have *adverse* political ramifications by inhibiting the development of state provision and undermining linkages between states and citizens in some contexts and historical moments.

1

Mapping Social Welfare Regimes beyond the OECD

Ian Gough

This chapter maps welfare regimes across countries that are not members of the Organization for Economic Cooperation and Development (OECD). Building on earlier work with Geof Wood and Miriam Abu Sharkh, I distinguish three types of welfare regime: "welfare states," "informal security regimes," and "insecurity regimes" (Abu Sharkh and Gough 2010; Gough et al. 2004). The chapter illustrates the wide and at times puzzling variation to be found among the middle-income group of informal security regimes that are the focus of this volume. At the same time, this exercise is hampered by a severe lack of comparable international quantitative data on many aspects of non-state welfare provision. It thus illustrates the signal importance of this book in exploring this territory.

This chapter is organized in four sections. First, the welfare regime concept is theorized and the three metaregimes identified. Next, these are crudely operationalized and a series of regime clusters are mapped across sixty-five countries. The third section identifies correlates of these clusters to begin to explain some of the differences between them. The final section then draws on the introductory chapters and case studies in this volume to illustrate the diversity of contexts in which different non-state welfare providers operate across the developing world, before drawing some conclusions.

The support of the UK Economic and Social Research Council (ESRC) is gratefully acknowledged. This chapter was part of the program of the ESRC Research Group on Wellbeing in Developing Countries at the University of Bath.

The Concept of Informal Security Regimes

I start from our earlier work on welfare regimes in developing countries (Gough et al. 2004; Wood and Gough 2006). This in turn built on Gøsta Esping-Andersen's influential book *The Three Worlds of Welfare Capitalism* (Esping-Andersen 1990), which proposed the idea of welfare state regimes. His approach remains a fruitful paradigm for thinking about social policy across the developing as well as the developed world for several reasons. First, it situates modern "welfare states" within a wider *welfare mix*: governments interact with markets and families to produce and distribute welfare. Thus it pays attention to some forms of non-state welfare—but by no means all—and their interaction with state systems and complements the typology of NSPs presented in chapter 2. Second, it pays attention to welfare *outcomes*, the final impact on human security, need satisfaction, and well-being. Third, it is a sociological or political economy approach that embeds welfare institutions in the "deep structures" of social reproduction: it forces researchers to analyze social policy not merely in technical but in power terms. Welfare regimes spring from particular "political settlements" (such as that between labor, capital, and the state after World War II) that define the shape of welfare state regimes and then provide positive feedback, shaping political coalitions that tend to reproduce or intensify the original institutional matrix and welfare outcomes. As a result, this framework also posits a strong thesis of path dependence.

Esping-Andersen (1990) developed the welfare regime framework as middle-range theory. Studying developed, capitalist, democratic nations, he argued that there are "qualitatively different arrangements between state, market, and the family" and rejected simplistic rankings on one dimension. In this way he distinguished three worlds of welfare capitalism: the social democratic world in the Nordic countries, the liberal world in the Anglophone countries, and the conservative or corporatist world in many western European countries. Others posit the existence of distinct southern and central European worlds, but the basic model as applied to advanced Western economies has received considerable empirical support over the last two decades (Castles et al. 2010).

Though there have been attempts to apply the regime framework to other parts of the world, most of these, apart from numerous single country studies, adopt the original conceptual framework developed to understand the OECD world (e.g., Lee and Ku 2007). Rudra's ambitious study (2007) uses cluster analysis to distinguish between "productive" and "protective" patterns of welfare effort in developing countries. Protective policies are designed to shield or decommodify labor against risks, whereas productive policies aim to invest in labor to make it more employable in open competitive economies. This is an important distinction in developing countries, but it remains focused on the public sector as do all her variables. One study stands out: Haggard and Kaufman's (2008) comparative study of development, democracy, and welfare states in Latin America, East Asia, and eastern Europe. A wealth of data is gathered on twenty-one middle income countries in the three regions and analyzed using both cross-section and time-series methods. At the same time, Haggard and Kaufman recognize throughout the profound importance of long-term historical processes and utilize a wealth of qualitative knowledge about the individual countries. This historical perspective and the continuing significance of regional factors sets up their regional comparison, but these regional "models" are not so much an outcome as a presupposition of the exercise. They also adopt several aspects of welfare state regime studies in the developed world: the focus remains on *government* social programs in health, education, and social security, and their conceptual framework adopts and extends factors common in studies of welfare states: distributional coalitions, the growth and organization of the economy, political institutions ranging from democracy to authoritarian, and welfare legacies. Their work is of outstanding importance in understanding the welfare state in middle income countries, but it does not significantly broaden our understanding of welfare regimes (a phrase they hardly ever use).[1]

Gough et al. (2004) contend that to apply the welfare regime paradigm to the nations and peoples in developing countries requires a radical reconceptualization in order to recognize the very different realities across the world. In essence, there must be a broadening of focus from *welfare state regimes* to *welfare regimes*. In particular, the welfare mix must be extended beyond "the welfare state," financial and other markets, and family/household systems. The important role of community-based relationships must be recognized, ranging from local community practices to NGOs and clientelist networks. In addition, the role of international actors cannot be ignored as it often has been in the welfare state literature: this embraces aid, loans, and their conditions from international governmental organizations, the actions of certain transnational markets and companies, the interventions of international NGOs, and the cross-border spread of households via migration and remittances. The result is an extended *welfare mix* or *institutional responsibility matrix* as illustrated in table 1.1.

On this basis, we posit the existence of two other meta-welfare regimes in the modern world: an informal security regime and an insecurity regime (Gough et al. 2004).

Informal security regimes describe institutional arrangements where people rely heavily on *non-state* institutions and relationships—including private markets, community, and family—to meet their security needs (though to greatly varying degrees). These institutions and relationships are variegated and have evolved over long periods of time. However, in the contemporary period they increasingly interact with state institutions and power inequalities. Wood argues that they are often hierarchical and asymmetrical. This often results in

---

1. Another notable contribution is Jeremy Seekings's (2008) work on welfare regimes in developing countries.

TABLE 1.1.
Components of the institutional responsibility matrix or welfare mix

	National	Supranational and extranational
State	National and local government; quasi-governmental institutions	International governmental organizations, national donors
Market	Domestic markets and economic actors	Global markets, multinational corporations
Community	Community practices and organizations, NGOs, patron-client networks	Transnational NGOs
Household	Household transfers, services and strategies	International household transfers, services and strategies

Source: Gough 2004, 30.

problematic inclusion or "adverse incorporation," whereby poorer people acquire some short-term assistance at the expense of longer-term vulnerability and dependence (Wood 2004). The underlying patron-client relations are then reinforced and can prove extremely resistant to civil society pressures and social policy reforms along welfare state lines. Nevertheless, these relations comprise a series of informal "rights" and afford some measure of security. The bulk of the NSPs examined in this book operate within this type of system, in which some public welfare institutions operate, albeit imperfectly, alongside an array of non-state actors.

Insecurity regimes describe institutional arrangements that block the emergence even of stable informal security mechanisms, and thus generate gross levels of insecurity and poor welfare outcomes. These regimes often arise in areas of the world where powerful external actors interact with and reproduce weak state forms, conflict, and political instability (Bevan 2004). The result is a circle of insecurity, vulnerability, and suffering for all but a small elite and their enforcers and clients.

The focus of this book is the "middle" category of informal security regimes.

Mapping Informal Security Regimes

Esping-Andersen (1990, 26) writes: "The linear scoring approach (more or less power, democracy or spending) contradicts the sociological notion that power, democracy, or welfare are relationally structured phenomena. . . . Welfare-state variations are not linearly distributed, but clustered by regime types." Regression analysis using cross-sectional data is not well suited to identifying recurrent patterns and "stickiness" in national patterns (Abu Sharkh 2007). For this reason Miriam Abu Sharkh and I (2010) claim that cluster analysis is the most suitable method to test these arguments (see Abu Sharkh and Gough 2010 for full details and arguments).

To map welfare regimes, we need data on at least two of the dimensions originally theorized by Esping-Andersen (1990): the welfare mix and welfare outcomes. The *welfare mix* describes the entire pattern of resources and programs that can act to enhance welfare or security in a nation state. However, to operationalize this across the non-OECD world is exceptionally difficult, not least because of lack of data. Thus we could find no valid, reliable, and comparative measures of: privately provided pensions and services (except for health purchases); community and NGO-provided welfare; the role of households and wider kin groups, except for overseas remittances; and little on the role and influence of transnational actors, except aid donors. Given this unfortunate fact, we are reduced at this stage to *inferring* the nature of informal and insecurity regimes from the data that are available.

To capture the extent of *state* responsibility for critical social resources, we use two pairs of variables covering expenditure/revenues and service delivery. This reflects the concern of Esping-Andersen that public expenditure is a poor indicator of welfare regimes. We must perforce rely on this given data inadequacies in developing countries, but we are able to complement it with information on public service *outputs* (to be distinguished from welfare *outcomes* below). The first pair are:

- Public spending on education and health as a share of Gross Domestic Product
- Social security contributions as a share of total government revenues (as a proxy for provision of social insurance benefits).

This provides us with indicators of both of Rudra's (2007) "productive" and "protective" forms of social spending. The second pair are:

- Immunization against measles: a fairly restricted social policy target
- Secondary school enrollment of females: a higher, more extensive output target.

To represent international aspects of the welfare mix we have measures of two external transfer flows:

- Official aid
- Remittances from overseas migrants.

To measure welfare *outcomes* we wanted to use the classic human development indicators of life expectancy, literacy, and poverty. However, because of doubts about the reliability of poverty estimates[2] we relied on the first two indices:

- Life expectancy at birth
- The illiteracy rate of young people aged 15–24 years.

---

2. See UN Statistics Division: http://unstats.un.org/unsd/mdg/Metadata.aspx?IndicatorId=0& SeriesId=584

Miriam Abu Sharkh and I (2010) use cluster analysis to map the patterns of these variables for sixty-five non-OECD countries in 1990 and 2000. We undertook cluster analysis in two stages: hierarchical cluster analysis and k-means cluster analysis. All variables were standardized before beginning the analysis. Hierarchical cluster analysis identifies relatively homogeneous groups of countries according to the selected variables based on an algorithm that starts with each country in a separate cluster and combines clusters until all form a single cluster. Dendograms are generated that provide a visual aid to assess the cohesiveness of the clusters formed and the appropriate number of clusters to keep. Yet the final choice of the number of clusters remains a judgment call.

Hence we use a second stage k-means cluster analysis to improve this judgment (another contrast with Rudra [2007]). This is designed to identify relatively homogeneous groups of cases based on selected characteristics, using an algorithm that requires one to specify the number of clusters in advance: this number can be generated by theories or by previous observations. In this case, the number was generated by observation of the dendograms generated by the hierarchical clustering. Following numerous trials, we settled on ten clusters, of which two comprise single countries, leaving us with eight (see Abu Sharkh and Gough 2010 for more details). A k-means cluster analysis also calculates the distance between cluster centers, which enables us to order the clusters, as described below.

Our data sets exclude the OECD world: these rich countries are sufficiently distinct that their inclusion can diminish discrimination within the rest of the world. In order to avoid large numbers of smaller states, we also exclude countries with a population of less than three million people. This left potentially 127 countries and a final tally of sixty-five countries with sufficient data. This analysis generates eight country clusters, which can be ordered according to the distances of their final cluster centers from the OECD welfare states (see table 1.1). The cluster with the highest scores for public expenditure, public provision, and welfare outcomes is labeled A. Most remote from this cluster are clusters G and H. The main findings for the year 2000 are summarized in table 1.2.

Our main findings were as follows.

Countries in *cluster A* exhibit some characteristics of Western welfare states and may be labeled *proto-welfare states*. These countries share in common relatively extensive state commitments to welfare provision and relatively effective delivery of services plus moderately extensive social security programs and superior welfare outcomes (by, it must be stressed, the standards of the non-OECD world). Apart from Israel, Costa Rica, and Tunisia, this cluster comprises two distinct geographical zones and historical antecedents: the countries of the former Soviet Union and its bloc members and the relatively industrialized countries of southern South America. Both developed European-style forms of social protection policies in the middle of the twentieth century, and both suffered degradation of these in the late twentieth century through the external imposition of neoliberal programs.

TABLE 1.2.
Cluster means and country membership, 2000

Cluster Identifier	A	B	C	D	E	F	G	H
No. of Countries	**14**	**16**	**7**	**5**	**5**	**7**	**5**	**4**
Foreign aid per capita/GNI (percent)	0.81	2.08	2.98	2.59	6.22	3.96	12.05	27.19
Workers' remittances/GNI (percent)	0.64	0.66	9.20	0.03	0.34	1.54	2.30	0.99
Public expenditure on health + education/GDP (percent)	9.35	6.77	5.77	8.63	4.35	4.80	5.44	5.17
Social contributions as percent of total public revenue	29.46	7.06	6.78	1.05	1.72	1.19	1.29	0.43
School enrollment, secondary, female (percent)	91.99	76.05	63.64	59.70	29.70	28.27	12.39	14.00
Immunization, measles (percent of children < 12 months)	90.50	89.19	92.86	76.40	62.80	65.14	58.40	78.75
Life expectancy at birth (years)	72.32	69.57	70.30	44.17	53.74	56.90	46.32	41.30
Youth illiteracy rate (percent of those aged 15–24)	1.28	2.20	13.39	7.29	6.65	35.57	48.21	27.42
	Argentina Belarus Brazil Bulgaria Costa Rica Croatia Estonia Israel Lithuania Poland Romania Tunisia Ukraine Uruguay	Bolivia Chile China Colombia Iran Kazakhstan Korea, Rep. Malaysia Mexico Moldova Paraguay Peru Philippines Tajikistan Thailand Turkey	Dominican Republic Ecuador El Salvador Jamaica Morocco Nicaragua Sri Lanka	Botswana Kenya Namibia South Africa Zimbabwe	Cameroon Congo, Rep. Ghana Indonesia Tanzania	Bangladesh Côte d'Ivoire India Nepal Pakistan Papua N.G. Togo	Benin Burundi Ethiopia Mali Senegal	Mozambique Guinea-Bissau Rwanda Zambia

Source: See Abu-Sharkh and Gough 2010.
Note: GNI = Gross National Income.

Cluster B exhibits the second-best level of welfare outcomes and social service outputs coupled with low levels of state social spending (and low reliance on external flows of aid and remittances). This interesting combination suggests that security and welfare are abetted by fast-growing average incomes or by other domestic, non-state, informal institutions, or by both. This combination is found in three major world regions: (1) China and most countries in East Asia from Korea through Thailand (except Indonesia, which dropped out of this group in 2000 having suffered most from the 1997 crisis); (2) the remaining countries of South and Central America not in cluster A; and (3) some countries in western Asia (Iran, Turkey, and Tajikistan).

Cluster C is mainly distinguished by great reliance on remittances from abroad, which account for 9 percent of gross national income on average and which constitute an informal functional alternative to public transfers. It comprises small countries in the Caribbean and Central America, plus Ecuador, Morocco, and Sri Lanka.

In southern and east Africa (South Africa, Namibia, Botswana, Zimbabwe, and Kenya) a distinct *cluster D* exhibited in 2000 relatively extensive public social policy (in both expenditures and outreach and literacy levels), but with poor health outcomes. The latter could be explained by the HIV-AIDS pandemic in this zone of sub-Saharan Africa and by high levels of inequality.

Cluster E comprises another small group of countries in sub-Saharan Africa (plus Indonesia, which "fell" into this cluster from cluster B in 1990 following the severe impact of the 1997 crisis). This is a heterogeneous group with relatively high foreign aid, low rates of girls' schooling, and paradoxically high levels of youth literacy.

Cluster F, with at its core the countries of the Indian subcontinent—India, Pakistan, Bangladesh, and Nepal—exhibits high levels of illiteracy and low numbers of females in secondary education. These are by no means "failed states": India is proclaimed as a future economic giant. Moreover, they boast a plethora of targeted social programs and informal security mechanisms. However, the absence of effective schooling, health, and social protection policies coupled with highly gendered outcomes, according to such indicators as the population sex ratio, betokens high levels of insecurity among the mass of the population.

Clusters G and H, mainly countries in sub-Saharan Africa, exhibit low and in some cases falling life expectancy alongside relatively weak states with low levels of public responsibility, indicated both by spending levels and social outputs, and higher dependence on overseas aid. The prevalence of poverty is also high and persistent.

Explaining Informal Security Regimes

One way to take our analysis further is to analyze the societal correlates of these different clusters. It does not amount to explanation but it can provide a framework for the subsequent chapters in this volume. Five key variables are suggested by current scholarly research on welfare systems in the South (Alesina et al. 2003; Huber and Stephens 2001; Kenworthy 1999; Rudra 2007), and one indicator of each is specified:

- Stage of economic development (GDP per capita)
- Societal inequality (the Gini coefficient of income inequality)
- The level of democracy (using the Gurr index)
- The degree of cultural diversity within countries (the ethno-linguistic fractionalization index)
- Historical antecedents (employing Goran Therborn's four distinct "roads to modernity").

Table 1.3 presents cluster means for the three largest informal security regime (ISR) clusters—B, C, and F—plus as a comparator the proto-welfare states of cluster A (see Abu Sharkh and Gough 2010 for details). The results are as follows.

Economic development. Do the regimes identified here simply reflect different levels of development? In 1990 this was indeed the case; there was a clear and significant gradient in income per capita as we move down the alphabet in the clusters. However, by 2000 this range is closing. Apart from incomes per capita in cluster F, which remain significantly lower, there is no significant difference between the average income per capita in cluster B and C, and that between A and B is only just significant at the 5 percent level. By the new millennium the middle range of clusters do not simply reflect different levels of development.

Income inequality. The Gini coefficient of inequality does not vary in a linear way across the welfare regime types; rather it is an inverse U-shaped relationship. Clusters B and C are significantly more inegalitarian (as is the distinctive high spending / low life expectancy cluster D in southern Africa) than the proto-welfare states *and* group F centered on South Asia.

Democracy. The Gurr indicator of democracy that we have used records a global spread of democracy between 1990 and 2000. One result is that by 2000 there were *no* evident linkages between democratic practices and clusters.

TABLE 1.3.
Cluster means: Structural and cultural descriptives, 2000

	A	B	C	F
GDP per capita (current intl. $)	8,789	5,799	3,999	1,823
Gini index	37.7	45.1	42.6	38.2
Democracy (Gurr index)	6.50	4.62	7.17	3.86
Ethno-linguistic fractionalization	.168	.430	.281	.703

Within the informal security regimes, cluster C scores moderately well on democracy and welfare, D and E on welfare but not democracy, and F on democracy but not welfare. The imposition and rapid spread of Western models of, at least nominally, democratic practices since 1990 have undermined any previous correlations with regime type. Put another way, in 2000 there appears to be no significant link at the cluster level between civil-political and social rights.

Fractionalization and "horizontal" inequality. Turning to cultural variables, the effects of cultural diversity on economic development have been extensively studied using measures of "fractionalization." Table 1.3 shows least cultural diversity among the proto-welfare states of cluster A, and most in cluster F. Most of the differences in ethno-linguistic fractionalization scores between clusters are significant, supporting the hypothesis that high cultural diversity within nations is associated with weak institutionalization of mechanisms of welfare.

Historical antecedents or "roads to modernity." We use Therborn's (1992) four "roads to modernity," which can be used to test for the influence of historical-distal factors on emerging welfare regimes, as Haggard and Kaufman recommend. The four routes are (1) the first, West European route that later embraced eastern Europe and Russia; (2) the "settler societies" of the New World including both North and South America, as well as Australasia and southern-eastern Africa; (3) the colonial zone of sub-Saharan Africa and much of Asia; and (4) the countries of "externally induced modernization," where nominally independent states in the face of Western pressures undertook autonomous strategies of development (including such nations as Japan, China, Thailand, Egypt, and Turkey).

We allocated countries to these four groups using the *Times Concise Atlas of World History* as a basic source (Barraclough 1982). Since this is a noncontinuous variable, we simply cross-tabulated the results. The countries in cluster A are all members of the first two routes to modernity: central and eastern Europe and Latin American "settler" countries. The most successful ISR clusters (B and C) embrace all four routes and display no clear historical background; however, the majority of the countries of "externally induced modernization" are in cluster B (China, Korea, Thailand, Iran, and Turkey). The remaining clusters E-H with poorer welfare outcomes have all had a history of Western colonization.

To summarize, by 2000 the link between welfare regime clusters and income was weakening and there was no clear relation with levels of democracy. The most significant and persistent correlates are the least tractable: historical path of development and internal cultural diversity. This provides an interesting starting point for the subsequent case studies in this book.

Informal Security Regimes and Non-state Welfare

Thus we find a highly variegated pattern of welfare—and illfare—systems across non-OECD countries. We conclude that different groups of countries in the developing world face divergent threats to human well-being and divergent potentials for social policies to mitigate these. In central Europe, parts of eastern Europe, and parts of South America, despite serious erosion of their traditional welfare systems, we see a potential for new forms of social citizenship. These cluster A countries may be labeled *proto-welfare states*. In much of sub-Saharan Africa, what social programs there are have been eroded and submerged beneath a rising tide of human need. This remained around the turn of the century a zone of high insecurity and illfare, and clusters G and H may be labeled *insecurity regimes*.

However, the "middle" group of informal security regimes, in which the NSPs examined in this book are situated, is very varied and requires unbundling. All ISRs have in common lower-middle income per capita and low levels of state expenditure on welfare. But they vary greatly, for example in democracy ratings and historical antecedents. These contribute to a wide spectrum of welfare outcomes ranging from the creditable to the very poor; in sum, from successful to failing systems of non-state welfare. I discuss them here focusing on the countries analyzed in this volume and the different structures of non-state welfare they exhibit.

The case studies in this book cover three countries of the former Soviet Union (FSU)—*Russia, Kazakhstan, and Azerbaijan.* Reflecting a lack of data only, Kazakhstan appears in our cluster analysis, where it declined from cluster A in 1990 to B in 2000. Unfortunately, Russia is not included but the database does cover several other member states of the FSU: four more Western states—Estonia, Lithuania, Belarus, and Ukraine—which emerged in cluster A and three others—Moldova, Kazakhstan, and Tajikistan—in cluster B. The Russian Federation includes features of both and would likely mirror the decline observed in Kazakhstan. Linda Cook (chapter 11) argues that the welfare regime in *Russia* falls between those of the OECD countries and the informal security regimes we describe above. On the one hand there is a dense legacy of institutions and interests (at least in health services) from the communist period. On the other hand, the extreme neoliberal experiment foisted on the ex-Soviet Union led to a rapid collapse of standards in many areas of state welfare provision and a process of spontaneous privatization and shadow commercialization. Though the main institutions remained, they were increasingly accessed by informal brokerage partly operated by public employees. The outcomes, she concludes, have been "abysmal" and inegalitarian. This reflects a countermove away from comprehensive, if inadequate, state welfare in the second half of the twentieth century to its chaotic degradation and partial replacement with NSPs and informal brokerage in the final decade. Pauline Jones Luong's study of *Azerbaijan* and *Kazakhstan* (chapter 3) reveals another pattern following the 1991 collapse: the growing role of foreign oil companies in providing services to specific groups and localities within these oil-rich territories. These suggest new forms of *substitution* whereby evolving NSP capacity displaces state provision as the legitimate driver of development.

The other continent that mainly straddles clusters A and B in our typology is Latin America, and this exhibits certain parallels with the FSU. The relatively industrialized countries of the southern cone of Latin America developed European-style forms of social protection policies in the middle of the twentieth century, and suffered degradation of these in the late twentieth century through the external imposition of neoliberal programs. The latter were pioneered by the Pinochet regime in *Chile* following the 1973 military coup and were introduced in *Argentina* in 1989, culminating in a severe economic and social crisis starting in 2000. Yet Argentina remained a proto-welfare state in 2000 according to our analysis and there is a strong case for placing Chile here too. With a social protection system mandated by governments but administered privately, the contributions of employers and employees will not figure as government expenditures or as social security contributions in the global data we use. If our data were more sensitive, Chile's social expenditures would likely push it into cluster A.

However, the ability of such systems relying on private suppliers and vouchers to provide secure universal welfare remains quite open to question. Alejandra Mizala and Ben Ross Schneider (chapter 10) show how the central state in Chile has gradually recovered major regulatory powers in response to public concerns about quality, equality, and legitimacy in education. Alison Post (chapter 4) shows how the Argentinian state retained legal and regulatory powers over private suppliers of water and sanitation services. In democracies like these privatization does not remove politics or the state. The editors of this volume, in chapter 2, table 4, regard both countries as exhibiting high state capacity for delivering and regulating social welfare (in relation to the non-OECD world), distinguishing them from all other countries covered in this volume. This, together with high NSP capacity, leads the editors to argue that state and non-state welfare can develop in tandem using a coproduction or delegation model of finance and service delivery.

Lebanon, the subject of Melani Cammett's study (chapter 7), is also unfortunately absent from our database. However, as a medium development economy with very substantial workers' remittances (accounting for 14 percent of GDP in 2001 and as much as 20 percent later in the decade) it would very likely fall into our cluster C. Here relatively good social outputs are achieved alongside quite low public expenditures, signaling the existence of functional alternatives to the welfare state. Our analysis focused on the role of remittances, but Cammett also demonstrates the burgeoning role of sectarian organizations, such as Hezbollah, in Lebanon and notes the importance of other NSPs such as NGOs and religious charities in the Lebanese welfare regime. Although NSPs play a critical role in providing crucial services, given the absence of state provision and the disruptions of war and political conflict, they inhibit the construction of a coherent national social policy.

We place *Kenya* in cluster D, a small group of "ex-settler" countries in Africa that exhibit high levels of state activity as measured by taxation, public spending, social outreach, and literacy levels, but coupled with poor life expectancy. If the HIV-AIDS pandemic is the major cause of the adverse health trends, these can be regarded as relatively strong states in many other respects. However, Jennifer Brass (chapter 5) shows that the Kenyan state has little capacity to reach much of its territory and that NGOs are 97 percent financed by international donors. State provision accommodates to, rather than administers, the burgeoning NSPs. This is a case where our cluster analysis is belied by detailed (and more recent) research on the ground.

Tanzania, Ghana, and Côte d'Ivoire feature in clusters E and F in our analysis, characterized by low levels of state activity and relatively poor school enrollment and health outcomes. All are ex-colonial countries in which Christian missions and faith-based organizations (FBOs) have played a leading historical role. Though independence brought about a rapid expansion of public social provision, the long decades of economic crisis in the 1980s and 1990s decimated much of this, resulting in newer NGOs augmenting the older FBOs. The result is characterized by the editors as "appropriation" where low NSP capacity exists alongside low state capacity, generating local brokerage systems to control access. However, Lauren MacLean (chapter 8), in comparing Ghana with the Côte d'Ivoire, does demonstrate the continuing salience of the inherited Anglophone and Francophone colonial administrative systems on this mix.

Finally *India* and the other countries of South Asia (except Sri Lanka) comprise a distinctive cluster in our analysis that we label high-illiteracy failing ISRs. India boasts a plethora of public social programs and informal security mechanisms but with continuing relatively poor outputs and outcomes in terms of education, nutrition, and health. This in turn fosters power struggles and collusive practices among local power brokers, who then control access to the mix of public and NSP services and benefits. Further compelling evidence for several states in northern India is provided by Anirudh Krishna (chapter 9). The case that these informal brokers provide vital assistance to poor villagers in accessing the welfare mix is a strong one. But it is hard to deny that such networks are blocks to more effective and democratic forms of social provision.

Conclusion

This chapter has presented a cross-national cluster analysis to identify different welfare regimes across non-OECD countries, in order to situate the variety of NSPs presented in this volume. But it has been hampered by lack of relevant data about non-state welfare! It was not possible to find valid, reliable, and comparative measures of: privately provided pensions and services (except for health purchases); community and NGO-provided welfare; the role of households and wider kin groups, except for overseas remittances; and little on the role and influence of transnational actors, except aid donors. Given this unfortunate fact, we have had to *infer* the nature of informal security regimes from the data that are available. This suggests that attempts to characterize the role of non-state providers in welfare regimes must necessarily involve historically grounded analyses, as employed in the chapters in this volume.

Nevertheless, the clusters do provide a useful framework for what follows. The countries at the most "formal" end of our ordering (in clusters A and B) have witnessed predominantly private for-profit and commercial CSR initiatives. In both Latin America and the former Soviet Union space for these was created by the partial dismantling and erosion of earlier state systems of welfare. But the extent to which these forms have displaced the public sector has depended on the strength of the residual public institutions and interests. These have proved strongest in Latin America and weakest in parts of the FSU such as Kazakhstan. In Kenya (cluster D) a relatively extensive state apparatus has been confronted with an explosion of NGOs, which have not displaced but reinforced the public administration of social policy.

Turning to countries with lower capacity state sectors we see clearer examples of displacement and substitution by NSPs. In Lebanon a history of war and political conflict has fostered powerful sectarian organizations and prevented a coherent social policy from developing. In the three countries of sub-Saharan Africa, colonial inheritance of faith-based missions coupled with inherited community-based reciprocity has nourished much more informal welfare provision, especially following the disruption of public provision in the 1980s. Here again, inherited state structures play some role, witness the well-established comparisons of Francophone and Anglophone Africa (Geschiere 1993; MacLean 2010; Miles 1994). Finally, in the northern states of India, a plethora of both public and non-state providers in the presence of a weak state has generated a network of local power brokers who provide or deny access to these services.

Finally, an important conclusion is the need to distinguish forms of social welfare *provision*, which exist in every country whether in state or non-state forms, from a coherent, universal, rights-based social *policy*. The history of welfare states in the West suggests that a necessary condition for the latter is mobilization from below (rather than imposition from above or outside) and some form of political settlement between major classes and interest groups. Without this, individual social programs, however numerous and extensive, are unlikely to be legitimate or sustainable. The issue for different forms of non-state welfare is whether they contribute to, or detract from, the emergence of such a unified social policy (Gough and Therborn 2010).

2

The Political Consequences of Non-state Social Welfare

An Analytical Framework

Melani Cammett and Lauren M. MacLean

As Ian Gough details in the previous chapter, "informal insecurity" welfare regimes are the norm in many developing countries. Within this broad category, the state participates in the direct provision of social protection to varying degrees. As Gough acknowledges, non-state social welfare is a vital component of welfare regimes across the developing world, but it is virtually impossible to capture the nature and extent of NSPs in large-N, cross-national studies of welfare regimes. Comparable quantitative data on non-state welfare are scarce, particularly in the context of weak state capacity to collect information in many developing countries, and simplified measures cannot illuminate the substantive nature of interactions between citizens and NSPs. To assess the political consequences of non-state social welfare, we therefore focus in the rest of the volume on the linkages between NSPs and citizens at the micro-level.

An emphasis on the relationship between NSPs and citizens reveals in stark terms that the rise and consolidation of non-state providers is not just a technical solution to the problems of delivering services to populations, but is instead deeply political. The nature of non-state provision and its role in a given national welfare system can shape the political and social life of the national community in fundamental ways. As we argue in more detail below, the type of NSP and its relations with the state affect whether NSPs limit or expand access to social services; diminish or enhance accountability to citizens; and promote or undercut state capacities related to social provision and other public functions.

We first develop a series of propositions regarding the political ramifications of non-state provision. These propositions are not meant to be determinative.

Rather, they point to possible conditions under which citizens enjoy enhanced access to services, greater provider accountability, and more effective public authorities when NSPs are big players in their systems of social protection. The next sections conceptualize the key variables and theorize the relationships between them. First, we define and specify the political consequences of non-state social welfare provision. We focus on three outcomes, including access to services, accountability, and state capacity. We then present the building blocks of a theory of the political consequences of non-state welfare, emphasizing four key components of NSP characteristics: the degree of organizational formalization, proximity of operation, profit motives, and eligibility criteria. We next present a framework for characterizing state-NSP relations, ranging from more collaborative to competitive configurations. Our propositions below tease out how these four dimensions of NSP characteristics combine with the different modes of state-NSP relations to produce divergent political outcomes for access, accountability, and state capacity.

Explaining the Varied Political Consequences of Non-state Social Welfare

Specific characteristics of NSPs along with relations between the state and NSPs shape access to social benefits, accountability, and state capacity to provide social welfare, as we elaborate in more detail below. First, the degree of formalization, locus of operation, profit orientation, and eligibility criteria of an NSP affect the political consequences of non-state welfare provision. Second, the modes of NSP-state relations, which can be more cooperative or conflictual, also shape the political ramifications of non-state welfare for citizens. (See tables 2.3 and 2.4 below.) How do these two sets of factors jointly affect the political consequences of non-state welfare?

To begin, NSP form has direct effects on the first outcome: access to social welfare. We expect that more formalized, locally rooted, and inclusive NSPs that do not operate according to profit maximization principles will afford greater access to social welfare for citizens. Almost by definition, more inclusive eligibility criteria reach and attract a broader pool of beneficiaries. Different types of NSPs are more or less likely to serve broadly as expressed in their formal mandates and informal practices. Some NSPs explicitly aim to serve the largest possible array of beneficiaries while others effectively serve a more narrow pool of beneficiaries. Even after accounting for resource endowments, which constrain all but the wealthiest providers, some NSPs prioritize specific communities or categories of citizens, whether by race, ethnicity, religion, gender, or other forms of social stratification.

More formalized and less personalistic organizational management also limits discretion in the allocation of benefits and perhaps even encourages more people to seek assistance in the first place, thereby broadening access to welfare. In general, more formalized organizations have more transparent and institutionalized administrative practices, which clarify eligibility criteria. Providers that are rooted in their communities are more likely to understand the needs of the community and may therefore initiate programs that address local concerns more effectively and appropriately. Local embeddedness also enables citizens to obtain more direct knowledge of programs and to establish or benefit from ties with staff members, which may enhance their willingness to seek and receive services. Finally, for-profit providers are more likely to prioritize or incorporate financial concerns in the allocation of benefits, putting the poor and marginalized at a distinct disadvantage.

The relationship between NSPs and the state may also affect access to services. To the extent that the NSP-state relationship is collaborative—or at least not competitive—it may improve both access to services and citizen experiences of seeking services. To the extent that NSPs and public agencies work together, the total pie of programs and benefits may be enlarged. Furthermore, more cooperative and institutionalized ties between direct providers and the state facilitates the process of supplying services and improves the state's capacity to regulate other suppliers, which in turn can enhance citizen access to social welfare.

NSP type also has implications for the second outcome of accountability. In the ideal world, all providers—NSPs included—accept responsibility for both citizen experiences in accessing services and for the quality and outcomes of their programs and benefits. Which types of NSPs are more likely to be responsive to and accept liability for their interactions with citizens? We expect that more formalized and locally rooted NSPs with clear eligibility criteria are more likely to be accountable to citizens. Profit orientation may promote accountability to individual citizens but can also reduce responsiveness to the broader public. On the one hand, the profit motive can make for-profit institutions more responsive to their "clients," who can take their business elsewhere if they are not satisfied with their service experiences. On the other hand, the power embodied in consumer choice is the privilege of those with means, excluding the majority of less fortunate citizens from accessing services or at least placing them at the mercy of the provider.

The relationship between NSPs and the state may also impact the accountability of NSPs to citizens, although the particular configurations of NSP-state relations under which accountability is improved are not clear-cut. When the state has and exercises existing abilities to monitor and sanction the actions of non-state providers, whether in a relationship of coproduction or state domination, NSPs are likely to be more responsive to citizens. When state capacity to regulate NSP activities is low, NSP accountability to citizens can be reduced. Indeed, higher state regulatory capacity may be a necessary albeit insufficient condition to create accountable relationships between NSPs and citizens.

Finally, different aspects of NSPs, and especially their relations with the state, can affect the state's *future* capacity to provide, finance, and regulate the provision of social services. All things being equal, collaborative state-NSP relations can enhance state capacity. This implies that coproduction, the most clearly positive-sum NSP-state relationship, is most likely to boost state capacity. When the state and NSPs work together productively, this can improve the state's ability to regulate and even provide social welfare by freeing up state resources for other pressing public needs and by facilitating the task of regulating the provision of social services by NSPs. Conversely, in more competitive NSP-state relationships, state capacity may be diminished, whether because states expend resources to outbid NSPs or because mutual antagonism complicates the task of state regulation of non-state provision. Again, there is nothing automatically conflictual about relationships of appropriation and substitution but they are more likely than other patterns to generate competitive interactions between NSPs and states. Coproduction and delegation reflect the most obviously positive-sum relationships between NSPs and states while state domination is virtually by definition less characterized by competitive dynamics because states hold the upper hand in their exchanges with NSPs.

The Political Consequences of Non-state Social Welfare

Now that we have outlined our theoretical propositions, it is essential to further specify each of the three dimensions of political consequences that we treat in the book, including access to social welfare, accountability, and state capacity. Table 2.1 summarizes these outcomes.

Access to Social Welfare

Access to social welfare assesses the degree to which people are able to meet their needs for basic services such as medical care, education, and social assistance. *Equity* and *sustainability* are central to the question of access to social services and benefits.

Both the quantity and quality of social services received by citizens determine the equity of access to social welfare (Castro-Leal et al. 2000; Pritchett 2004; Sarker and Davey 2009; McGuire 2010; Hill et al. 2012). If services are available and affordable, but of such low quality that recipients decline to use those services or do not receive adequate and appropriate care, then the equitable distribution of social welfare is de facto reduced.[1] For example, in many developing and postcommunist countries, citizens believe that public facilities offer lower quality services than private providers. In effect, then, those who cannot afford private services may feel that they have inferior access to health

---

1. On the low quality of health care by various providers in developing countries, see Berendes et al. (2011), Das (2011), and Das, Hammer, and Leonard (2008).

TABLE 2.1.
The political consequences of non-state social welfare provision: Access, accountability, and state capacity

Concept	Dimensions	Possible Indicators
Access	Equity	– Equity of access to social welfare by gender, ethnicity, age, religion, income, partisanship, geography, and so forth.
		– Equity of access to high quality of social welfare by gender, ethnicity, age, religion, income, partisanship, geography, and so forth.
	Sustainability	– Duration over time of service provision
		– Stability and renewability of financial support for services
		– Cultural appropriateness of services
		– Social embeddedness of services in community
Accountability	Ability of citizens to hold providers responsible for the experience and quality of service provision	– Existence of liability mechanisms for the quality of services rendered or not supplied
		– Rule-based vs. personalized procedures for lodging complaints and receiving compensation
State capacity	State capacity to provide, finance, and regulate welfare	– Human capital (number of staff, education levels of staff)
		– Spending per capita
		– Proportion of total delivery of social welfare services
		– Quality of services provided
		– Effectiveness of regulation of service provision

care, schooling, and other basic services. Multiple factors may influence the ability to access requisite quantities and qualities of non-state social services, including gender, ethnicity, age, religion, wealth, partisanship, geographic region, and other social categories.

Access to social welfare is also contingent on the sustainability of access. Here the notion of sustainability refers to the durability over time of a provider—in this case, NSPs—in a given policy domain. This understanding of the term goes beyond a minimalist idea of a long-lasting organizational structure by including the stability and renewability of financial support for non-state actors. For example, Scott Allard (chapter 12) highlights variation in the continuity of service activities delivered by nonprofit versus for-profit institutions in the United States. He argues that because most for-profit organizations rely more on private fees for services than on charitable gifts or grants to supplement public funds, they are less exposed than nonprofits to the vicissitudes of public support.

The concept of sustainability also incorporates the extent to which non-state provision is socially embedded, where communities and citizens have some ownership in the delivery process and are invested in the future. For example, based on a detailed comparative analysis of two Central Asian countries, Pauline Jones Luong (chapter 3) emphasizes this dimension of sustainability, arguing that multinational corporations (MNCs) that are committed to CSR are likely to have a positive impact when they can both enforce their contracts and form viable partnerships with local communities. At the same time, her chapter cautions against romanticizing the effects of CSR on local development. Even when all propitious conditions are present, delegating the role of public goods and social service provision to MNCs has its downsides, notably unequal citizen access to benefits. In her discussion of privatization in Argentina, Alison Post (chapter 4) demonstrates that domestic firms with significant operations within the jurisdiction of their contract (provinces, in the case of Argentina) can negotiate more effectively with local governments than either domestic firms without significant local operations or foreign firms. Locally rooted domestic firms therefore can establish longer-term and, hence, more stable operations than MNCs or domestic firms without local operations. Thus, according to Post, the type of investor shapes the degree to which privatization succeeds in improving the reach and quality of water services, as well as the political viability of privatized provision, in the long run.

Accountability

The second dimension of the political consequences of non-state social welfare examined in this book addresses how non-state provision affects accountability for citizens. Accountability with respect to social welfare entails the ability of citizens to hold providers liable for the quantity and quality of services received and, more fundamentally, for the process and experience of seeking and obtaining services.

Non-state provision may affect whether and how citizens demand accountability around their access to social welfare. At the most basic level, NSPs do not have the same obligations that, at least theoretically, bind states to citizens. To the extent that NSPs tend not to have mandates to serve broadly or indiscriminately, they are less accountable to beneficiaries and the communities where they operate. Depending on the terms of their establishment and eligibility criteria, NSPs often have no obligation to serve all citizens universally, even those with demonstrated need or who lack alternative welfare channels. As a result, it may be harder for people and especially the poor and vulnerable to identify providers or to demand recompense for insufficient or poorly rendered services.

The social ecology of non-state welfare may also diminish the accountability of providers to citizens. NSPs are often small and operate in a fragmented terrain of social service providers, particularly in welfare regimes with greater numbers of non-state actors. Smaller institutions—even those whose staff have the best of intentions—may lack the administrative capacity and scale to institute mechanisms to ensure accountability to community members. This problem is compounded in the context of fragmented systems of social service delivery, which make it harder for citizens to locate appropriate providers and, if necessary, to assign responsibility to and seek compensation from specific entities. Fragmentation among NSPs can be addressed through the formation of larger umbrella associations, but Rose (2006) finds that these associations usually favor more established NSPs serving more elite populations. Non-state provision, then, potentially diminishes the responsiveness of providers to beneficiaries and, in turn, may make access to services less equitable.

The logics of these arguments appear to presume that states are necessarily superior in providing social protection; however, the reality in many developing countries is often more complicated. Many states lack the administrative and financial capacity to meet the basic needs of their citizens or corrupt and negligent rulers may disregard populations while favoring segments of elite supporters. In general, however, accountability is easier to attribute in sectors with a smaller number of providers than in a fragmented sector with many small providers. In addition, by the twenty-first century, norms (although perhaps not realities) of state guarantees of minimum levels of social protection have spread globally, particularly among middle-income countries (Seekings 2008). Furthermore, to the extent that states adopt even a rhetorical commitment to rights-based citizenship, then populations are more likely to hold public providers accountable for their welfare experiences. As a result, welfare regimes with multiple NSPs can be less conducive to accountability than systems with greater state involvement, as credit and blame are easier to attribute to a smaller number of actors that have at least nominal commitments to the public.

Non-state provision may also have second-order effects on citizens' everyday practices of political participation and relationships with their states. Encounters with NSPs may mobilize and empower (or demobilize and frustrate) citizens to new frequencies and intensities of political participation and may affect whether and how they demand accountability from their governments. Standard definitions of political participation emphasize voter registration and voting, but less sporadic and more everyday nonelectoral activities, such as attending a community meeting or contacting a politician for help with an issue, are also important modes of participation.[2] If states neither provide nor receive credit for the provision of basic social services for their populations, citizens

---

2. See MacLean (2011b) for an analysis of how the differential quality of public versus non-state service provision affects electoral and nonelectoral forms of participation in eighteen African countries. See Bleck (2011, 2013) for a comparison of how Islamic versus secular schooling shapes a range of types of citizen participation in Mali.

may feel that their governments do not serve them and, as a result, will be less politically engaged and even trusting of public institutions and authorities.[3]

State Capacity

Since the 1990s, scholars have expressed considerable concern about the consequences of non-state provision for the state itself. The predominant line of thinking has been that the provision of services by non-state actors undermines the capacity of the state (Whaites 1998; Khan 1999; Martin 2004; Obiyan 2005). The logic here is that the provision of these services prevents states from developing their own internal capacities and revenue generation ability. De Walle (1997) and Uvin (1998) offer even more critical perspectives. They argue that the provision of services by non-state actors not only allows weak states to persist but that these are politically charged interventions, not at all neutral, which essentially permit human rights abuses to continue unabated.

Other scholars challenge this interpretation, arguing that the provision of services by non-state actors actually enables weak states to continue functioning by targeting their minimal resources to other areas (Brown 1998; Brinkerhoff 1999). Non-state provision may not be a simple zero-sum game with the state, but instead may substitute for or complement public welfare functions.

Both perspectives have their merits. The effects of non-state provision likely depend on the nature of state-NSP relations as well as the goals and actions of NSPs themselves. Before elaborating these arguments in more detail, it is essential to specify the building blocks of our theory. In the next section, we describe and analyze the different types of NSPs and categorize distinct patterns of state-NSP linkages.

NSP Characteristics and NSP-State Linkages

In order to understand the political consequences of non-state social welfare, it is essential to know more about the diversity of NSPs, including their distinct relationships with states. These properties of NSPs potentially shape access to welfare, accountability for citizens, and state capacity. Obviously, the direct linkages between states and citizens also affect these outcomes, but these dynamics have been more thoroughly analyzed by the existing literature on the

---

3. On the politics of credit-claiming and the role of public perceptions of service delivery in fostering trust in government, see Sacks and Larizza (2012).

welfare state in the advanced industrialized countries and state social policy in developing countries (Esping-Andersen 1990; Gough et al. 2004; Rudra 2007; Castles and Obinger 2008; Haggard and Kaufman 2008; Seekings 2008; Brooks 2009; Castles et al. 2010). This volume complements studies of the welfare state by uncovering the dynamics of relationships between NSPs, states, and citizens.

A Typology of NSPs

What is the range of NSPs operating around the world? A diverse array of NSPs interacts with citizens and states to provide social protection, with varied implications for the politics of non-state provision. This volume covers a wider spectrum of non-state providers than most analyses, which tend to focus separately on one type at a time and particularly on NGOs. Table 2.2 depicts the spectrum of domestic and international organizations and actors involved in non-state provision, including for-profit institutions, secular organizations, ethnic and sectarian groups, faith-based organizations, informal brokers, community-based organizations, and family networks. The horizontal axis arranges NSPs according to their degree of formal institutionalization, with multinational corporations or international secular NGOs on the more formal end of the spectrum, and organizations such as community-based groups and family networks on the more informal end of the continuum. The vertical axis divides types of providers according to their locus of operation, notably whether they are primarily domestic or international actors. Each of these NSP types may have distinct relationships with citizens and states, in turn producing distinct implications for access to services, accountability, and state capacity. Collectively, the chapters in this volume examine almost every type of NSP depicted in table 2.2.

Table 2.3 describes the four dimensions of NSP form and the range of variation found, which we conceptualize as continua rather than dichotomously. The discussion of each NSP form below emphasizes its specific characteristics along these four dimensions, including the degree of organizational formalization, locus of operation, profit orientation, and eligibility criteria. Each of these factors, as we argue in more detail below, has specific implications for the political consequences of non-state provision.

First, the degree of organizational formalization within the NSP influences the NSP-citizen dynamic, with direct implications for inclusion and accountability. Some NSPs operate on a very informal, highly personalized basis whereas others function according to formal, rule-based interactions. When informal organizations have less transparent and institutionalized decision-making processes, it is more difficult for community members to understand why and how resources are distributed and to present claims or requests. In general, informality complicates efforts to understand allocation processes and

TABLE 2.2.
Types of non-state providers

	Formal ↔ Informal						
	Private sector organizations	Secular NGOs	Ethnic and sectarian organizations	Faith-based organizations	Community-based organizations	Informal brokers	Family and friendship networks
International	Multinational corporations (Jones Luong; Post)	International nongovernmental organizations (Brass; Jennings)	Transnational ethnic organizations and networks (Cammett)	International church-based charities (Jennings)	–	–	Transnational family networks, migrant remittances (MacLean)
Domestic	Domestic for-profit firms (Post; Mizala and Schneider; Allard)	Domestic NGOs (Brass; Allard)	Ethnic and sectarian political groups (Cammett)	Local faith-based organizations; local churches (Jennings; Mizala and Schneider)	Village or neighborhood-based associations (MacLean)	Naya netas in India, private providers in Russia (Krishna; Cook)	Family and friendship networks (MacLean)

TABLE 2.3.
Characteristics of NSPs

Dimensions	Range of Indicator
Level of personalization	Formal/rule-based ↔ informal/personalized
Locus of operation	Local ↔ international
Profit orientation	Not-for-profit ↔ for-profit
Eligibility criteria	Inclusive ↔ exclusive

may deter those outside of connected social networks from seeking support in the first place. As a result, NSPs that incorporate personal factors in their interactions with citizens likely serve more circumscribed communities.

Second, the locus of operation or proximity to communities potentially shapes the ability of citizens to access social services or demand and receive accountability from providers. When NSPs are highly international and less locally embedded, it can be more difficult to trace the avenues of benefit provision or mechanisms for claim-making. The distinction between domestic and international types can be fuzzy. For example, some NGOs operate internationally or receive extensive funds from foreign states and donors but are firmly rooted in a particular domestic setting and are considered "local" actors.[4] This is also true for less formal institutions, such as family networks, in which members may move across or span international boundaries. Citizen experiences with international and local organizations, however, can vary. If members of the community actually know the key decision makers who run the office in their area, they may be more inclined to seek services from them, even if their financing comes from abroad.

Third, the profit orientation of providers has potential political effects by establishing new boundaries of inclusion and exclusion in welfare systems. For-profit providers are more likely to be inaccessible to the poor than institutions that do not need to maximize financial returns. The rise of private schools and medical centers catering to emerging middle classes who are not satisfied with the crumbling public welfare infrastructure is evidence of the growing importance of for-profit providers in many developing countries. These institutions are largely out of bounds to those who lack the means to pay for their services (Laurell and López Arellano 1996; Bennett, McPake, and Mills 1997; Dror and Jacquier 1999; Steketee 2004; Horwitz 2005; Mendoza and Thelen 2008).

---

4. Obiyan (2005) discusses the difficulties of determining which NGOs are foreign versus local and highlights the importance of the organization's headquarters versus the operations of NGOs.

Finally, the eligibility criteria for receiving services are of obvious importance. NSPs exhibit distinct norms and practices of social inclusion and exclusion in the delivery of services. The empirical chapters show how some NSPs are more exclusionary, while others are more egalitarian. NSPs that explicitly or implicitly favor some potential beneficiaries over others—whether based on class, gender, ethnicity, religion, partisanship, or other forms of social stratification—provide more limited access to their services than universal, citizen-based programs theoretically offer. Furthermore, some NSPs have visible and transparent eligibility criteria, enabling citizens to readily assess their likelihood of obtaining services; others have more opaque requirements, making it difficult to determine the prospects for social welfare access and increasing the discretionary power of providers in allocating benefits. Not only does the transparency of criteria for access affect the ability of citizens to gain access to services, but it also shapes the likelihood that citizens demand accountability from their providers.

The following reviews of each NSP type note general characteristics vis-à-vis the dimensions of NSP form delineated in table 2.3. Although the typology of NSPs in table 2.2 indicates how each case study in the chapters to follow illuminates the dynamics of a particular type of NSP, this should not imply that these are the sole provider types in the countries in question. In any given country or even subnational community, multiple types of NSPs inevitably operate. Nonetheless, in some contexts, particular types of NSPs may dominate or play a critical or growing role in social welfare provision.

Private sector organizations. The first NSPs in our typology are private sector organizations such as domestic businesses and multinational corporations. Both domestic and international private sector firms play an increasingly important role in social welfare provision in the communities where they do business. Whereas private sector organizations all share the same fundamental for-profit motive for service provision, private providers fall into three different categories, each of which has distinct relationships with host governments. First, private firms may provide social services as a *supplement* to or alongside their main, profit-making activities, either because they anticipate this will improve relations with local communities, or because governments demand this as a condition of entry. Second, governments may delegate service provision to the private sector via contracts. Third, private providers may create markets for services traditionally offered by the state, capitalizing on the realization that households will pay for these services.[5]

Corporate social responsibility, which has gained prominence in the United States and other industrialized countries in recent decades, exemplifies the first

---

5. We are grateful to Alison Post for emphasizing these distinctions within the category of for-profit, non-state providers.

type of relationship between the state and the private sector. CSR refers to the self-regulation of corporations to ensure their adherence to legal and ethical principles as well as standards and norms of good corporate citizenship (Bowen 1953; Lodge and Wilson 2006). In broad terms, the principles and norms of CSR include attention to the environmental impact of corporate activities on the places where they produce or market their goods and services as well as on the workers and communities affected by the corporation's activities. At a minimum, CSR calls on corporations to refrain from harming the planet or people affected by their activities and may even entail that firms strive to improve the communities where they operate (United Nations 2012). In some developing countries, MNCs even undertake the financing, provision, or construction of infrastructure for the provision of basic services such as health care, education, or water purification.

CSR is controversial. On the one hand, social programs sponsored by corporations can have tangible benefits for residents and the poor and may be the only real source of social assistance in the context of deficient domestic welfare regimes. On the other hand, CSR may be little more than a fig leaf for corporations seeking to boost their global reputations among watchdog NGOs and relatively wealthy citizens in industrialized countries who incorporate ethical considerations into their consumer choices (Petras and Veltmeyer 2007). Furthermore, as a self-regulating process with standards set by the firms themselves, industry groups or international agreements such as the U.N. Global Compact,[6] CSR has virtually no compliance and enforcement mechanisms. Firms adopt standards on a voluntary basis with little incentive beyond threats of consumer boycotts, which are notoriously difficult to launch and sustain, or the specter of bad press as a result of exposure by watchdog groups (Shamir 2004; Vogel 2005; Blowfield and Murray 2008).

Pauline Jones Luong's chapter in this volume presents a nuanced view of the relationship between CSR promotion and development outcomes, focusing on the petroleum-producing states of Azerbaijan and Kazakhstan. Both countries have significant foreign direct investment in the oil and gas industries, yet MNCs investing in the two countries have varied commitments to CSR, with firms investing in Azerbaijan far more engaged in local development initiatives than their counterparts in Kazakhstan.

---

6. Adopted in 2000 with over fifty-three hundred participating businesses in 130 countries, the UN Global Compact is the largest voluntary corporate social responsibility initiative. Based on various international agreements and conventions, the agreement focuses on human rights, labor, the environment, and anticorruption measures, and aims to generate "shared understandings" of how companies can help promote UN principles within corporate domains. The compact does not include sanctions for companies who violate its principles nor does it verify or monitor companies' actions. Nonetheless, the agreement arguably raises the possibility of reputational risk for noncompliers. On the main principles of the UN Global Compact, see http://www.unglobalcompact.org/AboutTheGC/TheTenPrinciples/index.html.

The role of for-profit organizations in non-state welfare provision is not limited to multinational firms committed to CSR, however. Alison Post reveals the important role of private *domestic* firms when the water sector was privatized in Argentina. During the 1990s throughout Latin America, large private companies increasingly gained long-term contracts to manage and invest in state infrastructure. Post shows why certain domestic firms were more successful than multinational ones in bargaining with the state, and, ultimately, in expanding access to safe drinking water, an important component of the public health infrastructure.

Second, private for-profit and not-for-profit institutions may have contractual relationships with public agencies to offer services. Focusing on the rise of NSPs in the United States, Allard analyzes the variation between domestic for-profit firms and nonprofit organizations for the equity and sustainability of access by the poor.[7] NSPs play a vital role in ensuring social protection in the United States, yet greater dependence on grants and donations can make nonprofits more vulnerable to economic downturns than for-profit institutions.

Finally, private organizations may capitalize on market opportunities to establish new types of social service provision. For example, private, for-profit schools have emerged in China to target the children of the "floating population," or migrant workers who lack residency permits in the places where they find employment and therefore cannot enroll their children in public schools (Yang, Rong, and Deng 2008). In this volume, Alejandra Mizala and Ben Schneider demonstrate the increasing role of private schools, some of which are for-profit, in the provision of primary and secondary education in Chile after the implementation of a national voucher system. These private schools in Chile are primarily domestic, but often affiliated with larger international organizations such as the Catholic Church. The authors show how these changes have important ramifications for citizen efforts to hold providers accountable.

Secular nongovernmental organizations. The second type of NSP in the typology is the secular nongovernmental organization. Secular NGOs, both international nongovernmental organizations and domestic or local NGOs, have received the most attention in scholarly and policy debates about the role of non-state actors in fostering development (Korten 1990; Smith and Lipsky 1993; Edwards and Hulme 1996a, 1996b; Salamon and Sokolowski 1999; Bebbington, Hickey, and Mitlin 2008; Lewis and Kanji 2009). Defining NGOs is challenging because the category encompasses diverse types of actors. Multiple terms have been coined to describe them, with a corresponding alphabet soup of acronyms (Najam 1996; Lewis and Wallace 2003). Secular NGOs are nonprofit entities with a secular normative orientation,

---

7. Milward (1996) conceptualized the term "hollow state" to emphasize the systemic governance risks when governments increasingly contract services out to the private sector.

distinguishing them from faith and other identity-based organizations, which we address separately below. As Lewis and Kanji (2009) note, NGOs are generally associated with either the delivery of basic services to people in need, the focus of this volume, or public advocacy for social change.[8] Over time, the role of NGOs has broadened substantively and geographically to encompass activities ranging from disaster relief to the promotion of democracy and human rights, which often transcends national boundaries (Khagram, Riker, and Sikkink 2002). Although NGOs are by definition nongovernmental, they may receive extensive government funding, again significantly blurring the lines between the state and non-state actors.[9]

Advocates of NGOs underscore the vital role they play in improving the well-being of the poor and other disadvantaged populations, particularly in the developing world where states may be unable or unwilling to provide the physical and programmatic infrastructure for meeting basic needs. Furthermore, proponents claim, government-NGO partnerships can be beneficial for development and NGOs can serve a critical bridging role in linking governments and communities (Reilly 1995; Brown 1998; Brinkerhoff 1999; Brinkerhoff 2002; Andersson 2004; Batley 2006; Keese and Argudo 2006; Batley and Mcloughlin 2010; Rose 2010).

Yet critics question the ability of NGOs to provide social welfare and, more broadly, to promote development on technocratic and, increasingly, on political grounds. First, it is not clear that NGOs can deliver public services and infrastructure such as water, sanitation, education, or health as effectively as the public sector itself. Most NGOs lack the scale needed to ensure efficient and equitable delivery, although this claim is contingent on the nature of the service in question. Second, as Wood argues (1997), the outsourcing of basic public functions to NGOs can reduce state accountability to citizens.[10] A vicious cycle ensues with a reduced state role in society, leading to increased exit options and decreased voice opportunities for citizens in the system, thereby undermining the need for states to practice "good governance" (Wood 1997). Furthermore, NGOs can employ opaque management structures and processes and, by definition, are less directly accountable to an electorate than governments (Gariyo 1995). Proponents of NGOs as the locus of social welfare provision may

---

8. Salamon and Anheier (1992) adopt a "structural/operational" definition, which characterizes organizations from the "third sector," or institutions that are neither governmental nor market based, as "formally constituted, nongovernmental in basic structure, self-governing, nonprofit distributing, and voluntary."

9. Gazley (2011) highlights these blurred boundaries in her analysis of tax-exempt entities that raise philanthropic funds for public services in the United States, including libraries, fire and police departments, and public parks.

10. Gugerty and Prakash (2010) investigate how NGOs attempt to address the problem of accountability through voluntary self-regulation in an accountability club, where NGOs join together to collectively establish regulatory rules and monitor each other.

overlook the fact that NGOs can be hierarchical and nondemocratic, act as mouthpieces for the powerful, serve to replicate larger patron-client relationships in society, and focus more on reporting to donors than on catering to the needs and demands of beneficiaries (Fowler 1995; Gariyo 1995; Mercer 2003).

In this volume, the chapter by Jennifer Brass addresses secular NGOs as providers of social welfare most centrally. Focusing on the role of secular NGOs in service provision in Kenya, Brass documents a shift from antagonism and conflict during the regime of Daniel arap Moi (1978–2002) to collaboration and mutual assistance under President Mwai Kibaki (2002–present). In a vastly different context, the United States, Allard, too, highlights the critical role of secular NGOs in service provision. Ironically, the United States has more in common with developing countries than is often assumed. As Allard argues, over the past four decades the provision of social welfare assistance by nonprofit organizations has become prevalent in American cities and towns where the state is notoriously weak as a provider of services (Hacker 2002).

Ethnic or sectarian organizations. Ethnic or sectarian organizations[11] are the third type of NSP in the book's typology. In some countries, ethnic and sectarian organizations are vital to meeting the basic needs of populations, and, as a result, social welfare can become a terrain of contestation when these identity-based cleavages are politicized. However, research on welfare regimes has not addressed these types of providers systematically. In parts of South Asia and the Middle East, including Afghanistan, Pakistan, India, Sri Lanka, Egypt, Iraq, Jordan, Lebanon, Morocco, and Palestine, to name a few examples, ethnic and sectarian political parties and organizations run their own welfare institutions and serve as gatekeepers for access to services provided by the state or private providers (Hefner 2000; Shadid 2002; Flanigan 2008; Berman 2009; Cochrane 2009; Thachil 2014; Cammett 2014). Meanwhile, in many parts of Africa, ethnic or "hometown associations" provide financial assistance to support the construction of schools and clinics in urban neighborhoods and rural villages (Woods 1994; Honey and Okafor 1998; Mercer, Page, and Evans 2008). These associations are frequently organized by the sons and daughters of the hometown who have moved to larger urban capitals or even migrated overseas for educational and work opportunities.

It is generally assumed that ethnic organizations cater to their own, a claim supported by the literature on ethnic politics and public goods (Habyarimana

---

11. Definitions of ethnic or sectarian parties either focus on the ethnic or religious identities of constituents (Horowitz 1985) or the messages and actions of party leaders, such as the degree to which they employ ethnic symbols and language in their self-presentation, events, and pronouncements (Chandra 2004). Both criteria may apply simultaneously in characterizing an organization as ethnic or sectarian. Drawing on insights from constructivist approaches to ethnicity (Chandra 2006), we view ethnic and sectarian politics as the expression of historically contextual political struggles rather than the product of innate cultural differences.

et al. 2009). From a distinct vantage point, the "terrorism studies" literature holds that welfare provision by organizations such as the Tamil Tigers, Hezbollah, or Hamas is largely directed at supporting militias and violent forms of political engagement (Flanigan 2008; Berman 2009). But such groups may also expressly seek to serve members of other communities, depending on their broader political goals and the historical evolution of intergroup relations in the national context, and are rarely so unidimensional that they focus exclusively on military initiatives (Cammett and Issar 2010).

The chapter by Cammett traces the origins and evolution of welfare provision by sectarian parties and movements in postindependence Lebanon, demonstrating the manner in which the welfare regime has evolved in a series of distinct political moments. In the postwar period, militias and local bosses, some of which were rooted in particular religious communities, consolidated wartime gains and transformed themselves into political parties and movements. Their affiliated welfare networks tend to serve supporters and in-group members, but under certain conditions they reach out beyond their core bases.

Meanwhile, ethnic or hometown associations, groups organized to maintain reciprocal ties between urban migrants and their natal towns, are also instrumental to meeting basic needs in many developing countries. The chapter by MacLean reveals how ethnic hometown associations were organized quite differently in similar regions of neighboring Ghana and Côte d'Ivoire. The ethnically rooted rural-urban linkages produced more concrete benefits in the Ivoirian villages than in the Ghanaian ones but had troubling consequences for ethnically based political participation.

Faith-based organizations. The fourth category of NSP in the typology is faith-based organizations. With long lineages that predate the establishment of modern welfare states by centuries (Singer 2008; van Kersbergen and Manow 2009), faith-based organizations refer to groups that are characterized by administrative, cultural, or financial connections to religious communities, traditions, or places of worship (Cnaan, DiIulio, and Fass 2002; Wuthnow 2004). Here, the book distinguishes faith-based organizations from both for-profit organizations as well as secular NGOs. Faith-based organizations generally refer to charitable organizations linked to a religious institution, such as a soup kitchen run out of a neighborhood Catholic church or mosque, rather than to the broader religious institution itself, that is, the Catholic Church or Islamic religious authorities. The degree of overt religiosity varies by organization; some faith-based organizations integrate faith and religious elements into program administration and interactions with beneficiaries, including through proselytism, while others refrain from incorporating religious messages or materials into their activities even if staff members view their work as part of their private expressions of faith.

Importantly, as our typology indicates, we also differentiate between faith-based and sectarian organizations, although both are rooted in particular religious communities. The main source of difference between these two types of NSPs relates to their engagement in politics. Sectarian organizations have political foundations, goals, and orientations and tend to operate where religious cleavages are politicized and may even be institutionalized in the political system. Faith-based organizations are generally not involved explicitly as official actors in formal politics and focus on religious and charitable endeavors more exclusively.[12] This distinction is empirically important because, at a minimum, it may affect the ways in which these two types of organizations interact with beneficiaries and shape de facto eligibility criteria for services.

The chapter by Jennings makes a strong case for treating faith-based organizations as a subtype of NSPs unto themselves. The analysis traces the historical roots of the NSP sector in Tanzania, where NSPs have increased exponentially in the past four decades, and shows how faith-based organizations have shaped the social terrain occupied by secular NGOs in the contemporary period.

Community-based organizations. The fifth type of NSP explored in the book is the community-based organization. Community-based organizations have gained prominence as service providers at the local level, particularly as donors increasingly view them as more committed and effective in reaching the poor than other providers, including governments. Community-based organizations refer to self-organized grassroots associations formed to serve the shared, vested interests of the members of a neighborhood or community. Community-based organizations often arise out of existing institutions such as schools, churches, ethnic groups, or youth, sports, or cultural associations (Open Society Institute 2010). Community-based organizations also include mutual aid or cooperative organizations formed by farmers or producers of certain products, such as cooperatives for dairy or beer producers.

We place community-based organizations toward the more informal end of our typology of NSPs. They range from very small, informal groups with just a handful of members that might meet irregularly, to more formalized associations with twenty to thirty members. Generally, community-based organizations operate on a limited scale, are frequently staffed by volunteers, and rely on self-funding mechanisms, although their financing structures have evolved with growing donor interest in their activities. Because they interact with local communities on a daily basis, and their staff or group members usually come

---

12. In practice, the lines between sectarian and faith-based organizations are often blurred. Pious practices can be political, even if participants do not engage explicitly in formal politics (Mahmood 2005). Furthermore, some U.S. charitable organizations linked to churches, which are commonly referred to as "faith-based," have inserted themselves in electoral politics, for example by urging constituents to support socially conservative candidates (Quadagno and Rohlinger 2009). Nonetheless, the analytical distinction between sectarian and faith-based organizations reflects meaningful distinctions in the behavior and practices of these two types of NSPs.

from or reside in the same communities as beneficiaries, community-based organizations are well-positioned to develop cooperative ties with the communities they serve, gain trust at the local level, and assess local needs and tailor projects accordingly.

Some scholars are less sanguine about the role of community-based organizations. Agrawal and Gibson (1999) highlight the domination and division within community-based development initiatives. Still others contend that the growing reliance on and exaltation of community organizations both reflects and perpetuates the hollowing out of the state. As Kamat (2003) argues, "With the imposition of structural adjustment programs and neoliberal economic policies in Africa, Latin America, and South Asia, CBOs have become useful and even essential to the functioning of international donor institutions." In comparing community-based organizations in similar regions of Ghana and Côte d'Ivoire, MacLean finds that while these organizations are more active on a daily basis in the Ghanaian region, their financial resources have been so depleted over the past two decades of economic crisis that their activities have little consequence for the provision of social welfare.

Informal brokers. Informal brokers by definition operate separately from—albeit alongside—formal institutional channels of welfare. Our claim that informal brokers constitute "providers" could be contested on the grounds that they themselves do not possess the physical, material, or technical resources to directly deliver social services. Nonetheless, given their de facto importance in mediating access to services offered by third-party institutions, they are an important and often unrecognized component of welfare regimes in many developing countries. As the label suggests, informal brokers operate between ordinary people and providers, acting as agents who enable citizens to gain access to benefits, whether state "entitlements" or privately provided services. In some contexts, their very existence indicates that welfare states often do not provide legally enshrined social rights, compelling the needy to seek alternative sources of social protection.

Krishna's contribution to this volume on the emergence of *naya netas*, or "new leaders," in India illustrates the vital roles that informal brokers play in welfare regimes in many developing countries. The *naya netas* are informal actors who earn fees for linking villages with powerful actors at higher levels and conveying information and preferences between ordinary citizens and state officials. Cook's analysis of postcommunist transitions to privatized health care and pension insurance also underscores the importance of informal mediation in facilitating citizen access to services in higher income countries. Although the public sector retains an important de jure role in the provision and financing of social welfare in the Russian Federation, in practice access to services has undergone a process of "spontaneous privatization," in which ostensible state entitlements are accessible only through under-the-table payments to private providers. Although she does not focus explicitly on informal brokers,

Cammett's chapter on social welfare provision by sectarian organizations also highlights the importance of informal mediation in the Lebanese welfare regime. Although only the larger and more resource-rich sectarian organizations run their own welfare agencies, all serve as intermediaries to third-party services and particularly to certain ostensibly public entitlements for the needy.

Family and friendship networks. The final component of our typology of non-state providers highlights the role of family and friendship networks. Families are key components of social safety nets in most contexts but, given the relative underdevelopment of formal public welfare functions and insurance markets, they play—or are expected to play—a particularly vital role in many developing countries (von Benda Beckmann et al. 1988; Gough et al. 2004). Scholarship on international remittances has highlighted how overseas family members send significant levels of resources back to their family members to finance social welfare needs (Adams 1991; Manuh 2006). In the context of structural adjustment and the retrenchment of state social programs, it was often assumed that families would compensate for shrinking social safety nets.[13] MacLean's analysis of the effects of economic reforms in rural communities in two similar regions of Ghana and Côte d'Ivoire reveals the limits of these assumptions by revealing how divergent histories of state formation have produced different understandings and patterns of family in the two regions.

This overview of distinct NSPs highlights variation in NSPs with regard to multiple criteria that shape the political consequences of non-state welfare. As the discussion indicates, NSPs vary according to their degree of formalization, locus of operation, profit orientation, and eligibility criteria. In addition to the above factors, the relationship between a given NSP and the state can also affect citizen access to welfare, accountability, and, especially, state capacity to provide, regulate, and finance social services. The dynamics of these relationships are discussed below.

State-NSP Relations

The relationship between NSPs and the state can take multiple forms ranging from more collaborative to more antagonistic and competitive interactions. Table 2.4 presents a framework for characterizing different patterns of NSP-state relations premised on the variable capacities of each actor to finance, deliver, and regulate social welfare.

State capacity refers here specifically to the state's ability to provide social welfare, a more narrow definition than most political science definitions of this concept, which tend to privilege the provision of security and the ability to generate tax revenues (Weber 1946; Levi 1989; Lieberman 2003). Our

---

13. See World Bank (1994) for a critique.

TABLE 2.4.
Modes of NSP-state relationships

		State capacity to deliver and regulate social welfare	
		Low	High
NSP capacity to finance and deliver social welfare	Low	Appropriation (NSPs control access to state resources through brokerage, patronage, credit-claiming) Examples: India, Ghana, Côte d'Ivoire, Lebanon, Russia	State domination (state control over financing and delivery of services) Example: China
	High	Substitution (NSPs take over when state does not perform or provide) Examples: Tanzania; Kenya, Central Asia; Lebanon	Coproduction (joint financing and delivery of services by state and NSPs) and delegation (authority granted to NSPs to finance and/or deliver services) Examples: United States, Argentina, Chile

understanding of state capacity emphasizes not only the state's ability to finance and deliver social welfare services directly but also, critically, its power to monitor and regulate the non-state actors involved in social welfare provision within its borders. NSP capacity is captured by the scale and formalization of the network, group, or organization that provides or finances social services; the quantity and quality of human capital in the NSP; and the level of financial capital available for social welfare provision (Fowler 1997; Tandon and Bandyopadhyay 2003; Banerjee 2006; James and Haily 2007; Huyse et al. 2012).

Table 2.4 illustrates how the various combinations of low versus high state capacity with low versus high NSP capacity yields four different patterns of NSP-state relations. When state capacity and NSP capacity are both low, a relationship of *appropriation* emerges.[14] Appropriation describes a situation in which NSPs control access to state resources by serving as brokers for state-provided benefits or by distributing public services as a form of patronage. Appropriation may even entail credit-claiming by NSPs for services that they do not actually provide, or finance, themselves. The book's chapters on India, Russia, Lebanon, Ghana, and Côte d'Ivoire highlight the dynamics of

14. For stimulating our thinking here, we thank Robert Kaufman and other participants in the conference on the Politics of Non-State Social Welfare Providers sponsored by the Academy Scholars Program at the Weatherhead Center at Harvard University in May 2009.

appropriation in state-NSP relations. For example, in India middlemen have emerged to facilitate access to state services and resources for poorer citizens.

When state capacity is low, but NSP capacity is high, the ensuing pattern is *substitution*. Here, NSPs are able and willing to take over social welfare functions from the state when it is not performing or to provide services that the state never provided in the first place. The empirical chapters on Tanzania, Kenya, Lebanon, and Central Asia demonstrate this model of substitution. In her chapter on Kenya, for example, Brass highlights how non-state actors provide an increasing number of services that the state does not have the infrastructure to supply.

Not many developing countries exhibit high state capacity for the delivery and regulation of social welfare, but there are some relative exceptions. In Table 3.4, the inclusion of the category for high state capacity exposes the similarities and differences between advanced industrialized countries, highlighted in Allard's chapter on the United States, versus those middle income states with higher capacities to regulate NSPs, such as the book's empirical chapters covering Chile or Argentina. When state and NSP capacities are both high, the resulting pattern can range from *coproduction* to official *delegation*.

In contrast, when high state capacity combines with low NSP capacity, the dynamic is one of *state domination*. For example, the state in China is the principal provider of social welfare in the contemporary era, strictly controlling the activity of NSPs at the village level (Dillon 2011; Tsai 2011). Given the rarity of state domination of welfare regimes in most developing countries, even under conditions of authoritarian rule, the chapters in this volume do not address this pattern of NSP-state relations.

The four ideal types of NSP-state relations that we present in table 3.4 cannot be characterized necessarily as either collaborative or zero-sum, but some are more likely to reflect more competitive interactions between non-state actors and public agencies and officials. When relatively high state capacity combines with high NSP capacity, the pattern is more cooperative, and ranges from a relatively balanced situation of coproduction between NSPs and the state to a more lopsided style of delegation in which NSPs are primarily responsible for welfare delivery, albeit heavily financed and tightly regulated by the state. The chapters on Argentina and Chile exemplify patterns of coproduction and mid-range delegation on the spectrum of cooperation, while the chapter on the United States typifies the more extreme dynamic of delegation. In relationships characterized by appropriation or substitution, in which NSPs take on roles that citizens in most middle- and upper-income countries would expect their states to play, states can feel more threatened by non-state providers. This dynamic is less likely to arise in more collaborative relationships of coproduction or delegation, in which states and NSPs explicitly work together to provide services, and under conditions of state domination, in which states clearly have the upper hand in the relationship.

This book is premised on the assumption and empirical observation, however, that most developing countries have relatively weak state capacity. Hence, the majority of cases covered in the volume are lumped together in table 2.4 on the top and bottom of the left side of the theoretical framework, which represent state-NSP relations characterized by appropriation and substitution. In a smaller number of cases, state-NSP relations may also be characterized by coproduction and delegation. Obviously, other factors beyond state and NSP capacities shape relations between these two sets of actors. For example, regime type may influence the degree to which the state tolerates NSP activities. In more authoritarian contexts, states may be more wary of permitting NSPs to operate freely and to engage in more than very basic service provision. Depending on NSP types and their interactions with the state, authoritarian rulers may also be wary that NSPs will upstage their governments in meeting social needs.[15] For example, Brass highlights how the increasing political liberalization from the Moi regime to Kibaki has stimulated the emergence of a new, more collaborative era of state-NGO relations in Kenya. Furthermore, in countries with more etatist historical traditions, states are more likely to adopt a proactive and interventionist role in offering social services.[16]

The next part of the book presents case studies of varied NSP types across the developing world. The empirical material in these chapters provides valuable insights into distinct NSP forms and enables preliminary assessments of the validity of our propositions. In the book's second part, we further probe the extent to which our propositions are valid in countries with emerging markets or more advanced industrialized economies. We finally revisit our propositions in the conclusion when we take stock of the ways in which the empirical chapters support and do not support our arguments and highlight additional questions that emerge from the book.

---

15. Tandon (cited in Clark 1992) highlights how three different categories of regimes present dramatically different environments for NGOs. See also Clark (1995) and Bratton (1989).

16. Von Benda-Beckmann and Kirsch (1999) underscore the importance of an even broader type of normative framework that defines the rights and obligations for the provision of social security from all sources, not only the state.

Part I

States, Non-state Social Welfare, and Citizens in the Developing World

3

Empowering Local Communities and Enervating the State?

Foreign Oil Companies as Public Goods Providers in Azerbaijan and Kazakhstan

Pauline Jones Luong

The image of foreign oil companies as having a decisively negative effect on the developmental prospects of mineral-rich countries, and hence the daily lives of their citizens, still dominates mainstream discourse on foreign investment in the petroleum industry (e.g., Asiedu 2006; Estrada, Tangen, and Bergesen 1997). And yet, since the 1990s foreign oil companies (FOCs) have had a much greater *potential* to play both a more direct and positive role in improving social and economic conditions in petroleum-rich states by providing crucial public goods and social services. The expanded role of FOCs can be attributed directly to increasing pressures from international nongovernmental organizations (INGOs) and international financial institutions (IFIs), beginning roughly in the late 1980s, to embrace new norms associated with corporate social responsibility.[1] Whereas in the 1960s and 1970s the focus of INGOs and IFIs was on insuring that host governments captured a larger share of the rents from FOCs, which they then could harness for their own economic developmental priorities, by the 1990s a recognition had emerged not only that this was insufficient to achieve desirable outcomes but also that these rents might actually be better spent by socially responsible FOCs than states that lacked Weberian bureaucracies.[2] Of course, the question remains whether encouraging FOCs to

---

1. The origins of CSR can be traced to Bowen 1953.
2. This growing disillusionment with the state as the primary source of rent allocation was widely shared (see de Soto 1989). For a full explication of the pathologies associated with centralized control over resource rents, see Jones Luong and Weinthal 2010, esp. chaps. 3 and 6.

play such a role can have a positive impact. In fact, scholars and practitioners have expressed a healthy degree of skepticism that the global push for CSR can produce *any* tangible benefits in petroleum-rich states—particularly for the local communities most affected by foreign investment in the oil and gas sector (e.g., Frynas 2000, Idemudia 2009, Jenkins 2004).

In this chapter I present a more nuanced view of the relationship between CSR promotion and development outcomes in petroleum-rich states. Drawing on the divergent experiences of Azerbaijan and Kazakhstan—two new oil and gas producers in the developing world with significant foreign direct investment—to illustrate, I specify the conditions under which and identify the mechanisms whereby FOCs' expanded role is most likely to promote social and economic outcomes positively associated with development. In sum, when FOCs that are strongly committed to CSR can both enforce their contracts and form viable partnerships with local communities, FOCs are likely to have a positive impact because they have greater control over the size, scope, composition, and level of transparency of their fiscal burden.[3]

And yet, as the case of Azerbaijan demonstrates, even when these conditions are all present—that is, under the "best case" scenario—there are inherent trade-offs involved in delegating the role of public goods and social service provision to external actors when it comes to state capacity and equitable access for citizens. First, although FOCs are likely to be able to provide goods and services of both higher quantity and quality than the host government, particularly in weak states, some citizens are likely to benefit more than others because their provision tends to be geographically concentrated. Second, while viable partnerships between FOCs and local communities can increase the latter's ability to influence how the proceeds from petroleum sector development are allocated, these partnerships also shift the locus of accountability away from the host government. Finally, while FOCs can improve a petroleum-rich country's prospects for social and economic development by both providing better goods and services to and forming partnerships with local communities, they may also undermine its political development.

The contribution of this chapter is twofold. By focusing on external actors as non-state providers of public goods and social services, it highlights the influence of international factors on the political origins, dynamics, and hence the effects of non-state welfare provision in the developing world. Specifically, it argues that structural and normative changes at the international level have affected both the relative capacity of FOCs vis-à-vis the host government in mineral-rich states and the expectations for FOCs to play a more direct role

---

3. Conversely, when governing elites can unilaterally renege on the contracts of FOCs that are not committed to CSR, we are likely to find that the FOCs' fiscal burden is large, unstable, and nontransparent, thereby enabling the state to eschew the formation of a domestic tax base outside the mineral sector, and contains spending requirements aimed at fulfilling governing elites' pet projects (for details, see Jones Luong and Weinthal 2010, chap. 6).

in providing public goods and social services to the citizens of these states. Whether their expanded role has a positive impact, however, also depends on how committed FOCs are to fulfilling these expectations, which in turn affects their desire to engage local communities in determining the content of local development programs. Thus, while this chapter provides further corroboration that the relative capacity of NSPs to the state and community relations are key factors in gauging the impact of non-state welfare provision, it also illuminates the direct influence that NSPs' own intentions can have on welfare outcomes.

The Role of Foreign Oil Companies in Historical Perspective

FOCs have been involved in the exploitation of oil and gas in almost every petroleum-rich country since the late nineteenth century and throughout the twentieth century.[4] The extent and potential impact of their involvement, however, has varied over the twentieth century in response to fundamental changes in the global historical context in which they operate. As this section will substantiate, it was not until the 1990s that FOCs became a potential source of public goods and social service provision in mineral-rich states. In short, this decade marks both the emergence of new strategies among FOCs to prevent host governments from reneging on the terms of their contracts and the proliferation of new international norms concerning the obligations of FOCs to host countries alongside INGOs and IFIs seeking to impose these norms. Both trends had a direct impact on the contractual relationship between FOCs and host governments.

The size, scope, composition, and degree of transparency of FOCs' fiscal burden has changed dramatically over the course of the twentieth century owing to two major shifts in the set of actors and norms that dominate the international petroleum industry. This created three distinct time periods: (1) the period from 1900 to 1960 was characterized by a small number of large FOCs (aka the "Majors") who dominated the international petroleum market; (2) the period from 1960 to 1990 saw the rise and proliferation of smaller FOCs (aka the "independents"), who eroded the Majors' control over the global supply of oil and facilitated the foundation of the Organization of Petroleum Exporting Countries (OPEC), which toppled the Majors' oligopoly pricing structure (Morse 1999; Keohane and Ooms 1972); and (3) the period from 1990 to the present has been characterized by the emergence of new norms regarding the way that businesses should conduct their operations abroad and by the entrance of INGOs and IFIs that have sought to play a more pronounced role in petroleum revenue management by exerting influence on the relationship between FOCs and host governments and promoting the adoption of CSR.

---

4. For details, see Jones Luong and Weinthal 2010, appendix B.

As a result, there has been not merely a quantitative but also a *qualitative* difference in the nature of the FOCs' fiscal burden across mineral-rich states over time. First and foremost, this is manifested in dramatic changes to the "model contract," which has dictated the terms of exchange between FOCs and governing elites in host countries since petroleum exploration in the developing world began in earnest. Its main purpose has continued to be establishing the rights and duties of both parties with regard to the exploitation of mineral wealth. Yet, its form and content have been distinct in each of these three time periods.

During the first time period (1900–1960), it was possible to describe the model contract as a truly international template because its terms were universal. Beginning with the D'Arcy Concession with the shah of Persia in 1901, the FOCs carried out their business operations with oil producers in the developing world according to an internationally recognized system of isomorphic concession contracts that grossly favored the FOCs' preferences over those of the host governments. These contracts granted the FOCs huge tracts of land for extremely long periods of time wherein the FOCs not only acquired the rights to develop the petroleum in the ground but had full control over production schedules; the host governments, in turn, only received payment upon actual production but not a share of the profits (Hartshorn 1967; Smith and Dzienkowski 1989). The terms remained virtually unchanged until 1950, when Aramco agreed to split the profits 50–50 with the Saudi Arabian government; this became the predominant formula for profit-sharing (Wells 1971; Odell 1968). The model contract nonetheless continued to favor the FOCs disproportionately (Tanzer 1969).

During the second time period (1960–90), contractual relations between the FOCs and governing elites have largely been defined by the standardization of a new model contract—the production-sharing agreement (PSA). In contrast to the uniformity in the prior concessionary system, there has been and remains more variation among PSAs, largely depending on how quickly the FOCs' costs are recouped and how the profits are divided between the FOCs and the government (Bindemann 1999; Johnston 1994). Generally speaking, under a PSA the host government contracts an FOC to undertake exploration and production, and in return for carrying the initial risk the FOC receives a share of the oil produced as payment (Johnston 1994). The first major PSA signed in Indonesia in 1966, based on a 65/35 split of oil profits in the government's favor, henceforth became the predominant template in all oil-producing regions except North America and Western Europe, and thus marked the shift to an international template that deliberately favored the host governments (Bindemann 1999). This model contract differed sharply from its predecessor not only in that the level of taxation and royalties were more generous to the host governments. It also could include nominal spending provisions for the FOCs known in the industry as "local content," which required FOCs to reserve a portion of fuel production for the local economy, employ a certain share of the local workforce, or purchase locally made good and services (Smith and Wells 1975).

During the most recent time period (1990–present) the model contract retained its basic form as either a PSA or concessionary agreement that largely advantages the host government regarding taxation. However, its basic content changed fundamentally. In addition to automatically including "stability" and "international arbitration" clauses to protect the FOCs against expropriation (Smith and Dzienkowski 1989), it automatically contains explicit spending provisions for the FOCs that solidify the "local content" requirements that were only sometimes specified in their contracts during the 1970s and 1980s. These spending provisions also exceed the token and charitable spending requirements for FOCs that characterized the preceding time period; they encompass broad social spending that both sides anticipate (Radon 2007). Thus, by the last decade of the twentieth century the terms of the model contract had become even more auspicious to host countries. From the start of the negotiations it is presumed that host governments can require FOCs to pay not merely royalties, taxes, and bonuses but also fines for violating stringent environmental, health, and safety regulations and the costs associated with providing training, jobs, and basic public goods and social services to the communities surrounding their operations (Smith and Dzienkowski 1989).

Second, the FOCs' fiscal burden since the 1990s is distinct from that of the preceding time periods not only in its size and scope but also in its composition and level of transparency. Just as the model contract has changed in response to major shifts in the international petroleum industry, so too have societal expectations regarding the degree to and the manner in which they should benefit from their country's natural resource wealth. This is largely a function of the increasing visibility and publicity surrounding petroleum production in the developing world over time, which has served to elevate societal expectations vis-à-vis the FOCs.[5] During the first time period, foreign activities in the petroleum sector were essentially hidden from public view. There was little or no expectation, then, that FOCs would do more than provide minimal benefits for their own employees within what were essentially "closed towns." The second time period coincided with much greater public awareness of foreign investment in the petroleum sector due to the tremendous fanfare with which host governments ratified exploration and production contracts with FOCs. This fostered a broad expectation that FOCs would both accept a much larger tax burden at the national level and assume some limited responsibilities for spending beyond their enclave at the local level, for example, by building or repairing basic infrastructure and engaging in *symbolic* forms of philanthropy to benefit the surrounding community. The third time period is characterized by greater visibility concerning the impact of foreign investment in the petroleum

---

5. For details, see Jones Luong and Weinthal 2010, chap. 6.

sector, which INGOs and IFIs have promoted largely through their focus on transparency. They have thus targeted fiscal transactions within the mineral sector, scrutinizing the way that royalties, income taxes, and bonuses are paid to the host governments through such prominent campaigns as Publish What You Pay and the Extractive Industries Transparency Initiative (EITI).[6] This contributed to a dramatic shift in societal expectations vis-à-vis FOCs since the 1990s. These heightened expectations, however, can also be attributed to international actors' active promotion of CSR in the petroleum sector and their efforts to empower local communities in petroleum-rich states.

New norms associated with CSR proliferated in the 1990s (Gereffi, Garcia-Johnson, and Sasser 2001). The broad mandate was to encourage foreign investors not only to improve the transparency of their fiscal transactions with the host government but also to engage in activities that would better promote economic development, social welfare, and conflict prevention in the countries where they operate (Bennett 2002). In the petroleum sector, this has entailed actively and publicly pressuring FOCs to improve their own business practices vis-à-vis host governments and to expand the scope of their social and economic activities in host countries. Many of the aforementioned transparency initiatives, for example, require FOCs to cooperate by agreeing to make the terms of their contracts publicly available. At the same time, INGOs have emphasized FOCs' responsibility toward local communities where they operate by raising international awareness of the plight and protests of those most affected by the negative externalities of oil exploration and production (e.g., Ikelegbe 2001). They have also enlisted the support of IFIs, encouraging them to use their financial leverage to help persuade FOCs to invest locally in social welfare and environmental protection (e.g., Watters 2000). Overall, they have promoted CSR as a way to ensure that revenue flows within the mineral sector are not only more transparent to the population but are also channeled into a natural resource fund that explicitly directs revenue toward poverty relief in the short term and sets aside revenue for future generations over the long term (Haufler 2006; Gary and Karl 2003).

INGOs and IFIs have endeavored to empower local communities in petroleum-rich states through three basic channels. The first is linked directly to their focus on transparency, which is also aimed at providing the citizens of host countries with better information about how their "national wealth" is being utilized and for whose benefit. Second, they have increasingly encouraged local populations in petroleum-rich states to demand that FOCs play a direct role in fostering social and economic development (e.g., Treakle 1998). Finally, they have encouraged FOCs to build transnational alliances with local activists in the countries where they operate in order to make their spending

---

6. For more information, see http://www.publishwhatyoupay.org/english/, and http://www.eitransparency.org/.

programs more responsive to local needs (Jordan and Van Tuijl 2000; World Bank 2004a).

FOCs' fiscal burden since the 1990s, therefore, has amounted to much more than higher tax payments ensuring that "[they] . . . get only a fair rate of return" (Stiglitz 2007, 44). It has also become reasonable to contractually require FOCs both to engage in broad social spending at the national and local level and to assume social obligations at the local level that go beyond these ex- plicit *ex ante* requirements (i.e., to spend "beyond compliance"). Indeed, both local populations and host governments have come to expect FOCs to provide an array of public goods and social services for the benefit of entire communi- ties that surround their operations, which may include building roads, hospi- tals, and schools along with providing subsidized fuel to local consumers. At the same time, FOCs are also being asked to play a direct role in promoting transparency by disclosing the terms of their contracts. Emblematic of this is the 2005 production sharing contract signed with the Nigeria–São Tomé and Principe Joint Development Authority, which includes a "transparency clause" that requires every signature and production bonus to be published on the Au- thority's website (Save the Children 2005, 21).

Can FOCs Positively Impact Development?

In sum, what makes the third time period (1990–present) so unique from the two preceding ones is that FOCs have a much greater *potential* to play both a more direct and positive role in improving social and economic conditions in petroleum-rich states by providing crucial public goods and social services. A skeptical view would argue that this potential is so limited that FOCs' ex- panded role can only help at the margins, if at all, and may even make things worse. Indeed, this appears to be the conventional wisdom (e.g., Bakan 2004; Frynas 2000). Even those who are optimistic about the prospects for foreign direct investment to promote social and economic development in general dis- miss such a possibility for petroleum-rich states (Klein, Aaron, and Hadjimi- chael 2001; Lodge and Wilson 2006).

This pessimism is rooted in the distinction often made (explicitly or implic- itly) between "micro CSR" and "macro CSR" and the relative weight assigned to each in generating positive developmental outcomes. Micro CSR refers to a FOC's role in generating employment and providing education and health care for the communities surrounding their operations. It is widely presumed both that this is the form that FOCs are *most* likely to adopt because it has clear (and relatively low cost) reputational advantages and that it only pro- duces "immediate" benefits. In other words, such activities can have a positive impact on the local population in the short-term but are unlikely to promote long-term development (e.g., Frynas 2005). Macro CSR, in contrast, refers to a FOC's role in mitigating "the effect of oil revenues on corruption, human rights controversies, and lack of democratic progress in developing countries" (Skjaerseth et al. 2004, 6–7) and can thus range from making information regarding their payments to host governments publicly available to championing the adoption of policies that advance "accountability, good governance, anti-corruption programs, human and social rights, and democrati[zation]" in the host country (Gulbrandsen and Moe 2005, 55). It is thus heralded as an alternative way to promote social and economic development, and yet it is widely considered to be the form of CSR that FOCs are *least* likely to adopt because FOCs are unwilling to incur the political risks associated with advocating policy change (e.g., Skjaerseth et al. 2004, 7).

The distinction between "micro CSR" and "macro CSR," however, serves to obscure rather than to illuminate the role that CSR can play in fostering development. First, it underestimates the intrinsic value of FOCs' financial contributions at the micro-level. By providing basic social services that the host government either cannot or does not supply adequately, local expenditures directed at poverty reduction and human capital formation can have a notable impact on alleviating poverty, creating opportunities, and simply improving the quality of citizens' daily lives. Even if such benefits are relatively short-lived, in many countries they guarantee that citizens will receive a greater share of the proceeds from the petroleum sector in the form of improved living standards than they are likely to have received otherwise given the dismal historical record of governments in mineral-rich states to effectively allocate rents so as to improve the lives of their citizens. The appropriate counterfactual to be posed when evaluating the effects of CSR that focuses on the micro level, therefore, is not whether the local population in oil-rich states would be better off if the FOCs in question focused on the macro level instead but whether these communities would be better off *without* the involvement of FOCs engaged in CSR at all. And the track record of petroleum-rich states under state ownership in the 1970s and 1980s in which FOCs were either only minimally involved in developing the industry or directly involved but not engaged in CSR suggests that the answer is no.[7]

Second, this distinction also underestimates the instrumental value of so-called micro-CSR for achieving the goals of so-called macro-CSR. In other words, the provision of basic social services at the local level (micro-CSR) can have a direct and positive impact on the long-term developmental prospects (macro-CSR) in those communities that would otherwise be the most adversely affected by petroleum exploration and production. This is particularly the case if we conceptualize development in broader terms. If, for example, we conceive of "development as freedom" and the way to achieve development as mitigating "unfreedoms" (Sen 2000, 3) via "the expansion of the 'capabilities'

---

7. For details, see Jones Luong and Weinthal 2010, chaps. 3 and 6.

of persons to lead the kinds of lives they value" (18), then such services would not only be constitutive of development but also essential for development to occur. And yet, the activities characterized as "micro-CSR" and "macro-CSR" are integrally related even if we rely on conventional understandings of development. It is difficult to imagine, for example, how citizens in petroleum-rich states can take full advantage of FOCs' providing public goods at the national level, such as greater transparency and accountability regarding the flow of petroleum revenues, without access to primary education and basic health care at the local level. It would be equally problematic for FOCs to openly condemn national governments for their human rights record or undemocratic institutions if they are not respecting human rights and supporting democratic processes in the areas surrounding their operations.

Finally, this distinction places too much emphasis on FOCs' willingness rather than their capacity to engage in both forms of CSR. The degree of commitment to the norms embodied in CSR, which varies considerably across FOCs, is undoubtedly an important determinant of whether a given company's activities at either the micro or macro level will contribute to development.[8] Those FOCs that display a high degree of commitment, however, also tend to approach CSR holistically—that is, to view their activities at the local and national level as integrally related in the manner described above (Olson 2002). It is thus unlikely that if FOCs are not engaging in CSR at the macro level they are in fact engaging in CSR at the micro level. At the same time, while a high degree of commitment to CSR is necessary, it is not sufficient. In order for FOCs to successfully carry out CSR they must be capable of "managing" their own fiscal burden—that is, exercising control over the size, scope, composition, and level of transparency of their tax payments and social expenditures. Engaging in CSR, for example, requires not merely that FOCs make financial contributions at the local level in compliance with their contracts but also that they work closely with local community representatives in order to consciously and consistently direct their expenditures toward providing the social services that a particular community needs most. FOCs must therefore also be able to resist the attempts of national as well as local governments to redirect funds away from community development projects. Likewise, FOCs must be able to oppose governments' efforts to arbitrarily alter the terms of their contracts in order to extract additional funds for building large "national prestige" projects, financing public sector debt to avoid restructuring the economy, or expanding the state's coercive capacity—all of which can undermine long-term development prospects.[9]

---

8. The Goldman Sachs Energy Environmental and Social Index provides a good benchmark for assessing these differing levels of commitment (for details, see Goldman Sachs 2004).

9. For example, these were the spending priorities of OPEC countries in the 1970s and 1980s, which have been linked directly to "double-digit inflation, cost overruns on vast public projects, . . . and high levels of state debt," among other things (Karl 2000, 5; see also Amuzegar 2001).

I adopt a more nuanced view of the relationship between CSR and development in petroleum-rich states. First, based on a holistic approach to CSR, I place equal emphasis on FOCs' contributions at the micro- and macro-level regardless of the prima facie magnitude and duration of their impact. Second, I specify the conditions under which and identify the mechanisms whereby FOCs committed to CSR are most likely to promote social and economic outcomes positively associated with development.

As noted above, although most FOCs have at least acknowledged CSR, they have not embraced the norms embodied in CSR to the same degree. Whether or not those FOCs that are strongly committed to implementing CSR can actually do so, however, depends on two other factors: (1) their bargaining power relative to the host government; and (2) the history of their relations with both the host government and particular communities.

Another distinguishing feature of the third time period is that the dominant actor in the negotiations between FOCs and host governments cannot be identified *ex ante*. In the first half of the twentieth century, when the Majors effectively exploited the world's oil fields, the combination of solidarity among these FOCs (Lipson 1985) and gunboat diplomacy from their respective home governments secured the predominance of FOCs (Mommer 2002). FOCs could therefore unilaterally enforce the initial terms of their contracts. After 1960, with the intense competition brought on by the emergence of the independents, the creation of OPEC, and the increasing reluctance of home governments to intervene on behalf of FOCs, bargaining power shifted decisively to host governments (Tanzer 1969). Indeed, these changes ushered in an era characterized by the "obsolescing bargain," whereby host governments automatically gain leverage in their contractual relations with FOCs once the latter's costs are sunk and use their advantage to constantly rewrite FOCs' contracts in order to capture a greater share of rents (Vernon 1971). By the end of the 1980s, however, some FOCs began to develop strategies to counter the inevitability of the obsolescing bargain. In particular, where they could effectively form a united front vis-à-vis the host government—that is, overcome the collective action problem[10]—they could also prevent the state from unilaterally reneging on the terms of their contracts.

The capacity of FOCs to carry out CSR-based initiatives also depends on the history of their relations with both the host government and particular communities. Simply put, this is because a *minimum* requirement for implementing effective local development projects is a viable partnership with representatives of the community in question, which in turn necessitates a certain degree of trust concerning FOCs' intentions as well as the longevity of their project. Where an FOC's past is tainted by its collaboration with corrupt governments

---

10. It is has become quite common, for example, for FOCs to form petroleum associations to lobby government agencies collectively for the harmonization of laws and regulations (Prattini 2007).

or blatant disregard for the environment, this is difficult to achieve. Despite a concerted effort to gain an international image as a socially and environmentally conscious company since the late 1990s, for example, Shell has not been able to overcome its devastatingly negative reputation in Nigeria (Amadi, Germiso, and Henriksen, 2006).[11] And conversely, building trust is easier to achieve when either the FOC's reputation has not been tainted by prior operations within the country or the country or community in question is a new petroleum producer. It is no surprise, then, that the only successful community development project inaugurated in Nigeria to date (in Akassa) has been directed by Shell's main competitors Statoil and BP both of which are relative newcomers to the country and to the Akassa community (World Business Council for Sustainable Development 2005).[12] This is not to say, however, that trust is unattainable where past relations are poor or that trust will be automatic where past relations are favorable. Statoil and BP's success in Akassa, for example, has been attributed to its proactive outreach; in other words, the companies started to engage the local community in a continuous dialogue before their operations even began (Amadi, Germiso, and Henriksen 2006).[13]

The "best case" scenario, then, is when FOCs that are strongly committed to CSR can both enforce their contracts and form viable partnerships with local communities. It is under these conditions that FOCs are most likely to play a direct role in improving both the quality of citizens' daily lives and the long-term developmental prospects of mineral-rich states. But how does this occur? There are three basic mechanisms. First, FOCs can promote budgetary transparency and stability by publicly revealing their payments to the host government and limiting its ability to alter the size and scope of their fiscal burden. Second, FOCs can ensure that crucial public goods and social services are provided by exercising greater influence over how their expenditures are allocated. And finally FOCs can empower local communities by giving them a more decisive role in how petroleum sector proceeds are actually spent. In other words, where these conditions are present, FOCs are most likely to have a positive impact because they have greater control over their fiscal burden's size, scope, composition, and level of transparency. Where these conditions are not present, FOCs are least likely to have a positive impact—even if they are committed to CSR—because they have little or no control over their fiscal burden. The contrasting cases of post-Soviet Azerbaijan and Kazakhstan serve to illustrate.

---

11. Shell is second only to BP on the Goldman Sachs Index (cited above).

12. Although Shell and other FOCs have been active in Nigeria since the mid-1950s, Statoil signed its first PSAs in the early 1990s with BP, which had left Nigeria in the 1960s and returned only in 1993 to explore new offshore fields.

13. Arco adopted a similar approach in Ecuador in the 1990s vis-à-vis the indigenous communities near the Villano oil field after gaining a negative reputation for its operations in this country in the 1980s (Sawyer 2004, 64–68).

Azerbaijan versus Kazakhstan:
The Best- and Worst-Case Scenarios

Azerbaijan and Kazakhstan are an ideal set of cases for comparison not only because they share the same political and economic legacy due to their common Soviet past but also because they emerged as new oil and gas producers in the same international context (i.e., 1990–present) in which FOCs have historically had the greatest potential to foster outcomes that are positively associated with development (broadly understood). Thus when both countries signed extensive exploration and production contracts with FOCs in the early 1990s,[14] there was good reason to expect that, ceteris paribus, these FOCs would be engaged in a similar level of social welfare provision. And yet, over a decade later, the evidence suggests that they have not. The key to understanding why is that whereas Azerbaijan depicts the "best case" scenario described above, Kazakhstan depicts the "worst case" scenario.

Origins of FOC Social Welfare Provision in Eurasia

Azerbaijan and Kazakhstan are unique among their petroleum-rich counterparts in Eurasia in that they welcomed a large degree of direct foreign involvement in their petroleum sector when they gained independence following the Soviet Union's dissolution in 1991. In Azerbaijan this has taken the form of PSAs,[15] the first of which was signed with great fanfare on September 20, 1994, and was widely referred to in the popular press as the "Contract of the Century." This historic PSA was reached with a consortium of major international oil and gas companies known as the Azerbaijan International Operating Company (AIOC)[16] to develop the Azeri, Chirag, and deep-water portion of the Guneshli oil fields with estimated reserves of over six billion barrels of oil. Another monumental PSA[17] was signed shortly thereafter (in June 1996) for the Shah Deniz giant natural gas and condensate field, which is considered to be one of the world's largest natural gas field discoveries in the last twenty years.

In Kazakhstan, contracts with FOCs have taken two basic forms. Up to the mid-2000s, the majority of oil and gas production occurred in fields under concessionary contracts. This includes Tengiz, one of country's three largest

---

14. For details, see Jones Luong and Weinthal 2010, chaps. 7 and 8.

15. Azerbaijan stands out as having signed the largest number of PSAs in Eurasia; by 2005 it had concluded over twenty-five PSAs with approximately thirty FOCs.

16. The AIOC partners included BP, ChevronTexaco, State Oil Company of Azerbaijan Republic, Inpex, Statoil, ExxonMobil, Turkish Petroleum Overseas, Devon Energy, Itochu, and Delta/Hess.

17. This consortium consisted of BP, Statoil, State Oil Company of Azerbaijan Republic, Lukoil, National Oil Company Iran, Elf, and Turkish Petroleum Overseas.

fields in terms of reserves and the single largest producing field (approximately 35% of total current production), as well as several older, smaller fields (Aktobe, Emba, Kumkol, and Uzen) that have much smaller reserves but together account for approximately 50 percent of total current production. But since the late 1990s there has been an increasing number of PSAs with large consortia of FOCs. The first was signed with British Gas (32.5%), Agip (32.5%), Texaco (20%), and Lukhoil (15%) to exploit the giant Karachaganak oil and gas condensate field located onshore in western Kazakhstan. The second PSA was signed with the Offshore Kazakhstan International Operating Company[18] to develop the Kashagan deposit in the Caspian Sea shelf, where the majority of the country's future production is expected to lie.

Dynamics of FOC Social Welfare Provision in Eurasia

Under BP's leadership, the FOCs exploiting Azerbaijan's petroleum sector have displayed a high level of commitment to CSR, maintained a clear bargaining advantage over the central government, and encouraged the active involvement of the local community. With the highest participation rate of all the FOCs, BP is without question the predominant FOC involved in exploring and producing Azerbaijan's oil and gas fields.[19] BP is also the operator of several consortia of major international oil and gas companies, including the two most important projects producing petroleum mentioned above (AIOC and the Shah Deniz Consortium), as well as the Baku-Tbilisi-Ceyhan pipeline.

BP's dominant position has been buttressed by the proliferation of consortia with overlapping memberships, which has not only fostered cooperation among FOCs but also led them to recognize the value of a hegemon that could harmonize their interests and act as their unanimously recognized chief negotiator. The FOCs clearly realized early on the power of a unified front. As David Woodward, President of BP Azerbaijan, explained, "Following the merger of BP Amoco [in 1999], it was recognized that BP Amoco had, by far, the largest shareholding in AIOC (34%). The partners saw the value of having a single company responsible for the operation rather than having it managed by the consortium and agreed that BP Amoco should take on this role commencing in June 1999."[20] As a result, they were able to avert the obsolescing bargain by forming a united front vis-à-vis the Azerbaijani government.

On the taxation side, this has enabled the FOCs to maintain a stable rate of taxation even after their costs were sunk in the late 1990s—that is, when the

---

18. The name was later changed to Agip KCO—Agip Kazakhstan North Caspian Operating Company.

19. By 1998, BP had signed five PSAs with the Azerbaijani government (for details, see Bindemann 1999, 71–72). Its participation shares in these contracts increased when it merged with Amoco that same year.

20. Interview with David Woodward in Azadliq, August 20, 2002.

obsolescing bargain is presumed to take effect. During the bust in 1998, when the price of oil fell below $10 a barrel, for example, the FOCs were able to cut back dramatically their investment expenditures and reduce their operational budget for 1999 rather than having to increase production to make up for budgetary shortfalls (Auty 2006, 61). The FOCs' capacity to avoid arbitrary tax increases has not only imposed some degree of budgetary stability on the government but also provided it with an incentive to pursue broad-based tax reform. As oil prices began to rise in the early 2000s, for example, foreign tax analysts expressed continued surprise that "Baku [the capital of Azerbaijan]— unlike Astana [the capital of Kazakhstan]—has not (yet?) attacked the tax provisions of PSAs and reform of the tax administration under IMF auspices continues to edge forward" (Townsend 2002).

On the expenditure side, forming a united front with BP at the helm has enabled the FOCs to direct their social spending toward their own priorities and to withstand pressure from both national and local officials to support projects that did not accord with these priorities.[21] While skeptics argue that such influence has a minimal impact because the government share of petroleum revenue is so much greater than the FOCs, this actually varies by contract and over time based on changes to the real rate of return. In the case of Azerbaijan, for example, the government's share of profit oil (the oil that remains after the contractor covers its costs and is usually divided between the contractor and the government) had only reached 30 percent from 2003–07 and was expected to rise precipitously in 2008 (Bagirov 2008). Thus, even if FOCs controlled only their own spending, the potential impact would be significant. And yet, in addition to this, they have exercised control over their voluntary contributions, which will be discussed further below.

Importantly, BP has also utilized its role as hegemon to promote CSR. BP is both widely recognized for having embraced CSR and credited for being one of its earliest and most vocal advocates in the oil industry (Goldman Sachs 2004; Save the Children 2005). BP has also vigorously pursued a pro-CSR agenda from the signing of its initial contract in Azerbaijan. As early as 1995, Terry Adams (the first president of AIOC) pledged: "We're committed to making sure our business process is transparent to the industry at large" (Adams 1995). BP's efforts have received the greatest amount of attention (and praise) regarding transparency of petroleum sector revenues—both internationally and in Azerbaijan. BP was one of the first MNCs to endorse wholeheartedly the principles espoused by EITI and Publish What You Pay. In Azerbaijan, it has willingly revealed its royalty and tax payments to the state budget and encouraged other FOCs, including the national oil company (State Oil Company of Azerbaijan Republic), to do the same.[22]

---

21. For details, see Jones Luong and Weinthal 2010, chap. 7.
22. Ibid.

Beyond increasing public access to information regarding the amount of revenue that the government receives from the petroleum industry, their combined commitment to transparency has had two concrete effects. The first concerns the increasing openness with which Azerbaijan's natural resource fund—the State Oil Fund of the Azerbaijan Republic, created in 1999—has accumulated FOCs' payments and deposited them in "highly reputable financial institutions" (Petersen and Budina 2002), and thus earned a reputation as "the most transparent government body in Azerbaijan"(Economist Intelligence Unit 2006, 26).The second is the Azerbaijani government's decision to reach "EITI Compliant" status, which requires both the government and the FOCs to regularly submit reports on revenue flows from the petroleum sector to an internationally reputable accounting firm (Economic Research Center 2006).[23]

The FOCs' unified commitment to the core principles of CSR has also been manifested in how they have directed their spending—particularly at the local level. In sum, they have followed BP's lead in both adopting an "investment" approach to development and "partnering" with representatives of the local community toward this end.[24] FOCs in Azerbaijan, for example, have not only targeted their local-content spending at creating growth opportunities for local businesses and providing basic social services and public goods but also increased the level of their spending beyond compliance to meet the needs of local communities. BP in particular has routinely volunteered to renovate schools and overhaul water supply systems in order to improve the education, health, and general welfare of the population residing in the districts surrounding its operations. Together with its partners, BP has also agreed to finance several comprehensive development initiatives that were conceived and are being implemented through active dialogue with multiple local stakeholders, for example, along the Baku-Tbilisi-Ceyhan pipeline route.[25] One such initiative was the Human Development Program associated with AIOC's Sangachal Terminal Expansion Program through which AIOC supported local projects aimed at improving the health, economic development prospects, and educational opportunities in most of the local communities in the Garadagh district (Bayatly 2003). A clear indication that these efforts have not been in vain is that according to independent surveys BP is viewed favorably among local NGOs for its "capacity-building projects, community development initiatives and the contributions [it] make[s] to the economy" (British Petroleum 2006, 14; see also, e.g., Economic Research Center 2006).

The role of FOCs actively involved in Kazakhstan's petroleum sector is in stark contrast to that of Azerbaijan. First and foremost, unlike their counterparts

---

23. On March 15, 2005, it became the first oil producing country to achieve this status. For details, see http://eitransparency.org/Azerbaijan.

24. For details, see Jones Luong and Weinthal 2010, chap. 7.

25. By 2006, they had invested approximately $6.7 million in the social sector, of which $3.2 million was spent on "community development investment projects" (British Petroleum 2006).

in Azerbaijan, FOCs in Kazakhstan have failed to either create a viable institution or anoint a hegemon through which they could prevent the government from arbitrarily increasing their taxation and spending obligations.[26] They have thus fallen prey to the obsolescing bargain. Although their initial contracts clearly stipulated tax obligations and offered stability assurances against fluctuations in the country's general tax code, these terms were routinely violated within a few years. For example, it was not unusual for FOCs to be exempt from value added taxes (VAT) by contracts signed in the mid-1990s but then be forced to pay VAT during the late 1990s due to alleged budgetary shortfalls. Whereas the central government's favorite tactic seemed to be withdrawing tax exemptions to cover budgetary shortfalls in the 1990s, local officials (*akims*) became notorious for imposing hefty fines for alleged noncompliance, late payments, and environmental damage.[27] The absence of a stable tax code in Kazakhstan was both a cause and a consequence of this dynamic since it enabled various tax authorities to conduct frequent audits of the FOCs—ranging from 6–15 times a year to several times a week—which generated little incentive to pursue broad-based tax reform. Frequent audits, in turn, served as a vehicle for both the central and local government to extract other concessions from the FOCs, such as supplying the domestic market with subsidized oil and gas or absorbing redundant employees. The threat of a compulsory review of all existing contracts served a similar purpose since wary FOCs would agree to pay additional royalties "voluntarily" in order to avoid this fate. FOCs have also been subjected to increasing demands at both levels of government to make expenditures outside their contractual obligations. Local officials, for example, would insist that FOCs finance their pet projects, ranging from annual celebrations to sports complexes, as a condition for continuing their operations unimpeded. Such "requests" became so common by the late 1990s that a large number of FOCs simply opted to make a lump sum contribution directly to the local *akimiyat* (administration) each year that could be used at the sole discretion of the *akim*.

The fact that FOCs' tax payments have become increasingly opaque, moreover, has also contributed to the lack of transparency within the mineral sector. Many of the initial bonuses the government received, for example, were placed in offshore bank accounts and not formally reported in the state budget, "undermining the validity of fiscal data" (Ramamurthy and Tandberg 2002, 12). Only in 2002 did Prime Minster Imangaly Tasmagambetov reveal that in 1996 a $1 billion "bonus" payment from an oil contract was surreptitiously siphoned off into a "top-secret Swiss [bank] account under Nazarbayev's direct control" that was created for this very purpose (Global Witness 2004, 15–16).

---

26. For details, see Jones Luong and Weinthal 2010, chap. 8.

27. One indication of the frequent use of fines to extract more revenue from FOCs is that environmental fines alone increased by approximately 400 percent between 2003 and 2004 (Najman, Pomfret, and Raballand 2008, 119).

In short, since the mid-1990s the Kazakhstani government has been increasingly able to unilaterally determine the size, stability, composition, and degree of transparency of the FOCs' fiscal burden. Its ability to do so is compounded by the fact that the FOCs are only weakly committed to CSR.[28] In fact, the FOC that has occupied the dominant role in Kazakhstan since the early 1990s, and thus, could potentially perform the role of hegemon—Tengiz Chevroil[29]—is notorious for its blatant disregard for CSR (Yessenova 2008, 195). FOCs in Kazakhstan have thus exhibited a lukewarm approach to international transparency initiatives such as EITI; in contrast to those in Azerbaijan, only half of the FOCs in Kazakhstan that were identified as candidates for EITI implementation agreed to participate (Makhmutova 2005). This has affected both the Kazakhstani government's willingness to join EITI and its subsequent halfhearted efforts to harmonize its legislation with the international principles and criteria of EITI (International Crisis Group 2007, 25). More concretely, it has resulted in the creation of the Natural Resource Fund of Kazakhstan, which, in contrast to the State Oil Fund of the Azerbaijan Republic, does not promote the transparent flow of petroleum revenues from the FOCs to the government.

FOCs in Kazakhstan have displayed a similar lack of enthusiasm when it comes to monitoring the impact of their operations or the quality of their expenditures on the local communities (e.g., Gulbrandsen and Moe 2005). Tengiz Chevroil's lack of leadership has helped to perpetuate not only a common disregard for revenue transparency but also a common notion across the FOCs' representatives that have no obligation to the domestic population.[30] For example, the consortium developing the giant Karachaganak oil and gas condensate field located onshore in western Kazakhstan[31] has refused to respond to local community concerns that they have both been denied access to basic information on the field operations and environmental impacts and redress for widespread illnesses among the local population. Rather, when it comes to their social spending, what seems to have mattered most to FOCs was whether it benefited the *akim*. Most FOC representatives openly acknowledged that their financial contributions at the local level were "wasted" or would "essentially disappear" but few seemed troubled that these expenditures were not actually fostering socioeconomic development.

This has had several negative consequences for the impact of FOCs' expenditures in Kazakhstan. First, although they have intensified over time (as in Azerbaijan), FOC expenditures have focused solely on the subnational level and primarily on projects that are highly visible projects in the main urban areas or

---

28. For details, see Jones Luong and Weinthal 2010, chap. 8.
29. Tengiz Chevroil is the main operator of the Tengiz field (described above). Chevron holds a 50 percent interest in the company.
30. For details, see Jones Luong and Weinthal 2010, chap. 8.
31. Partners included British Gas (32.5%), Agip (32.5%), Texaco (20%), and Lukoil (15%).

in close proximity to their production fields.[32] Second, also in contrast to Azerbaijan, FOCs' spending in Kazakhstan has been less directed toward achieving specific developmental goals such as poverty alleviation. Instead, they have readily agreed to support such ventures as a regional football team for the sum of $50,000. Third, due largely to ongoing requests at both the subnational and national level for additional funds to finance pet projects, FOCs' expenditures have been characterized by a high degree of instability and arbitrariness And, finally, FOCs' expenditures have spawned poor results for poverty alleviation in the oil-rich regions that contrast sharply with the tremendous strides that Kazakhstan, as a whole, has made toward reducing poverty (Agrawal 2008). In 2004, for example, the overall poverty rate was less than 16 percent of the population, whereas poverty rates in the oil-rich regions of Mangistau, Atyrau, and Kyzylorda still exceeded 20 percent with 29.1 percent recorded in Atyrau (United Nations Development Program 2005, 19, 28).

The Political Consequences of FOC Investment in Social Welfare

As the contrasting cases of Azerbaijan and Kazakhstan demonstrate, FOCs are most likely to have a positive impact on development when they are strongly committed to CSR and can both enforce their contracts and form viable partnerships with local communities. And yet Azerbaijan's experience also suggests that—even under this "best case" scenario—delegating the role of public goods and social service provision to external actors involves inherent trade-offs for development. First, because the primary mandate is for FOCs to provide public goods and social services to the communities surrounding their operations, there is a strong likelihood that the benefits of FOCs' direct role in social spending will be unevenly distributed within the country—making some local areas better off than others. In Azerbaijan, for example, the Garadagh district of the capital city (Baku) and several districts along the Baku-Tbilisi-Ceyhan pipeline route have received the lion's share of community development funds. A more even distribution of these benefits would require a greater amount of coordination and fiscal discipline than most states, including Azerbaijan, are equipped to handle. Second, although partnerships with FOCs enable local activists to influence how petroleum revenue is spent within their respective communities—and thus, to help ensure that they receive a greater share of the benefits—these partnerships also encourage them to circumvent the state. Local communities in Azerbaijan, for example, have not only come to expect FOCs to provide public goods and social services but also to view FOCs as their preferred supplier. By both providing better goods and services to and forming partnerships with local communities, then, FOCs may actually

---

32. For specific examples, see *Kazakhstan International Business Magazine*, various issues 2003–05.

undermine the state's own capacity to promote social and economic development. Rather, their expanded role has fostered the emergence of a proxy state, whereby international actors both replace various forms of local organization as mediators between the state and society and displace the state as the legitimate driver of development.

4

The Politics of "Contracting Out" to the Private Sector

Water and Sanitation in Argentina

Alison E. Post

In the wake of the Washington Consensus, many governments throughout the developing world "contracted out" social welfare and health services to private firms. In doing so, they delegated responsibility for service provision, while retaining the power to award contracts and regulate compliance with contractual terms. In the explicit and formal nature of state delegation of responsibility to the private sector, this form of private sector provision differs dramatically from the other two types of private provision discussed in this volume, entrepreneurial efforts by individual firms to provide services in areas or sectors where the state provides services inadequately and corporate social responsibility programs launched by private firms to complement their primary operations in sectors such as mining or manufacturing.

This chapter examines the origins, dynamics, and consequences of contracting with private firms for the management of and investment in state-owned urban water and sanitation systems. These systems constitute an important aspect of the welfare state in the developing world. Whereas cities of the developed world built the physical foundations of their public health systems—networks of water and sewer pipes and water treatment plants—during the nineteenth century, much of this "hard" infrastructure has yet to be built in developing countries, with enormous public health repercussions. Problems are

Bernardo Deregibus, Hernán Flom, Eugenia Giraudy, and Lindsay Mayka provided excellent research assistance for this project. I also thank Melani Cammett, Debbie Cheng, Kathryn Hochstetler, Lauren MacLean, James McGuire, and Wendy Pearlman for extremely helpful comments on preliminary drafts.

particularly acute in the mushrooming cities of the developing world, where water and sewer network expansion has failed to keep pace with rapid population growth. The empirical focus of the chapter is Latin America, and in particular provincial-level contracts in Argentina, the first Latin American country to privatize in the sector and one of the countries that privatized most extensively.

In this chapter I make three arguments. First, scholars of the developing world should expand their definition of the welfare state to include investments in "hard" infrastructure that contributes to health, such as water and sanitation services. Second, the contracting out of management and investment obligations to private firms transforms rather than enfeebles the state's role in the sector. Finally, the dynamics and consequences of private sector service provision depend critically on the *type of investor* to whom contracts are awarded. Domestic, and especially locally diversified, investors are better able to navigate the complex and volatile politics in the sector that emerge following privatization than domestic investors with few local operations or international investors, because they structure operations to be less vulnerable to economic and political volatility, are accustomed to informal means of dispute resolution, possess informal ties with the local political establishment, and enjoy a more multidimensional relationship with the state, which lengthens their time horizons. In the medium run, differences in ownership have contributed to uneven institutional legacies, with privatized provision surviving more often in jurisdictions where services are managed by local investors. The preponderance of contract renegotiations has also contributed to waning public support for private sector service provision.

Infrastructure a Vital Component of Social Welfare Regimes

The standard definitions of social welfare regimes employed by the recent wave of research on welfare states in developing countries borrow heavily from traditional concepts formulated to describe the European and North American welfare state. Esping-Anderson (1990) focused on social and health insurance and services in industrialized democracies, and recent studies of Latin America and other regions (Gough et al. 2004; Segura-Ubiergo 2007; Haggard and Kaufman 2008) analyze similar types of services.

In the developing world, however, the definition of social welfare policy should be expanded to include physical infrastructure that prevents the spread of disease. Access to clean water yields improved health outcomes, particularly reduced rates of child illness and mortality.[1] Unfortunately, there are

---

1. On the link between clean water access and health outcomes, see Merrick (1985); Behrman and Wolfe (1987); Esrey et al. (1991); Cebu Team (1991); Lavy et al. (1996); Lee, Rosenzweig, and Pitt (1997); Jalan and Ravallion (2003). Scholars have found that individuals must be educated in personal hygiene and the nature of disease transmission in order for health improvements to be fully realized (Green 2003, 230–1).

major coverage deficits in developing countries: according to United Nations estimates, 46 percent of the world's population currently lacks piped household water connections, while 48 percent lack access to improved sanitation through flush toilets, latrines, or composting toilets.[2] The main reason that scholars of public policy in the industrialized world do not include water and sanitation infrastructure in their definitions of the welfare state is that they take it for granted: these countries achieved almost universal coverage during the nineteenth and early twentieth centuries, with investments in new purification technologies massively reducing the spread of diseases such as cholera and typhoid.[3]

Just as the Latin American welfare states analyzed by Huber (1996), Segura-Ubiergo (2007), and Haggard and Kaufman (2008) have covered workers with formal sector jobs and have failed to provide social and health insurance and services for those in the informal sector, the failure of state urban and water systems to keep pace with urban growth has yielded a similar division between system insiders with subsidized access to the water and sanitation network maintained by large state bureaucracies and outsiders dependent on alternative, less formal sources. State water companies have often not enforced payment for those with subsidized access, further aggravating the insider-outsider divide.[4] Network outsiders, on the other hand, must rely on other sources, including household wells of dubious quality, and private water vendors that typically charge between ten to twenty times as much a liter (Estache, Gomez-Lobo, and Leipziger 2001, 1185). Even in developing countries that have constructed extensive welfare states, significant portions of the population live outside the formal water and sanitation network. Argentina is a case in point. The Argentine census measures water and sanitation access in a number of categories—ranging from household access to the formal public network to access from a stream or river.[5] When one includes only the population receiving services through the formal network within one's household or property, rates of access for 1991—that is, before privatization—were surprisingly low: 66 percent. Moreover, provincial-level access data on household connections testifies to significant differences across regions; while higher income provinces such as Capital Federal, Tierra del Fuego, and Santa Cruz reported water access rates above 90 percent, comparatively poor provinces such as Chaco,

---

2. Figures from UNICEF-WHO (2008, 6, 23). An additional 33% of the population obtains access to other "improved sources" of water such as standpipes, boreholes, and protected dug wells or springs.

3. See Cutler and Miller (2005) and Macassa et al. (2006).

4. See Savedoff and Spiller (1999, 1–17) regarding the political difficulties that plague public sector management in developing countries.

5. The categories include access to water through: (a) the public network; (b) a motorized well; (c) a manually operated well; (d) a perforation in the ground; (e) rainwater; (f) a cistern; (g) a river or stream; h) unknown. Instituto Nacional de Estadísticas y Censos (INDEC), Series B, table V6, 1991.

Formosa, and Santiago del Estero left more than half of the population without formal household connections.[6] Coverage gaps were even more striking in the case of sanitation. This data suggests that even in countries that Wood and Gough (2006) would categorize as "actual or potential" welfare state regimes, such as Argentina, significant portions of the population lacked access to basic public health infrastructure that is a vital component of preventative health care systems. To make matters worse, these figures do not convey any information about service quality. In many contexts, water quality provided by formal systems may be substandard or water pressure only sufficient to provide service for a few hours a day.[7]

The Statist Origins of Water Privatization

Developing countries enlisted the private sector to address water and sanitation coverage deficits during the 1990s in the context of sweeping market reform programs. Throughout Latin America, this shift marked a return toward more sophisticated versions of the long-term contracts for infrastructure development utilized during the late nineteenth and early twentieth centuries. Both preexisting institutional legacies and conscious choices by politicians (and trusted technocrats) shaped the *extent* and *form* of privatization. First, the institutional legacy of decentralized responsibility in the sector meant that privatization occurred more unevenly than would have been the case if the sector had been controlled at the national level. In addition, privatization contracts typically retained the main institutional features of public sector provision, including service area boundaries, tariff formulas, and labor codes. More strikingly, politicians *consciously chose* a particular mode of privatization—long-term management and investment agreements called "concession contracts"—that contained very explicit government commitments to quality services for a far greater portion of the population than enjoyed services under the status quo. They also chose to privilege certain types of investors in the privatization process.

For much of the postwar period, Latin American governments provided water and sanitation infrastructure, making impressive headway expanding networks in the face of rapid urban growth.[8] National government involvement followed an earlier, less sweeping wave of investment beginning in the late nineteenth century, when local and national governments financed their nascent systems through foreign loans or granting franchise contracts to private

---

6. Connection percentages for each province were calculated from municipal-level data on the population served through the public network either within one's dwelling or on one's property. Municipal totals taken from INDEC, 1991 Census (table V6, series B).

7. Habitat (2001, 122–26).

8. Foster (2005) describes the institutional setting for service provision in six Latin American countries prior to 1990.

companies (Hardoy 1998, 109; Gilbert 1998, 108).[9] By the 1980s, however, the Latin American debt crisis made it increasingly difficult for national water companies to keep financing network expansion and maintenance. In response to these difficulties, most states chose to decentralize the administrative responsibility for service provision during the 1980s and early 1990s.[10] Investment levels slowed because local governments often did not have sufficient revenues to subsidize services, and service levels in many cases deteriorated as a result.[11] Outside the service areas of the large state companies, a range of non-state actors provided complementary services: user-owned cooperatives and private companies operating small, networked-based systems (primarily located in small towns and peri-urban areas), as well as mobile water vendors such as tanker trucks or trucks selling containers of water of varying volumes. A 2005 World Bank study estimates that roughly one-quarter of Latin America's urban population continues to receive water and sanitation services from small-scale, non-state providers, including for-profit and nonprofit ventures.[12]

National-level politicians in Latin America decided to invite *the private sector* to fund investment in and manage state-owned systems during the 1990s against this messy backdrop of decentralized governance, disinvestment, and informal provision on the urban fringe. The attractiveness of water and sanitation privatization to national politicians can be explained by standard political economy arguments regarding the sources of market reform. These stress the importance of international financial pressures (Stallings 1992; Henisz, Guillén, and Zelner 2005) and the important role of technocrats and practically minded politicians, who had reached a consensus regarding the promise of market-oriented approaches to problems of disinvestment and poor administration (Domínguez 1997; Teichman 2001; Madrid 2003; Kogut and MacPherson 2004; Weyland 2005). Systems were starved for investment and domestic sources of finance were limited. Multilateral bank sector loan programs also promoted institutional changes within the sector, such as the establishment of regulatory agencies, granting concession contracts with private investors, and the transfer of services to state-owned, but legally distinct, service companies (Goldstone 2006).

The policy consensus regarding the advantages of private sector management, however, did not translate automatically into a uniform privatization

---

9. For examples of early franchise agreements, see the cases of Buenos Aires (Bordi de Ragucci 1997) and Córdoba (Boixadós 2000) in Argentina.

10. By 2008, municipalities were individually or jointly responsible for drinking water provision in Argentina, Bolivia, Brazil, Colombia, the Dominican Republic, Ecuador, Guatemala, Honduras, Mexico, Nicaragua, Paraguay, Peru, Uruguay, and Venezuela (World Bank and United Cities and Local Governments 2008), 190–91.

11. Ordoqui Urcelay (2007, 8–9) chronicles this history in the Argentine case.

12. The respective percentage for African cities is estimated to be nearly 50% (Kariuki and Schwartz 2005, 6 and 18).

wave. Because the Washington Consensus period followed or coincided with decentralization in the sector, if national politicians wanted to privatize, they needed to work with subnational governments. This increased the potential number of veto players in the privatization process and the number of politicians who needed to be willing to assume the associated political risks.[13] So while fifty-eight low- and middle-income countries privatized some portion of their urban water and sanitation infrastructure between 1990 and 2005 (PPIAF-World Bank 2007), uptake of privatization at the subnational level varied. In Argentina, for instance, the national government required provinces signing the Fiscal Pact of 1993 to privatize services administered at the provincial level, such as water and sanitation.[14] The Argentine national government had few means of forcing follow-through, however, other than steering World Bank and Inter-American Bank loans to fund water and sanitation system upgrades to provinces that adhered to the national program. Despite the fact that twenty-one out of twenty-three provinces signed the 1993 Fiscal Pact, only thirteen provinces privatized in the sector.[15] In Latin America, 15 percent of urban water consumers came to be served by large-scale private providers. Chile brought almost its entire water sector under private sector management, Argentina roughly 65 percent, Bolivia almost a third, Ecuador a quarter, and Mexico a fifth (Foster 2005, 1).

Firms, on the other hand, saw sufficient potential in the nascent market to bid for contracts in Latin America and other developing countries. As Wells and Ahmed argue (2006, 6), international firm interest in the infrastructure sector grew considerably during the 1990s, confidence buoyed by a new set of international property rights guarantees including international arbitration provisions contained in bilateral investment treaties between developed and developing countries. Moreover, the attractiveness of emerging markets like Latin America to European utility firms grew as the European Union began to deregulate its internal market, thereby exposing firms to greater competition within their home markets (Clifton, Comín, and Díaz-Fuentes 2007, 5, 221; Fridenson 2007, 65–68; Guillén 2005, 71–75). Furthermore, after initial periods of opposition, domestic conglomerates in Latin America came to view privatization programs as an opportunity to reconfigure their domestic portfolios (Corrales 1998).

Institutional legacies and conscious choices by politicians not only influenced the *extent* of privatization but also the *form* that it took. First, politicians

---

13. These included, but were not limited to, electoral concerns (Murillo 2009) and the chance that the provincial branch of the union would attempt to block the effort, which in turn depended on the independence of the local union chapter from the central hierarchy.

14. See Article 9 of the Pacto Federal para el Empleo, la Producción y el Crecimiento, signed August 12, 1993.

15. Provinces with Peronist governors, more centralized water and sanitation systems, loyal union chapters (locals), and larger revenue constraints were more likely to privatize (Post 2008). Water and sanitation systems were typically bundled in the same concession.

that privatized chose to do so most often via *concession contract*, or detailed management and investment contracts that by definition left infrastructure assets under state ownership.[16] Privatization via concession contract is similar to the "contracting out" of social services to private companies or nonprofit organizations except that investment in hard infrastructure is also delegated to the private provider. Privatizing governments generally preferred this model because large sums were not expected from asset sales, and because it allowed them to establish very specific contractual targets with respect to investment and expansion for particular firms.[17] Before granting concessions through a competitive tendering process, governments typically established regulatory agencies charged with monitoring firm compliance with contractual targets (Foster 2005, 1).

A close examination of the eleven provincial-level concession contracts entered into in Argentina during the 1990s illustrates the extent to which pre-existing policy and institutional legacies influenced the particular form that concession contracts took at the local level. First, because water and sanitation services had already been decentralized to provincial (and in a few cases, municipal) governments during the previous decade, privatization occurred at the provincial level.[18] Governors decided whether or not to privatize, presided over the drafting of regulatory laws and model contracts, and established regulatory agencies at the provincial level. Second, provincial governments chose to structure the concessions as privatizations of the existing state-managed companies, which typically serviced the majority, but not the entirety, of the provincial population. For the vast majority of the concessions, the geographic boundaries of the concession area closely matched the remit of the provincial utility that was privatized. (Cooperatives, small entrepreneurs, small municipalities, and private vendors continued to cater to the portion of the population not served by the state company or service provider both inside and outside of the concession area boundaries.) Contracts also required investors to assume a large fraction of the existing workforce of the provincial companies, and respect long-standing labor agreements.[19] Finally, the detailed rate formulas used to determine charges for individual households bore very close resemblance to—and often mirrored exactly—progressive formulae employed by the state

---

16. Between 1990 and 2008, Latin America witnessed 108 concessions in eleven countries, twelve divestitures in three countries, forty-five greenfield projects in ten countries, and thirty management and lease contracts in six countries (PPIAF-World Bank 2008).

17. It should be noted that policy documents published by the World Bank outlined a range of institutional options for reform, but that the concession contract model was typically singled out as a model. See, for instance, Idelovitch and Ringskog (1995).

18. The exception is the concession for the Buenos Aires metropolitan area, where a national-level state company had continued to operate following the decentralization wave of the early 1980s.

19. A subset of the former provincial company's employees was typically transferred to the new regulatory agency.

companies.[20] The institutional and policy legacies from the prereform era, in other words, are many and striking.

Although many aspects of the preexisting system were maintained, Argentine governors and their public works ministers did make explicit political choices regarding the contractual goals for private water operators. Whereas early Argentine privatizations involving the sale of state-owned enterprises, such as state telephone monopolies, were often structured so as to secure high prices from investors, later privatizations via concession contract in less remunerative sectors such as water and sanitation followed a different pattern. Argentine governors and their advisers framed the concession contracts to make public commitments to improving the quality and reach of services. The model contracts drafted by the provincial public works or economy ministries and their consultants contained *very specific and ambitious targets* for the expansion of the water and sanitation networks within concession area boundaries. To cite just one example, the contract for the province of Santa Fe required the concessionaire to expand water coverage from 74 percent to 100 percent of the population within concession area boundaries by the eighth year of the concession and sewerage coverage from 30 percent to 100 percent by year ten of the concession.[21] Contracts also included explicit quality, service continuity, and water pressure standards that grew more demanding over time, as well as expectations regarding the time frame within which customer complaints should be resolved. The contracts also typically specified the type of fine or sanction the provincial regulator could impose if the concessionaire failed to meet any of its contractual obligations. In the clarity and specificity of these contracts, and the government's clear regulatory role as an enforcer of the contracts, the provinces were making public commitments to extend quality services to a much broader proportion of the population. The assumption was that concessionaires' access to foreign capital would allow provincial systems to improve dramatically.

Argentine provincial governments also exercised a great deal of control over the types of investors that won the concession contracts. Provincial public works agencies typically established demanding financial and technical requirements during the prequalification rounds of the concession bidding processes. It was assumed, after all, that multinationals had the technological knowledge and access to financial resources required to improve systems within short periods. This meant that international firms with previous experience in the

---

20. These characterizations are based on examination of the contract appendices for each of the concessions. Charges for individual households were based on proxies for household income.

21. These goals are included in appendix X of the "Pliego de Bases y Condiciones Generales y Particulares para la Concesión del Servicio Público de Agua Potable y Desagües Cloacales en el Ámbito de la Dirección Provincial de Obras Sanitarias," December 1994. All eleven contracts examined contained explicit, ambitious coverage targets with the exception of the Salta contract, which contained peso-denominated investment goals.

sector were best positioned to submit winning bids—either on their own or by heading consortia that included domestic partners.[22] As a result, concessions in the most prosperous provinces—markets in which international companies expressed greater interest—were secured by consortia led by foreign companies. Concession contracts in economically peripheral provinces were awarded to consortia led by international investors if any bid for the contracts, and if not, to consortia of domestic investors. All in all, while greatly encouraged by international admonishments to privatize services, conscious political choices and state legacies shaped both the extent and form of privatization in the Argentine case.

Investor Type and Postprivatization Accountability Politics

The state maintains a strong role following privatization as well, both as the regulator of firm compliance with its contractual obligations and as the party with whom agreements regarding contractual revisions must be reached. This section will argue that—contrary to the expectations of many reform proponents— privatization has rendered the politics of local water and sanitation delivery both more salient and more volatile, especially in competitive political contexts. Importantly, local investors have proven better able to navigate this "volatile politics of accountability" than international investors or domestic firms with few local operations in the contract jurisdiction, though even under local investors these arrangements remain politicized.

The privatization process sets in motion a contentious post-privatization politics through two institutional changes. First, privatization creates an institutional separation between the political establishment and the private provider, which in turn sets up an oppositional dynamic between the two. Political responsibility for service quality following privatization can be squarely attributed with the monopoly service provider; the government, even if it has legal obligations under the contract and regulator framework, is no longer seen as responsible for problems. This shift in responsibility provides opportunities for politicians to make names for themselves by defending consumer interests; since services are no longer managed by political appointees named by the party in power, this means that not only political challengers have an incentive to make a name for themselves by highlighting service problems and noncompliance with contractual goals but also that ombudsmen, regulatory agency directors, legislators, and others affiliated with the party in power can gain political prominence by castigating firms (Post 2008).

Second, individuals receiving services view themselves differently following privatization. Following politicians' efforts to sell privatization with promises

---

22. The average number of bids per concession was 2.4.

of quality and coverage improvements and companies' comparatively greater efforts to make consumers pay their bills, consumers come to feel entitled to higher quality services. This tendency becomes more marked as memories of service quality under public provision fade and prices rise (Baker 2009). The fact that private operators earn profits by delivering services, meanwhile, has become increasingly controversial with international NGOs' campaigns advocating a human right to water; earning profits while service deficits persist appears unconscionable to many, after all. Overall, the establishment of an oppositional politics and greater consumer consciousness creates a "volatile politics of accountability" in the sector, in which providers are subjected to high degrees of political scrutiny by the mass public, especially during politically competitive periods when politicians can attract attention by highlighting service problems.[23] This scrutiny makes it very difficult for governors and mayors to uphold contractual and regulatory provisions designed to help firms move toward cost recovery.[24]

The politics of private water and sanitation provision becomes yet more contentious in developing countries because it is impossible to write complete contracts for outsourced social or infrastructure services: not only are economic environments typically volatile, but the political sphere also tends to be less institutionalized than in the developed world. This makes it impossible to specify how every possible contingency might be dealt with beforehand, especially over the twenty-to-thirty-year period that most contracts cover. Firms, encountering changed market conditions or infrastructure in a different state of repair than they expected, may desire to renegotiate aspects of their contracts. Politicians will likely encounter prompts to renegotiate as well. They often find that contractual provisions designed to make projects commercially viable for private providers are more controversial than originally anticipated, especially during politically competitive periods. Normal patterns of political turnover can also bring new officeholders with different preferences to power. Although some newly elected politicians may be ideologically disposed to continue with private sector participation, new officeholders in countries with strong currents of economic nationalism may choose to revise, or even end, contracts with concessionaires.

Just as important, politicians' preferences can change dramatically with improved access to finance. When they have little access to finance, they face incentives to invite the private sector to build infrastructure and regulate in a fashion that ensures providers will invest. When commodity booms or changes in external lending conditions improve their access to funds, politicians may

---

23. Murillo (2009, 43–44) also analyzes the effect of political competition on utilities regulation, arguing that regulators are more likely to privilege consumer interests during competitive periods if utilities policy is salient.

24. Rhodes (2006, 27, 33) and Savedoff and Spiller (1999, 7) make a related point, arguing that the monopoly nature of service provision makes utilities an identifiable target.

prefer to control infrastructure investment themselves because of the political benefits associated with expanding service and granting contracts to supporters and because, in some cases, of the opportunities for kickbacks such large projects present. This means that while they will usually prefer that the politically risky responsibilities associated with service delivery stay with the private sector, they will desire to renegotiate contracts so as to transfer infrastructure construction back to the public sector.

In the wake of unforeseen events or changes in firm or government preferences, firms and host governments tend to renegotiate the terms of privatization agreements directly rather than turn to third parties. In weak institutional environments, there are usually no parties both governments and firms would view as unbiased arbiters in the face of disputes over contract terms. Firms will tend to view interventions by the judiciary with skepticism because of concerns regarding judicial independence, while governments often view the international arbitration processes preferred by firms with suspicion because of concerns that firm interests are favored in such proceedings.[25] Yet the inevitability of contract renegotiations renders the politics surrounding private provision yet more volatile, as contract renegotiations muddy the clearly articulated goals publicized in original privatization agreements and sour public opinion. Governors and mayors tend to sideline regulatory agencies during these processes as well, further damaging public opinion regarding the efficacy of regulatory agencies and raising suspicions of corruption.

Domestic investors have distinct advantages in managing the oppositional, volatile politics in the sector—especially in the context of renegotiations following shifts in political preferences. First, conglomerates from developing countries tend to diversify across sectors and contract little debt, which makes them less vulnerable to political and economic volatility, and are accustomed to the informal means of dispute resolution characteristic of developing countries. They are also more likely to sense what types of measures are politically viable at a given point in time because of their greater familiarity with domestic politics. (For instance, a set of small, staged tariff increases might be more viable politically than one large adjustment.) Although international firms may be more willing to contract debt to finance up front investment, their access to international legal guarantees and greater ability to pull out of the market lead them to pursue more legalistic and brinksmanship-type negotiating strategies, which ultimately works against the political institutionalization of privatization.

Investors that are not only domestic but that also possess diverse, additional holdings in the local contract jurisdiction are best positioned to survive

---

25. In other words, the countries studied in this volume have weak institutional environments, and do not possess the sorts of institutional checks and balances described by Levy and Spiller (1994) as fundamental for the effective functioning of standard types of regulatory institutions.

in the water and sanitation sector in the long run. They have a more multidimensional relationship with the state, which lengthens their investment time horizons and broadens the set of carrots and sticks at their disposal during contract renegotiations with the state. Their local presence also keeps them more attuned to political threats to operations, and gives them more ties with the political establishment. Overall, this allows local investors to negotiate *more resilient* shifts in responsibility between the public and private sector that reflect the changing preferences of both parties. Even if negotiations do not yield settlements that allow local firms to earn substantial returns within the sector, local investors can enjoy more synergies between sectors and find it advantageous for political or long-term economic reasons to maintain loss-making operations in the water sector.

To what extent do the dynamics outlined above capture the dynamics of private water provision in Latin America, and in Argentina more specifically? Data collected by the World Bank on the water sector in Latin America and the Caribbean suggests that contract renegotiations are extremely frequent: 74.4 percent of the water and sanitation contracts entered between 1985 and 2000 were renegotiated.[26] Furthermore, contracts have been renegotiated on average within 1.6 years of contract award, despite the fact that most are for twenty- to thirty-year periods.[27] Returning to the Argentine cases discussed in the previous section, similar trends are evident. Of the six concessions analyzed as primary cases in Post (2008)—Buenos Aires, Santa Fe, Tucumán, Formosa, Mendoza, Salta—four contracts were formally renegotiated or changed significantly via regulatory resolutions within the first four years. In the two remaining cases, relationships between the government and the international operator had deteriorated to such an extent that conflict had migrated to the courts or national government pressure to renegotiate failed to produce a workable agreement. Although privatization may have yielded contracts that included clear statements regarding firm and governmental responsibilities regarding service expansion and quality, these goals quickly became muddied in contract renegotiations, the results of which were not always published in as clear terms as the original contracts on regulatory agency websites. Importantly, these provincial cases represent the full range of social, economic, and political environments in the country.

Analysis of the trajectories of provincial-level privatizations in Argentina also illustrates the varying abilities of different types of investors to navigate the "volatile politics of accountability" in the sector described in the preceding paragraphs. The following contrast between the experiences of two different types of investors in the same concession contract illustrates the greater ability

---

26. Guasch (2004, 13). Percentages are based on a sample of one thousand private infrastructure contracts.
27. Ibid., 14.

of local investors, compared with efforts by international investors, to negotiate politically acceptable shifts in responsibilities and financing mechanisms as circumstances change.

The Córdoba Concession under International and Local Investors

The Córdoba concession, managed first by the French multinational Suez and subsequently by a local investor, provides an instructive illustration of the dynamics of regulation and contract renegotiation under different types of investors. The province constituted a propitious environment for contracts led by international investors. First, Córdoba is a relatively affluent province. Second, the governor who came to power shortly after the privatization, José Manuel de la Sota, was a supporter of neoliberal policies and disposed to work constructively with private sector operators of privatized firms. The concession covering the provincial capital's water system was granted to Suez, a French firm that was a leader in the global water industry, in 1997. Although Suez possessed two water concessions in other Argentine provinces, its water concession constituted its main asset in Córdoba Province.

The Córdoba concession, like others operated by multinationals, faced important challenges following the Argentine crisis. Suez had invested heavily in the concession prior to the crisis, drawing on a large, dollar-denominated loan from the European Investment Bank.[28] When Argentina devalued its currency in early 2002, the size of the concessionaire's interest payments relative to its income stream increased dramatically. Meanwhile, the provincial government followed the national government's lead and suspended existing privatization contracts, opening them up for renegotiation. To concessionaires, the conclusion of a renegotiation agreement represented an improvement on the status quo, because agreements could provide for consumer rate increases, adjustments to investment programs, and other changes that could shift part of the burden of adjustment after the crisis away from firms. Like other foreign investors in Argentina's water sector, Suez filed an international arbitration claim to bring the provincial government to the negotiating table, and pushed for a large, one-off consumer rate increase that would return its operations back to profitability. With its only Argentine assets concentrated in the water sector, it had little to lose through such brinksmanship. From the firm's perspective, any deal reached had to make the water sector profitable once again.

Although the Córdoba political context provided favorable conditions for negotiations in comparison with most other provinces, the concessionaire's

---

28. The Córdoba concessionaire invested $35 million during its first year, a sum that exceeded the amount proposed in its bid for the concession and that represented 71.5% of revenues. Ratio calculated from investment figures reported in "Aguas Cordobesas: Bajo Análisis," *La Nación*, March 14, 1998, and revenue levels reported in Ente Naciónal de Obras Hídricas y Saneamiento (ENOHSA) and Consejo Federal de Entidades de Servicios Sanitarias (COFES) (1999).

foreign owners did not manage to obtain approval of a revised contractual agreement that would allow them to stay in the province. Suez managed to secure a provisional agreement with the government in 2005, but its insistence on a single and very significant rate increase—rather than the sorts of staged, more moderate tariff increases secured by concessionaires controlled by domestic investors—ultimately proved its downfall.[29] There was a public outcry in February of 2006 when households received the first bills including the increases.[30] Newspapers carried stories alleging errors in how the company had applied the new tariff formula, and Governor de la Sota's main political opponent in the province, the mayor of the capital city of Córdoba, seized the opportunity to mobilize against his rival. De la Sota backed down in the face of pressure from his opponent, the public, and the national government.[31] The public outcry was so strong that it was necessary to fire his public works minister. Over the next few months, de la Sota's vice governor worked out an alternative contract under which one of Suez's minority partners, the Roggio Group, would be willing to assume control of the concession. The Roggio Group had grown from a small, Córdoba-based firm into one of the largest Argentine conglomerates, active in areas such as construction, rail and highway concessions, and garbage collection.[32] Committed to the local market in the long run and sensitive to the provincial political climate, the Roggio Group took an alternative approach to negotiations. Rather than push for a single large consumer rate increase, this local group pushed for an alternative, less politically salient set of policies that would address the concessionaire's financial difficulties. Following the lead of local investors operating in other provinces, the Córdoba-based firm negotiated a transfer of investment responsibilities to the state and a series of small—and therefore, less noticeable—rate increases that eventually totaled more than the amount demanded by Suez and returned the concession to profitability.[33] The firm's numerous other holdings in the province provided it with longer time horizons in negotiations, which made this gradual realization of rate increases more acceptable. Possessing other operations in the province, and keen to retain the possibility of managing Argentine infrastructure concessions in the future, the firm had stronger incentives than Suez to be more moderate in

---

29. Domestic investors in other provinces tended to push incrementally for small increases rather than adopt an all-or-nothing negotiating stance of the sort Suez and other foreign investors with access to international arbitration did.

30. "Ola de protestas por la suba del agua en Córdoba," *La Nación*, February 19, 2006.

31. "Frenan alzas en Córdoba," *La Nación*, February 24, 2006; "De la Sota rectificó el aumento del agua: Será de 15% promedio," *La Voz del Interior*, March 20, 2006.

32. "Roggio assume la conducción de Aguas Cordobesas," *La Voz del Interior*, December 22, 2006.

33. Local investors in Corrientes and Salta had already demonstrated the utility of this sort of approach. The cumulative size of these rate increases has been higher than the amount Suez pushed for earlier in the decade. Regarding the firm's profitability, see "La Provincia financió la ganancia de Aguas Cordobesas," *La Voz del Interior*, September 17, 2007. Regarding applications for the new inflation adjustments, see "Hoy, audiencia por aumentos," *La Voz del Interior*, April 14, 2008.

its requests of the provincial administration. All in all, the Córdoba case illustrates the greater ability and willingness of local investors to manage contract renegotiations within a volatile political environment compared with efforts by multinationals and domestic firms with few local ties.

The Short- and Medium-Run Effects of Private Sector Service Provision

Existing empirical evidence regarding the effects of privatization in developing countries suggests that the effects of water and sanitation privatization differ in the short and medium run.[34] The short-run *effects upon service access and quality* appear to be varied. Meanwhile, the short-run *political effects* tend to be fairly uniform: increased consumer, NGO, and court mobilization and participation in the sector, and decreasing levels of public support for private service provision. In the medium run, the political fragility of private sector management becomes more visible. Private sector provision appears to be most sustainable when contracts are held by local investors, especially as public attitudes toward private provision sour and states regain access to resources with which to fund investment on their own.

Existing empirical studies of the effects of water privatization, as well as comparisons between provincial-level concessions in Argentina, suggests that while private sector management has tended to improve utility efficiency, impacts on coverage and service quality have proven to be more mixed (Clarke, Kosec, and Wallsten 2004; Gassner, Popov, and Pushak 2008; Andrés, Guasch, and Foster 2008; Marin 2009). The Argentine case suggests that this variation does not stem from differences in country-level political variables, but rather factors such as investor type and the extent to which local political systems endured periods of intense political competition, which provide local officials with incentives to deliver less favorable policies to utilities. Table 4.1 compares progress in network expansion achieved by concessionaires that entered contracts in Argentina by 1995.[35]

While the French firm Suez expanded network coverage in Buenos Aires and Santa Fe via a substantial debt-financed investment program, much more impressive is the progress made by a local investor in Corrientes, where the rate of growth in the main urban agglomeration was 22 percent.[36] In contrast,

---

34. We cannot yet examine the long-run effects of private sector management, as the first privatizations occurred only in the early 1990s, and were structured as thirty-year contracts.

35. Data for these particular contracts are displayed because data from the last two censuses, taken in 1991 and 2001, is more likely to reflect investments made by concessionaires than data for concessions started in the late 1990s.

36. This compares with 5% population growth in the Buenos Aires metropolitan area, 10% in Santa Fe (Rosario metropolitan area), 18% in San Miguel de Tucumán, and 34% in Formosa. Data from INDEC, 1991 and 2001.

TABLE 4.1.
Expansion rates in Argentine concessions entered by 1995

Province	Lead investor type	Concession start date	% of population with water connection 1991*	% of population with water connection 2001	% of population with sewer connection 1991	% of population with sewer connection 2001
Corrientes	Domestic (local and diversified 1996 onwards)	1991	73	85	35	51
Buenos Aires (metro area)	International	1993	73	82	54	56
Formosa	Domestic, not local or diversified	1995	71	79	33	36
Tucumán	International	1995 (canceled 1997)	82	85	34	38
Santa Fe	International	1995	79	88	34	45

*Percentage covered refers to the percentage of the population *residing in the concession area* with service. Municipal-level ("departamento") population connection data from Instituto Nacional de Estadísticas y Censos (INDEC), census for 1991 and 2001, series B, table V6. Population is considered covered if they receive services from the public network (within the household, property, or outside of the property). Municipalities are coded as falling in a concession area if at least 50% of the population receives services from the concessionaire. Data on municipalities falling within particular concession areas is taken from Sistema Permanente de Información de Saneamiento (SPIDES) and the concession contract appendices, following Galiani, Gertler, and Schargrodsky (2005).

only modest progress was made in Formosa, where the concession was held by a domestic investor without local holdings, and in Tucumán, where the French firm Vivendi was never able to negotiate effectively with the new gubernatorial administration and legislature that came to power just a few months after the concession was granted. In many cases, greater progress was made with respect to water than sanitation. The presence of such varied outcomes in a single country underlines the fact that it is crucial to examine the drivers of varied outcomes under private and public management rather than to focus on the average differences in performance between private and public management.[37]

The short-run political effect of privatization has been to generate higher expectations regarding service quality and greater levels of political mobilization among consumers. Data for the concession contract for the Buenos Aires metropolitan area illustrates the changing attitudes and activism of consumers

---

37. This is the approach taken by Galiani, Gertler, and Schargrodsky (2005) for the Argentine water and sanitation sector. Their study reports more significant decreases in rates of child mortality in jurisdictions under private sector management than under public sector management.

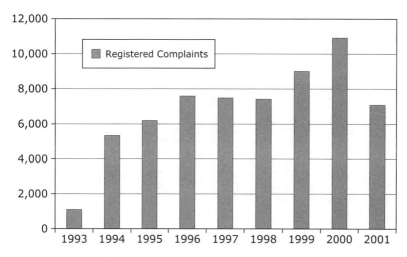

Figure 4.1. Complaints registered with the Buenos Aires water regulator (ETOSS).
Source: ETOSS. Includes water, sanitation, and commercial complaints regarding Aguas Argentinas, the private concessionaire, for the precrisis period.

in the first eight years of private sector management. Figure 4.1 shows that consumers registered complaints with the water and sanitation regulator, ETOSS, with increasing frequency between the 1993 privatization and the 2001–02 Argentine crisis, at the same time that water services expanded to over 1.8 million new users and water pressure levels improved dramatically.[38] This increase reflects the creation of a new entity charged with registering and responding to consumer complaints (the regulator), and increasing expectations among consumers. Increased consumer expectations and mobilization coincided with a gradual disillusionment with privatized provision, spurred at least in part by contract negotiations that sidelined the regulatory agencies supposedly charged with protecting consumer interests. Figure 4.2 reflects the decline in public support in Argentina for the private provision from over 50 percent in 1995, two years after the prominent privatization of services in Buenos Aires, to less than 40 percent during the first set of contract renegotiations in 1998.

In the medium run, public support for private sector provision has declined more precipitously in Argentina; Latinobarómetro surveys suggest that support for private provision dipped below 20 percent in 2008. Similar declines were observed in Bolivia, which also privatized extensively: the percentage of Bolivians supporting private sector management declined from 51 percent in 1998 to 24 percent in 2008. Note that these trends contrast with fairly stable support for privatization in most other countries in the region. One must attribute this at least in part to a longer and more extensive experience with

---

38. Coverage increase figures from Aguas Argentinas.

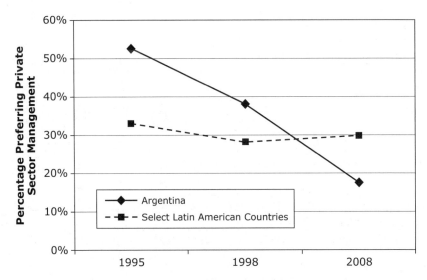

Figure 4.2. Support for private sector management of drinking water. "Select Latin American Countries" summarizes survey results for all Latin American countries with data for each time period: Argentina, Brazil, Chile, Mexico, Paraguay, Peru, Uruguay, and Venezuela. The percentage displayed reflects the average of country-level averages, with each country weighted equally irrespective of population size. Note that data for Bolivia, the country that experienced the most controversial privatization, is unavailable for 1995 and therefore not included in the Latin American averages. *Source:* Latinobarómetro.

privatization in the Argentine case; in the Bolivian case, the failure of the Cochabamba concession had great resonance as well. (Chile, which eventually privatized management of all its major water utilities, only entered this process in earnest in the late 1990s.)

In addition, governments have regained access to finance in much of Latin America due to the commodity booms of the early to mid-2000s. This has given governments the option of financing infrastructure investment on their own. As the preceding section suggested, certain types of investors have proven able to adapt to this new political reality more effectively than others. This, in turn, has yielded important institutional effects: the retention of private sector management where local investors manage services, and a tendency to return to state provision (or transfer to local investors) in other cases. Table 4.2 documents patterns of investor exit and their repercussions in the Argentine case. Importantly, local investors' superior ability to manage relations with host governments is evident in both poor and relatively prosperous provinces, as are international investors' difficulties.

Although data on local (as opposed to domestic) ownership does not exist on a cross-national basis, one observes a stark difference between the failure rates of contracts held by domestic and international investors in Latin

TABLE 4.2.
Rates of exit by lead investors in Argentina's water concessions, 1991–2010

	Domestic investor	International investor
Investor with additional local holdings	33% (1/3)	No Cases
Investor *without* additional local holdings	78% (3.5/4.5)	89% (8/9)

Source: Post 2008.
Notes: Figures refer to exits by lead investors holding a majority of concessionaire shares. When concessionaire ownership was split 50–50, an observation was created for each investor and weighted by 0.5.

Domestic investors with diverse local holdings: Investors in Corrientes and Córdoba (Roggio, 2006–present) still in place in 2010. Investors in Mendoza (half local ownership) and Salta (half local ownership) exited when contracts were canceled and the public sector took over services.

Domestic investors without diverse local holdings: Investors persist in Santiago del Estero, but exited concessions in La Rioja, Salta (half nonlocal ownership), and Formosa when their contracts were canceled and the state took over. Investors also exited in Corrientes (sold to a local investor in 1996).

International investors: Investors in Misiones continue, but exited concessions in Mendoza (two international investors with half of shares, first set sold shares, and second exited following contract cancelation), the Buenos Aires Metropolitan Region (contract canceled), Buenos Aires Province (two contracts, both canceled), Tucumán (canceled), Santa Fe (canceled), Córdoba (sold to local investor), and Catamarca (canceled).

America. Contracts held by international investors have been cancelled at four times the rate of those with domestic investors: thirteen of the forty-eight concession contracts with international investors had been cancelled before term by May 2008, whereas only one of fifty-two contracts with domestic investors had been cancelled prematurely.[39] In addition, patterns of market entry and exit suggest that while international investors are pulling out of the sector after becoming disillusioned with the market, domestic conglomerates are continuing to enter concession contracts at an impressive rate. Not only are many international investors attempting to find domestic buyers for their shares in Latin American concessions. According to the World Bank's Private Participation in Infrastructure (PPI) data set, of the twenty-nine concession contracts and divestitures on offer in Latin America *after* the Argentine economic crisis of 2001–02, only two winning consortia included investor participation from outside the region.[40] This ratio is minuscule compared with the forty-six out of eighty-four projects with foreign participation prior to the crisis (55%). Decisions by domestic investors to enter new contracts following the Argentine crisis reflect a confidence in their ability to navigate post-privatization politics. Whereas the short-run political effects of privatization appear to be higher consumer expectations and mobilization, this appears to destabilize private sector provision in the medium-run, with local firms better able to manage the "volatile politics of accountability" coming to dominate the sector.

---

39. Base data from the Private Participation in Infrastructure Database, PPIAF-World Bank, downloaded May 2008. Base data updated by author.
40. Ratio calculated from the PPIAF-World Bank (2008).

Conclusion

Motivated by desires to rein in costs and improve service quality, as well as pressure from international financial institutions, governments throughout the developing world contracted with private firms for the delivery of important social and health services during the 1980s and 1990s. This chapter has examined the origins, dynamics, and consequences of "contracting out" for management and investment in urban water and sanitation systems.

Several general points emerge from this analysis of the politics of "contracting out" in the water and sanitation sector. First, water and sanitation infrastructure should be considered a key pillar of social welfare systems in the developing world, due to the importance of access to safe water and sanitation for health outcomes. Second, privatizing services does not remove politics (or the state) from service provision. The Argentine experiences described in this chapter show that, to privatize, political elites must first define goals and conditions for private sector operation. Following contract award, they possess the legal authority to sanction providers and amend contracts. Third, the act of delegating service provision to a separate entity *not* overseen by political appointees tends to raise the salience of and level of acrimony animating the policy area; incumbent public officials are quicker to blame a private firm for quality problems than one of their own. Politicization can increase yet further with contract renegotiations, which—though often unavoidable—tend to muddy original contractual goals and arouse suspicions of unfair dealing. If the water sector provides any guide, "contracting out" has led to fluid and constantly changing responsibilities between the public and private sector that can accommodate changing corporate and political preferences rather than greater transparency and clear, arm's-length contracts. Given the importance of managing long-term relationships with the state and consumer expectations, it should come as no surprise that local firms have been better able to manage the politics associated with regulated private provision than have international providers or domestic firms with few local ties.

To what extent would we expect to observe these same tendencies when governments contract with private firms for the provision of other types of social and health services? First, one would expect the politics of private service provision to be more salient and volatile under monopoly service provision. Whereas voters will find it straightforward to place blame for service problems with monopoly providers, responsibility becomes more opaque to citizens when service provision is delegated to numerous providers. This creates a paradox: while less concentrated market structures may be able to facilitate competition on the basis of cost or quality among providers, it can actually weaken political monitoring, leading to ambiguous effects on service quality. Second, long-term contracts will be more susceptible to contractual incompleteness than short-term contracts; as a result, "contracting out" in policy areas where it is possible to write short-term contracts may be less contentious and likely to deliver the results originally stipulated by politicians in contracts.[41] Finally, "contracting out" is likely to be simplest and yield results most in line with expectations in policy areas in which government goals can be clearly specified (Donahue 1989; Sclar 2000); for instance, while it is straightforward to specify service coverage and quality targets for water and sanitation providers, standards are much more difficult to define with respect to child care. Overall, it is clear that contracting out is not a panacea; its effects are likely to be varied. Nor does it represent an end to government involvement in the policy areas where it is undertaken. A strong government role is inevitable during and after privatization, and politics is inescapable.

---

41. Long-term contracts are typically granted in sectors requiring up front investment that firms would recoup over time. It is easier to find investors willing to sign short-term contracts that do not include major investment obligations.

5

Blurring the Boundaries

NGOs, the State, and Service Provision in Kenya

Jennifer N. Brass

With no NGOs, there's more of government hanging around the office. When there's strong NGOs, more can be done, more impact. Then government gets out there, to the field.
—Kenyan civil servant, 2008

People consider us government. They are confused about where government starts and [our NGO] stops.
—NGO worker, 2008

Over the past two decades, the number of not-for-profit nongovernmental organizations in the developing world has grown dramatically. Although estimates on the existing number of organizations vary widely, the *Economist* reports the quadrupling of international NGO numbers between 1990 and 1996, and there are thought to be over one million organizations in India alone (McGann and Johnstone 2006). In Kenya, the government began registering NGOs in 1991, at which time there were four hundred operating in the country (National Council of NGOs of Kenya 2005).[1] By the start of 2012,

---

1. According to the government of Kenya, an NGO is defined as "a private voluntary grouping of individuals or associations not operated for profit or for other commercial purposes but which have organized themselves nationally or internationally for the benefit of the public at large and for the promotion of social welfare development, charity or research in the areas inclusive but not restricted to health, relief, agricultural, education, industry and supply of amenities and services" (Government of Kenya 1992).

that number had grown nearly twentyfold, to over seventy-five hundred.[2] In this chapter I seek to explain the *origins* of NGO growth, the *dynamics* of NGO-government relations, and the *consequences* of NGO involvement for processes of service provision at the local level, using Kenya as a case study. The chapter focuses on how NGOs affect decision-making and implementation *processes*, rather than outputs such as the number of children in school or boreholes (water wells) in a village. Although these outputs are important, understanding processes is also crucial for development outcomes.

Theoretically, this chapter contributes to two debates regarding the role of NGOs in development. First, I investigate claims that NGOs are replacing the state in the provision of services (Matthews 1997), taking seriously Obiyan's (2005) question, "Will the state die as NGOs thrive?" and assertions of a "roll-back of the state" amid NGO growth (Campbell 1996, 2–3). Second, I address contestation regarding the impact of NGOs on accountability in developing countries. When NGOs first gained prominence on the international scene, scholars lauded them for publicly championing participatory approaches, teaching populations about civic rights, lobbying governments to administer transparently, providing a voice for the disempowered, and pressing for democratization (Clark 1991).[3] More recent work, on the other hand, has cautioned that NGOs are not a "magic bullet" miraculously instilling civil society and consolidated democratic governance (Edwards and Hulme 1996a). Indeed, NGOs can be short on internal democracy processes (Edwards and Hulme 1996b; Bebbington 1997; Edwards 2000) and particularly accountability to the impoverished people they claim to serve (Mercer 1999, 2002).[4]

Research for this chapter conducted between 2005 and 2012 in Kenya, however, demonstrates that under certain conditions NGOs both complement the administrative objectives of governments and positively influence the politics of how services are provided. I find that, under the conditions detailed below, NGOs do not replace the state or let the government "off the hook" in providing services. Instead, NGOs and the state actively collaborate to provide services. The line between government and NGO blurs, as NGOs jointly implement service delivery with government offices, aid the state in decision making, and have their plans integrated into government plans. As such, NGOs

---

2. Data come from Bratton 1989, National Council of NGOs (2005), NGO Coordination Board (Government of Kenya 2006; Government of Kenya 2012b), and an NGO expert in Kenya (2008–58). Note that references in the latter format represent an interview respondent whose identity is concealed in accordance with protection of human subjects' requirements.

3. See also Hyden 1983; Meyer 1997; Mercer 2002, 8–10; Bratton 1990; Sanyal 1994; Ndegwa 1994; International Center for Non-profit Law 1995; Salamon and Sokolowski 1999; Besley and Ghatak 1999; Garrison 2000; Cannon 2000; Martin 2004, 25.

4. This can usually be attributed to incentives created in the competition for foreign donor funding (Fowler 1991; Cooley and Ron 2002; Martin 2004).

reinforce the process of public service provision. Regardless of their internal dynamics, moreover, NGOs encourage a nascent spirit of democratic accountability among Kenyan civil servants (Brass 2012a).

What are the conditions under which NGOs have this impact? In Kenya, key determinants have been a relatively open political climate, in which freedoms of association and speech are normally assured; a central government that grants autonomy to service providers; a majority of NGOs focused primarily on service provision rather than governance; street-level civil servants motivated to work with NGOs; and a willingness to engage with and learn from non-state actors in service provision. A history of shared goals between the government and NGOs contributed to these conditions in Kenya, which began to arise during the 1990s and came into sharp relief after the democratic transition of 2002.

This is not to say that these conditions are universal within Kenya or that NGOs are an unmitigated good. NGOs remain critical of government's general lack of follow-through, frequent corruption and misuse of resources, and politicians' tendency to take credit for work done by NGOs. Government officials critique NGOs for profligate spending on relative luxuries and for seeking out public counterparts only after a problem arises, rather than from the start of a new program. Yet tensions, which were the norm in the 1980s and 1990s, have been the exception in the 2000s. Moreover, these findings do not mean that service provision outcomes and development levels have drastically improved as a result of NGO involvement. The fact remains that relative to the government, NGO resources are small and their impacts often indirect.

In this chapter, I explain conditions under which collaboration between NGOs and government officials has or has not succeeded, and I describe methods of interaction when it has. I focus on successful interactions deliberately, since others have discussed problematic relations extensively. The chapter begins by detailing the history of service provision and origins of nongovernmental organizations in Kenya. It then explains the dynamics of NGO-government relations over time, examining changing conditions from the Moi administration (1992–2002) to those of the Kibaki one (2002–13). The chapter describes the patterns of collaboration between NGOs and government in service provision, painting a picture of what NGO-government complementarity looks like. Finally, I analyze the political consequences of this expanded role of NGOs.

In so doing, this chapter resonates with the findings of Anirudh Krishna in this volume, showing the democratizing impacts of non-state service provision. It also accords with the theoretical arguments in this book that the history of state development critically shapes the political dynamics of non-state provision, and that non-state provision can transform (if slowly) mechanisms of accountability and participation. Finally, the chapter confirms the volume's observation that highly dichotomized variables (state/non-state, national/international) are often actually fuzzy or blurred in real contexts.

Methods and Data

Most case studies in comparative politics explore the "causes of effects"—taking a puzzling outcome and explaining it. This research takes the opposite approach: I examine a new phenomenon and seek to determine its impact—the "effect of causes" method. Thus, I analyze one independent variable, the proliferation of NGOs, examining its bearing on service provision. The focus on interactive processes of service implementation at the local level is deliberate. I analyze processes because the ways that NGOs and government interact to provide services have important implications for long-term outcomes. I focus on service provision because the vast majority of NGOs in Kenya work in this arena—only 4 percent in Kenya focus primarily on governance issues of human rights, corruption, and democratization (Brass 2012b). And I largely study street-level interactions in rural districts because most Kenyans live in small towns and rural areas, and because individuals are affected by the everyday acts of low-level civil servants and local politicians—not just decisions made by elites in the capital city. Local government actors are often overlooked in studies of NGOs.

This chapter uses the informed-observer method, drawing on over one hundred semistructured interviews with NGO leaders and workers, civil servants, politicians, and Kenyan citizens conducted between 2005 and 2012. NGO respondents were selected initially from the government's registry of NGOs, and then using snowball sampling. Government respondents were representatives present in government offices during drop-ins by the author. Both sets of respondents were asked about the services NGOs provide, whether and how NGOs work with government ministries and politicians, and relationships between the two types of organizations.

Approximately half of the interviews took place in the Machakos and Mbeere districts of Eastern Province in late 2008. Because less than a year had passed since the ethnically charged violence following the 2007 presidential elections, I controlled for the violence by selecting districts that experienced little violence and had similar presidential voting patterns over time. I did this because I sought to understand NGO effects on service provision, not the impact of ethnicity on NGO-government relations. The rest of the interviews were done with respondents from a range of ethnicities, mostly in Nairobi, but also in Rift Valley and Nyanza provinces. The interviews thus represent four of the eight districts of the country, though they are neither proportionately nor randomly distributed.[5]

---

5. Interviews were conducted during the following periods: May–July 2005, September–November 2006, January–April 2007, September–November 2008, and June 2012. They were conducted throughout Machakos, Mbeere, and Nairobi districts, and in a limited fashion in Naivasha, Nakuru, Molo, Kisii, Rongo, and Bomet districts, many of which experienced ethnic violence in 2008.

Respondents' throughout the country reported similar patterns, regardless of ethnicity or district. This may be explained by the fact that most workers in NGO offices at the district level come from the local area, therefore sharing ethnic identity with the people and politicians of the area. The government, moreover, often stations civil servants outside their home district, placing them among people who do not share their ethnic identity. This disrupts the stereotypical politics of distribution; while in the capital, distribution occurs along ethnic lines, this tendency may be reduced among street-level civil servants in small towns and rural districts.

The chapter also employs data from an original survey of 501 Kenyans from Nairobi, Machakos, and Mbeere, completed in October 2008: 150 individuals each were randomly sampled from the whole of Machakos and Mbeere districts; 100 and 101 people in Machakos town and Nairobi, respectively. The survey asked respondents about the services they receive, their contact with and views of NGOs, and their views on government.[6]

Service Provision and the Origins of NGO Involvement

Since independence, African governments have predicated their legitimacy on the promise of distributing developmental services and employment to the populace (Young 1988; Bratton 1989; Fowler 1991; Kanyinga 1996; Schatzberg 2001; Owiti, Aluoka, and Oloo 2004). In the 1960s, when state-led development was de rigueur and commodity prices were booming, governments expanded rapidly, creating thousands of new jobs in the civil service, state-owned enterprises, schools, clinics, and infrastructure projects.[7] Growing numbers of university-educated students saw the civil service as their future employer (Prewitt 1971; Barkan 1975) and, in many countries, were actually guaranteed employment (van de Walle 2001).

The period of expansion did not last long. Most African states governed largely through patronage, which meant distributive goals, not long-term investment, determined economic policy. Over time these development policies resulted in low or negative profits, perverse incentives within organizations (Ekeh 1975), and the withdrawal of farmers from commercial markets, reducing tax revenues (Bates 1981). Added to this were a series of economically toxic factors in the 1970s and early 1980s: oil shocks, plunging world market commodity prices, and a string of debilitating droughts. States became increasingly reliant on foreign aid and loans. By the late 1980s, international policymakers began to insist on economic liberalization as a precondition to additional loans and grants. Donors required, among other things, budget reductions, privatization, and deregulation.

---

6. See Brass (2010) for additional information and results from the survey.
7. By 1979, 42% of formal employment in Kenya was in government (Hazlewood 1979).

The role of government in service provision changed dramatically. Governments not only stopped expanding, they retreated from free public and welfare goods provision. This allowed them to reduce public expenditure, and to acquiesce to donor promotion of private organizations, including NGOs, as service providers. In Kenya, public spending on education dropped from 18 percent of the budget in the 1980s to 7.1 percent in 1996. In the health sector, government spending decreased from $9.82 million in 1980–81 to $6.2 million in 1993 and $3.61 million in 1996 at the same time as HIV/AIDS was spreading rapidly (Katumanga 2004, 48).

As Michael Bratton noted at the end of the 1980s, "Governments often have had little choice but to cede responsibility for the provision of basic services to a church, an indigenous self-help group, or an international relief agency" (Bratton 1989, 569). Indeed, NGOs have sought to fill the lacuna and deliver many of the services promised by African governments. Over the years, they have moved from supplemental charity and relief work to basic development and service provision (Brodhead 1987). This has been facilitated by their favored status among donors, who tout their services as more efficient, effective, flexible, participatory, democratic, accountable, and transparent than their government bureaucracy counterparts. As proof of their status among donors, the World Bank increased the percentage of projects involving NGOs from 21 percent in 1990 to over 80 percent by 2011 (World Bank 2011).

In Kenya, non-state actors working in the country are not new—both local self-help groups and international missionary organizations have been around since colonial times. Yet the number, scope, and the sources of funding of NGOs have changed. Today, civil society organizations employ more than three hundred thousand people full-time in Kenya—2.1 percent of the economically active population, 16.3 percent of non-agricultural employment, and the equivalent of 45 percent of the 660,000 people employed by the Kenyan government (Kanyinga 2004, 17). Most NGOs in Kenya—regardless of where they are established—are funded via international sources.[8] Of the $213 million raised by the NGOs that submitted an annual return in 2005, 91 percent of funds come from international sources, and only 1 percent originates in the Kenyan government.[9]

The Dynamics of NGO-Government Relations

In Kenya, the government has not always viewed NGOs as positively as have donors.[10] Indeed, government-NGO relations moved over the course of the

---

8. This is in contrast to Latin America, where national governments tend to fund NGOs (2009–6).

9. This figure derives from the author's analysis, independently verified by a research assistant, of information available in the NGO Coordination Board's database as of December 2006.

10. For an expanded view of this section, see Brass (2012a).

1990s and 2000s from a state of intimidation during the Moi administration to one of integration during the Kibaki presidency (Brass 2012a). The political conditions of the country as well as the contrasting administration leadership styles of the two presidents help to understand this change. Conditions during Moi's autocratic, highly centralized rule resulted in antagonism between NGOs and government, while Kibaki's more open political regime, his alignment with NGOs during the Moi years, and his hands-off approach to ministry administration created the conditions necessary for collaboration.

Politics and administration during the Moi regime were highly centralized in the person of the president. By the 1990s, when NGO numbers began growing rapidly, Moi had ruled a one-party state for over a decade. Media freedom was curtailed, extrajudicial detentions were common, and opposition leaders were often jailed for years—if they did not die under dubious circumstances, as happened to several prominent men. Fear of government was the order of the day.

In large part, this fear extended to NGOs. One NGO leader in Nairobi reported that during the Moi years she dared not stray from the government curriculum at her organization's primary school—the idea of introducing "civics" classes was particularly anathema to her. She believed the government shut down organizations whose programs taught critical thinking skills (2007–26) (references in this format represent an interview respondent whose identity is concealed for reasons of anonymity and confidentiality). This was a rational apprehension, considering that Moi publicly described NGOs conducting civic education as "a threat to the security of the state" whose "activities must be curtailed" (U.S. Department of State 1998). The government didn't target only NGOs working on human rights and democratization: poverty-relief organizations were also at risk. As an agriculture-focused NGO leader in Mbeere said, "For a long time, lifting people out of poverty was seen as threatening" (2008–54), explaining that the Moi government felt that wealthier, educated people would have the tools necessary to confront the state should they wish to do so (2008–54). A Rift Valley-based NGO leader agreed; contrasting his energy provision NGO's current conditions to the Moi regime, one said, "There was a time when they [the government] were not friendly. . . . For a long time, we were seen as troublemakers" (2012–8).

The antagonism between the government and NGOs largely stemmed from Moi's autocratic governing style. After the Berlin Wall fell in 1989, both donors and civil society pressed for political liberalization, which Moi opposed. Although he appreciated the health care and poverty relief some NGOs provided, his government largely lumped them with NGOs pushing for democracy. He saw all NGOs acting autonomously as threats to both government legitimacy and sovereignty (Kameri-Mbote 2000). Kenyan scholars writing at the time were not surprised when the state cracked down on NGOs since "NGOs were using donor funds to contest state legitimacy through delivery of services" (Kanyinga 1996, 82).

Relationships between the Moi regime and the international donors exacerbated the government's perception of NGOs. In the 1990s, most donors not only withheld aid from the Kenyan government in an attempt to cajole Moi into embracing liberal democracy but also diverted as much as 30 percent of bilateral aid to NGOs (Chege 1999). At the same time, the donors pressured governments throughout Africa to allow nongovernmental actors to participate in state decision making (Brautigam 1994, 59). The Moi government became concerned that donors favored NGOs over it (Owiti, Aluoka, and Oloo 2004).

The Moi government centralized control over NGOs through legislation passed in the late 1980s and early 1990s. The government required NGOs to register with the state, submit their plans and budgets, and to channel funds through the government. Regulations also set up a state agency, the NGO Coordination Board, to organize and monitor NGOs, and to deregister those that were noncompliant. These regulations allowed the government to reinforce its command-and-control hierarchy, leaving little autonomy to NGOs.

According to Kameri-Mbote (2000), the government used these regulations as justification for harassing NGOs. As prominent examples, the government threatened and then deregistered Nobel Peace Prize winner Wangari Maathai's Green Belt Movement and a research organization, CLARION, for their roles in prodemocracy activities or research. In Moi's last year in office, 304 NGOs were deregistered, with fewer than twenty successfully appealing (National Council of NGOs 2005). Other organizations saw their registration processes repeatedly delayed, halting their ability to work openly (2008–10).

In 2002, however, Kenya's presidential elections saw the ruling party, KANU, defeated for the first time, by Mwai Kibaki's National Alliance Rainbow Coalition, with 62 percent of the vote. The change of power brought about conditions necessary for NGO integration into public service provision: a relatively open political climate; street-level civil servants motivated to work with NGOs; government and NGOs willing to engage with and learn from each other; and a central government that grants autonomy to service providers. Donor support for collaborative relationships and NGOs' focus on basic needs provision also facilitated the change.

Since Kibaki took power, the political climate in the country has become more open, moving from an average Freedom House score of 6.0 (not free) during the last decade of Moi's administration to 3.5 (partly free) in 2012.[11] Although Kibaki failed at political openness during the 2007 election and its violent aftermath—most accounts assert that he stole the election, prompting weeks of interethnic violence that ended with a power-sharing settlement between Kibaki and his rival candidate, Raila Odinga—he did accept the electoral rejection of his proposed new constitution in 2005, as well as the 2010 passage of a constitution limiting presidential power. Notwithstanding the events of the 2007 election, the Kibaki government rarely interfered with what has become

---

11. Freedom House scores rate political and civil liberties, ranging in score from 1 to 7, where 1 is the most free and 7 the least.

a lively media space and, unlike Moi, allowed public satire of the government. Academic freedom became the norm during the Kibaki administration, as did freedom of assembly and speech, leading to an engaged civil society (Freedom House 2012). As a result, NGO representatives now feel able to speak openly, saying, "It's not like when it was a dictatorship!" (2008–19). NGOs' opinions and ideas are welcome. As one NGO leader described, "We're free to voice issues, say what [we] want" (2008–12). As another explained, "It's sincerely a very cohesive relationship" (2008–11).

One might hypothesize that NGO involvement in service provision allows a government to shirk its responsibilities as part of the "retreat of the state" (Matthews 1997). Stereotypes of African bureaucrats would suggest the same. According to a district officer, however, street-level bureaucrats have become more motivated to work: "2002 catalyzed people—they want to move forward. Once change comes, it's hard to stop" (2008–36). An NGO worker agreed, saying that civil servants "became now more proactive. They really try to do their jobs since 2002" (2008–14). The democratic change in power after forty years of single party rule brought a newfound vigor to many Kenyans, who saw the turnover as the first of many transformations to come.[12] A generational change in the civil service also brought new ideas to public administration (2008–14).

The Kibaki administration not only tolerated NGO involvement in service provision after 2002 but also actively engaged with non-state actors to change the legacy of Moi's bureaucratic mind-set. Kibaki allied with members of the opposition to Moi who had taken refuge in NGOs during the 1990s. In 2002, he invited a number of these civil society leaders to direct government departments. Integrating capable, demanding leaders into public administration meant that the "do-gooder" mentalities, participatory decision-making mechanisms, transparent spending practices (developed by successfully navigating donor accountability requirements), and push for democratization common to NGOs were brought into government offices, sometimes for the first time. As one NGO leader said, "Civil society was all swallowed by government, so government is thinking like NGOs. Government employees are all from [NGOs]" (2008–33). Former thorns in the side of government were included, shaking up the status quo. For example, John Githongo, founder of Transparency International's Kenya office, became the government's "anti-corruption tsar." Maina Kiai, former director of the nongovernmental Kenya Human Rights Commission, became head of the government's own human rights agency.

Many of these changes can be attributed to the differences between Moi and Kibaki's leadership styles. Where Moi micromanaged the state, Kibaki

---

12. UC Berkeley economist Ted Miguel has noticed a similar transformation in Kenya's economic conditions (Miguel 2009), where the economy has grown considerably since Kibaki took power.

took a largely hands-off approach to line ministries dealing with health, water, sanitation, and other services. The central government grants considerably autonomy to them, according to many informed observers. They attribute the laissez-faire attitude to personality differences between Moi and Kibaki, to the fact that Kibaki is a PhD-educated and long-time technocrat, and, less charitably, to a 2007 car accident and stroke that left Kibaki "vague, distracted, struggling to maintain a coherent chain of thought" (Wrong 2009, 71)—making him physically and mentally unable to micromanage.

Donor support for collaborative relationships adds another condition facilitating NGO integration. The Kibaki administration has maintained a better relationship with donors than did his predecessor. Leading multinational institutions such as the Global Fund to Fight AIDS, Tuberculosis and Malaria and the President's Emergency Plan for AIDS Relief require the government to work with NGOs in order to receive funding. People throughout the government were therefore influenced by a global pattern encouraging collaboration. As one senior NGO employee said, "That's the new global approach—you must involve everyone now!" (2008–26). A senior district administrator agreed: "Things are changing dramatically: *everyone* is being brought on board!" (2008–41).

Finally, the fact that most NGOs in Kenya focus foremost on meeting Kenyans' basic needs has facilitated the positive working relationship between NGOs and government. Although a number of prominent NGOs in the capital exist primarily to critique the government's record of corruption, human rights, and governance, the overwhelming majority of NGOs work on issues of health care, education, economic development, and general welfare improvement (Brass 2012b). These organizations help relieve the burden of service provision for the government.

NGOs since 2002: Extending the Government's Arm

Under the political conditions just described, NGOs can have positive, mutually enforcing effects. In Kenya, we see this through several types of mechanisms. NGOs complement the government's administrative agenda through joint implementation of services, participation in government decision making, and integration of NGO plans into government plans. NGOs sometimes also literally take the government farther than it would have gone on its own. One consequence of this is that many civil servants and ministries have begun to adopt tools of accountability that have long been employed by NGOs.

This is not to say that positive mutual enforcement always occurs in Kenya. In this partial democracy, public services remain extremely weak, many civil servants view government employment as a tool for personal resource accumulation, and considerable friction remains between NGOs and the public sector. NGO leaders remain vocal in their critiques of government: all is certainly not rosy. Informed observers from NGOs accused the government of making policy, but failing to follow through on implementation (2008–13, 2008–14, 2008–30, 2008–47); misusing resources and corruption (2008–16, 2008–19, 2008–31, 2008–35, 2008–44, 2008–54); taking credit for the work that an NGO had done (2008–19, 2008–31, 2008–47); and being overly suspicious of NGOs and their activities (2008–43).

From the government perspective, moreover, both civil servants and politicians are wary of the way NGOs spend resources, especially on training and "capacity building" activities. Concurring with this view, I have seen poor rural Kenyans served lavish breakfasts and lunches—meals that cost more than the average district resident earns in a month—at NGO trainings in rural district headquarters. Civil servants also complained of some NGOs collaborating only when "they have problems or need something. *Then* they come" (2008–39). Government employees become frustrated with NGOs when they cause avoidable problems. For example, an agricultural officer complained about NGOs encouraging crops that require access to markets for profitability, but then disappearing after the plants had been grown, but before a market could be found (2008–38). She said that her office tries to partner with NGOs so that the farmers are not hurt in the process. Clearly, many problems remain.

Joint Implementation by NGOs and Government

When successful collaboration does occur, however, interpenetration takes several forms: joint implementation, decision making, and long-term planning. The first of these, joint implementation, involve partnership between NGOs and government. In a joint project, the government might provide technical expertise, while NGOs provide funds, transportation, and logistical support. When this happens, the line between government and NGO blurs. For example, in one district's blood donor program, the government provides social mobilization, sends technicians to collect blood, and contributes 25–40 percent of funding. Its partner NGO gives logistical support, provides the remaining funding, and seconds an employee to the government hospital to coordinate the program (2008–14). Another NGO works hand in hand with four different ministries on an "orphans and vulnerable children" community-based care program (2008–29). To complete one element of this program, training fifty community-based health workers, the government provided the curriculum and educators, while the NGO funded the program. This NGO also collaborated on a condom distribution program for HIV/AIDS prevention. The government provided condoms and hospital staff, and the NGO gave logistical support and transportation. A similar merger in another district saw an NGO facilitate the government's deworming program in schools: the government sent an officer and drugs, while the NGO covered transportation and per diem expenses for that worker. According to an NGO representative, "The government has the drugs, but they just expire if they don't get facilitation. So we add *that*" (2008–52). On occasion, many organizations collaborate: for a water program, one NGO might conduct training while another pays for a dam to be built, and the government provides a dam specialist (2008–17).

Embedding government personnel in NGOs and vice versa is a second way that interpenetration occurs, facilitating partnership and collaboration. The Ministry of Water and Irrigation often embeds staff in NGO projects. In particular, water engineers are seconded to NGOs to provide expertise on locating the water table and drilling boreholes (2008–14, 2008–30, 2008–46). Sometimes these engineers work on a single well, while others are based in an NGO for a period of years (2008–14). NGOs working with other ministries, such as health, agriculture, and livestock, occasionally locate their office within line ministry buildings (2008–11).

Certain NGOs design their programs with the *explicit* goal of enabling ministries to enact their mandates, a third method of NGO-government integration. Several examples illuminate this trend: because the Ministry of Education lacks sufficient funding to train public school management committees and hold in-service trainings, an NGO in Machakos district runs this program for the ministry, providing transportation, fuel, meals, supplies, and an honorarium for trainers (2008–32). It has similar programs in four other line ministries. Another NGO supports the Ministry of Agriculture mandate by sharing famine and relief distribution data (2008–25), and a third pays for the Ministry of Livestock offices in Machakos to have Internet access (2008–38). NGOs also sponsor governmental special events and ministry stakeholders' meetings (2008–11, 2008–39). During the postelection violence of early 2008, the government relied on NGOs for statistics on internally displaced people in some provinces, rather than collect the information internally (2008–14).

Even when a program is not explicitly designed to meet government objectives, NGO and government often try to work in different locations, or when in the same place, as complements rather than duplicates (2008–23, 2008–11, 2008–18). This allows NGOs to extend government services by bringing existing programs to areas for which the government lacks resources. Due to budgetary constraints, many line ministries receive adequate funds to cover only a subset of the locations in a district in a given year (2008–38).[13] One division-level civil servant reported that she receives funds to cover only three of the nine locations in her division each year. Support from a local NGO, however, allowed her to reach two more (2008–40). Another government office listed over twenty NGO partner-organizations, saying, "They sponsor us to go down to the community to advocate" (2008–37). Likewise, for computers-in-schools programs, it is often the case that government gives some funds for these, but "then the NGOs bring again more" (2008–51).

---

13. A location is a formal administrative unit of government in Kenya; it is smaller than a province, district, and division, and larger than a sublocation.

Both NGO representatives and civil servants emphasized that government staff are extremely pleased with these service extensions. Without them, they often rest idle, "just writing reports in the office" (2008–39; 2008–30). A children's officer concurred: "[NGOs are] helping us a lot a lot a lot a lot. Imagine there are four of us! We cannot be everywhere. There are 6,291 sq km in this district, and 142 people per square km. We very much rely on these NGOs! We don't even have a vehicle here!" (2008–37).

The government has begun to contract out services to NGOs, a fourth mechanism integrating NGOs into public administration of services. In 2008, the Ministry of Planning, Development and Vision 2030 contracted out the activities of a pilot sensitization program called "Localizing Millennium Development Goals (MDGs)," part of the "NGO-Government Partnership Program," to NGOs in twenty-two districts (2008–29; 2008–41). NGOs worked with District Development Offices to teach *wananchi*[14] about the MDGs and the government's goal to implement them by 2030. One such NGO organized workshops at the district, division, and location levels, conducted trainings with line ministries on sector-specific MDGs, and organized local-language radio broadcasts of MDG public service programming for 15–20 minutes each day for two months, while the ministry performed monitoring and evaluation for the program. The head of this NGO said that they reached considerably more people working together than either they or the government could have done alone (2008–29).

The government has also contracted NGOs to disseminate information on citizens' rights and obligations regarding service provision during its annual Kenya Public Service Week, discussed in greater detail later in the chapter (2008–26). And it has enlisted NGOs to perform monitoring and evaluation for some of its distributive programs, including decentralized funds (2008–24). Other NGOs interviewed have been commissioned by the Ministry of Health for HIV/AIDS campaigns; by the Constitutional Review Commission to conduct civil education; by the Ministry of Justice to implement national participation on a new human rights policy; and by the Ministry of Agriculture to carry out a drought-resistant crop experiment and a fruit tree development program. According to a leader from an NGO that focuses on agriculture, this type of engagement "co-opted [the NGO] into the Ministry [of Agriculture] and their activities" (2008–50).

NGOs Help the Government Make Decisions

In addition to joint implementation, under the Kibaki administration NGOs have been invited to directly participate in government planning and lawmaking

---

14. *Wananchi* is a Swahili word meaning "people of the country." It has become a term in Kenyan English meaning "common people."

regarding services at the national and local level. NGOs regularly sit on policy-making committees within government ministries.[15] Although by no means exhaustive, several representative examples give a flavor of interwoven decision making: two NGOs lobbied the Ministry of Agriculture to change its policy on farm inputs, and worked with it to create new rules. Instead of distributing free seeds and fertilizer, the government now subsidizes farm inputs through a voucher system, thereby nurturing the development of agricultural markets (2008–9, 2008–11). Likewise, another NGO worked with two government agencies on a project meant to make access to the lucrative dairy market more accessible to smallholders. This collaboration led in 2005 to the introduction of the Dairy Development Policy, in which the government agreed to license informal milk producers and legalize small-scale marketing, which accounts for 85 percent of milk sold in Kenya (McSherry and Brass 2008).

Another NGO that works on youth[16] issues has been involved not only in the development of a National Youth Policy with the Ministry of Youth Affairs, it has also represented youth interests for the Ministry of Housing's annual report, worked on reforming water policy as part of the national Kenya Water Partnership, contributed to the draft National Lands Policy, and sits on the steering committee of the Millennium Development Goals implementation (2008–24). Yet another NGO is a member of the Review Committee of the Local Government Act (2008–10) and collaborates on policy with seven other government agencies, including the police. The head of one of Kenya's largest NGOs sits on approximately thirty government policymaking bodies in the Ministry of Health, where her organization helped to create a code of ethics for the Kenyan health sector (2006–3).

Most NGOs are involved at the subnational level. Nearly 20 percent of NGO representatives interviewed volunteered that they are members of their District Development Committee, a governing body overseeing the district's economic and social development. An NGO representative on the Mbeere District Development Committee said this makes them "part and parcel of government procedures" (2008–52). NGOs interviewed brought up over a dozen other local planning bodies on which they sit.

These changes reflect a fundamental shift in modes of interest representation in Africa. Rather than only "Big Men" representing their affinity group clients, NGOs now also speak on behalf of *wananchi* to government. This might sound familiar to students of interest group politics of the 1950s in the United States, with NGOs taking on the role interest group lobbyists played in industrial democracies. More recently, it mirrors the dynamics that Theda

---

15. Students of organization theory might note that these relationships conjure Philip Selznick's (1949) as well as more recent discussions (Tripp 2001; Mercer 2003) of co-optation. Here, I agree with Tripp (2001) that these relationships should be seen primarily as inclusion, not co-optation.

16. In Africa, "youth" denotes fifteen to thirty-five year olds.

Skocpol (2003) describes, where American civil society has reorganized, moving away from mass mobilization toward interest group representation through advocacy groups and nonprofit organizations.

NGO Plans Blended into Government Plans

Besides their involvement in planning and policymaking, NGOs have also been recognized in the country's District Development Plans (DDPs). DDPs, akin to Soviet five-year plans, have been used in Kenya since the 1970s and are a good measure of the pulse of a district. The 2002–08 DDPs introduced across-the-board integration of NGO plans, as well as elaboration of the role that NGOs will play during the plan period.[17] The integration of NGOs' plans and budgets means that when district-level governments list their revenue and expenditures, they now include funds raised by NGOs. Before this time, DDPs were written by and for government only. One civil servant expresses the idea behind the change: "You can't implement a plan you didn't help to make!" (2008–41).

The sense of *reliance* on NGOs for service provision is present nationwide. In Butere-Mumias District, NGOs are *expected* to provide "credit, grants and material support" to cooperatives, and to manage and promote good governance, and to undertake agricultural extension services jointly with government (Government of Kenya 2002a, 27–29). They are *required* to provide financial support and capacity-building in Nyando (Government of Kenya 2002f, 43); they *will provide* "credit facilities, physical infrastructure, educational and health services" in Kakamega (Government of Kenya 2002b, 50); and are "*expected* to continue complementing the Water Department's efforts" in Rachuonyo (Government of Kenya 2002g, 34).[18] Very frequently, plans plainly state that NGOs will do such things as "Supplement extension services; Carry out training and awareness campaigns" (Government of Kenya 2002c, 36); or provide "textbooks, bursaries and physical facilities" (Government of Kenya 2002d, 48). Makueni District proposes 149 projects to be undertaken; of these, forty-four (just under 30%) explicitly involve NGOs in implementation or funding, or both (Government of Kenya 2002e, 71–86). The presence of these statements in districts spanning the country suggests that NGO-government collaboration is not limited to districts that share ethnic affiliation with the president or other specific powerful politicians, as theories of patronage-based politics in Kenya would have us believe.

The DDPs clearly recognize the importance of NGOs for effective service delivery. The West Pokot DDP states explicitly, "Lessons Learnt: Projects that were implemented with assistance from NGOs and other development agencies

---

17. Some older DDPs mention NGOs, but the countrywide emphasis began in 2002.
18. Emphasis added.

performed better than those that were implemented by the government alone. There is thus need to collaborate with all stakeholders during the preparation of the current plans" (Government of Kenya 2002h, 17). Government actors desire to improve the quality of services they provide, and they recognize that they can learn from NGOs in this regard.

The Consequences of NGO Involvement in Service Provision

Since 2002, government actors have very slowly begun to change the way they provide services, mimicking NGOs' calls for participatory development, transparency, and accountability. Most key informants interviewed for this essay— even *after* the violent election period in early 2008—were convinced that the change represents a slow-moving, long-term turn toward democratic governance in service provision, with widening participation in policymaking and increased efforts at accountability. According to one authority on international development, this is one of NGOs' greatest abilities—to change the attitudes and practices of local officials (Clark 1995).

Although the international donor community has also pushed governments toward greater accountability, NGOs have played a role on the ground. Government offices began to adopt new strategies after developing closer contact with NGOs, after former NGO leaders entered the Kibaki administration, and after noting the positive response that local people have toward NGOs.[19] Government officials credit NGOs for this explicitly: "It's NGOs that made government open our eyes. We have made a lot of changes" (2008–37). As a result, as one senior civil servant optimistically reports, "Government is more of an NGO than NGOs are!" in terms of levels of participation and accountability, which NGOs are known for in Kenya (2008–33). In developing these new patterns of service provision, government agencies and actors have very slowly begun to adopt more democratic practices than are usually associated with African public administration. This is not to say that Kenya has democratic service provision practices—only that there has been a slow movement *toward* political opening. As proof of both the changes and the remaining issues, one civil servant was excited to point out that "you have to report to duty now"—a rather grim reminder that public administration in Kenya has a long way to go before accountability is achieved (2008–41).

Some new government initiatives are exact replicas of existing NGO programs. Over thirty government ministries have introduced a "scorecard" system, publicly posting citizen responses to service provision by that agency. The scorecards are nearly identical to an NGO's "report cards" started several years earlier (2008–10). Government employees, including some politicians,

---

19. See Brass (2010), chaps. 5 and 6.

now have performance contracts used to judge their effectiveness (2008–35). Each year they set precise targets for various activities and are judged on how well they achieve them, sometimes competing with civil servants in other districts or provinces (2012–14). As one observer reported, "Service contracts are new in government, but are old at NGOs" (2008–52).

Line ministries have also reinvigorated "demand-driven development," adding the type of participatory elements that NGOs popularized.[20] For example, the Ministries of Agriculture and of Livestock reported that in their extension services, "It's taking root! Sixty percent of people come and demand" (2008–41). Instead of disbursing ministry-chosen agricultural inputs, they now develop action plans with communities: they analyze area conditions, then float possible strategies to farmers, and finally allow the community to decide a course of action. The ministries then provide training on these agricultural techniques (2008–38, 2008–39). These ministries also sponsor food security, agroforestry, water development, and livestock improvement programs for self-help groups and private businesses to implement. Potential projects are discussed and chosen publicly in an effort to ensure that government is "now being held accountable" (2008–41).

The Kibaki administration's ambitious *Vision 2030* plan to implement the Millennium Development Goals by 2030 verbally showcases that a "participatory approach is one of our new 'core values,' " according to a senior district administrator (2008–41). The plan "advocated a consultative approach . . . involving as many ordinary Kenyans and stakeholders as possible . . . from all levels of the public service, the private sector, civil society, the media and nongovernmental organizations" (Government of Kenya 2007, 3).

Service charters describing the mission, range of service, clients, commitments to delivery, and complaint mechanisms are another introduction to line ministries, and are prominently displayed throughout government offices. The Ministry of Livestock service charter, for example, is designed as "a tool to enhance awareness on the range of services offered by the Ministry . . . and to express our commitments to offer satisfactory services to all our clients. [It] represents a paradigm shift in the manner in which public services will be delivered, now and in future" (Government of Kenya 2008b). Government service provision offices now have suggestion boxes and even staffed customer care desks.

Also meant to enhance citizen awareness is the Kenya Public Service Week, held annually in each provincial and district headquarters. This program represents "a shift towards 'openness' in service delivery to the public encouraging

---

20. Scholars writing on Kenya during the first decades of independence note that demand-driven development is not new (Leonard 1977). It is interesting that young civil servants and NGO workers *believe* it to be new. It may be the case that these programs declined during the Moi administration and have been reinvigorated in the 2000s.

citizens to demand better services. . . . It is also to build recognition of the role public officers play towards achievement of efficient and effective service delivery to citizens" (Government of Kenya 2008a). As one politician reports, the Kenya Public Service Week is an accountability measure designed to let citizens "know that their taxes are getting plowed back" (2008–35).

Even leaders of NGOs who were strongly antigovernment during the 1990s struggle for democracy acknowledged the movement toward democratic processes in government programs and have begun to work more collaboratively with government. For example, a representative of a nationwide NGO that fought the Moi administration as the "voice of the voiceless" described her organization engaging with the Kibaki administration, saying, "Government has not asked us to compromise ourselves" (2008–26).[21] In the past, however, provincial administrators sent her on "wild goose chases," and forced her into working clandestinely to avoid harassment. This has ended, she says. "Now . . . I'm able to work" (2008–26). As Aili Tripp (2001) noted elsewhere in Africa, this suggests a relationship of inclusion, not co-optation, between government and nongovernmental actors.

Demonstrating this change, the government contracted her organization, alongside several other NGOs, to coordinate the National Policy and Action Plan (NAP) to reform human rights policy in Kenya—something that would have been unimaginable during the Moi years. The NAP uses a participatory approach, in which "regional hearings [are] held . . . in all provinces . . . [to] discuss with the residents their human rights concerns, challenges and priorities towards informing the human rights policy and action plan" (Kenya National Commission on Human Rights 2009). Organizers of this process in one province revealed that hundreds of NGOs and community groups presented planning documents, group opinions, and memoranda at a forum held for public involvement.

Another organization representative involved in the NAP program told a similar story. Even though his NGO is a critical, outspoken watchdog of government, it was contracted to conduct NAP activities in Eastern Province. This NGO's mission was to mobilize people to "Raise concerns! Be lively! Demand to know!" at government meetings (2008–27). Working with critical organizations rather than stifling them represents a significant opening in governance patterns.

Kenyans seem to appreciate NGOs, seeing them as looking after their interests. When 501 people from three districts were asked by the author, "To what extent do you think NGOs have the interests of the people in mind?" 70 percent of respondents answered positively, and only 20 percent responded negatively.[22] In a similar study in Uganda, Barr, Fafchamps, and Owens (2005, 676)

---

21. This organization is not politically affiliated with Kibaki or his Kikuyu ethnic group.

22. The response options were "usually," "sometimes," "rarely," or "never." The remaining 10% had no answer or didn't know.

report that NGOs are generally well regarded, particularly when they are accessible to their beneficiaries.

Conclusion

Evidence from Kenya since 2002 supports the theory that civil society can improve government performance (Putnam 1993; Tocqueville 1863). The relations between NGOs and the government today suggest that the state has not retreated from the governing scene to be *replaced* by non state actors, as some have worried. Instead, it has been *joined* by non-state actors in the governing process and has been bolstered by the combined efforts. As a result of government-NGO collaboration on service provision, the total amount of services is higher than it would be in NGOs' absence (2008–38). NGOs collaborate with line ministries on joint programs, provide their own services, supplement the services of government, bid for government contract work, and, by example, influence the government to provide services in a more participatory manner.

The overarching trends suggest a blurring of the boundary between government and nongovernmental actors in the delivery of services. As one NGO worker put it, "People consider us government. They are confused about where government starts and [our NGO] stops" (2008–14). Indeed, many government officials consider the work of NGOs to be part of the work of the Kenyan state. Even when they do not yet see NGOs as fully integrated with government, some civil servants hope that this will one day be the case: "NGOs and the Ministry will be streamlined, so they are working in the same same[23] direction" (2008–38).

This state of affairs is neither universal in Kenya, nor did it arise independently from the broader political conditions of the country. On the contrary, NGOs have been able to complement the administrative aims of the state due to several key factors, including a relatively open political climate, a central government that grants autonomy to service providers, a majority of NGOs focused primarily on service provision rather than good governance; street-level civil servants motivated to work with NGOs; and a willingness to engage with and learn from non-state actors in service provision. Under these conditions, several methods of mutual reinforcement occur: joint implementation, decision making, and planning in particular.

Scholars describing the situation elsewhere in Africa have come to similar conclusions, asserting that collaborative NGO-government relations can facilitate service provision (Obiyan 2005, 319) and even expand the scope of the

---

23. Kenyans often repeat words intentionally for emphasis. Thus, "same same" means "exact same."

state's reach (Sandberg 1994, 13). Many NGOs "work with almost every ministry because our programs are close to [those of] government," according to one NGO leader (2008–53). Experts on Western public administration should be familiar with this trend, having noted that public-private partnerships are a common strategy for improving governing capacity in weaker states (Peters and Pierre 1998, 233). Collaborative efforts occur on both the planning and implementation sides of service provision, blurring the line between public and private NGO provision.

6

Bridging the Local and the Global

Faith-Based Organizations as Non-state Providers in Tanzania

Michael Jennings

Since the gradual rolling back of the state from the 1980s non-state providers have come to play a particularly dominant role in service provision and broader developmental activity in sub-Saharan Africa. Yet it is a sector that remains poorly understood and, with the exception of one particular element of the broader NSP "type," rather underresearched in the region. As a result, a number of its characteristics remain rather opaque: the emergence of this sector (as opposed to atomized, individual NSP actors); the nature of its relationship with governments, donors, and other national, regional and international organizations; the evolution and ongoing transformation of the sector in its activities, character, and modes of operation; and the ways in which this sector is funded and resourced. Although this chapter is not an attempt to map the landscape and contours of the NSP sector in sub-Saharan Africa in general, it does seek to widen the analytical focus somewhat, by examining an element that has often been forgotten, ignored, or misunderstood: faith-based NSP actors.

Although the sub-Saharan African NSP sector comprises a mix of public and private actors, voluntary organizations (of which faith-based organizations are a component part) play a significant role. However, the literature has tended to look to one type of voluntary organization above all others: the non-governmental organization (NGO). Goran Hyden, for example, has described how the voluntary sector "has become known in Africa as the NGO sector, named after its principal actors—non-governmental organizations" (Hyden 1995, 35). Alan Fowler epitomizes this approach when conflating the (conceptually distinct) terms voluntary sector and NGO: "voluntary development

organizations (NGOs) are normally united around a vision of more economically equitable, socially just and globally sustainable societies than exist at
present" (Fowler 1995, 53). However, while the analysis of the constraints,
challenges faced, and potential opportunities offered by NGOs is useful, the
modern secular NGO is not the only NSP actor,[1] and the experiences of other
types of organization might offer a different perspective and add nuances to
our understanding of the NSP sector more widely.

It was faith-based and religious organizations that initially carved out the
space into which the NSP sector would emerge and evolve in large parts of
sub-Saharan Africa during the colonial period. And it is these same organizations, with the addition of new faith-based actors emerging in the postcolonial environment, that have continued to shape the form, function, scale, and
relationships of the NSP sector. Mapping out this space, without reference to
the longer history of action and engagement, and without placing faith-based
organizations and religious-linked organizations at the fore, risks failing to
adequately account for the non-state sector as a whole.

The importance of the faith-based organization (FBO) sector, both historically and contemporaneously, also reminds us of the importance of distinguishing between different non-state actors. Where FBOs have been included in
the analysis of the NSP sector in sub-Saharan Africa, they have often been
regarded as NGOs—their faith aspect sidelined or ignored as irrelevant or dis-
tracting. But founding beliefs of agencies do impact the nature of their relationship with the local communities in which they are based, the government with
whom they work, and the range of bilateral and multilateral donors, creating
distinctive patterns of engagement and impacts.

Just as secular NGOs differ in organizational, ideological, and functional
role, FBOs come in many forms. Some resemble modern NGOs, focusing on
their development function, while others put greater stress on proselytizing
alongside (or as part of) their social action (European donors remain wary of
World Vision, for example, seeing it as an evangelizing, more than development-
oriented, organization). Some FBOs are openly sectarian while others serve all
regardless of their beliefs and faith. But the common thread, what binds them
together and allows us to see in them a distinctive "type," is the strong thread
of faith running through them. Religion lies at their core, whether implicit,
or more explicit, and this distinguishes them from secular NGOs (even where
the impact on project selection, delivery of services, and overall policy closely
resembles other, nonreligious NGOs). This raises an obvious question: If an
organization conceptualizes itself and behaves as an NGO, how important

---

1. Not all NGOs are secular: there are faith-based organizations that see themselves, and are
largely perceived, as NGOs rather than FBOs. This is especially the case where their religious identity is less overt than their developmental and humanitarian one. The use of the word "secular"
therefore is problematic. However, faith-based NGOs are largely presented in the literature (and
present themselves) as secular-in-approach, hence the distinction being made here.

is the religious element? The relevance faces both upwards and downwards: up, because it gives the organization a constituency it can look to for support (financial but also in values), linking it into globalized networks of faith denied to avowedly secular organizations; down, because it enables the organization to engage in a discourse that is relevant to the lived experience and worldviews of the vast majority of people with whom they engage. Faith and religion are important factors in understanding how certain organizations function (and their areas of comparative advantage) and the nature of the relationships they establish with other actors and communities. FBOs are different from NGOs, not just a subset of that sector, despite fuzzy boundaries on all sides.

This upward and downward face of the FBO is important for understanding its power. The extent to which FBOs are able to draw on their rootedness within communities at the same time as being linked into global networks of faith enables them to create particularly powerful modes of operation at many levels. This potent combination of localism and globalism, coupled with a leadership role at both levels, gives FBOs both power and prestige within local communities, with government leaders (at local and national levels), and with international organizations.

But the consequences of this global-local power and leadership can be problematic. Sectarianism or (faith) exclusivity in service provision, can contribute to intercommunal tensions. Moreover, where faith values clash with developmental ones (such as gender equity, family planning and choice, and sexual rights), the leadership role played by FBOs and faith leaders can undermine efforts to promote alternatives. Nonetheless, the presence of FBOs and religious-linked organizations are a reality. Nor are the potential limitations and problems necessarily confined solely to organizations linked to faiths. Ignoring them risks ignoring a core component of the NSP sector and a group of organizations that play tremendously important roles (for good and for bad) in the lives of the poor.

Religion and NSP Action

The place of religion and faith, and through this that of faith-based organizations, in development and service provision is problematic for writers who see development as essentially a secular project. Amartya Sen, identifying himself as "a strong believer in secularism and democracy" (Sen 2006, 19), warns against, for example, "trying to redefine the religions involved in terms of political and social attitudes." This "downgrades," he suggests, the "civic initiatives" people (who happen to be religious) make in what are "essentially political and social," and by implication not religious, problems (Sen 2006, 78). The equivocal position of religions on human rights and equality similarly presents problems (a point reinforced not least by Pope Benedict XVI's comments on the British Equality Bill, in particular on its implications for the Catholic

Church's stance on homosexuality [Butt 2010, 3]). As Maxine Molyneux and Shahara Razavi argue, "More radical attacks on human rights and women's rights agendas have also resulted from the resurgence of religious identities that include the assertion of 'traditional' gender roles and systems of authority that intrinsically violate women's rights." "When religious authorities become the spokespeople for nations and ethnic communities," they continue, "and where no guarantees exist for equality, democracy or human rights protection within the political context, there is little scope for contestation and dialogue" (Molyneux and Razavi 2006, 18).

Some of this analysis rests on a notion that there has been a broad global resurgence in religion since the 1980s, in particular a more muscular and assertive form of religious engagement in social life. Barr and colleagues, for example, argue that faith-linked development is based on new forms of religious engagement, notably "evangelical churches and Muslim communities" (Barr, Fafchamps, and Owens 2005, 657). Others have looked at the rise of a more politicized, socially-aware faith from this period. Casanova, for example, suggests religion changed around the 1980s from a focus on the inner, individual, realm to "the public arena of moral and political contestation" (Casanova 1994, 3). Religion had adopted a new social role: "We are witnessing the 'deprivatization' of religion in the modern world. By deprivatization I mean the fact that religious traditions throughout the world are refusing to accept the marginal and privatized role which theories of modernity as well as theories of secularization had reserved for them" (Casanova 1994, 35).

Religions were refusing "to restrict themselves to the pastoral care of individual souls" in their challenge to state and markets (Casanova 1994, 5). At a broader political level, the influence of Huntington's clash of civilizations hypothesis (Huntington 1993 and 1996), which posited the escalation of social tensions and violence as incompatible faith systems came up against each other, has reinforced the tendency to look to the negative impact of this revival of religion.

However, underpinning this debate is a lack of understanding of the place of religion and faith-based organizations as non-state providers. The notion of a religious revival, and the associated "shift" into the public realm by faith leaders and organizations, ignores the extent to which religion has played a critical role in non-state action in service delivery, welfare, and care for the poor and marginalized across cultures and time, from ancient Egypt, through medieval Europe, to nineteenth and twentieth century Ethiopia (Jennings 2008a, 13–18). Over the twentieth century and into the twenty-first, world religions have consistently sought to maintain relevance and influence in social and political affairs as well as the spiritual realm, recasting their social role in diverse and changing ways in order to maintain that relevance. What perhaps changed in the 1970s and 1980s was the global visibility of such public engagement, not the engagement itself.

In East Africa faith-based service and welfare provision preceded the creation of the colonial state. Christian missions (whose dominance of this sector was to be cemented by support from the colonial state) built schools, clinics, and hospitals; they provided training in skills and income-generating activities, food relief in times of famine, and shelter in times of war and instability. Faith organizations delivering vital services, social support, and development and humanitarian assistance have been an enduring feature of East African life, especially rural East Africa, since the late nineteenth century.

The Rise of the FBO-NSP Sector in Tanzania

For much of the twentieth century—right up to the end of the 1970s—religious and faith-linked organizations dominated service and welfare provision in East Africa, and were the most substantial of non-state actors in social development programs. A more pervasive and deeply rooted presence than both colonial and postcolonial states, embedded within the communities in which they provided services, the mission, the mosque, the independent church, and other religious agencies provided care and assistance to the poor and needy. The growth of the NGO sector somewhat eclipsed these agencies from the gaze of both donors and analysts during the 1980s and afterward, but they did not disappear nor see their importance as NSP actors diminish. Indeed, one consequence of the liberalization of health and education provision in Tanzania from the mid-1990s was a renewed expansion of religious-based welfare service.

Within colonial Tanganyika,[2] faith-based organizations, in the shape of missions, were the most important non-state actors in welfare and development. As a result, it was their engagement in this area, and their relationships with the state (and the response of the state to their engagement), that shaped the NSP sector in Tanzania. The emergence of legislation, institutional structures, and funding mechanisms to control and direct non-state action reflect this history of engagement by FBOs, a legacy that would be inherited by the postcolonial state and by the emerging NGO sector from the 1960s and, especially, from the 1980s.

Faith-based NSP action was initially the province of the Christian missions, present in ever increasing numbers across East Africa from the middle of the nineteenth centuries and firmly embedded within colonial Tanganyika by the 1920s. Early mission activity (pre-1930s) was highly individualized, based on the priorities and policies of the individual organization with little reference to the work of other missions. However, by the 1930s, greater efforts to coordinate mission activities in social welfare were taking place, as missions sought to create an officially recognized space in which they operated and received support from the state for their work. In doing so, they laid the foundations

---

2. Tanganyika will be used when referring to the country during the colonial period, and Tanzania thereafter.

for the NSP sector into which NGOs and other providers would emerge beginning in the 1960s, establishing a relationship with the government reflecting mutual reliance, and occasional suspicion on both sides, that would similarly frame experiences after independence and up to the current period. In 1961, as an indication of the dominance of the missions in social welfare, despite fifteen years of expansion of state-run and delivered services, missions ran 287 hospitals, dispensaries, and clinics across Tanzania compared to the government's seventy-three (Government of Tanganyika 1962, 12–15, 24). They dominated maternal and child health services and provided training to African nurses and other medical personnel (Jennings 2006, 2008c). Missions were more important than the state in education, controlling around 75 percent and 56 percent of primary and secondary education places, respectively (Iliffe 1979, 546).

The initial impetus for greater coordination in the 1930s came from within the mission organizations themselves. The main Protestant missions operating in the territory established the Tanganyika Mission Council in 1934 as an umbrella group representing Protestant mission interests (the Catholic Church attended meetings on an informal basis). The Tanganyika Mission Council, and its subcommittees focusing on particular aspects of mission welfare activity, sought to secure greater cooperation between missions and the colonial state. The Medical Mission Committee (established in 1936), for example, worked to establish "closer cooperation between medical missionaries and the Medical Department of the Government,"[3] seeking to integrate more fully mission medical services into the colonial health system.[4] Through these institutions, missions were seeking to assert a broader "mission" identity, above and beyond individual mission organization identities, and in doing so established a "mission sector" in terms of service provision.

If the impetus had occurred within the newly established mission sector, colonial governments nonetheless recognized the importance of working with (and co-opting) missions as formal welfare service providers. As Ana Madeira notes in relation to education: "The missionary zeal in promoting vocational education was thus seen by the State as a practical economic investment in the sense that convergent ideology and consistent practice were saving the central government the trouble of having to spend a considerable part of the budget on financing education in the colonies" (Madeira 2005, 38).

In Tanganyika, the state had long used mission facilities to fill the gaps left by the paucity of colonial state services. Often located in rural areas, remote and isolated from government-run services, missions were in many instances the sole Western medical service provider in their area. As a result, mission

---

3. Director of Medical Services, to the Chief Secretary, February 25, 1937. Tanzania National Archives (TNA) 24848.

4. Muller, "Medical Mission and its Relations to Government," TNA 450 692 v.1. No date or author, but Muller is referred to as the author in Agenda of the TMC (Tanganyika Mission Council) meeting, July 9–11, 1936. TNA 21247 v. 1.

medical services were called on in public health campaigns, such as managing and monitoring sleeping sickness, and vaccination campaigns following the outbreak of epidemics (Jennings 2008c). In areas such as maternal and child health care, the colonial state effectively withdrew and left missions almost solely responsible by the mid-1930s.[5]

But by formally recognizing the new umbrella mission institutions, and more important in granting them a place in policy debate and formation, in moving from a system of ad hoc grants to support particular services to regular grants-in-aid, the colonial state acknowledged the division of welfare service provision into state and non-state sectors. Mission medical services, education services, and broader social action were no longer to be considered part of their Christian missionary activity and efforts to proselytize, but as essential components of colonial services. The result was the creation, by the end of the colonial period, of a distinct NSP sector. The state still controlled overall policy and direction, set standards, and provided oversight to the range of individually provided (but still coordinated through the mission representative organizations) services. But it had recognized NSP service provision was not just an extra layer, but an integral part of public welfare in Tanganyika.

Such recognition did not mean relations were always smooth, or that the government willingly embraced a new set of partners. The colonial state was reluctant to allow the new NSP sector too much influence over policy, and constantly sought to limit its own financial contributions, just as the missions pushed for an increase in both influence and cash. But it created a recognizable landscape of public and nonprofit provision of services that would be picked up again in the late 1980s and 1990s as national reforms and international development discourse pushed NGOs onto the center stage as NSP actors.

Independence in 1961 coincided with the emergence of a burgeoning NGO sector in Europe and North America with a view to move into international development and relief assistance. But even as new secular NSP actors moved into the public space already created by their mission forerunners, religious organizations continued to play a key role. Indeed, the 1960s were a critical period for faith-based organizations globally. Just as secular NGOs in this period shifted their focus from funding disaster relief and emergency projects to "development" interventions, so too religious leaders, FBOs, and other organizations within the "faith sector" similarly reconceptualized their social role. As Ian Linden notes, the Vatican moved toward embracing the newly emerging development discourse and the postcolonial global order (Linden 2008). At the national level, religions similarly sought to engage in new ways in the changing space wrought by decolonization and the establishment of new nations. In Tanzania, not only did the "faith sector" widen to include other religions (especially Islam), but faith-based and religious organizations began to move

---

5. Secretariat minutes, March 30, 1936. TNA 10834.

away from welfare service provision alone to embrace social development as part of a wider social mission.

The Christian Council of Tanzania (which replaced the Tanganyika Mission Council in 1949 as the umbrella organization for the main Protestant churches) outlined this change in 1963: "In the past the Churches have engaged in medical, educational and various welfare services in which they have demonstrated their concern for man but generally they have regarded these as secondary to the work of evangelism. Today in our situation we need to widen the scope of Christian concern and action to match the new opportunities for showing forth the love of God to our neighbours in the midst of a new nation."[6]

In 1968, the Christian Council of Tanzania declared: "Traditionally, the Churches have built and maintained schools and hospitals. . . . Now the time has come to help equip our people for rural development."[7] During the 1960s and 1970s, then, faith-based organizations in Tanzania began increasingly to use the rhetoric of "social development" as the means for putting their social ministry into action, and as the basis of their relationship with the state.

If the role of faith-based non-state actors in service provision and broader development has remained relatively constant over the course of the twentieth century, and into the twenty-first, the extent of power held by faith-based NSP actors in relation to the state has fluctuated both over time and within particular sectors, largely as a result of the relative resources available to both them and the state. When the state has relied more heavily on resources (whether capital, infrastructure, or influence) controlled by FBOs, then FBOs have been able to wield more influence in the formation of policy and in directing the shape of the services they offer. Conversely, where the state has been able to exercise greater control over policy setting and implementation, it has been able to resist FBO demands for a greater say. But such fluctuations have not been absolute: greater control for either the government or FBOS in one sector does not imply control in all sectors.

One can see this in the shifting dynamics in colonial period welfare provision. In education, the colonial regime was aware it lacked sufficient resources to offer a state-run service. It was therefore prepared to allow missions to take the lead and to pay them for their contribution. In health, government was more reluctant to allow mission domination. It had to fund mission services, given the large gaps in its own provision, especially in the rural areas where many missions were based. But it was able to maintain more control over the direction and coordination of mission health services than it was in education.

---

6. Christian Council of Tanzania, Rapid Social Change Study, Preliminary Report Study Commission A, "The Christian Contribution to a Dynamic Society in Tanganyika," May 1973, 18. Christian Aid Archives (CAA) CA/A/6/7.

7. Christian Council of Tanzania AGM minutes, June 20–21, "Report of the Relief and Service Division," 1. CAA, CA/A/7/2.

Relations between government and mission were therefore complicated. Missions perhaps had the upper hand in education, but less so in health care.

In the first decades of independence, despite the nationalization of health and education services (enhancing the power of the state), voluntary (faith-based actors) remained key players, continuing in the health sector to run their own clinics, hospitals, and other services. The rate of non-state expansion may have slowed down, but faith-based health services remained critical to meeting the needs of the national health system. The state could not simply supplant faith-based actors. Indeed, foreign NGOs seeking to operate in the country noted the difficulties of finding non-state, nonfaith partners.[8]

Also shifting were the relations between faith-based actors and the state, reflecting internal and external power balances. During the colonial period, the faith sector had functioned as a proto civil society. Despite its close relationship to the colonial state, and its inability to claim to be truly representative of Tanzanian society, the faith sector did challenge state policy in a range of areas, in particular over state welfare provision, arguing for a greater commitment to meeting the needs of Africans. In the postcolonial period, the (now broader) faith sector moved closer to the state, granting it a powerful voice in the center, but at the expense of this tentatively critical role. Religious-based efforts served to reinforce state domination, rather than challenge it. Faith leaders were given a voice at the center: Christian and Islamic leaders regularly met with the president and other senior government officials as part of the (informal) Baraza la Wazee (literally, "Meeting of the Elders").[9] At the local level, faith leaders often had close relationships with district and regional commissioners. While the NSP sector flourished, its ability to challenge or critique the government, or function in a truly independent way, was (willingly) subsumed to ally non-state action to state policy (Jennings 2008b, 105–10).

From the late 1980s, as the Tanzanian state (as with other African states) lost power as a result of structural adjustment and related donor policies, the relative power of faith-sector NSPs (and the new NSP agencies that had been created) once again rose: they secured greater freedom and control over services, which now were as likely to be funded from external sources as directly from the government. Religious leaders became more prominent in criticizing government policies and interventions, both in Tanzania and in sub-Saharan Africa more widely. In Benin, Gabon, Togo, Congo, and Democratic Republic of Congo (then Zaire), senior Catholic clergy led the prodemocracy

---

8. Oxfam, a large British NGO working in Tanzania in this period, found that most partners it worked with were church-based. Efforts to identify new, secular partners in the 1970s were only partially successful, and missions and church-linked organizations continued to receive significant amounts of Oxfam funding in this decade. Interview with Oxfam's Tanzania field director during the 1970s, April 30, 1996.

9. Around one-third of the population is Muslim, and around 60 percent are Christian. Zanzibar is overwhelmingly Muslim.

movements of the early 1990s (Gifford 1994, 513). In Kenya, the National Council of Churches was prominent in the push for multiparty democracy, and faith leaders publicly criticized President Daniel arap Moi's government for human rights abuses (Jennings 2008b, 112). Faith leaders and FBOs began, from the 1990s, to move more fully into orthodox civil society, not at the expense of retaining close ties to the state (at the leadership level) but with their uncritical support no longer guaranteed.

As the shift of faith leaders and organizations into a more critical stance in relation to the African state from the 1990s onward shows us, their influence rests on more than just resource capital. Even where the state has the upper hand (in terms of control over funds, policy, and infrastructure), faith leaders and organizations retain considerable power (still fluctuating, but less so, perhaps, than the fortunes of secular civil society organizations). This "moral" power, a power that gives considerable clout to the pronouncements and deliberations of FBOs and faith leaders, rests on a key characteristic of the FBO: its global-local hybridity, the consequences of which are discussed in the next section.

FBOs as Global-Local Hybrids

In part, the strength of the FBO sector in NSP provision reflects this history: the decades of engagement and working with governments (colonial and post-colonial) in shaping the NSP space. It also reflects the continued dominance of faith-linked organizations, institutions, and actors in the region, and their presence in almost every part of the country in the form of the village church(es) and mosque(s), easily outweighing in scale the number of government posts and officers.

However, the importance of FBOs also reflects some important characteristics of this type of NSP that distinguish it from their secular non-state counterparts. In particular, FBOs exhibit a global-local hybridity. FBOs tend to operate within highly global faith networks, at the same time as they remain deeply embedded in local communities.

NGOs have both transnational and local characters, but seldom (to a meaningful extent) within the same organization. International NGOs (INGOs) are, by their nature, transnational. But rarely could such organizations be considered to be "local" in the sense of belonging in the local community. While national NGOs and (especially community-based organizations) might be "local" in this sense, their transnational character is potentially more limited (mediated, as it often is, through an INGO partner).

The Very Local?

A 2003 World Bank survey of sixty thousand people across sixty countries found that faith-based organizations emerged as vitally important institutions for the rural poor in particular. FBOs, Deepa Narayan has noted, "emerge frequently in poor people's lists of important institutions. They appear more frequently as the most important institutions in rural rather than in urban ones. Spirituality, faith in God and connecting to the sacred in nature are an integral part of poor people's lives in many parts of the world. Religious organizations are also valued for the assistance they provide to poor people."

Moreover, the survey concluded that "religious organizations feature more prominently than any other single type of state institution" (although it also noted that FBOs "do not disappear when ineffective institutions are mentioned") (Narayan 2000, 222). Faith-based organizations operate on a level that can be much more immediate than secular counterparts, both a physical immediacy (based within the local community, run from or by a local church or mosque) *and* an ideological intimacy. This immediacy brings with it two key aspects of the FBO: a shared language of problems, challenges, and the aims of "development"; and secondly, a level of leadership that many secular NGOs, even if also based in the local community, find it difficult to generate.

FBOs often possess a shared worldview with the communities in which they are based, one that often extends beyond the confines of its own faith community. The language of development practice (including welfare service provision) is distancing, jargon-led: a world of rapid rural appraisals, target-driven outputs, participatory approaches, social capital, and so on. Development discourse operates within a dualist perspective, with the modernist tropes of progress versus backwardness, willingness to embrace change versus conservative fear of the new, still firmly embedded within it.[10] FBOs have found a space between the narrow dualism of Western development discourses and the more holistic understandings of African societies (or, indeed, society more generally), in which to express ideas of improvement, well-being, and change.

As Ellis and Haar (2004) point out, the lack of recognition for the realm of the spiritual does not accord with the social realities of many Africans. The reluctance of secular organizations to acknowledge the nonmaterial is to fail to engage fully with what are perceived of as realities. In the mid-1950s a mission hospital in a coastal district of Tanganyika was ordered by the colonial government to stop holding public prayers in the wards in order not to upset local Muslim opinion. In response, the local chief, a Muslim, wrote the provincial commissioner requesting the ban be overturned. Muslims, the chief argued, appreciated the fact that mission hospitals recognized the presence of God, something ignored in the strictly secular government hospitals.[11] Mission hospitals in colonial Tanganyika remained popular, despite their small fees, even when a government health center was situated in the same area offering free consultation. The acknowledgement of the spiritual world gave mission

---

10. Cosmopolitan discourse, a self-proclaimed endeavor to move away from such Manichean dialogue, seems to rather more fully entrench such distinctions and divisions within the language of development.

11. Interview with Victor Evans, government medical stores officer, Dar es Salaam, 1954–62, November 5, 1999.

hospitals greater symmetry with African notions of health, sickness, and well-being, accounting in large part for their popularity among Christians and non-Christians alike.

The local aspect of the FBO is also reflected in the particular leadership role that such organizations can have within a community, a region, or even a nation. As Robert Garner notes, religious organizations possess both 'extensive' and 'intensive' power that can be mobilized to modify, encourage, or discourage certain types of behavior (Garner 2000, 50). Religious leaders are invested with not only spiritual power but often significant temporal power, giving added weight to their pronouncements and teachings.

Governments have sought to mobilize this leadership role in rolling out national anti-HIV and AIDS programs. In Uganda, Muslim leaders were brought into the fight against the disease early on, as were imams in Senegal. Studies in sub-Saharan Africa have suggested a positive correlation between active Islamic faith and lower levels of infection, leading some to suggest that Islamic proscriptions on the consumption of alcohol and extramarital affairs, rules requiring ritual washing and cleanliness, and the widespread practice of male circumcision are responsible for providing a greater degree of protection to Muslims (Gray 2004, 1751–55). Similarly, studies by Isaac Addai in Ghana have suggested that women members of evangelical Christian churches were less likely to engage in premarital sex than members of other Christian denominations (Addai, in Takyi 2003, 1222). While compelling evidence of faith adherence and lower risks of infection is complicated and difficult to prove, leadership by faith organizations and individuals has been seen as tremendously important in the fight against HIV and AIDS, and in achieving other developmental goals.

But leadership is a double-edged sword. It is regarded as effective when it is oriented to goals that are not counterproductive or even dangerous. The power of faith and religious leaders can also, as demonstrated by the Vatican's regular fulminations against the use of condoms, be used to exacerbate risk, as well as to lessen it. As Takyi notes, "the network of relationships and church-based social ties" could facilitate the "diffusion of new ideas." But equally, it could limit change where actions are believed to go counter to religious tenets (Takyi 2003, 1222). Thus faith leaders have exhorted their members to remain faithful within marriage, to not succumb to the desires of the flesh outside marriage, but in their refusal to countenance the use of condoms directly (by asserting that their use goes against religious rules) or indirectly (by simply not mentioning them), they can in fact increase the risk for those who stray from their best intentions.

Transnational Agency? Global Networks of Faith

As the example of the Vatican's stance on condoms as part of an anti-HIV and AIDS strategy demonstrates, leadership is also a factor at the global level, for

FBOs are embedded within international networks of faith (organized, semi-organized, and personal) that can give a local FBO a transnational character. Since the early 1990s, transnational civil society has emerged as an increasingly powerful force, assisted by advances in communications technology. Global networks of similar-focused organizations are not, of course, confined to the faith sector. Southern NGOs often have close relationships with international NGOs, or form part of global advocacy networks or groupings that function at the international level. But faith networks have played a significant part in this expansion, and inter- and intrafaith networks have a long history. Missions in nineteenth-century Tanganyika sought to mobilize funds for their welfare work in ways immediately recognizable to modern-day NGO marketing strategies (including sponsorship, the use of stories of hope and despair, and campaign appeals).

Faith-based networks are able to foster links at the highly personal level, as well as the institutional. Thus we have the World Council of Churches, bringing together many Protestant churches (linking to national Christian Council organizations and to individual churches); the important role of the Vatican and pontifical councils in shaping policy, giving advice and channeling funds to Catholic groups and organizations; or the Islamic Gulen movement, which claims to have established over five hundred places of learning in ninety countries, and the more radical and controversial Muslim Brotherhood, whose organization and its affiliates play a large role in linking Muslims and Muslim NSPs throughout the world. At the level of the personal, the Parish Twinning Program of the Americas seeks to establish close partnerships between North American parishes and those especially in Haiti (Hefferan 2009, 69–82).[12] Individual preachers regularly visit developing country parishes for mass rallies, with audio- and videotapes and DVDs of sermons circulating globally (and, more recently, the vast number of Internet-related resources on websites such as YouTube).

The most obvious role of global faith networks is as a source of capital for NSP action in developing countries. Four large faith-based development agencies—CIDSE (Coopération Internationale pour le Développement et la Solidarité), APODEV (Association of Protestant Development), World Vision International, and Caritas International—had between them combined resources of around $2.5 billion in 1999–2000, or just over 60 percent of the budget for the U.K. Department for International Development for 2000–01 (Clarke 2006, 841). The Aga Khan Development Network, an Islamic charity had an income of $253 million in 2006, spending some $120.1 million on program grants and assistance (Aga Khan Foundation 2006, 49). In 2009 alone, World Vision International spent $2.6 billion (World Vision International

---

12. For more about the Parish Twinning Program of the Americas, see http://www.parish program.org/.

2009),[13] more than the aid budgets of Switzerland, Belgium, and just under that of Australia, for example.[14] On a smaller scale, the UK's Muslim Aid had an income of £15.6 million ($22.9m), and spent £14.6 million on charitable activity in 2007 (Muslim Aid 2007, 15). Even in smaller, more personal networks, significant sums can be transferred. The Parish Twinning Program of the Americas, for example, has established some 340 linkages and sent around $22 million to mostly Haitian parishes since its establishment in 1978.

These figures, illustrative of the importance of transnational faith networks as sources of development income, point to one of the key strengths of the faith sector: it is significantly less reliant on official donor funds than are many NGOs. As the income of many modern NGOs shifted in the 1980s to include a significantly larger proportion of funding from donors (signaling, for critics, the beginning of the contracting era), faith-based organizations also benefited from such funding streams. However, they also continued to have access to the huge resource flows within transnational faith networks, whether from large international FBOs or the smaller, but numerous, individual links between parishes, mosques, and so on. Arguably, this has served to maintain a strong faith identity among these types of organizations, and preserve a degree of independence from national governments and international donors, reinforced by the formal and informal authority often accorded to spiritual leaders by communities of faith and nonfaith alike. Access to such global funding sources thus allows FBOs to avoid reliance on (still unreliable and changeable) official funding sources, and enables them to potentially offer more sustainable solutions (see the chapter by Allard in this volume).

A second feature of the transnational nature of the FBO has been to give it a power that can serve to mobilize action at a global level. The apparent victory of the Christian Right in the United States in lobbying for a financial commitment to abstinence-only programs as part of the U.S. President's Emergency Plan for AIDS Relief (PEPFAR), and the alliance of Christian and Muslim groups in criticizing family planning policies that include abortion, demonstrate the power of faith leaders to affect international policy. Critics would rightly use such examples to highlight the negative aspects of faith engagement. However, there are more positive actions where faith-motivated social action has helped shape policy, such as the Jubilee 2000 campaign. Established in 1996 by church groups to campaign for debt relief for developing countries, it lobbied governments in Europe and North America, and had an organizational presence in over sixty countries. It was, moreover, successful in not just raising debt relief as a potent issue in public discourse but in mobilizing huge public support and social action. The launch of a $4 billion bond to finance global

13. World Vision International, *2009 Review* (World Vision International 2009), 5.

14. OECD-DAC, international development statistics online database, http://www.oecd.org/dac/stats/idsonline.htm.

immunization programs for the under-fives by British prime minister Gordon Brown in November 2006 was given moral and financial support by faith leaders: representatives of Pope Benedict XVI, the leader of the Anglican Church, (Archbishop Rowan Williams), the British chief rabbi, the Muslim Council of Britain, the Hindu Forum of Britain, and the Network of Sikh Organizations purchased the first six bonds.

Local-level leadership is critical for mobilizing action at the community level. But at the transnational level it gives faith organizations immense power to lobby governments and international organizations. Global faith networks also mobilize among rich country congregations, generating broader faith-based civil society action across a range of issues of importance in development.

Political Consequences of FBOs in Sub-Saharan Africa

The presence, dominance even, of FBOs as service providers in sub-Saharan Africa, has consequences for state capacity, for equity of access to social welfare, and also for experiences of citizenship, although the interplay between them is complex and not liable to lead to a single outcome (nor one that is fixed).

The presence of a large FBO sector in welfare provision certainly has implications for state capacity in service provision. The critique of NGOs in sub-Saharan Africa—that they have acted as the agent through which the privatization of welfare goods has been pushed, under the New Policy Agenda[15] (Hearn 2007)—might equally be applied to the FBO. That in accepting donor funding for, and channeling funds from alternative sources to, private (albeit nonprofit) schools, hospitals, food-for-work programs, and so forth, they have undermined the claims of the state to be the main provider of such goods. However, unlike NGOs who took advantage of shifts in donor funding policies in the 1980s to expand their role in this area, faith-based providers in much of Africa have historically dominated service provision: it is the state that is the latecomer, not the minaret or the steeple. In the former British and Belgian colonies especially[16] the history of service provision is one that began with, and was dominated by, faith providers. State-run services have formed a relatively small part of the narrative of the past one hundred years or so.

Thus while FBOs have certainly had an impact, and continue to do so, on issues around state capacity, it stems from their function as non-state actors, rather than as faith-based ones. The policy reforms from the 1980s—Washington Consensus–led structural reforms, the rise of the New Policy Agenda, and so on—shifted the balance between private and public service

---

15. The New Planning Agenda brought together neoliberal economics with a stronger focus than the Washington Consensus on institutions and the structures of governance.

16. French African colonial territories were characterized by greater state involvement. However, faith providers did nevertheless make a contribution to welfare.

provision. FBOs were not complicit as an individual sector in the attack on state capacity that this entailed, but they did so alongside NGOs and other nonprofit actors. Indeed, as actors embedded within the local community, forming part of local structures of governance, and potentially subject as a result to greater oversight of their actions than external actors, they arguably have had less of an impact on state capacity than NGOs.

However, the consequence of FBO-based provision of welfare goods is certainly more problematic in the areas of equity of access, and on the more nebulous area of ideas around citizenship and the relationship of society to the state. FBOs have been accused of fostering sectarian identities, creating possibilities for the fragmentation of welfare goods as a result of exclusive (or excluding) relationships within the communities in which they are based. Certainly, there are examples of FBOs that work solely within a particular faith community. However, the evidence does not point to this being a general consequence of increasing faith-based provision. First, following Gerard Clarke's distinction between "passive," "active," "persuasive," and "exclusive" FBO typologies, only the latter type engages solely with a single community (Clarke 2008, 34) There are some FBOs that do fall within the "exclusive" category (Hezbollah in Lebanon, for example), but many FBOs, whether they seek to proselytize alongside their welfare activity or not, explicitly reject a strategy of focusing only on their own faith communities. Second, official funding for welfare provision is generally made on the basis of nonsectarian, entirely open provision. Norwegian state funding for the Norwegian Missionary Society, for example, is predicated on a formal split between its development/welfare activity and its missionary work, with the former to be accessible by all (although, as Ingie Hovland reminds us, such distinctions between religious and development activity are harder to maintain in practice) (Hovland 2008). There is always a danger of any value-based organization seeking to exclude others based on those values (including faith), suggesting that caution needs to be applied to further engagement with FBOs in welfare provision.

The particular values of some faith- and religious-linked organizations could have implications in areas such as gender equity in the area of health. The lobbying of evangelical Christian organizations in the United States over both the President's Emergency Plan for AIDS Relief (PEPFAR) and the Mexico City Policy (which prohibited organizations in receipt of U.S. Agency for International Development funding from providing, promoting, or otherwise engaging with abortion services), and the significant increase in funding of FBOs that accompanied this, appears to have had an impact on sexual and reproductive health care provision in many parts of sub-Saharan Africa. Where a faith-based hospital, clinic, or other health facility serves as the sole (or main) provider in a particular area, the values of that organization in relation to questions of sex and family-planning services may affect the level and type of services, potentially undermining gender equity in health-care provision. Moreover, to return to Molyneux and Razavi (2006), paternalistic organizations may struggle to identify structural barriers to women accessing particular types of health care.

The consequences of faith-based provision of welfare goods on questions of national citizenship and loyalty to the state are harder to understand or predict. As others in this volume have suggested, the privatization of service provision has implications for the relationship of citizens to the state, potentially drawing allegiance away from that state to the non-state provider. Such arguments are based on a rather restrictive understanding of identity and citizenship (seeing a zero-sum game in the quest for loyalties). But are there particular issues at play with religious organizations, above and beyond their role as non-state actors? Until the end of the 1980s, relationships between FBOs, religious leaders more widely, and the state were largely cordial, with faith-based non-state actors allying themselves to the objectives and strategies of state-led development. As FBOs (and the non-state sector more widely) changed to become perceived as a civil society actor, rather than a contracted service provider, the relationship with the state (and from that questions about citizenship) became more complex. FBOs, as civil society actors, were now part of the broad alliance designed to challenge and critique the state, to mobilize among its faith community on issues that might conflict with state priorities and policies. One question that emerges, one faced centuries earlier by post-Reformation leaders of Protestant countries in Europe in relation to their Catholic population, is to whom do people owe their first loyalty: to their government (as citizens), or to their God (and the religious representative of spiritual power)? And what happens when there is a conflict between the demands of the two?

This links into a growing debate in sub-Saharan Africa over the position of traditional elites and their role in governance. Are they a potentially divisive force, undermining the strength of the elected government to impose its authority and lay claim to the loyalty of its citizens, or is African governance more complex, nuanced, and multifaceted than normative models allow for? As with chiefs and other traditional leaders, religious leaders have both spiritual and temporal power. The latter has often been situated within official structures, or increasingly within a civil society space. But spiritual power carries real weight, and must not be ignored. The experience of Somalia demonstrates the potential for spiritual leadership to hold on to loyalties more than a secular (albeit new) state. But that of Rwanda, where some religious leaders have been implicated in perpetuating hate and violent rhetoric that supported the genocidal campaign in 1994, shows most potently the murderous consequences of combining spiritual and temporal authority in support of a regime determined to do anything to retain power.

Conclusion

For donors in particular, faith-based NSPs remain problematic. They have been linked to sectarianism, to values that oppose, or at least create problems for, wider developmental objectives and values such as gender equity, family planning, sexual rights, recognition of certain minority groups, freedom of speech, and so forth. Some donors have also seen in the resurgence of religion the dangers of violence and extremism, with the impact of Somalia's political vacuum and radical religious groups being felt across East Africa. Secular-minded development thinkers and writers, too, have sought to present the dangerous face of religion in the twenty-first century, demonstrating the incompatibility of faith and religion with the secular development project.

And yet, as I have argued in this chapter, religion and FBOs are not inimical to development, welfare, and service provision. How could they be, given their role in establishing and shaping the non-state provider sector that has contributed so much to this? FBOs, initially in the shape of Christian missions before being joined by a myriad of faith and faith-organizational types, dominated welfare and service provision in Tanzania and East Africa throughout the twentieth century, and continue to do so today. Their importance in this region rests not only on the scale of their current role but also on the historical trajectory of faith-action over more than century. For it was from faith-based action that the NSP sector emerged in Tanzania and in much of Africa, and it was these organizations that created the space that the modern NSP sector occupies. The types of relationship they established with governments, and the fluctuations and shifts in that relationship, affected the NGO sector when it first emerged in sub-Saharan Africa. Their experience of service provision and social development intervention left its imprint on non-state action, influencing the types of organizations that emerged and where they saw themselves fitting in.

FBOs are, as their critics assert, problematic. Their engagement carries potential risks of undermining basic rights, and the position and opportunities open to women. Their faith values can even dangerously undermine key health messages, placing people at risk, rather than offering protection. The power held by faith leaders, unelected and often unaccountable, creates dilemmas not just for the impact they may have in their communities or influence within government but over questions related to national sovereignty, loyalty to and the continued legitimacy of the state (although, it is not only faith leaders who have been subject to concerns in this regard).

But FBOs remain a core, dominant even, component of non-state action in Tanzania and across much of sub-Saharan Africa. To ignore this sector and exclude it from the analytical gaze of those working on the NSP sector would be to thoroughly distort the presentation of how that sector is formed, how it works, and how it relates to other state and non-state actors. In considering how the contracting era has reshaped the public–private balance in Tanzania and sub-Saharan Africa, in trying to understand the implications of the strength of international NGOs over both local organizations and even within government circles, and in seeking to examine both what the NSP is in an African context and in what ways it might evolve in the future, an awareness of the history of this sector is critical. And it is a history dominated by faith-based social action.

7

Sectarian Politics and Social Welfare

Non-state Provision in Lebanon

Melani Cammett

> When the war ended in 1992, the state said, "You can't come into the
> southern suburbs." Our response was: "We would be glad to step aside
> and we would welcome the government with roses if it would provide."
> Until the government provides, Hezbollah needs to be there providing.
> —Hajj Hussein Shami, director, Al-Qard Al-Hassan, Hezbollah

In an interview on the social programs of Hezbollah, Hajj Hussein Shami,
the head of the organization's credit association and the former director of its
Islamic Health Unit, told me that his organization would gladly scale back
its welfare operations if it were replaced by public programs in the areas it
serves.[1] Whether Hezbollah would actually retrench its programs in the face of
expanded public welfare functions is a matter of speculation, but his remarks
point to the fact that the Lebanese state plays a minimal direct role in the provision of social services. The relative absence of a public social safety net and the
(not coincidental) prevalence of non-state providers are defining features of the
Lebanese system. In particular, various local political and religious organizations, some of which are labeled "sectarian,"[2] are integral to social provision,

---

1. Author interview: Hajj Hussein Shami, director, Al-Qard Al-Hassan (Hezbollah credit association), Bir al-Abd, Lebanon, June 19, 2004.

2. Although based on "descent-based" attributes (Chandra 2006), sectarian identity and,
hence, sectarian organizations are flexible categories that manifest themselves and operate differently in distinct political moments and in the presence of varied audiences. In this analysis,
I distinguish between religious and sectarian organizations. Although expressions of religiosity can
be profoundly political (Mahmood 2005), in my usage sectarian organizations engage directly in
contests over state power whereas religious organizations may not aim to control state institutions
directly.

particularly for lower-income families. What role do sectarian organizations play in the Lebanese welfare regime and how have their activities evolved over time? What are the implications of the provision of social welfare by these organizations for citizen access to basic services, accountability to beneficiaries, and broader processes of state-building? Focusing on the health sector, the main contention of this chapter is that sectarian organizations provide crucial and otherwise unavailable services but, at the same time, may perpetuate inefficiencies and inequalities by limiting the construction of a more coherent system of social protection and by allocating social assistance on a discretionary basis.

In this chapter I focus on the major sectarian organizations in Lebanon, including the predominantly Sunni Future Movement, the Shia Hezbollah, and Amal Movement, and the three main Christian parties—the Free Patriotic Movement, the Kataeb, and the Lebanese Forces. Each of these organizations runs some forms of social programs and all receive funding from public social welfare entitlements. The three Muslim organizations administer their own health programs and schools as well as smaller social assistance programs while the Christian parties generally do not operate their own facilities but rather broker access to services offered by third-party providers.[3] The research for this chapter draws on in-depth interviews with representatives of these parties and other elites in the public and private sectors (n = 175) and with "ordinary" citizens from the main sectarian communities (n = 135). The interview data are supplemented by archival materials and secondary source literature.[4]

The next section presents a historical overview of the construction and evolution of the welfare regime in Lebanon to trace the origins of sectarian providers in the system. Focusing on the respective roles of state and non-state providers in the health sector, the analysis is structured around three historical moments in the construction of the Lebanese welfare system—the immediate postindependence period from the creation of the independent state in 1943 to the mid-1970s, the civil war period from 1975 to 1990, and the post–civil war period from the early 1990s to the present. The third section describes the dynamics of social provision in Lebanon, and the fourth section points to the implications of the Lebanese welfare regime for social protection. The analysis

---

3. The Christian Kataeb Party, however, runs eight clinics either solely or in conjunction with various state agencies.

4. This research is derived from a book manuscript that relies on multiple quantitative and qualitative forms of data analysis (Cammett 2014). The fieldwork, which I conducted between 2006 and 2009, involved the compilation of an original data set of the spatial locations of welfare agencies coded by affiliation and population characteristics in corresponding geographic units; the execution of an original national household survey on access to welfare and political behavior; interviews with elites from diverse types of welfare institutions, political parties, and state agencies; interviews with Lebanese citizens from diverse sects, socioeconomic backgrounds, and regions; and archival data.

focuses most heavily on two types of consequences—the overall operation and efficiency of the public health system and the potential effects on citizen access to health care. The concluding section suggests areas for future research.

Social Welfare in Postindependence Lebanon

Since independence, the Lebanese political economy, including the welfare regime, has entailed minimal if any state intervention and a dominant role for private, non-state actors (Gates 1998). The historically limited state role in social provision in part derives from an entrenched historical experience of community organization along sectarian lines (Makdisi 2000; Meo 1965), but the effects of civil war from 1975 to 1990 consolidated the provision of welfare along sectarian lines and undercut efforts at state-building. This section traces the history of state efforts—and non-state efforts—to institutionalize health policies and the concomitant construction of parallel health networks by sectarian organizations from independence through the postwar period.

Social Welfare from Independence to the Civil War (1943–1975)

Lebanon has a long historical tradition of religious philanthropic organizations dating back to at least the Ottoman period (Fawaz 1994; Hanssen 2005, 116; Abouchedid and Nasser 2000; Makdisi 2000; Sbaiti 2008). Although the French and British authorities attempted to establish a rudimentary public health system in order to create a more secure environment for foreign investors, public welfare functions were minimally developed on the eve of independence in 1943 (Hanssen 2005, 117, 122, 127–128). Under the first two postindependence administrations of Bishara el-Khoury (1943–52) and Camille Chamoun (1952–58), the government did not prioritize socioeconomic development, despite some efforts to develop basic infrastructure and to expand and standardize public schooling (Bashshour 1988, 48; Salibi 1966, 212–13). State penetration of areas outside of Beirut was limited, particularly in South Lebanon, the Bekaa in the east, and Akkar in the north, reinforcing the control of the *zu'ama*, or traditional leaders, over rural areas (Attié 2004, 53; El Khazen 2000, 57).

State development efforts accelerated markedly during the presidency of Fu'ad Shihab (1958–64), who launched an ambitious state-building effort and tried to undercut the authority of traditional local and communal leaders (Hudson 1968, 297; Traboulsi 2007, 139). For Shihab, social policy was a key tool for national integration. After the civil war of 1958, which some attributed to regional inequalities, the Shihab administration extended government schools and roads as well as the delivery of basic public goods throughout the country. Shihab also established community-based dispensaries and rural hospitals across Lebanon, although a dearth of trained medical professionals hampered the effectiveness of these institutions (Dagher 1995, 61–64; Hudson 1968, 311, 321; Salibi 1976, 18–19).

Among Shihab's enduring legacies was the establishment of the National Social Security Fund (NSSF), a national social insurance program initiated in 1965 (El Khazen 2000; Traboulsi 2007, 141).The fund was designed to provide medical, maternity, and disability insurance as well as family allowances, end-of-service indemnities, and pension benefits to employees of formal sector firms.[5] As I discuss below, the NSSF, which grew over time to incorporate more segments of the workforce and to provide an expanded array of benefits, became an important source of health care financing in Lebanon.

Under subsequent administrations, social development did not advance significantly and public spending slowed, in part due to opposition from within the government and by powerful social groups. As a result, the Lebanese public health infrastructure did not develop extensively after independence, despite sporadic efforts to improve the system and to expand health care facilities in rural areas.

Civil War, Militias, and the Consolidation of Non-state Provision (1975–1990)

The civil war brought about the partial and, for some programs, total breakdown of public social welfare institutions established in the 1960s, weakening the already feeble state administrative capacity and enhancing the importance of non-state social provision. In part as a response to state failure, which was deliberately precipitated by some of the warring militias, confessional groups in all of Lebanon's religious communities initiated or further developed their own social welfare programs while NGOs, both domestic and international, proliferated in the domain of social provision (Hanf 1993, 352–55, 359).

The civil war took a heavy toll on the public health infrastructure, in part due to the physical destruction, looting, and desertion of government-run facilities. Protracted conflict also undercut the nascent primary health care system and permitted the unrestricted growth of private health services. Basic components of the system, such as health workers, databases, and broader planning efforts, were deficient and the role of the public sector in direct provision was diminished. Public hospitals were important sites for treating injured civilians and fighters during the civil war, but the conflict contributed to the decline of the public hospital sector (Kasparian and Ammar 2001, 20). Thus, between 1975 and 1991 the share of public hospital beds dropped from 26 percent to 10 percent of the total (Mehio-Sibai and Sen 2006, 848). In the same period,

---

5. Modeled after the French system, the NSSF contributed 25 percent of the financing, while the remainder was supplied by contributions from employers and employees (Hudson 1968, 324; Traboulsi 2007, 141). Informal sector employees and agricultural workers, however, were not included in the scheme (International Labor Organization 2004).

more than 50 percent of private hospital bed capacity was established and was concentrated in high-cost curative care.

By the end of the war, government provision was concentrated in secondary and tertiary care and targeted only the most disadvantaged as well as government employees covered by specific insurance schemes. Because most public hospitals had been destroyed or were shut down, the state was compelled to purchase services from private, for-profit institutions, while NGOs became important providers of primary health services, particularly for those who could not afford the fees of private physicians.

The territorial division of the country into about a dozen cantons controlled by wartime militias posed direct challenges to the coherence and sovereignty of the national state. Militias took over basic state functions by levying taxes and collecting customs duties in the territories they controlled, depriving the state of badly needed revenue and boosting the national debt (Beyoghlou 1989, 34–36; Corm 1991, 13–15; Snider 1984, 22–23; Traboulsi 2007, 232–233). Some militias established welfare programs to serve militia fighters and residents in their spheres of influence (Corm 1991, 17; Hanf 1993, 359). During the war, four organizations—the Christian Lebanese Forces, Druze Popular Socialist Party, and Shia Amal Movement and Hezbollah—were the main militias engaged in social welfare provision (Harik 1994, 8).

The variable development of militia social welfare programs created and exacerbated regional disparities in access to public goods and services in war-torn parts of the country. In general, the Lebanese Forces and the Popular Socialist Party had more developed programs, largely because they had longer historical roots in Lebanon and initially commanded the most resources. Beginning in the early 1980s, however, Amal and Hezbollah progressively developed social welfare networks in areas with heavy concentrations of Shia residents. While Christian, Druze, Shia, and other militias divided up the country, Rafiq al-Hariri, a Lebanese Sunni from Sidon who made a fortune in Saudi Arabia during the 1960s, gradually came to dominate politics in the Sunni community, in part by co-opting or marginalizing established Sunni religious institutions.[6] Although he started his charitable initiatives in the predominantly Sunni city of Sidon, Hariri later funneled aid to NGOs throughout Lebanon and distributed scholarships to Lebanese of all sectarian backgrounds.[7] The wartime surge in

---

6. The Future Movement, the political organization associated with the Hariri family, was not formally established until 2007, but Hariri established his political machine in the 1990s, if not earlier. Author interviews: professor, Department of Political Science, American University of Beirut, Beirut, June 23, 2004; development consultant, Beirut, July 7, 2006; official, Makhzoumeh Foundation, Beirut, November 2, 2007; executive director, Lebanese Association for Democratic Elections (LADE), Beirut, December 10, 2007; president, Islamic Charitable Projects, Beirut, January 23, 2008. See also Johnson (1977).

7. Author interview: former official, Hariri Foundation, Beirut, November 9, 2007. The charitable wing of the Future Movement, the Hariri Foundation was first established in Sidon in 1979 as the Islamic Institute for Culture and Higher Education. The foundation adopted its current name in 1984, when it moved its headquarters to Beirut.

non-state provision of public services had important legacies for the postwar welfare regime by fostering and consolidating parallel social welfare networks along sectarian lines.

Sectarian Organizations in the Postwar Welfare Regime (1990–Present)

After the Ta'if Accords formally ended the Lebanese civil war in 1989, some social welfare programs initiated by militias evolved into institutionalized welfare agencies with branch offices and networks of social centers. Organizations linked to sectarian political organizations that either did not have militia wings during the war or did not emerge until the postwar period also launched their own welfare programs.

The experiences of Muslim and Christian political groups and parties-cum-militias diverged in the postwar period. The Christian Lebanese Forces and Kataeb did not immediately transform wartime social institutions into postwar party institutions and welfare agencies largely due to repression by Syria, which retained forces in Lebanon until 2005.[8] At the same time, most Muslim political organizations initiated or expanded their welfare networks. The Hariri Foundation originally focused exclusively on education but in the late 1990s it rapidly expanded its health-related activities, a trend that continues today. The expansion of the Hariri Foundation's social, health, and educational programs coincided with Hariri's increasing turn toward participation in national politics. After running in the first postwar elections held in 1992, Hariri was appointed prime minister, a post reserved for a Sunni in Lebanon's power-sharing system.

The two major Shia political groups, Hezbollah and Amal, transformed themselves into political parties while expanding their social programs in the postwar period. The social welfare institutions of Hezbollah developed far more extensively, in part thanks to generous funding from Iran. The organization initiated or expanded a variety of formal institutions with diverse mandates, including social programs targeted at militia fighters and their families, construction and agricultural development agencies, loans for income-generation projects, health centers, hospitals, schools, and social assistance programs for the poor. The Amal Movement, which has a smaller resource base and relies more on state patronage for its social initiatives, has less developed welfare programs than Hezbollah, although it too developed and expanded its networks of schools, medical institutions, and social assistance programs in the post–civil war period.[9]

---

8. The Free Patriotic Movement did not emerge formally until decades after the two other main Christian organizations. Established in 2005 by General Michel Aoun, the Free Patriotic Movement has launched some social programs and received some support for these efforts from Hezbollah following the establishment of an official alliance between the two parties in 2006.

9. The next section provides more information on the contemporary health and welfare institutions of these organizations.

The number of NGO-run health clinics and dispensaries, or small health centers that distribute pharmaceuticals, also expanded rapidly during the civil war and postwar periods, with NSPs accounting for 80 percent of these facilities across the country by the late 1990s (Ammar 2003, 21). By 2006, NGOs, sectarian parties, religious charities, community groups, and family-based institutions operated roughly eight hundred health clinics, of which about 450 were fully functional while the remainder operated more sporadically and lacked trained medical personnel or adequate facilities.[10] Non-state providers account for about 90 percent of the delivery of services and about 60 percent of health spending. The next section describes the dynamics of the contemporary Lebanese welfare regime in more detail with a particular focus on the role of sectarian organizations in the system.

The Dynamics of Health Care Provision in Lebanon

Historical legacies of non-state provision have produced a complicated mix of public and private involvement in the Lebanese welfare regime, as exemplified by the health sector. As this section describes, the public sector has played a minimal role in the actual delivery of health services but has provided extensive financing for the system. A combination of weak state capacity and resistance to reform by multiple stakeholders, including sectarian organizations, which hold great sway in public institutions, has curtailed efforts to build effective public regulation of the health sector. As a result, state agencies and social programs have evolved into lucrative sources of patronage for non-state providers, creating entrenched interests in the status quo. The relationship between the state and sectarian organizations in the health sector is almost parasitic. This state of affairs results from the power balance between the state and non-state actors, in which sectarian organizations, local feudal leaders, and religious charities with independent social bases face minimal restrictions on their activities and penetrate state institutions at all levels. With underdeveloped regulatory capacity, the state faces major challenges in coordinating the fragmented field of providers in the health sector.

Non-state organizations of various types are integral to health care provision in Lebanon. Figure 7.1 depicts the distribution of health clinics and dispensaries by affiliation, classified according to partisan, religious, and other types of affiliations in the mid-2000s.

The figure shows the numerical importance of sectarian parties and religious charities—especially, Christian charities—in the provision of primary care. Although Christian political parties run relatively few institutions of their

---

10. Author interviews: chief executive officer, YMCA Lebanon, Sin El-Fil, April 13, 2006; official, Ministry of Public Health, Beirut, June 13, 2006.

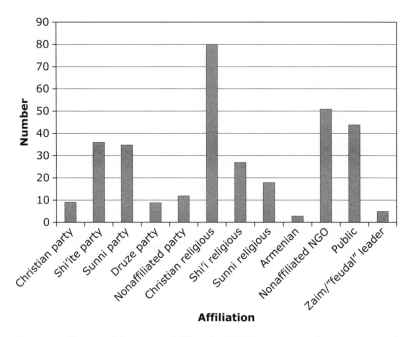

Figure 7.1. Clinics and dispensaries affiliated with different state and non-state providers (2008 estimates). *Sources:* Ministry of Health 2006, YMCA 2006, author interviews.

own, they compensate by facilitating access to services in clinics run by coreligionist charities, which operated about eighty clinics and dispensaries, as well as from private medical practices headed by sympathetic doctors. Shia and Sunni parties directly administer about thirty-six and thirty-five clinics, respectively, while coreligionist charities also run many clinics and dispensaries. Although it is impossible to code which religious charities are linked to coreligionist parties, it is well known that organizations such as the Future Movement and Hezbollah either directly control or strongly influence charitable institutions in their corresponding sects. Given that Lebanon has had at most about 450 operational clinics, sectarian parties collectively operate or control important shares of the primary care infrastructure in Lebanon. Sectarian parties and religious charities also play an important, albeit even more indirect, role in secondary care. All sectarian organizations obtain preferential treatment for supporters in facilities run by coreligionist charities and public institutions. Thus, as is the case for primary care, the scope for their influence in hospitalization extends beyond consultations and treatment supplied in their own institutions and the number of dispensaries, clinics, and hospitals in their official networks.

According to the National Health Accounts Survey conducted in 1998 by the Ministry of Public Health in conjunction with the World Health

Organization and World Bank, facilities run by sectarian parties and religious charities constituted a relatively small percentage of total medical visits—about 12 percent—and an even smaller percentage of total health expenditures— about 2 percent, which reflects the low cost of the services they provide. But these organizations play a crucial role in primary health care. The study found that NSP-run centers accommodate up to 20 percent of total primary care visits (Ammar et al. 2000). The figure has undoubtedly increased as the number of centers has grown, political organizations have expanded and upgraded their health services, and economic decline has compelled a broader share of the population to seek lower cost medical care at NSP facilities.[11] In 2009, the cost of a routine visit to a private physician cost between 30,000 Lebanese livre (LL) and 50,000LL, or about US$20 to US$33, but a consultation at a clinic run by an NSP cost about 5,000LL, or about US$3.35. Furthermore, as noted above, the weight of political parties in primary care exceeds services provided in their own clinics. Because political parties use their connections to obtain subsidized care for supporters in private and nongovernmental institutions run by coreligionist charities or in private practices run by sympathetic physicians, their influence is broader than the number of health facilities that they administer directly.[12]

Although non-state organizations predominate in the *provision* of health care, the public sector is the major source of *financing* for the health system. In 2006, the state accounted for almost 47 percent of total health expenditures while out-of-pocket expenditures amounted to about 39 percent of health spending. Employers and donors supplied about 10 percent and 2 percent, respectively, of spending on health. Public spending on health care has risen steadily since the civil war. A decade earlier, in 1996, government spending was only about 28 percent of total health spending while out-of-spending accounted for about 55 percent of total health expenditures (Ammar 2003, 9, 46; Mehio-Sibai and Sen 2006; World Health Organization-Statistical Information System 2012). Thus, the share of the public sector in total health expenditures rose substantially between the mid-1990s and mid-2000s, in part because the state foots the bill for some services provided by NSPs.[13]

The vast majority of government spending on health is devoted to the public hospitalization program, which is administered by the Ministry of Public Health. Established in 1961, the program covers 85 percent of hospitalization

---

11. A document provided by a Hariri Foundation official indicated that between 2000 and 2006 the organization's Directorate of Health and Social Services had received a total of 238,616 patients, which constitutes an important percentage of Lebanon's total resident population of approximately four million. However, it was impossible to independently verify this figure.

12. Author interviews: chief executive officer, YMCA Lebanon, Sin El-Fil, April 13, 2006; official, Ministry of Public Health, Beirut, June 13, 2006. See also Tabbarah (2000, 11–12).

13. Out-of-pocket expenditures on health have declined in the past five years (personal communication with Dr. Walid Ammar, director general, Ministry of Public Health, Beirut, April 25, 2013).

fees[14] as well as 60 percent of high-tech ambulatory services such as MRIs and CT scanners and 100 percent of cancer drugs. Additional drugs are covered on a discretionary basis. In 1992, the Ministry of Public Health extended its program to cover all expenses for cancer treatment, renal dialysis, open-heart surgery, and organ transplantation (Kronfol 2004, 174, 178).The public hospitalization program was largely responsible for the exponential growth of public health spending (Ammar 2003, 4; Tabbarah 2000, 8–9; Ammar et al. 2000, 9).

Hospital administrators emphasize that state coverage is an important source of income, even if reimbursements are increasingly delayed; however, the degree of dependence on state funding varies across institutions. For example, the Imam Musa Foundation, a Shia religious charity based on the southern city of Tyre, receives only about 10 percent of its annual funding from government sources, while the Druze Ein Wazein Hospital in the Chouf receives about 97 percent of its revenues from the government. For other hospitals, such as the American University Hospital, the Greek Orthodox St. George Hospital, and the Catholic Hotel Dieu Hospital, revenue bases are more diverse, including a mix of insurance and private sector funds. Additionally, some parties run clinics that have contracts with either the Ministry of Public Health or the Ministry of Social Affairs. Under the terms of such contracts, the center receives a budget from the ministry as well as access to subsidized medications. But government capacity to cover hospitalization costs has declined and, because of outstanding debt, some private hospitals routinely refuse to treat patients who do not have sufficient personal funds or private insurance to cover hospitalization costs (Balaa 2005; Chatilla 2007).

The NSSF has become a major source of health care financing and the most important public insurer in Lebanon. Over time, the program expanded its coverage to contracted staff in the public sector and members of a wide range of occupational categories, some of whom are not obliged to pay co-payments.[15] Official estimates from the NSSF hold that 26.1 percent of the population benefits from the Fund's health coverage, although the 1998 National Health Accounts Survey indicated a lower coverage rate of 17.8 percent (Kasparian and Ammar 2001, 22; Tabbarah 2000, 10). In practice, a far smaller percentage of the population likely benefits from the Fund's health coverage because the agency is almost bankrupt and providers increasingly refuse to accept patients insured by the NSSF (Chatilla 2007). Other government agencies, including the Cooperative of Employees, the Security Services, and the Ministry of Social Affairs are also important in financing the health care

---

14. Until 1992, the Ministry of Public Health covered 100 percent of hospitalization fees (Ammar 2003).

15. Beneficiaries include the individual as well as his or her spouse and children up to the age of twenty-five or permanently for disabled dependent children.

system (Ammar et al. 2000, 3). These funds are more generous than the NSSF, as they do not require contributions from employees and cover all ambulatory and hospital services.[16]

Data on health insurance coverage of the population are contested but all estimates indicate that more than 50 percent of the population is uninsured (Ammar 2003, 23–24, 43) and cost burdens, as measured by out-of-pocket payments, are not equitable (Kasparian and Ammar 2001, 9, 54; Salti, Chaaban, and Raad 2010). Nonetheless, through a patchwork of different funds, providers, and social support systems, the bulk of the population has access to basic health services, albeit with wide variation in the extent and quality of services. Non-state providers are the main reason for this broad access to medical care, especially for primary health services. Sectarian organizations, religious charities, NGOs, and for-profit institutions account for about 90 percent of the delivery of services and about 60 percent of health spending.

Some sectarian organizations have become important players in the health sector through their own welfare networks. In the current period, the most developed programs linked to sectarian organizations are run by Hezbollah and the Future Movement, although recent financial and political problems have allegedly contributed to the decline of the latter's welfare network. Other organizations, such as the Christian Kataeb Party and the Shia Amal Movement also run their own health and social programs. The Future Movement, initially led by Prime Minister Rafiq al-Hariri, who was assassinated in 2005, and now headed by his son, Saad al-Hariri, is the dominant political representative of the Sunni community in Lebanon and effectively controls many Sunni charitable institutions.[17] At various times, the Hariri Foundation, the social wing of the Future Movement, effectively controlled the public Rafiq al-Hariri Hospital in Beirut. In 1999, the Hariri Foundation established the Health Directory, which established over forty clinics and had ambitious plans to expand its network in the 2000s.[18]

Although Hezbollah established some social centers and medical facilities during the civil war, the bulk of its institutions were established after the war ended. By 2008, the organization directly operated twenty-four clinics through its Islamic Health Unit, four hospitals, a social service agency targeting extremely poor families (al-Emdad al-Islamiyya), and many other social organizations and programs.

---

16. Author interview: official, Ministry of Social Affairs, Beirut, June 9, 2004; official, Ministry of Public Health, Beirut, June 13, 2006; see also Tabbarah (2000, 13).

17. Author interviews: professor, Department of Political Science, American University of Beirut, Beirut, June 23, 2004; development consultant, July 7, 2006; official, Makhzoumeh Foundation, Beirut, November 2, 2007; executive director, LADE, Beirut, December 10, 2007; president, Islamic Charitable Projects, Beirut, January 23, 2008.

18. Author interviews: representatives, Directorate of Health and Social Services, Hariri Foundation, Beirut, June 15, 2007, and January 9, 2007.

Like the Future Movement and Hezbollah, the Shia Amal Movement has also established its own health centers and schools, but on a much smaller scale. In 2009, the Amal Movement health program operated thirteen health clinics, at least two of which were run in cooperation with the Ministry of Public Health and Ministry of Social Affairs. The Nabatiyyeh and Marjayoun hospitals, officially public institutions, are allegedly controlled by the Amal Movement, a perception consistent with the claim that the party derives much of its resources for patronage from state agencies.

The Christian Kataeb Party developed a much smaller network of social institutions than the Future Movement, Hezbollah, and the Amal Movement. As of 2009 the Pierre Gemayyel Social Foundation, the party's social wing (named after the assassinated son of the party's leader), ran eight health clinics, at least one of which was operated in cooperation with the Ministry of Social Affairs. The other major Christian parties did not operate their own health institutions.

As emphasized above, the number of health care facilities operated directly by sectarian organizations vastly understates their role in health care provision. Representatives of these organizations hold high-level positions in government agencies and are prominent members of their communities. Their social and political connections enable them to arrange subsidized or even free health care for supporters in both public and private hospitals, clinics, and medical practices. Although some health benefits, such as the coverage of hospitalization costs, are citizen entitlements, access to these services requires official authorization, providing opportunities for sectarian organizations to obtain favors for supporters while claiming full credit for public benefits.[19] The next section explores the consequences of Lebanon's fragmented social welfare regime for the efficiency of the health system and for citizen access to health care.

Social and Political Consequences

Given the realities of Lebanese politics, sectarian organizations and other brokers may be somewhat justified in claiming credit for health benefits because access to health care, particularly for low-income families, is subject to clientelist intermediation, particularly for needy citizens. At the same time, it is

---

19. Claiming credit for state-sponsored benefits can take multiple forms. For secondary care, sectarian organizations and other political patrons may secure hospital beds for their clients and pay only the remaining 15 percent of hospitalization costs not covered by the public program. After negotiating these arrangements, representatives of sectarian organizations may convey the impression to beneficiaries that they were indispensable for securing hospital stays and had covered the *total* cost of medical treatment rather than the outstanding 15% of charges (author interviews: director, official, Ministry of Public Health, Beirut, June 13, 2006; AinWazein Hospital, Chouf, July 10, 2006; journalist, international news agency, Beirut, November 9, 2007; board member, Al-Nejdeh Al-Shaabiyyeh, Beirut, December 12, 2007; official, Amal Movement, Ghobeiry, January 17, 2008).

these very actors that help to perpetuate the system and may even block reform efforts. At the macro-level, their diverse programs and health care institutions exacerbate existing inefficiencies in the system. On the micro-level, their actions create and maintain discretionary access to medical services and financial support for health care, contributing to societal health inequalities.

Inefficiencies in the Health System

Sectarian organizations and other vested interests sustain an important and largely unregulated role for private providers in the Lebanese health care regime. The combination of extensive private provision with minimal public oversight and generous state financing has produced inefficiencies in the health system and disparities in access to health care. As a result, international organizations cite Lebanon's highly inefficient, hyperprivatized system as a *negative* example for other developing countries (Oxfam 2009; World Bank 2004b).

Macroeconomic data suggest that Lebanon has underperformed with respect to basic health indicators, at least until recently. In 2006, Lebanon spent about 9 percent of its GDP on health, a level equivalent to total health care spending in the Scandinavian countries but with far inferior health outcomes. With a per capita health expenditure of $608 in 2006, life expectancy in Lebanon was seventy years and under-five mortality was thirty-one per thousand live births. In comparison, Costa Rica, with a similar level of economic development, spent 7 percent of its GDP on health in 2006 and achieved a life expectancy of seventy-eight years and under-five mortality of twelve per thousand live births (World Health Organization Statistical Information System 2012). Even when benchmarked against other countries in the Middle East with comparable or lower GDP per capita levels, Lebanon has lagged. For example, in 1990, Lebanon, Syria, and Jordan had similar life expectancy and child mortality rates; a decade later, however, Syria and Jordan exhibited superior health outcomes while Lebanon's rate of improvement stagnated, particularly for child mortality. Overall, the World Health Organization (2000) ranked health expenditure per capita in Lebanon forty-sixth but the prospects of child survival eighty-eighth and the performance of the health system ninety-first out of its 191 member countries.

The structure of health financing has created perverse incentives for the overall development of the Lebanese health care system. First, access to public coverage of hospitalization fees promoted an oversupply of hospitals, and particularly of small facilities that could not capitalize on economies of scale or provide adequate care. As a result, Lebanon has a comparatively high ratio of beds to population.[20] In 2009, Lebanon had four beds per 1,000 people,

---

20. Within Lebanon, there is wide regional variation in the ratio of beds to population, ranging from .86 in Nabatiyeh to 6.55 in Mount Lebanon (Ammar 2003, 37).

which is twice the regional average (two beds per 1,000) and almost as high as the average for OECD countries (five beds per 1,000) (World Development Indicators 2010).[21]

Second, with the dominance of private, for-profit providers, supplier-induced demand for high-tech, expensive equipment and diagnostic techniques has burgeoned, resulting in an imbalanced health system that does not cater to the needs of the bulk of the population.[22] Private insurers shift costs to the public sector wherever possible, while private providers invest disproportionately in high-tech services to the neglect of basic health needs. Because the Ministry of Public Health has effectively become the "insurer of last resort," some insurers dropped coverage for hospitalization and some high-tech services and providers had an incentive to submit inflated or fictitious bills (Ammar 2003, 6, 40; Tabbarah 2000, 18–21).

Third, the system neglects preventative medicine in favor of specialized and curative care, while primary care clinics run by sectarian organizations, religious charities, and NGOs, some of which have contracts with the Ministry of Public Health or Ministry of Social Affairs, do not coordinate their efforts effectively. The nature of health personnel reflects this imbalance: almost 75 percent of doctors are specialists rather than generalists. In addition, Lebanon has one of the highest concentrations of physicians in the world but a chronic undersupply of nurses, with 2.4 doctors per 1,000 residents but only 1.3 nurses per 1,000 residents (Tabbarah 2000, 16–32; World Health Organization Statistical Information System 2012). The relative neglect of primary health care as well as the absence of insurance schemes to cover the costs of basic pharmaceuticals have created a niche for non-state providers, including sectarian organizations, which use the situation to their advantage.

Sectarian organizations as well as private for-profit institutions, nonprofit organizations, and medical professional associations have developed vested interests in the system, blocking attempts at reform initiated by government officials and supported by international agencies (Ammar 2001, 5; World Bank 2000, 15). Since the end of the civil war, the Ministry of Public Health has launched multiple health system restructuring efforts, often in cooperation with international donors. Many of the goals of these reforms remain unfulfilled to this day. In 1993, the government launched a health sector rehabilitation and reconstruction program aimed at strengthening the institutional capacity of the Ministry of Public Health, improving primary health care by building a national system of public health centers, bolstering hospital management, and restructuring the health financing system. The World Bank granted $37 million to support

---

21. Data for the Middle East and North Africa and the OECD countries are from 2007 and 2008, respectively.

22. For example, in 2002 the number of facilities offering cardiac catheterization, a procedure to check blood flow to the coronary arteries and heart chambers, was the second highest in the world (Mehio-Sibai and Sen 2006).

the reform program, but by the end of the decade the primary goals of the plan were not met (World Bank 2004b). Since then, the Ministry of Public Health has launched additional reform programs, including an initiative to regulate and streamline the primary health care system. Under the terms of the program, clinics and dispensaries must register with the Ministry of Public Health and meet minimum standards to receive accreditation, which brings official budgetary support and access to free or subsidized medications.[23]

Patterns of social welfare provision and financing that developed both before and after independence have resulted in an inefficient and underperforming health care regime in Lebanon. A combination of weak government administrative capacity and opposition by both formal and informal societal groups, including sectarian organizations, has hindered reform of the system. Interestingly, high levels of state spending in the health sector defy social science expectations that more fractionalized societies exhibit lower social spending (Alesina, Baqir, and Easterly 1999; Easterly and Levine 1997; Habyarimana et al. 2007); however, the fact that the leaders of sectarian parties with affiliated non-state welfare networks are simultaneously high-level government officials helps to explain this apparent paradox. Because they have effectively carved up the state in a postwar compromise, they share an incentive to "cannibalize" the state, feeding off state patronage for political purposes and thereby pushing up state spending.[24] Deficit spending, substantial amounts of regional foreign aid, and some general tax revenues bolstered by overseas remittances facilitate these relatively high levels of public social spending.

Unequal Access to Health Care and Social Protection

The important role for non-state and, especially, sectarian organizations in providing health care in Lebanon shapes *access to health care* and the *experience of seeking and receiving medical treatment.* The relatively unregulated health care regime has facilitated the politicization of health care by political organizations, which use their influence with both public and private providers to gain favorable treatment for their supporters or run their own health care networks in which they can deliver services on a discretionary basis.

Sectarian organizations from all religious affiliations have connections to other private providers and to state officials who control access to public entitlements, allowing them to serve as mediators to third-party services and to act as gatekeepers to benefits that are supposed to be social rights available to

---

23. For an overview of some of these initiatives, some of which have led to improvements, see Ammar (2009). Author interviews: representative, Health Program, World Bank/Lebanon, Beirut, May 4, 2006; official, Ministry of Public Health, Beirut, June 13, 2006; project director, Ministry of Public Health, Beirut, June 24, 2006.

24. I am grateful to Roger Owen for providing this eloquent description of the relationship of sectarian actors to the Lebanese state.

all citizens with demonstrated need. Interviews with elites from government agencies, NGOs, and even sectarian organizations themselves confirmed this observation.[25] Interviews with ordinary citizens about their efforts to access health care offered complementary perspectives. Supporters of different political parties attested that they received preferential access to health programs run by these parties while others, who lack such close connections to political groups, complained of inadequate access to medical care.[26] For example, a woman whose husband was killed by a sniper at the end of the civil war attested that the Al-Shahid organization run by Hezbollah has provided comprehensive health benefits to her and her son. She noted, "When the Shahid took care of him, I would give [my son] his [vaccinations] there. . . . When the organization [Al-Shahid] expanded, they registered him with full medical services with everything [included]."[27] Conversely, a Shia woman who does not support Hezbollah emphasized that only the party's supporters benefit from its largesse: "Hezbollah only gives . . . aid to its people. Anyone can go to join the Hezbollah, act religious, and then have all the aid available."[28]

Other research supports these findings. Based on analyses of an original national survey that I conducted in spring 2008, a strong linkage exists between political activism and the receipt of health and other social services in Lebanon (Cammett 2011; Chen and Cammett 2012). Even after controlling for a range of demographic and other socially relevant factors, respondents were more likely to receive financial assistance for health care if they engaged in various forms of political participation such as declaring their support for a political party, voting, shuttling others to the polls on election days, volunteering for a party, or attending political meetings. The results suggest that partisanship and political behavior mediate access to basic assistance for health care. Given that the major sectarian organizations dominate the political landscape while other parties garner little support in national elections, the findings suggest that sectarian parties incorporate political considerations in offering or brokering access to health care. A full analysis of the political impact of service provision by sectarian parties is beyond the scope of this analysis, and citizens support these parties for diverse and complex reasons rather than mere quid pro quo transactions. Nonetheless, evidence suggests their social programs consolidate support for sectarian parties, in part because beneficiaries are grateful for their benefits and in part because they provide a sense of social protection and order that is otherwise absent for many Lebanese (Cammett 2014, chap. 6).

---

25. Author interviews: director, hospital, Chouf, July 10, 2006; official, Ministry of Public Health, Beirut, June 13, 2006; official, Imam Musa al-Sadr Foundation, Tyre, June 26, 2006; director, Health Service, Amal Movement, Ghobeiry, January 17, 2008.

26. Interview by Lamia Moghnie: Shia man, Chiyah, November 6, 2007.

27. Interview by Lamia Moghnieh: Shia woman, Chiyah, October 23, 2007.

28. Interview by Lamia Moghnieh: Shia woman, Bir Hassan, November 13, 2007.

The discretionary allocation of health assistance in response to political factors almost by definition contributes to health inequities in the Lebanese polity. Furthermore, Lebanese citizens are subject to a gap between de jure and de facto social rights: again, although needy citizens are eligible for public coverage of treatment for certain diseases and for hospitalization, in practice their access to these "entitlements" is mediated by politicians and political organizations that exert influence over relevant agencies.

The politicization of access to health care also affects the experience of seeking or receiving medical treatment. As the preceding discussion implies, the experience can be either smooth and agreeable or extremely unpleasant, depending on a citizen's relationship with the local elites, politicians, and political organizations that mediate access to care. Good connections with power brokers greatly facilitate the process of receiving higher quality and lower cost health services, introducing inequalities in the experience of access.

Political messages and activities may also shape the experience of accessing health care. The act of waiting for treatment in the reception room of a clinic can be a partisan experience. To varying degrees, political and religious influences are prevalent in institutions run by all the major party-based organizations in the form of religious symbols, photos of party leaders, posters promoting political organizations, pamphlets in waiting rooms, and other materials. For example, the Farah Social Foundation has photographs of Walid Jumblatt, the head of the predominantly Druze Popular Socialist Party, throughout the waiting room and administrative offices at its facility in Kfar Heem, even though the director claims that the organization has no political affiliation. Hariri Foundation clinics and schools display photos and other memorabilia of the late prime minister Rafiq al-Hariri and his son and successor, Saad al-Hariri. Similarly, Hezbollah clinics have photos of the Ayatollah Khomeini, other Iranian leaders, or Sayyed Hassan Nasrallah, the leader of Hezbollah. Clinics and schools run by religious groups that are not directly linked to political organizations also display religious symbols such as icons, Qu'ranic or biblical inscriptions, and photos and posters of holy sites. The impact of such materials on beneficiaries is not self-evident and is certainly not uniform. Nonetheless, their presence in health and other welfare facilities indicates that political and religious messages are embedded in the service experience, whether or not providers make overt pronouncements or urgings.

Conclusion

The fragmented and largely unregulated welfare regime in Lebanon provides ample opportunities for private actors and particularly sectarian organizations to supply, broker access to, and take credit for health and other social services. The minimal direct state role and the importance of sectarian groups and other non-state organizations in the welfare regime is the result of a complex mix of factors, including historical legacies of religious philanthropy and community-based service provision during the Ottoman period, the privileging of so-called laissez faire principles during the French Mandate and postindependence periods, and the effects of war and political conflict. Sectarian organizations with vested interests in the status quo both profit from and sustain the underdevelopment of public welfare functions. This situation helps to create and perpetuate inefficiencies that result in the relative underperformance of the health system. In addition, the discretionary allocation of health benefits along partisan and sectarian lines, particularly for low-income citizens, compounds existing socioeconomic inequalities in access to health care.

The findings and arguments presented in this chapter raise questions for further research. First, the discussion focuses largely on sectarian organizations, which are distinguished analytically from religious groups on the grounds that they engage in direct and overt competition to control state institutions. But charities rooted in diverse Muslim and Christian communities are also key providers of health and other social services in Lebanon. What criteria do religious charities linked to churches, mosques, charitable endowments, and other religious institutions employ in allocating social welfare? Under what conditions do they explicitly serve non-coreligionists in addition to or even instead of congregationists? How do citizens experience health care provision in religious institutions? These questions are particularly important in contexts such as Lebanon, where religious identity serves as both the foundation of representation in the formal political system through power-sharing arrangements and a key source of social identities. Furthermore, the analytical distinction between sectarian and religious groups is undoubtedly overstated. In Lebanon, the boundaries between some religious charities and sectarian political parties are blurred, calling for an analysis of the linkages between sectarian and religious providers in mediating access to health care.[29]

A second potential area for additional research focuses on the impact of receiving services imbued with political or religious messages. Clinics, hospitals, and other welfare institutions linked to sectarian organizations display symbols, pamphlets, and other materials promoting their corresponding leaders and parties. How, if at all, do the messages conveyed in these materials affect the attitudes and behaviors of beneficiaries? Do welfare institutions only attract existing supporters and sympathizers in the first place as a result of these messages, or do nonsupporters and the unaffiliated approach them for social assistance?

Lebanon is hardly the only place in the developing world where sectarian, religious, and comparable groups play a vital role in meeting the basic needs

---

29. The relationship between prominent Sunni philanthropic organizations such as the Maqased or Dar al-Fatwa and the Future Movement is a prime example. The Future Movement, which has dominated political representation of the Sunni community in the postwar period, increasingly controlled these and other charities and NGOs.

of citizens. In parts of South and Southeast Asia, sub-Saharan Africa and Latin America, ethnic, religious, and other identity-based organizations offer or mediate access to social welfare, sometimes in conjunction with state programs and sometimes through entirely separate channels. Given their importance in social welfare regimes and the relative deficiency of public social safety nets in many contexts, it is imperative to understand the roles of these types of locally rooted institutions in shaping the well-being of populations.

8

The Reciprocity of Family, Friends, and Neighbors in Rural Ghana and Côte d'Ivoire

Lauren M. MacLean

Given the persistence of hard economic times for many Africans, and the weakness of most African states, it is perhaps unsurprising that non-state actors would play a critical role in the provision of social welfare on the continent. Where earlier in this book Michael Jennings and Jennifer Brass examined the role of faith-based and secular non-governmental organizations in East Africa, in this chapter, I focus on the nature of informal networks for social reciprocity in rural West Africa. In these villages of Ghana and Côte d'Ivoire, informal community-based organizations and networks of family and friends did not actually deliver social services themselves, but, instead played a critical role in financing access to both public and private social service delivery.

The significance of informal social reciprocity to address unmet social needs in many parts of Africa is not only recognized by scholars but is expressed frequently in everyday life through the expression of popular African proverbs that similarly convey that "it takes a village to raise a child."[1] The meaning of these proverbs suggests that Africans historically have relied on the collective expertise and resources of their extended family, friends, and neighbors in the village to meet the needs of their youngest and most vulnerable group members.

And, yet, my analysis of similar villages in neighboring regions of Ghana and Côte d'Ivoire inhabited predominantly by people of the Akan ethnic group

---

1. In Akan Twi spoken in several regions of Ghana, one saying, "Obaakonhweba," means that it takes an entire group to look after a child. Another similar Akan proverb, "Oba da abusua mu," highlights the role of the entire lineage in raising a child. Personal communication with Dr. Samuel Obeng, Department of Linguistics, Indiana University.

finds that the informal institutions of social reciprocity among the extended family, friends, and village community is neither timeless, solidary, or homogeneous, differing in quite surprising ways at the local level.[2] In the Ghanaian region that was studied, fewer people were exchanging any kind of help at all, and when they did it was a much lower level of support to people from a wider array of social ties, particularly friends. In the Ivoirian region, greater numbers of village residents gave more significant amounts of help, but this was exchanged with a much narrower group of people, especially members of their immediate nuclear family.

The critical explanatory factor for this variation was the history of the state role in mediating risk. The local experience of state formation over time shaped both the extent and structure of the informal institutions of social reciprocity. Further, these different patterns of informal reciprocity have important political consequences for equitable access to social welfare, mechanisms of accountability, and the long-term construction of state capacity.

In this chapter I draw on over eighteen months of intensive field research in two carefully matched villages in each of two regions of neighboring Ghana and Côte d'Ivoire in the late 1990s.[3] This comparative research design controls many potential explanatory variables such as precolonial ethnic culture, levels of wealth, economic development, public infrastructure, and so on. The study combined quantitative and qualitative methods including original survey research (n = 400), focus groups, in-depth interviews, and oral histories in each of the four field-site villages. In addition to local fieldwork, archival research and extensive interviews were conducted in Accra, Abidjan, Dakar, Paris, and London.

The History of Non-State Provision in Rural Ghana and Côte d'Ivoire

What are the primary non-state providers in rural Ghana and Côte d'Ivoire? Historically, non-state actors played a much larger and earlier role in establishing the first schools and clinics in Ghana (which was known before its independence as the Gold Coast) compared to Côte d'Ivoire. As early as

---

2. See MacLean (2010) for a more extensive treatment of this subject. Agrawal and Gibson (1999) similarly describe the problems with assumptions about the "mythic community" in development policymaking.

3. Fieldwork was conducted from April to August 1997 and from October 1998 to October 1999 in two similar villages in Tano District in Brong-Ahafo region of Ghana, and in two similar villages in the Abengourou region of Côte d'Ivoire. Fictional names are used for these villages in the notes to protect the anonymity of the sources. The author gratefully acknowledges the support of a Fulbright-Hays Doctoral Dissertation Research Abroad fellowship and grants from the Social Science Research Council, Institute for the Study of World Politics, and the UC Berkeley African Studies Center.

the mid-sixteenth century, European trading companies had created "Castle Schools" to educate a small number of children of African merchants and local chiefs at the slave trading forts along the coasts in Ghana (George 1976). The company headquarters, based in Europe, provided only limited financing of these schools, so local fund-raising was often used.

Following this commercial opening, various European missionary groups began to found schools and health care clinics in conjunction with their evangelical work. In Ghana, Wesleyan (Methodist) and Basel (Presbyterian) missionaries arrived as early as 1828 and had built several schools by the mid-nineteenth century. The missionary schools in Ghana were primarily supported by the missions and received only limited assistance later by the British colonial government. In contrast, French Catholic missionaries were the first Europeans to arrive in Côte d'Ivoire, as early as 1637, but their presence was always much more limited than their Protestant colleagues in Ghana.

Throughout the 1800s, Britain and France fought African rebellions and struggled to consolidate their colonial territories in this part of West Africa. The colonial state did not attempt to provide social services directly in Ghana until the early 1880s, and in Côte d'Ivoire, in 1887 (George 1976; Clignet and Foster 1966). Even then, missionary schools and clinics were still dominant in Ghana. By 1931, only nineteen of the 347 schools in Ghana were completely government run; the huge majority of schools were affiliated and at least partially supported by missions. In comparison, the French colonial government provided full financial support for free services in all public schools and clinics through revenues generated from direct taxation (Clignet and Foster 1966; French National Archives 1951–52).

Even after the independence of Ghana in 1957, and of Côte d'Ivoire in 1960, churches continued to play a larger role in providing education and health services in Ghana than in Côte d'Ivoire. Despite the expansion of public financing for social welfare in both countries during the 1960s and early 1970s, the Ghanaian government still encouraged local governments and voluntary organizations to provide labor, materials, and financial support for their area primary and middle schools. In contrast, the Ivoirian government reinforced its exclusively centralized financing, delivery, and control of education. By the late 1990s, many Ghanaian schools and clinics retained some religious affiliation whereas the Ivoirian ones were more explicitly public facilities. In addition to this faith-based development of social welfare, secular nongovernmental organizations were active in improving water and sanitation services (see earlier chapter by Alison Post) and other related development or democracy-promotion activities. However, they were not engaged as frequently in the direct delivery of core social services in either of these Ghanaian or Ivoirian regions.

Another less formally structured type of non-state providers were the community-based organizations, such as village youth or women's groups, which organized collectively to address particularly acute welfare needs by their group members. In fact, these initiatives were rarely systematic and occurred rather infrequently during the time of fieldwork for this study. A fair amount of scholarship has also been dedicated to the role played by group-based savings associations in many parts of Africa (Janin 1995; Henry, Tchente, and Guillerme-Dieumegard 1991; Bortei-Doku and Aryeetey 1996). These groups are known as "susu" in Ghana and "tontine" in Côte d'Ivoire, but they were surprisingly few in number in the study villages. Instead, many village residents described seeking a loan at 50–100 percent interest in times of crisis from a moneylender based in the village or the next largest town.[4]

Overall, the most significant non-state actors in these regions of Ghana and Côte d'Ivoire were the family, friends, and neighbors who provided cash, food, clothing, housing, or labor to village residents in times of need. I conceptualize these informal social networks as informal institutions of reciprocity where shared rules govern social exchange between individuals and groups over a long period of time.[5] The reciprocal exchange of social support may involve gifts of money, labor, goods, or even emotional support, and include nuclear and extended family, friends, neighbors, other villagers, and members of the same or different ethnic groups. The exchanges may take place within the village or involve people in cities or even overseas. These exchanges are simple, dyadic relationships between two people in one time period but may involve generalized reciprocity that spans generations.

Building on earlier work theorizing the "economy of affection" by Goran Hyden (2006), I characterize the patterns of informal social reciprocity as (1) horizontal versus vertical, and (2) diversified versus concentrated.[6] First, more horizontal reciprocity involves people of similar age, wealth, or power, whereas more vertical reciprocal relations are between people of vastly different ages or political/economic resources. Second, I consider to what extent individuals spread their reciprocity over a large number of different types of relationships. Thus, informal reciprocity is more diversified when individuals spread their gift giving relatively equally among a large number of diverse social categories and more concentrated when reciprocity is focused on a smaller number of targeted social relations.

Considerable scholarly debate exists regarding the origins of these informal institutions of social reciprocity. But none of the existing theories about the importance of market failure (Dercon 2003; Deaton 1992; Stiglitz 2005; Alderman and Paxson 1992), state failure (Tripp 1997; Azarya and Chazan

---

4. Men's focus group (anonymous), tape recording, Barima, Ghana, March 1999; men's focus group (anonymous), tape recording, Makwan, Ghana, April 1999; men's focus group (anonymous), tape recording, Opanin, Côte d'Ivoire, September 1999; women's focus group (anonymous), tape recording, Opanin, Côte d'Ivoire, September 1999.

5. To conceptualize reciprocity, I build on a deep literature in anthropology and history as well as works by Scott (1976), Popkin (1979), Bates and Curry (1992), and Hyden (1980, 2006) in political science.

6. Hyden contrasts vertical with lateral, and open with closed in his typology.

1987; Chazan 1994; Dei 1992; Pellow and Chazan 1986), or the existence of a precapitalist economy (Hyden 1980; Scott 1976) explains how informal reciprocal institutions have changed over time in such different ways in two similar regions. In the next section, I turn to the dynamics of the informal institutions of reciprocity over time and highlight how the history of state formation has transformed the informal rules about who to help, when, and how in rural Ghana and Côte d'Ivoire.

Interactions between the State and the Informal Institutions of Reciprocity

In contrast to the conventional myth of the communal African village, unaltered and unreached by the state, informal institutions of reciprocity have certainly changed and been fundamentally transformed through their interactions with the state over time. Following the framework established in the introduction to this volume, these dynamics can be characterized as appropriation, where non-state actors broker access to state-provided benefits. In most instances, these informal social networks of mutual support were not supplanting the state provision of social welfare, but instead were mediating access to public (and private) services by providing needed cash. One Ghanaian woman described the need for money even in rural areas where farmers grew their own food: "Help is not only money . . . but with those of us in this village, who are farmers, everyone has food, and you can get some money to buy a cloth, but can't wear only that one cloth, and the food alone too can't help, so it's the money we need."[7] In other interviews, village residents in both regions of Ghana and Côte d'Ivoire confirmed the need for cash to help pay for such necessities as oil, sugar, soap, medicines, doctor visits, fertilizer, pesticide, school fees, and school uniforms, books, and supplies.

Although villagers in both regions emphasized the significance of the reciprocal exchange of cash assistance, the patterns of informal reciprocity they described were surprisingly different. In a survey question that asked hypothetically what source would give the respondent help if they were sick and in need, the first answer given by the majority of Ivoirian respondents was the nuclear family (59%). (See table 8.1.) In comparison, about a third as many Ghanaian respondents mentioned the nuclear family first. Basically, the nuclear family was perceived to be the one essential pillar of support in Côte d'Ivoire, whereas it served as one of several approximately equal pillars of aid available in Ghana. Notably, for Ghanaians, friends outpaced the role of both the nuclear and extended family when in need. In contrast, only 7 percent of Ivoirians mentioned friends first as a source of assistance.

---

7. Women's focus group (anonymous), tape recording, Barima, Ghana, March 1999.

TABLE 8.1.
First-cited source of help if respondents were sick in similar regions of Ghana and Côte d'Ivoire

	Ghanaian region (%)	Ivoirian region (%)
Nuclear family	23	59
Extended family	20	11
Friend	28	8
Church	8	0
Association	0	6
Rich person or moneylender	16	1
Government	0	0
Other	4	14

In a later set of survey questions that attempted to document individuals' actual behavior in giving and receiving informal social support, I found similar differences between the Ghanaian and Ivoirian regions.[8] Although the largest share of help was allocated to the nuclear family in both regions, this was particularly concentrated in Côte d'Ivoire, where over 69 percent of help was given to the nuclear family (which was conceptualized very minimally as the respondents' children only). When Ivoirians did give to the extended family, it was more likely transferred to parents or other elders rather than to siblings or peers. In comparison, village residents from the Ghanaian region gave help to a more diversified set of social categories overall, and in particular noted the importance of friends and siblings.

Not only did the survey data reveal divergence in the qualitative structure of reciprocity but also in the quantitative levels of the amount exchanged. First, a surprisingly high number of village residents in the Ghanaian region were not investing in any type of social exchange, neither as a donor nor as a recipient. Over 39 percent of respondents from the Ghanaian region reported that they did not give any type of help to anyone whereas only 6 percent of Ivoirians did not invest in any reciprocity. Second, the median amount of help given was significantly smaller in the Ghanaian region than in the Ivoirian one. Ghanaians gave on average under $29 per year as help to others to pay for

---

8. In the statistical analysis for this study, I used the self-reported value of help given for hospital fees, medicine, school fees, school supplies, and clothing over the previous twelve months. Of the more than seventeen different types of help investigated, these five types were generally the most memorable and reliable because the event was life-threatening; the gifts were given or received at the same times of year; and, the gifts were almost always given in cash. See MacLean (2010) for a more detailed description of the survey sampling, instrument, implementation, and analysis.

hospitals, medicine, school fees, school supplies, and clothing, while Ivoirians gave $117 per year, over four times as much.

What explains the development of such puzzling differences in the nature of informal reciprocity in such similar villages on either side of the Ghana–Côte d'Ivoire border? In both of these cases, the states were relatively weak and, at the time of the fieldwork, in the late 1990s, among the more highly consolidated democratic regimes in sub-Saharan Africa. Both regimes were relatively unthreatened by non-state actors, particularly by such small-scale, localized, and informal networks of reciprocity.

Faced with similar challenges, the state had historically pursued state formation in much different ways in Côte d'Ivoire than in Ghana. In particular, the different historical roles that the state played in mediating risk in political administration, social service provision, and agricultural policy transformed the informal institutions of reciprocity in the contemporary period in dissimilar ways. It is critical to investigate the state role across all three of these policy domains—and not just social policy—in order to develop a more nuanced explanation for the divergent patterns in the informal institutions of reciprocity.

The divergent nature of the colonial and postcolonial state institutions for political administration has shaped informal reciprocity. Here, the initial formation of central state institutions to administer the colonial territories entailed a normative construction of the appropriate state role vis-à-vis the family and the colonial subject. The new formal political institutions of the central colonial state did not necessarily crush or replace the preexisting informal institutions of reciprocity. Rather, the new formal state institutions and the informal institutions transformed each other over time in an iterative process of local, everyday interactions that differed markedly in the two regions. Thus, in the Ghanaian region the more decentralized colonial and postcolonial administrative institutions validated the authority and meaning of membership in the broader lineage, ethnic, and village community. The central state in Ghana was not the exclusive, or even primary, actor in mediating risk in the village. The result was a greater diversification of informal reciprocity among a wider variety of social ties, and localization of these ties within the rural village. Meanwhile, in the Ivoirian region, the more centralized administrative institutions eroded the authority of the precolonial system of chieftancy, and did not facilitate village-level organization or self-help. To these village residents, the central state was the primary player mediating the risk they faced. The consequence of this everyday experience of political administration was that the informal institutions of reciprocity became more narrowly concentrated on a smaller number of social ties, with the priority given to the immediate nuclear family in Côte d'Ivoire.

The second aspect of the state's role in mediating risk is in the area of social service provision itself. Here, the actual day-to-day provision of social infrastructure and subsidized delivery of social services has had unintended consequences on the informal institutions of reciprocity in these regions of Ghana and Côte d'Ivoire. Somewhat counterintuitively, the more historically active and centralized state role in mediating social risk actually stimulated a higher quantity of less-diversified informal reciprocal exchange in the late 1990s in the Ivoirian region than in the Ghanaian one. Thus, in Côte d'Ivoire, state investments in social service infrastructure and delivery began later than in colonial Ghana, but were more stable and of a higher quality between the late 1960s until the mid-1990s. As a consequence of this more active role in mediating social risk, the informal institutions of reciprocity were less diversified in Côte d'Ivoire than in Ghana. Furthermore, Ivoirians in this region had greater expectations of service utilization. Thus, when the Ivoirian state retrenched in the 1980s, Ivoirians turned with greater frequency and intensity to their informal social networks to replace the financial subsidies previously provided by a more provident state. In contrast, Ghanaians had much lower expectations of what the state should or historically had done in social service delivery since the late 1960s. Moreover, after a longer period of economic instability during the 1970s, many Ghanaians had already diversified and then depleted their informal reciprocity assets.

The final component of the state's role in mediating risk is in the area of economic policy, specifically agriculture. The history of the state role in supporting economic production, mediating market volatility, and taxing productivity directly stimulated divergent economic production decisions at the local level, which then indirectly influenced the structure of informal reciprocity. Thus, where states historically imposed heavy taxes on export agricultural production, individuals chose less land-intensive production strategies with shorter-term yields and subsequently diversified their investments in the informal institutions of reciprocity. This was certainly the case in these villages in Ghana. Farmers had long experienced more extractive agricultural policies for cocoa exports and chose to switch to tomatoes as the new cash crop for domestic markets.[9] Tomato's high inputs of strenuous labor for short growing seasons on small plots of land particularly attracted young farmers who began to exchange land, labor, and cash more frequently and more intensely with their peer relatives and friends. Additionally, because these younger Ghanaian tomato farmers did not need land as much as they needed labor, inheriting the cocoa plantation of one's father or uncle became less important than maintaining a wide network of family, friends and others. Production requirements have thus maintained the salience of diversified and youth-oriented informal reciprocity networks in this region of Ghana.

In the Ivoirian region, the Ivoirian state historically pursued a more moderate level of taxation on agricultural exports and facilitated labor in-migration. This history of state support gave farmers' greater confidence to replant and

---

9. For an analysis of Ghanaian agricultural policies, see Frimpong-Ansah (1991) and Stryker (1990). Sara Berry (1997) also examines the rise of tomato production in another region in Ghana.

expand such a permanent and long-term investment as a cocoa plantation.[10] Facing lower levels of risk from state intervention in agriculture, Ivoirian village residents developed informal institutions of reciprocity, which were more concentrated on the nuclear family, yet nevertheless more intergenerational than in the Ghanaian region.

This process of institutional transformation was clearly not a simple zero-sum relationship in which state retrenchment led automatically to an expansion of informal networks and voluntary associations.[11] What were initially theorized by other scholars as short-term coping strategies have evolved in different ways over time in different localities due to divergent colonial and postcolonial interactions with the state.[12] Even though the informal institutions of reciprocity were limited in both regions, the particular boundaries of social exclusion—who was included and who was left out of reciprocal networks—differed profoundly on either side of the Ghana–Côte d'Ivoire border. The informal institutions of reciprocity were critically mediated by formal state institutions, both past and present. The ways the state mediated risk in the areas of political administration, social service delivery, and agricultural policy shaped the composition of the new groups of winners and losers and how they came together to change the informal rules of the game.

Consequences for Equity, Accountability, and Long-Term State Capacity

The nature of the informal institutions of reciprocity has important consequences for the equity of access to social welfare, the local understandings by village residents of how to seek accountability, and state capacity.

Consequences for the Equity and Sustainability of Access

In the context of state retrenchment throughout much of the continent, many Africans have no longer been able to exchange help with their kith and kin as they did in the past (Von Benda Beckmann and Kirsch 1999). In both the Ghanaian and Ivoirian regions, the informal social relations of reciprocity were so debilitated during the period of the late 1990s that many village residents were left out entirely, or at best received such meager assistance from others that children were withdrawn from school, and elders were finally taken to the

---

10. Cocoa trees require approximately five years before they can be harvested for the first time. After peak production between five and fifteen years, yields begin to decline, and trees need to be replaced after thirty years.

11. See Chazan (1988); Azarya and Chazan (1987); Bratton (1994); and Dei (1992).

12. Guyer, Denzer, and Agbaje (2002) critique this earlier conceptualization of short-term coping strategies as inadequate for understanding the contemporary situation in urban Nigeria.

TABLE 8.2.
Comparison of equity of access through informal institutions of social reciprocity in similar regions of Ghana and Côte d'Ivoire

		Brong-Ahafo region, Ghana	Abengourou region, Côte d'Ivoire
Depth of access	Number of people participating in informal social reciprocity	Low	High
	Amount of reciprocity exchanged	Low	Moderate
Breadth of access	Concentration on nuclear family	Moderate	High
	Rural-urban linkages	Low (infrequent)	Low (restricted)
	Stringency of terms of reciprocity	Moderate	High
Summary		**More exhausted**	**More exclusive**

hospital only to die. Still, the study found that the ability of families, friends, and village neighbors to provide financial assistance to gain access to state services was very different. Overall, however, the informal institutions of reciprocity were more exhausted in the Ghanaian villages and more exclusive in the Ivoirian ones. (See table 8.2.)[13]

First, the survey data discussed in the previous section revealed that significant numbers of people, particularly in the Ghanaian region, were not investing in any type of reciprocal social exchange. These findings show that the shallow depth of informal networks was unevenly experienced by different social groups, with important consequences for equitable access to social welfare. In both regions, women were less likely than men to be excluded from receiving any help at all. In contrast, nonindigenous ethnic groups were more likely than Akan groups to be excluded from giving or receiving any assistance at all. The results for the poor differed more markedly, between the Ghanaian and Ivoirian regions, than for gender and ethnicity. In the Ghanaian region, a greater number of the poorest village residents, as compared to every other wealth category, at least gave some help. In contrast, the poorest villagers in the Ivoirian region had the lowest participation rates in reciprocal networks.

Second, for those who were able to give help, the amount of reciprocity exchanged was so low that it was doubtful whether they could adequately address minimum social welfare needs in either the short or long-term. Although the quantitative amounts of help given over the year (an average of $29 in the Ghanaian villages and $117 in the Ivoirian ones) represented a substantial proportion of the villagers' median annual income, the value of the help to the recipient was relatively low when one considers the cost of living and potential

---

13. The conceptualization and measurement of the equity of access is developed more fully in MacLean (2011a).

costs of social welfare needs. Thus, a Ghanaian might give all of the help he could give for the entire year and barely be able to cover the cost of secondary school fees for one child. Needless to say, this amount would not cover room and board, transportation, school supplies, or the costs of giving help to any other children, family members, or friends.

Third, informal reciprocity, particularly in the Ivoirian region, was highly concentrated on support given to the very immediate nuclear family. Ivoirians in this region not only seemed more immediately cognizant of the very concept of the nuclear family than Ghanaians, referring to it frequently in French as "la petite famille," or the little family, they also more easily acknowledged, without any seeming hesitation, that they would help their nuclear family first: "For the nuclear family, it's an obligation to help. It's required [forcé] while for the extended family, it's simply help. You are not forced because there are the others."[14]

While the nuclear family clearly came first, residents from the Ghanaian villages appeared to exchange reciprocity with people from a more diverse group of social ties, especially the extended family and friends within the same age group. During interviews, Ghanaians more often emphasized the superior role of friends as more sensitive, straightforward, and trustworthy than extended family relatives. One twenty-five-year-old Ghanaian man explained that he would help a friend before a relative because "this relative would not have helped me if I were in need, whereas a friend will always help."[15] In contrast, Ivoirians emphasized that one was not "obliged to help" friends, particularly since the friend "also has a family who can help him."[16]

Fourth, in addition to different patterns of concentration across various social groups, informal reciprocity varied in how the networks spanned geographic space. In general, Ivoirian reciprocal networks tended to extend vertically from the rural village to the regional and national capital cities, whereas Ghanaian reciprocal networks were more horizontally concentrated within the village itself. Thus, informal reciprocity in Côte d'Ivoire often connected the youth or aged residents of the small, rural village to the "successful" middle-aged patrons from their own extended families who lived in the city. These patrons usually wielded both political and economic power, facilitating access to the central government and providing critical financial support for school tuition or a visit to the hospital by individuals in need. In contrast, fewer hometown associations existed for the Ghanaian villages, where people hailing from the same village who lived in the capital cities would meet to organize community development initiatives back home. Overall, visits and social support to and from urban-based relatives seemed to occur much less frequently than in Côte

---

14. Men's focus group (anonymous), tape recording, Kyere, Côte d'Ivoire, September 1999.
15. Survey interview (anonymous) by author, Makwan, Ghana.
16. Survey interview (anonymous) by author, Opanin, Côte d'Ivoire.

d'Ivoire, where village decisions often were put on hold until someone could be dispatched to the capital city for advice, money, favors, and so on, from the "big man." In Ghana, social ties seemed to be more horizontally concentrated within the village and only occasionally extended to the district capital.

Finally, the terms of reciprocity were becoming less generalized and less long-term in both regions, but particularly so in Côte d'Ivoire. In both countries, gifts or grants that need not be repaid were becoming increasingly rare. Furthermore, while loans seemed to be increasingly the norm in both Côte d'Ivoire and Ghana, more of those loans were being charged with interest (and higher levels of interest at that) in Côte d'Ivoire than in Ghana. In interviews, Ivoirians reported in greater numbers that they were no longer able to reimburse loans in kind by working or "perhaps with a bottle of gin,"[17] and that it was no longer "obnoxious" but rather "expected" to charge interest on a loan today. As one Ivoirian man calmly explained: "Before, our relatives got along very well, and they helped each other. But [now] if you want a loan, it's with interest. There are no longer any presents. People don't love each other anymore."[18]

In contrast, Ghanaian village residents were noticeably more uncomfortable discussing the topic of interest on loans. Not only was the depth of investments in the relations of social reciprocity fatigued but the breadth of these networks of social relations was limited.[19] Importantly, the nature of the exhaustion and exclusion of informal reciprocity was occurring in different ways in the two regions of Ghana and Côte d'Ivoire, with significant consequences for who was able to access social support and secure their own welfare in a sustainable manner.

Consequences for Accountability and Long-Term State Capacity

In addition to the consequences for access to welfare, this chapter also reveals how the differences in the nature of informal reciprocity have shaped the local conceptualization of citizenship and the identification of the appropriate mechanisms of accountability in the two countries. In general, in both regions of Ghana and Côte d'Ivoire the first-level mechanisms of accountability for village residents relying on informal networks of reciprocity were not very transparent or certain. Usually, if an informal rule of reciprocity was violated, the inappropriate behavior was sanctioned through local gossip, social stigmatization, or even violence. For example, in these regions many village residents explained the increase in the use of witchcraft to punish those who had not

---

17. Men's focus group (anonymous), tape recording, Kyere, Côte d'Ivoire, August 1999.
18. Men's focus group (anonymous), tape recording, Kyere, Côte d'Ivoire, August 1999.
19. Hirtz (1995) also finds a narrowing of social solidarity in his study of social security in the rural Philippines.

TABLE 8.3.
Perceptions of most important individual or group leader for village development and
policymaking in regions of Ghana and Côte d'Ivoire

Category of leader or group	Derivation of authority	Ghanaian region	Ivoirian region
Most local state institu- tions	Based on elected or appointed political	HIGH	LOW
	office	Unit committee 82.1%	Sous-préfet 3.8%
Most local "traditional" institutions		District assembly 23.8%	Mayoral 5.8%
		Village chief 54.8%	Village chief 25%
		chief's elders 12.9%	chief's elders 4.5%
Local and nonlocal individuals	Based on personal po- litical and economic	LOW	HIGH
	power	bureaucrats 0%	bureaucrats 51.4%
		the rich 0%	the rich 16.4%
		big farmers 0%	big farmers 11.2%

Note: All statistics shown are cumulative amounts that combine results for first, second, and third mentioned responses.

shared their success with needy extended family members according to the locally understood informal rules of reciprocity. Any differences between the two regions in the types or intensity of stigmatization, or even the invocation of witchcraft, would have been extremely difficult to document and compare systematically and was not the primary objective of this study.

What could be investigated, however, was the next level of accountability mechanisms in the two regions. Which types of authorities did village residents identify as most salient when they needed to resolve a problem? If a village resident had an access problem with the informal networks of reciprocity, and the informal sanctioning mechanisms did not work, where might they turn for help? Here, the study found notable variations between the regions of Ghana and Côte d'Ivoire. When asked who were the most important individuals or groups in making decisions or developing policies for the village, Ghanaians most frequently cited village-level political institutions whereas Ivoirians noted, often by name, individuals who were based outside of the village in the urban capitals of Abengourou and Abidjan. (See table 8.3.)

In Ghana, an overwhelming number of respondents (82%) cited the village-level unit committee as among the three most important leaders of village development. In comparison, Ivoirians rarely mentioned the most local political authority, the sous-préfet (4%) or mayor's (6%) office.

Ghanaians also evaluated the village chieftancy as playing a more pivotal role than did Ivoirians. Over twice as many Ghanaians (55%) as Ivoirians (25%) cited the chief as one of the three most important leaders for development in their village.[20] Indeed, in Côte d'Ivoire respondents were almost never

---

20. Other survey and interview data suggests that the institution of the chieftancy was held in higher esteem than were most individual chiefs. Furthermore, many respondents distinguished

able to name the elders of the village. One non-Akan cocoa farmer who had been an officer in the village cocoa producer cooperative admitted, "Me for example, I have been here since 1984 (fifteen years), but I don't know who is an elder."[21]

In contrast, demonstrating a lack of confidence in local-level political institutions, most Ivoirians (51%) cited, often by name, wealthy civil servants ("cadres") as being the most influential person or group for the development of their community. These individuals may have been born in the village and have family members living there whom they visit occasionally, but they are generally based in the regional or national capital. Hence, when a local problem needed to be resolved, a village resident would travel to the regional or national capital to seek advice or mediation. In one of the Ivoirian villages, even the younger brother of the chief who seemed to serve as a village elder mentioned only an individual named Bonzou as the single most important leader for village development, not the chief. In comparison, in Ghana respondents never cited high-level civil servants or particular "sons of the village" by name. And accountability was pursued within the confines of the village itself.

I argue that an individual's experience of the informal institutions of reciprocity shapes their reading of the boundaries of the political community, reinforcing certain types of identities over others and changing the contours of political cleavage and coalition. This is important for how individuals seek accountability vis-à-vis other participants in their informal networks, in the village community, or with the state.

The local experience of informal reciprocity networks also has broader consequences for how village residents define themselves as citizens in a particular community. Ghanaians and Ivoirians had distinct ways of conceptualizing and practicing citizenship at the village level in the two analogous regions studied. First, in the Ghanaian villages, village residents articulated a more restricted, community-oriented notion of citizenship rights and duties whereas in the

---

between the chief's important role in community development as opposed to his assistance to individuals. In Ghana, 16% of respondents reported that the chief does nothing to help individual villagers in need. Many Ghanaian respondents commented, "The chief himself is finding life difficult; as such, he is unable to help anyone." Although there are a fair number of negative comments such as this one, a much greater number of Ivoirians (37%) responded that the chief does nothing, a difference that is statistically significant (significance = .000). Ivoirian comments also tended to be more immediate and forthrightly negative. "If you have a problem, he does not resolve it. He does nothing. . . . The situation is getting worse and worse too because often one resolves problems elsewhere." Survey interviews (anonymous) by author, Barima, Ghana, and Kyere, Côte d'Ivoire.

21. An argument could be made that since this man did not belong to the indigenous Akan ethnic group, that he would not have the same reasons to know the elders. Still, his highly public activity with the cocoa producer cooperative and his own role as an elder of his ethnic group in the village would have provided ample opportunity to come into contact with the Akan elders. Men's focus group (anonymous), tape recording, Kyere, Côte d'Ivoire, August 1999.

TABLE 8.4.
Comparison of rights of citizens in regions of Ghana and Côte d'Ivoire

	Ghanaian region	Ivoirian region
Perception of rights	Restricted list of rights linked explicitly to duties	Expansive list of entitlements
Nature of goods delivered by state	Public goods consumed by communities	Private goods consumed by individuals
Three most frequently mentioned rights	Social services (33%) Employment (24%) Roads/markets/electricity (21%)	Individual loans (28%) Cash grants to needy (20%) Housing (16%) Employment (16%)
Extremely low scores on "classic" citizenship rights associated with Western democracies	Provision of physical security (2%) Protection of private property (1.5%) Protection of equality (1%) Guarantee of freedom (0.6%) Freedom to participate in political processes (0%)	Provision of physical security (2%) Protection of private property (0%) Protection of equality (0.4%) Guarantee of freedom (2%) Freedom to participate in political processes (0.4%)

TABLE 8.5.
Comparison of duties of citizens in regions of Ghana and Côte d'Ivoire

	Ghanaian region	Ivoirian region
Perception of duties	Explicit notion of reciprocity	Concept of obligations more difficult to grasp
Nature of duties owed to the state	Performed together as a community or to benefit the community	Performed as an individual
Three most frequently mentioned duties	Develop the community/country (47%) Pay taxes (22%) Perform communal labor (21%)	Work on individual farm (58%) Participate in politics (10%) Develop community/country (10%)
Extremely low scores on other "classic" citizenship duties associated with Western democracies	Participate in politics (7%) Obey laws (3%) Serve in the military (0%)	Pay taxes (8%) Obey laws (7%) Serve in the military (0%)

Ivoirian villages villagers described a more expansive, individualized sense of entitlements.[22] (See tables 8.4 and 8.5.)

Thus, Ghanaians responded with a relatively restricted list of public goods that were frequently linked in the same sentence to corresponding duties. For example, one survey respondent replied, "I would do anything I am asked to

22. In order to explore the indigenous understandings of citizenship in the most unrestricted manner possible, I asked two open-ended questions at the very end of the survey questionnaire about the rights and then the obligations owed between an individual and the state. The local

do, be it payment of money [taxes], etc., if only that will help to improve education."[23] In contrast, Ivoirians had a much more expansive view of the state's role in their lives, often presenting a long list of privately consumable goods owed to them from an omniscient and omnipotent state. For example, one forty-year-old Akan man ticked off several things that the state should give him and then summarized blithely by saying that the state should provide "everything I need."[24] Another Ivoirian declared seriously, "The state should buy me a car, purchase me a refrigerator, and build a house for me."[25]

Whereas Ghanaians often linked rights and duties explicitly in their remarks, Ivoirians dwelled on entitlements and then struggled for awhile to even imagine the concept of duties given to the state. One Ivoirian exclaimed, "It's us that don't have anything. Who should help the state, and why?!"[26] And, when duties were described by Ivoirians, they were conceptualized as individual rather than collective contributions. Hence, Ivoirians would most often pause and then reply that their duty was to work on their individual farm (58%) whereas Ghanaians would respond more quickly that they should work to develop the community or country as a whole (52%). For example, one Ivoirian explained, "Every morning, I go to the farm. This is all that I can do for the state."[27] In contrast, a farmer in the Ghanaian region said, "I should work harder at my farming to produce more food to help feed Ghana."[28]

These differences in how Ghanaians and Ivoirians conceive of their rights and duties vis-à-vis the state might also suggest potential variations in the long-term consequences for state capacity. More Ghanaians in this region expect that the state should provide public social services, and a greater number of Ghanaians also readily identify their obligation to pay taxes as a primary duty to the state. This might reveal a lingering political constituency, at least in the rural areas of Ghana, to support the continued role of the state in social welfare provision. In contrast, Ivoirians seem to demand an expansive state role but without being willing to supply the tax base to support those state capacities. Although these speculations are necessarily very tentative given the limits of the data available, these questions should be more rigorously assessed in future research.

To summarize, the varied patterns of the informal networks of reciprocity had significant consequences. Village residents in these regions of Ghana and

---

language translation for "the state" was used rather than "Ghana" or "Côte d'Ivoire" in order to investigate not only the content but the nature of the political community, or the location of citizenship.
23. Survey interview (anonymous) by author, Barima, Ghana.
24. Survey interview (anonymous) by author, Kyere, Côte d'Ivoire.
25. Survey interview (anonymous) by author, Kyere, Côte d'Ivoire.
26. Survey interview (anonymous) by author, Opanin, Côte d'Ivoire.
27. Ibid.
28. Survey interview (anonymous), by author, Barima, Ghana.

Côte d'Ivoire had very different ways of gaining access to social support and thus social welfare. And, they not only pursued different avenues of accountability to resolve problems related to social welfare provision but they also conceptualized their rights and duties of citizenship differently vis-à-vis the state, with the potential for long-term consequences for state capacity.

Conclusion

This original research on the divergent patterns of informal social networks in such highly similar regions reveals the dynamism and potential for conflict within rural communities. Rather than assuming a vibrant and inclusive village, in this chapter I examine the history, dynamics, and consequences of these informal non-state providers of social welfare in rural Africa.

This chapter underscores a central contention in this volume, namely that we cannot understand the political consequences of *non-state* social welfare without first understanding the history of *state* social provision. We need to examine the local experience of state service provision over time and how those interactions have transformed even such informal non-state providers as the extended family, friends, and village community. State and non-state providers did not exist in a zero-sum relationship, for example, with extended family networks simply expanding to fill the gaps left by neoliberal state retrenchment. Rather, different histories of state provision have profoundly shaped the quantity and character of the informal institutions of social reciprocity in these neighboring regions and thus indirectly influenced the local meanings and everyday practice of citizenship in Ghana and Côte d'Ivoire. In the current effort to extend our analysis to include the non-state providers of social welfare, we must be careful not to ignore the history and consequences of state action, even that of relatively weak states in the developing world.

9

The *Naya Netas*

Informal Mediators of Government Services in Rural North India

Anirudh Krishna

A new group of political intermediaries has arisen in north India. By providing important services at the local level, they are better enabling ordinary citizens to gain access to the protections, opportunities, and benefits of the democratic state.

These *naya netas* (literally, new leaders) have taken on this role for the most part during the past thirty years. They help villagers gain voice and enforce accountability vis-à-vis government officials; they enable individuals to better obtain in practice the legal protections that are written in the laws; and they facilitate connections with service providers, often also helping hold corruption in check. By helping bridge the distance that still exists between ordinary citizens and the Indian state, *naya netas* help improve diverse governance outcomes for thousands, perhaps millions, of Indian villagers, among whom are some of the poorest people in the world.

Not all villagers avail themselves equally of the services offered by these informal providers. Poorer villagers, who have relatively little access to formal institutions, are more likely to engage in political transactions with the *naya netas*. But better-off villagers prefer other means, relying more often than poorer villagers on the mediation provided by *formal* institutions. Even within the same village community different means are utilized by diverse individuals to gain access to the same state services and programs.

Among poorer villagers, however, especially among historically disadvantaged groups, the emergence of this new set of non-state providers of mediation services has substantially improved the quality of interactions with state officials. Participation in various forms of political activity has risen alongside the expansion of mediation services at the local level. It would not be an exaggeration to state that poorer people's experiences of democracy have vastly improved. It is a matter of concern, however, that poorer citizens are relying in greater measure on noninstitutional means of engaging with democracy. How stable and reliable such mechanisms will prove remains to be ascertained.

The Rise of Naya Netas

Five sets of factors have been principally responsible for the origins of naya netas and the enhancement of their roles. Some of these have helped raise the *demand* for mediation services at the local level. Other factors, operating in parallel, have helped increase the *supply* of individuals capable of forging the required governance links.

Three factors are particularly important in accelerating the demand for non-state provision of mediation services. First, the structure of the Indian state, historically constructed from the top down, has left the proverbial last mile—linking villages to the lowest levels of state administration—substantially uncovered.[1] People in villages—two-thirds of all Indians—still have to travel considerable distances in order to make contact with their state. Individuals desirous of making connections with state officials have largely had to fend for themselves. Into this vacuum of institutional representation have stepped various actors at different times. Thirty years ago, dominant landlords and other local "strongmen" functioned as the key intermediaries, closely guarding access to the powers and resources of the central state.[2] The social origins of the critical mediators have changed in recent years, largely on account of other factors discussed below.

The historical need for mediation, due primarily to incomplete state formation and other structural factors, has been accentuated in recent times by a vast expansion of the social welfare programs of the Indian state. The budget for rural development and other welfare programs has increased tremendously over the past thirty years, greatly expanding the workload of the government machinery.[3] Especially at the lower levels, government officials are required to deal with an explosion of small-scale projects that have to be implemented over vast and often remote areas. Increasingly, they have looked for suitable intermediaries in villages. These "mates," *mistris*, and other informal local

---

1. Decentralization, as currently practiced, has not helped bridge this last uncovered mile, although it has certainly helped in many other ways, as we will see below.

2. See, for example, Bailey (1963); Frankel and Rao (1989); Migdal (1988); and Weiner (1989).

3. Government funding for rural development schemes increased sevenfold (in inflation-adjusted terms) in the period between 1980 and 1995 (Government of India 1998), and it has increased further in more recent years.

supervisors help make more manageable the burgeoning portfolios of rural development projects that government officials are responsible for implementing.

Simultaneously, political competition has also become more intense, providing additional demand for local mediators. The Congress Party, which dominated Indian politics for most of the first thirty years after national independence (in 1947), has lost ground in recent decades. The rise of an alternative coalition headed by the Bharatiya Janata Party along with the ascendance of a plethora of regional parties has resulted in making elections much more competitive and unpredictable; incumbents are regularly thrown out by voters. Despite this alternation of parties in power, political parties have rarely invested in building stable organizations linked organically from the bottom to the top. The nature of party formation has paralleled the process of state building. The last mile—of links to the villages—has been left largely uncovered as well by most party organizations (Kohli 1990; Krishna 2002). At the time of elections, parties reach out to influential individuals, capable of bringing in the vote. The need for local providers of mediation services—made large on account of the two previous factors—has been enhanced as well by intensified political competition.

These three demand-related factors (incomplete state building, burgeoning social welfare programs, and increased political competition) may not have sufficed to produce an army of capable intermediaries at the local level. Two supply-related factors help complete this explanation for the origins of naya netas. Principal among these is the growth, particularly over the past thirty years, of education in rural areas. Where before hardly any schools (and virtually no colleges) were located in villages, and villagers consequently were unlettered, by and large, more recently the welfarist notion of education for all, at least to the primary school level, has led the Indian state to establish schools in growing numbers across the countryside. The result has been a rapid acceleration of educational achievement.

The extent of this change can be visualized by comparing educational achievement across generations. Research that I conducted in the second half of 2005 in twenty villages of Rajasthan, located in the north of India, and another twenty villages of Karnataka, located in the south, gives evidence of a very positive and steadily rising intergenerational trend. Among villagers presently in the age group 31–40 years, that is, those who attended primary schools twenty to thirty years ago, no more than 32 percent in Karnataka villages and 29 percent in Rajasthan villages have five or more years of education. Contrast these numbers with the corresponding ones for the age group 11–20 years: 85 percent in Karnataka and 64 percent in Rajasthan villages have five or more years of education.

Intergenerational change in educational attainment is, thus, quite remarkable. Two generations ago, only a small minority of villagers—11 percent in Rajasthan and 15 percent in Karnataka—had acquired five or more years of formal education. One generation ago, the corresponding numbers were

29 percent and 32 percent, still a minority among their cohort. In the generation that is now coming of age—those aged 11–15 years—the vast majority of villagers, both men and women, are functionally literate.[4]

The growing availability of educated young people has expanded the pool from which local intermediaries can be supplied. Older people, brought up in an oral tradition, mostly do not have what it takes to engage meaningfully with the everyday state.[5] The new leaders who have come up as a result of all these changes are thus usually, in the words of a Congress Party leader, "between 25 and 40 years of age . . . [and] educated to about middle school [level]. They read newspapers, have contacts in government offices, and are experienced [in dealing] with the government bureaucracy and with banks, insurance companies, and such like. . . . Their caste does not matter . . . [they] can be of any caste, but they must have knowledge, perseverance and ability."[6]

To be sure, having education does not equip a person fully for becoming a naya neta; other personal qualities are also necessary. But without education it would be impossible to function in the written-down world of laws, policies, procedures, applications, and general paperwork common to government bureaucracies everywhere but perhaps more widespread and cumbersome in India.

One other supply-related factor has also played a role, albeit an indirect one, in the rise of the new intermediaries. The passage of affirmative action laws, particularly laws outlawing untouchability and other laws reserving quotas for scheduled castes and scheduled tribes in government recruitment and educational institutions[7] has to some extent raised the prospects of upward mobility among people of these groups.

A considerable part of the new local leadership has arisen from among younger members of these historically disadvantaged segments of society. In one Indian state, Rajasthan, where I investigated the roles and social origins of the new local leadership, I found that scheduled and backward castes are better represented than upper castes within the ranks of the naya netas. Upper castes constitute 16 percent of the population in all sixty-nine villages where

---

4. Similar results have also been reported by other recent studies. See, for example, Probe Team 1999. Unfortunately, educational attainment falls sharply when viewed at the high school level. Of all those currently aged 20–24, only 3.5 percent graduated from high school in these Rajasthan villages, and only 5.7 percent graduated in the Karnataka villages.

5. For a fuller explication of the "everyday state," connoting the day-to-day interactions of ordinary people with lower-level government officials, see Fuller and Benei (2000).

6. Congress Party leader Chunnilal Garasiya, cited in Krishna (2003: 1175).

7. Scheduled Caste refers to the former untouchables, and Scheduled Tribe to what are, loosely speaking, India's indigenous people. These categories are recognized by India's constitution, which provides schedules listing specific castes and tribes as Scheduled Caste and Scheduled Tribe, respectively. Backward Caste is a more recent administrative listing, and it refers to caste groupings that, while historically underprivileged, are not listed in the schedules for Scheduled Castes and Scheduled Tribe.

these data were collected, but only 9 percent of naya netas have emerged from within this caste group. On the other hand, scheduled castes (the former untouchables) constitute 22 percent of village population but 26 percent of naya netas come from this group. Upper and middle caste persons are underrepresented, and scheduled and backward caste persons are overrepresented, insofar as naya netas are concerned. The bonds between caste and the new leadership are loose and unpredictable insofar as the emergence and influence of particular naya netas is concerned.

The bonds between naya netas and political parties are also weak. Party alliances are a matter of expediency in these villages. Even as they engage in regular transactions with political parties and government officials, naya netas are not bound to any particular party politician. One never knows when a naya neta might not be willing to cross party lines.

Just as naya netas are not always bound to any particular political party, ordinary villagers do not have to be bound to any individual naya neta. They can choose to utilize the services and join the support group of some particular naya neta, and they may choose alternatively to remain aloof or join with another naya neta—or to transact business simultaneously with more than one of them.

Diverse motivations guide the actions and aspirations of naya netas. The great demand for their services gives them positions of influence within their village. However, new leaders cannot easily use their special connections with state agents and market operators to benefit at the expense of ordinary villagers. The spread of education and information among other, especially younger, villagers has given rise to a more widespread capacity for independent action. New leaders who are effective and honest in their dealings attract a sizeable following among their fellow villagers, but villagers are watchful and wary. Alternative naya netas are available in most villages, and any hint of cheating or diminished effectiveness can result in a transfer of allegiance by a majority of villagers.[8]

Leadership exercised in the spirit of service is more likely to create a fund of obligations. New leaders who have political ambitions or who aspire to higher social status are careful not to overcharge villagers for the services they provide. Not all new leaders behave in these laudable ways, but there is a significant percentage—more than half, as I could make out—who are in it for the long haul and who invest in building longer-term relationships at the grassroots. They acquire status and respect in their village by working seemingly selflessly on behalf of their neighbors—and status and respect are important motivations for people who hail mostly from quite humble origins. The hope

---

8. I have written elsewhere in greater detail about naya netas in north India. Others have written about their activities in different parts of India. See Krishna (2002, 2003, 2007, 2010). See also Jeffrey, Jeffery, and Jeffery (2008); Manor (2000); Mitra (1991); and Reddy and Haragopal (1985).

of acquiring high political position in the future also acts as an incentive. One naya neta recalled: "I have been working for the villagers for about ten years now. It is hard work. People come in the middle of the night, and I cannot refuse. I take them to the hospital on my motorcycle. I am available to them night and day. I have no time for my family. . . . But it has become my life now. If a day goes by when no one comes to my door, I cannot sit peacefully. I feel unwanted. . . . We get by all right. I have a small salary for the work that I do for the Cooperative Department. I will never be rich . . . but someday I might be MLA [Member of the State Legislative Assembly]. I came close to getting a ticket [party nomination] the last time elections were held."

Their role as intermediaries requires naya netas to remain faithful both to villagers and to government officials. They establish their status and leadership in the village by providing access to welfare benefits, including employment opportunities, to fellow villagers, so they are keen to keep faith with government officials who control this work and who appoint the village supervisor. Officials prefer to keep dealing with those naya netas who have in the past behaved in trustworthy ways, rejecting others whose work has been tardy or sloppy or which has elicited public complaints. Since villagers are free to select which among the newly educated youth they will have as their intermediary, it becomes important for the naya neta to keep faith as well with fellow villagers. Another new leader spoke of how this balance is maintained in practice:

> I was eight years old, and my mother and father were dead. There was very little land in the family, hardly two *bighas* [one-third of a hectare]. My uncle sent me to school for eight years. Then I had to go to work. I started by helping the village *sarpanch* [elected chairperson of the *panchayat*, or local government]. I supervised labor on [government-sponsored] works implemented by the village *panchayat*, and I looked after accounts for these construction projects. I could read and write well, and there were few such persons at that time in the village who were also willing to stand all day in the sun and work with laborers. Then a new NGO project was started in the area for farm forestry. They looked for a person in the village who knew some official procedures, who could work hard, and who was trusted by laboring villagers.
>
> Trust is important. Many times labor is not paid for weeks after the work is done, so they come to work only on the say-so of someone in the village whom they trust and who can compel these agencies to make payments on time. The NGO supervisor saw me laboring day after day in the hot sun. He came to me and he asked me to lead the new project in the village. . . . After that there have been other projects.
>
> We have a team now . . . we all work together. I convince the villagers that the project is sound and that they will be paid fairly, even if the payment is a little delayed. On my guarantee, the village shopkeeper gives *atta* [flour] and other goods to them against future wages. To government officials and NGO

supervisors, I promise a loyal and hardworking labor force. We protect these officials against complaints and inquiries—but they must pay the laborers fully and on time.

Dynamics of Non-state Provision with the Naya Netas

Social welfare programs of many kinds have been introduced from above by the Indian state, and many of these programs, such as those concerned with education, health care, and water supply, have universal eligibility, but not everybody obtains the benefits of these programs equally. Mediation is very often necessary when interacting with service-providing organizations of the Indian state. *Who* helps procure these benefits on behalf of some particular individual or group is a critical question; the nature of the intermediary matters as much as (and often more than) the quantity of benefits written in policy documents.

The rise of the naya netas has made available to poorer citizens a previously missing conduit to the everyday state. Weak formal institutions at the local level have historically helped richer and more powerful citizens leverage their advantages. Thirty years ago, only they could gain entry to the state. Even today, formal institutions at the local level are mostly utilized by better-off villagers. But the emergence of an alternative channel of access has leveled the playing field to a considerable extent. Poorer villagers and others deprived of access to formal institutions rely in large numbers on the services made available by naya netas.

It is helpful to begin this examination by looking at the beliefs that ordinary citizens have regarding their abilities to interact independently and directly, that is, without benefit of any mediation, with the agencies of the democratic state. Surveys that I conducted in rural areas of two Indian states—a northern state (Rajasthan) and a southern one (Andhra Pradesh)—showed how a majority of citizens still find it hard to gain access to organs of the state and how these encounters are usually fraught with feelings of anxiety and marred by low expectations.

A team of field researchers surveyed the opinions of village residents in four districts of Rajasthan and three districts of Andhra Pradesh.[9] These districts are neither the richest nor the poorest ones in these states; each district falls close to the median for its state in terms of diverse socioeconomic indicators.[10] Following a process of random sampling, a total of 1,898 individuals were interviewed (in 1997–98) in Rajasthan, and a total of 1,750 were interviewed

---

9. According to the latest population census, conducted in 2011, the population of Rajasthan was sixty-eight million, of whom 75 percent live in rural areas, and the population of Andhra Pradesh was eighty-five million, of whom 67 percent live in rural areas (http://www.census2011.co.in/).

10. Districts in Rajasthan include Ajmer, Bhilwara, Rajsamand, and Udaipur. Districts in Andhra Pradesh include East Godavari, Khammam, and Nalgonda.

(in 2004–05) in Andhra Pradesh.[11] A battery of pretested survey questions was administered to each of them, related to different aspects of public service provision.

These results show that despite having a great deal of faith in democracy, most citizens have a hard time making connections with public service providers. In response to the following survey question—What do you expect? If you were to make contact with a government official or political leader, will you get a response or will you be ignored?—57 percent of respondents in Rajasthan and 53 percent in Andhra Pradesh believed that they would *not* get a response and would be ignored.

People's past experiences are such that a majority of people in both states— a somewhat higher proportion in Rajasthan than in Andhra Pradesh—expect that their voices will simply go unheard by public officials, including those responsible for service delivery. As a result, relatively few take the trouble to express their demands directly. Responses to other survey questions tend to confirm this impression. As many as 83 percent of respondents in Rajasthan and 89 percent in Andhra Pradesh agreed or strongly agreed with the assertion that "things are run by a powerful few, and ordinary citizens cannot do much about it." Similarly, 79 percent in Rajasthan and 87 percent in Andhra Pradesh agreed or strongly agreed with the view that "people like me do not have any influence over what the government does."

In multiple ways, therefore, a vast majority of people in both states felt that they could do little, if anything, to change the way that things were being run. They expressed such a view despite the fact that in both states they had thrown the incumbent state government out of power at the most recent state elections. Changing ruling parties does little to change political dynamics at and just above the local level.[12]

When more than three-quarters of all residents—selected randomly in villages of two states—expect that their voices will simply go unheard, it becomes important to investigate the sources of this weakness. Previous scholarship provides some important clues. Scholars have found that ordinary people find it hard to engage with service-providing agencies of the state. "The state can and often does appear to people in India as a sovereign entity set apart from

---

11. Villages within each district were selected purposefully in order to have a mix of remotely situated and more central locations. Mixed-caste villages were selected in addition to others where a single caste group is more dominant. Within villages, individuals to interview were selected on the basis of random sampling from the most recent voters' lists. In general, these lists are comprehensive and complete. We did not come across any adult village resident whose name was not included in the voters' lists. Some selected individuals, less than 5 percent in all, were not physically present in their village at the time of the interviewer's visit (and one revisit). These names were replaced by others from a reserve list, also constructed as part of the initial random sample.

12. We have no comparable data from longer-established and better-institutionalized democracies. So it is not possible to claim that these numbers are conclusive of any particular political pathology.

society," state Fuller and Harris (2000, 23). "A local administrative office, a government school, a police station: to enter any of these is to cross the internal boundary into the domain of the state." The state, in turn, finds it difficult to reach out and connect with ordinary citizens or meet their demands. "In contemporary India," as Yadav (1999, 2399) asserts, "the chain that links peoples' needs to their felt desire to their articulated demand to its aggregation and finally to its translation into public policy is impossibly long and notoriously weak."

What is it about these contexts that helps produce despondent democrats, able to participate in electing their governments but unable to have a say in what governments do on an everyday basis? Poverty is an important background feature but it does not seem to be the only cause. Relatively rich and the relatively poor people gave somewhat different responses to the survey questions discussed above, but this difference was no more than a few percentage points. For instance, while 85 percent of the poorest quartile of villagers agreed or strongly agreed with the statement—"Things are run by a powerful few, and ordinary citizens cannot do much about it"—as many as 76 percent of the richest quartile also agreed or strongly agreed. There is very likely something deeper, something more institutionalized, which needs to be examined in greater detail.

How does one explain the paradox of widespread faith in democracy—accompanied by huge electoral turnouts, particularly among poorer citizens (Yadav 2000)—alongside depressingly low expectations about the likely results from a visit to the police station, school board, or public development agency? We feel justifiably elated to observe mass participation and consistently fair elections. Yet in the interim between elections many Indians do not speak and are not heard by officials. They are "citizens only in name [with] few meaningful channels of political participation," as portrayed by Diamond (2008).

Where in rural India does the breakdown in political communication occur? Citizens do not communicate directly with an abstract entity known as "the state." In reality, most political communication is mediated and indirect. Citizens make their voices heard through the mediation of party organizers, lower-level officials, civil society activists, local political entrepreneurs, news reporters, and other providers of mediation services. Their participation is engaged and their protests are organized, not individualistically, every citizen for herself, but usually through the agency of some intermediary. Mediated transactions characterize citizen-state relations in all democratic countries.

How do intermediary institutions fall short in these rural Indian contexts? And how can they be strengthened and service provision be improved, particularly for those who currently most lack voice? Better—and more grounded—responses are required to these key questions. The search for answers is hardly a simple one, even though parts of the literature can be read to suggest that solutions are readily at hand. In practice, one cannot blithely follow the communitarians and start investing in community organizations, nor can one assume that party building will resolve these problems in full.[13]

Different intermediary institutions work well within diverse contexts. They vary considerably in their agendas, their activities, and their influence. How and how effectively do different agencies identify key demands of ordinary people—especially the poor—and then transmit them upward to higher levels? Conversely, how do they help government service providers communicate with people at the grassroots? And what consequences do these actions have in relation to the welfare needs of different segments of village society?

Investigating the Dynamics of Mediation

Two sets of investigations helped provide some initial answers to these questions. The first investigation, which I carried out in Rajasthan, showed how different types of intermediary institutions are consulted at the grassroots for different kinds of interactions with the state. We made inquiries from individual respondents in relation to four different types of priority public services required by residents of these communities.

The first type of public service concerns individuals' dealings with the police, and with the state land administration agency that is responsible for maintaining the official records of land ownership and for regulating transactions in agricultural land. Land is the most important productive asset for people in Indian villages. More than 85 percent of all village residents are fully or in large part dependent on agriculture for their livelihoods. Thus, land administration is a very important public service.

The second type of dealings with higher-level institutions that we examined concerned obtaining a loan from a commercial bank.[14] Bank branches have spread out in rural areas, and particularly since the 1970s a huge expansion of banking activity has occurred. Better-off villagers seek bank loans in order to make improvements to their agricultural land. Less well-off villagers deal with banks for obtaining the subsidized programmatic loans that the Indian government has been making available under its numerous social welfare schemes. In either case, these transactions are not direct. As observed by Weiner (1963, 123) in the early 1960s, and as remains true to this day, some "expeditor is

---

13. For proposals suggesting an enhanced role for community organizations, see, for example, Etzioni (1998); Fung and Wright (2001); and Varshney (2001). For proposals related to party building, see, for example, Huntington (1968) and Kohli (1987).

14. It is mostly public-sector banks that have operations in rural areas of Andhra Pradesh and Rajasthan. They help advance various objectives of state policy, including reaching out to economically weaker sections of rural society and promoting agricultural growth and small business development. In practice, however, obtaining a loan from a bank is not a straightforward mission, especially for older villagers, most of whom are uneducated.

usually involved who may not be a man with any official power, but he is always someone who is familiar with the intricacies of administration."

The third type of dealing about which villagers were asked concerned replacing a poorly performing school teacher, one who frequently does not show
up for work or who pays little attention to his or her duties. The network of
public primary schools is even more widespread than the network of banks.
Apart from the most isolated and thinly populated villages, most others have
a primary school, which is funded by the state government and staffed by
teachers who are employees of the state. Villagers have relatively little control
over what schoolteachers actually do; responsibility for oversight is vested in
a vertical hierarchy of school inspectors. Because oversight is sporadic and
scanty in practice, absentee and otherwise poorly performing schoolteachers
have become the bane of many villages. All but the poorest villagers are keen
to have their children educated. At least through the primary level, more than
85 percent of children in Rajasthan villages attend schools (Krishna 2004).
All of them face, to varying degrees, the problems brought on by nonperform-
ing school teachers (Kremer et al. 2004). To whom do villagers usually turn
for assistance in dealing with this problem? How do they attempt to get their
children's right to a free primary education—promised and paid for by a democratic state—implemented in practice?

The last type of demand considered here relates to wage employment.
This demand is of particular importance for poorer villagers. Seasonal wage
employment in public construction projects makes up nearly 45 percent of
the annual income of poorer villagers (Krishna 2002). In response to demands from below, the Indian state has progressively enlarged its budget for
employment-generating public works, culminating in 2006 with the introduction of a program guaranteeing one hundred employment days each year for
adult members of poorer households as a hedge against destitution. These intentions of policy and statute are carried through in practice by bureaucracies that follow certain procedures for determining eligibility and need. Their
implementation is also influenced, and sometimes undermined, by local elected
officials, landowners, powerful local figures, contractors, and so on. How in
practice is the need of one village or one villager proved to be greater than the
needs of other competitors? Who helps mediate transactions related to these
important public services?

Table 9.1 provides the survey results from all four domains. A similar survey question helped frame the choices posed to the village respondents: Which
type of mediating agent do you turn to when attempting to deal with the concerned state bureaucracy? "No one" was a choice that hardly any respondent
selected, indicating that unmediated transactions, rather than being a norm,
are rare exceptions.

The results in table 9.1 show how formal institutions—that is, the ones
usually studied by political scientists, such as local governments or political
parties—are hardly the most important ones for obtaining public services

TABLE 9.1.
Who helps gain access to the state agency concerned with the following situations? (Rajasthan, 1997–98 data, in %)

	Party representatives	Panchayat leaders	Caste leaders	Naya netas
Dealing with the land administration agency or the police	6	5	20	62
Getting a bank loan	5	7	8	63
Replacing a nonperforming teacher	4	18	11	64
Getting wage employment	4	11	8	70

within these contexts. Only a small minority of villagers consults with party representatives or local governments (*panchayats*). It is not clear that strengthening party organizations or enhancing the role of *panchayats* will necessarily result in improving channels of political communication, particularly for poorer villagers. Another small minority engages with the kinds of caste associations and informal caste networks that are available in such villages.

When they need to make contact with state agencies concerned with any of these four services, the majority of villagers, poorer or richer, prefer, instead, to consult with naya netas, whose mediation on their behalf is expected to have more benefits and fewer costs. Such new grassroots-level leaders tend to flourish where systems of democratic decentralization are weak, and where political parties lack the capacity to penetrate effectively to the local level—which is true in a large majority of Indian states—because these conditions give grassroots leaders room for maneuver (Mitra 1991).

A plethora of social welfare services and poverty reduction programs have been introduced by the Indian state, as mentioned above. Villagers are keen to avail themselves of benefits from these expanding social welfare programs, but they are usually unable or unwilling to deal with state agencies directly on their own account. Because of ignorance or unfamiliarity with the Indian bureaucracy's complex procedures, or for other reasons—including lack of time, shortage of money for travel, unwillingness to suffer humiliation, and lack of faith that any government business can get transacted without some intervention—villagers usually prefer to have agents deal on their behalf with the government machinery. Where these agents are effective, they can help villagers gain larger benefits, individually and collectively, from government departments and market agencies. As one elected official told me: "Many different types of schemes and programs are in operation. If they cannot understand these schemes, then of what use are the leaders? Ordinary villagers do not have the means to know about what benefits exist. Leaders perform these functions [for them] . . . They meet with officials. They [should] know about schemes and programs. They place the villagers' demands before officials and politicians."[15]

Naya netas have stepped into the gap in the middle of the institutional chain that links state leaders with ordinary villagers. Those who succeed in performing these services effectively and honestly acquire prestige and influence at the grassroots—even if they come from traditionally nonelite backgrounds.

Variations in the Dynamics of Mediation

A follow-up investigation, undertaken in villages of Andhra Pradesh seven years later (in 2004–05), showed how different social groups preferred to consult with different types of intermediary agencies. In relation to the same social service, poorer villagers prefer to deal with one type of intermediary, while richer villagers consult with a different type.[16]

A random sample of villagers was interviewed, using a pretested questionnaire. Table 9.2 provides the responses given by the poorest villagers (the bottom three deciles in terms of this index) and by the best-off villagers (the top three deciles) to three survey questions about interactions with different service provision agencies of the state.

Seven alternative responses were offered in relation to each of these survey questions. Six of these choices referred to six types of mediating agencies—including official *panchayats*, informal (or customary) *panchayats* (traditional village councils composed of the hereditary leaders of the different caste groups that live within a particular village) political parties, new leaders (the term used in Andhra Pradesh for naya netas), caste leaders, and an unstated "other" type. Within this unstated "other" were recorded all responses claiming direct (i.e., unmediated) contact with the particular state agency. As before, in the case of Rajasthan, hardly any unmediated transactions were reported. The seventh choice was simply "Cannot do anything in this situation." Considerable differences are visible between the responses of the poorest and the best-off people.

In general, the official *panchayats* and political parties—formal and state-based providers of mediation services—are preferred by richer people in each of the three situations examined. On the other hand, poorer people prefer to consult with new leaders (equivalent to the naya netas whom we saw earlier in the case of Rajasthan) or they expect to receive no assistance from any agency.

---

15. Interview with Vandana Meena, zila pramukh (head of the district-level *panchayat* organization), Udaipur, March 10, 1999.

16. Levels of well-being were calculated using the Stages-of-Progress methodology (Krishna 2004, 2006), which relies upon an asset-based index to compute each household's current material situation. In addition, a community-generated poverty cutoff is also ascertained. Households located above this cutoff were considered as relatively rich, while those located below this cutoff were regarded as relatively poor.

TABLE 9.2.
Intermediaries preferred by richer and poorer individuals (Andhra Pradesh, 2004–05 data)

	Poorest (bottom three deciles)	Best off (top three deciles)
Having one's child admitted to a preferred public school	– New leaders (31%) – "Cannot do anything" (24%) – Caste leaders (17%)	– Official panchayat (37%) – Political party (24%) – Informal panchayat (11%)
Obtaining a bank loan	– "Cannot do anything" (27%) – New leaders (25%) – Caste leaders (22%) – Political party (8%)	– Official panchayat (41%) – Informal panchayat (21%) – Political party (18%) – New leaders (13%)
Getting a sick relative admitted to a public hospital	– New leaders (31%) – "Cannot do anything" (24%) – Informal panchayat (16%) – Official panchayat (11%)	– Official panchayat (44%) – Political party (38%) – Caste leaders (13%)

Note: Only responses given by at least 10 percent of respondents within each category (poorest and best off) are reported.

Roughly one-quarter of all poorer people picked the option "Cannot do anything" in each of these three situations.

Consider the first type of interaction examined, namely, gaining admission for one's child to a preferred government-run school. In such situations, a majority of better-off people would expect to have their communications mediated either by the official *panchayats* (37%) or by political parties (24%). The majority of richer people would tend to employ, therefore, formal providers of the types—such as political parties and local government officials—who are better recognized in the political science literature.

On the other hand, the majority of poorer respondents tend to employ forms of mediation services that are both non-state and not so well recognized. Relying either on new leaders (31%) or caste leaders (17%), this group of people, by and large, tends to use informal means. Their political communications with the state are mediated by individuals rather than by institutions. Another 24 percent felt that no means whatsoever would be available to them if they were required to deal with the public school administration.

Access to the state is mediated in nearly all cases. It is mediated by different agencies on behalf of different social groups. In respect of the other two survey questions as well, richer people tended to name official *panchayats* and political parties; poorer people continued to place their faith on more informal and personalized channels.

For instance, in relation to the third type of interaction with a state agency reported in table 9.2—getting a sick relative admitted to a public hospital, supposedly a matter of right, involving a free public service in much of India, including Andhra Pradesh and Rajasthan—hardly any villager felt it prudent to approach the hospital staff without availing themselves of the services of a state or non-state provider of mediation services. Once again, different types of providers are preferred by relatively rich and relatively poor individuals. A total of 44 percent of richer individuals preferred to contact *panchayat* leaders for these purposes, and another 38 percent of richer people stated that they would seek the mediation of political party officials, making for a total of 82 percent of richer individuals. Poorer people preferred, instead, to work with an entirely different set of mediating agents. Among the poorer group, 31 percent preferred to seek mediation from new leaders, another 16 percent mentioned informal *panchayats*, and 24 percent expected to be entirely helpless in such a situation.

Differences in the nature of mediation providers consulted by richer and poorer village residents were equally visible in the second type of interactions examined in table 9.2, involving a bank loan. In this case, as well as in the other two, richer villagers tended, by and large, to rely on formal and state-based channels of mediation, including official *panchayats* and party leaders, while poorer ones tended to prefer informal, non-state providers.

It would appear, therefore, that the formal channels currently in existence appear to work relatively better for richer people. The strengthening of *panchayats* has tended, with some important exceptions, to serve prosperous groups better than their poor and lower-status neighbors.

In terms of the agencies on which they rely for gaining access to the kinds of public services promised to all by a democratic state, poorer people still expect to seek help from more shadowy entities, shadowy at least in relation to the academic literature and policy pronouncements, which barely recognize the existence of these non-state providers or which refer to these agencies in disparaging terms.[17]

Conclusion: Consequences for Political Participation and Local Institution Development

Diamond (2008, 39) states that "for democratic structures to endure—and to be worthy of endurance—they must listen to their citizens' voices, engage their participation, tolerate their protests, protect their freedoms, and respond to their needs. For a country to be democracy, it must have more than regular, multiparty elections." It must, in addition, have strong channels of political communication at the grassroots. Where these channels are weak, democracy itself is made feebler; its durability is brought into question; indeed, its democratic-ness is in doubt—for if a majority of citizens do not have access

---

17. For instance, as Ananthpur and Moore (2007, 11–12) report, "social scientists who have conducted research in rural India . . . generally seem not to have appreciated how widespread, active and important [informal *panchayats*] are. Insofar as India's mass media have paid any attention, this has been to report the occasional scandal or atrocity for which [informal *panchayats*] are held responsible."

to reliable channels of political communication, then how will their voices be heard, their freedoms protected and their needs met?

Observing the large and important roles that naya netas currently play in rural India simply helps underscore the vast need that exists for strengthening institutional links in the middle. Institutions at the macro-national level have been given a great deal of consideration, and more recently institutional designs for the global and international levels are being scrutinized. Impressive work investigating local institutions has also been undertaken. Additionally, the sinews of democracy and development—the institutional channels in the middle that connect ordinary citizens with social service providers and with markets—need to become much better understood.

Which types of intermediate institutions are most suitable in any particular context requires careful empirical investigation and cannot be assumed. Studies of democracy have identified different types of intermediary institutions. Some analysts expect political parties to perform the task of mediating between citizens and the state (e.g., Huntington 1968; Kohli 1987). In many new democracies, such as India, however, political parties are quite weakly organized, do not penetrate effectively to lower levels, have little or no presence at the grassroots, and may not provide much support for the tasks of interest articulation, demand representation, and political communication (Kohli 1990; Krishna 2002). Civil society organizations and local governments have been proposed as alternative bridging mechanisms between poor communities and the state.[18] But the reach of such organizations, that is, the number of people with whom they interact, tends to be quite limited, even in developing countries that have a long tradition of civil society organization. Local (or municipal) governments have been mentioned in yet other studies,[19] but does decentralization, pursued in certain ways, actually help to enhance poor people's abilities to engage with democracy and improve social service provision—or does it, as in the Indian case discussed in this chapter, serve the needs more of richer rather than poorer citizens? Interest groups, residential organizations, producer associations, labor unions, and ethnic and religious groupings have also been suggested as contextually effective channels of political communication.[20]

But which among these different agencies helps make democracy more real and social services more easily accessible in any given context, and which population segments are better served by different intermediary types? Reliable

---

18. The general case is presented by, for example, Etzioni (1998); Fung and Wright (2001); and Putnam, Leonard, and Nanetti (1993). For the Indian context, see, for example, Satterthwaite (2006) and Varshney (2001).

19. These and other arguments for (and against) decentralization have been presented by, among others, Blair (2000); Crook and Manor (1998); Fox (1990); Manor (1999); Schönwälder (1997); Smith (1985); and Smoke and Lewis (1996).

20. See, for example, Heller (2001); Posner (2005); and Rueschmeyer, Stephens, and Stephens (1992).

answers to these questions are not as yet available, but they need to be developed if the system is to be made more democratic, just, and inclusive. Developing countries across the world are being exposed differentially to the same kinds of influences—rising urbanization and commercialization, increasing literacy, and a greater push toward decentralization, often at the behest of international funders. Yet, institutional deficiencies nevertheless continue to result in the exclusion of most poor people from wider access to channels for expressing demands and asserting rights within the economic, social, and political domains (Vilas 1997; World Bank 2006).

Through undertaking comparative field investigations in two states of India—with different levels of socioeconomic development—this chapter provides some initial answers to these questions, finding that naya netas, a homegrown product, provide for most people, especially poorer ones, in the contexts examined above their best available source of mediation services. Democracy and social welfare are made more real for the majority of these citizens because of what naya netas do. Diverse governance outcomes, including especially voice and accountability, service provision, and the rule of law, have been improved largely because of their services. Observing these effects of social and economic changes on local institutional development across states in India allows us to begin to understand how these trends might play out elsewhere.

Research efforts such as the ones reported on in this chapter need to be more widely undertaken. Examining what exists—and what is lacking—at the grassroots is an essential first step. In order for democracy to become more widely practiced and valued, intermediary institutions need to be made stronger and easier to access. Multiple types of intermediary institutions may be required simultaneously in particular contexts. It is quite possible, as we have observed in the case of India, that different population segments will prefer separate types of intermediaries.

Part II

The Politics of Non-state Social Welfare in Emerging Markets and the Industrialized World

10

Private Provision with Public Funding

The Challenges of Regulating Quasi Markets in Chilean Education

Alejandra Mizala and Ben Ross Schneider

Chile is one of the few countries in the world, and the only developing country, with a national voucher system for funding primary and secondary education. The central government allocates funding to schools—private or public—based on the number of students enrolled. The military dictatorship of Augusto Pinochet, inspired by Milton Friedman and neoliberal Chicago economics, created the voucher system in 1981. Center-Left governments after 1990 consolidated it. Over the decades students have gradually but steadily migrated from public to private schools. By 2009, around half of Chilean students were in publicly funded but privately owned and managed schools.

Non-state provision of education in Chile created new policy challenges and new stakeholders in the policy process. The challenges in Chile revolved largely around issues of optimal regulation, information, teacher incentives, and equality. The new actors were of course the private providers, but the existence of non-state provision also reshaped relations with and between other stakeholders, especially the teachers' union. Although many of the challenges and stakeholders would be common to all types of educational systems with substantial non-state provision, the particular constellation of partisan contention and the contested legacy of the Pinochet dictatorship (1973–90) also shaped the dynamics of policymaking.

We are grateful to the Tinker Foundation for support and to Melani Cammett and Lauren MacLean for comments on previous versions Alejandra Mizala is also grateful to Fondecyt (project No 1100308) and PIA-CONICYT (project CIE-05).

Ironically, even in this market decentralized system, the major stakeholders—parents, teachers, and politicians—continued to hold the central government responsible for educational outcomes. The reforms of the 1980s did, as policymakers hoped, decentralize a lot of day to day management to private schools. However, the central government maintained control over many other aspects of education policy including curriculum, teacher salaries in public schools, and of course the value of the voucher. Moreover, governments after the 1990s enacted a range of new policies designed to correct market failures and push other goals such as equity. Lastly, in part in response to this central government activism, local communities and governments did not mobilize to participate more actively at the local level. The active engagement of the central government also resulted in a significant investment in state capacity to regulate education through hiring more personnel and extending the ability of the Ministry of Education to collect and process information and use it to inform ongoing planning and public debate.

Despite its peculiarities, an analysis of the Chilean experience opens a revealing window for understanding non-state provision of education more generally. Chile is in the vanguard of privatizing the provision of education. Many countries in Latin America and elsewhere are moving in Chile's direction and have enacted reforms to expand private provision. Such measures have taken many forms, from private curriculum provision, to expanded subsidies to private schools, to charter schools (see Patrinos, Barrera-Osorio, and Guáqueta 2009, chap. 1). These shifts, even if marginal now, strengthen new stakeholders and shift relations among existing ones, as well as create new regulatory challenges similar to those confronted in Chile.

As a radical, sweeping, and now long-standing educational reform, the Chilean voucher system has justifiably generated a great deal of scholarly interest and research, both in Chile and internationally.[1] Most of this research has focused on issues of quality and equality, and in general there is consensus on both issues: that the voucher system has not of its own produced noticeably higher quality nor has it reduced inequality. Our purpose is not to enter into the debate on the causes of these outcomes, but rather to register that quality and equality continue to be, as they are in most countries, core challenges for educational policy, and to concentrate our attention on how the existence of private provision of education affects the policy process in ongoing efforts to reform and regulate the system.

Our overall goal is to analyze the dynamics of governance in a market-decentralized, non-state provision of education. Along the way, we make several more specific arguments on the workings of the Chilean system that may also apply to other decentralized market systems. In principle, market systems

---

1. See, among others, Cox (2003); Mizala and Romaguera (2000, 2005a), Mizala (2007); Hsieh and Urquiola (2006).

are designed to introduce non-state, uncoordinated pressures to improve quality, as families move from bad to good schools. In practice, in Chile, markets have not always fulfilled this promise, and government reformers have intervened in multiple ways to correct perceived market failures especially in terms of quality and equity. Voucher systems also create new stakeholders in the form of private school owners (supported by parents of children in them), which at a minimum complicates coalition building to promote reforms and in some instances establishes new veto players. Lastly, decentralized systems are generally supposed to shift political debate and mobilization away from central governments. This was not at all the case in Chile where stakeholders continued to mobilize to influence the central government.

In this chapter we first lay out the conceptual framework, describing three types of education systems—centralized, decentralized public, and decentralized private—and identifying the major stakeholders involved in education politics. We examine the general challenges that policymakers face in efforts to promote access, quality, and equality. We then turn to the case of private decentralized education in Chile to examine some of the policy reforms implemented since 1990, especially efforts to promote equality, teacher motivation, and effective use of information.

Conceptual Framework

Most educational systems can be categorized in three ideal types, which vary largely by their degree of policy centralization and type of ownership. A first common type is public and centralized. Primary responsibility for funding, curriculum, performance, and labor relations is centralized in national ministries or central educational agencies. Some countries that approximate this centralized type include France, other countries of southern Europe, and much of Latin America. A second ideal type is public but decentralized to the provincial or local level. In this type, provincial or municipal governments, or school districts, hold primary responsibility for funding, curriculum, hiring, and so forth. Examples include urban school districts in the United States, or provincial level control of school systems in Brazil and Argentina. A third model is also decentralized, but more market oriented, less hierarchical, and includes private schools. In voucher systems, the primary responsibility for funding is public, but schools or local districts are responsible for salaries, curriculum, and hiring. In addition, families are free to switch schools, and private schools can enter the market and compete for students.[2] Charter schools also operate

---

2. Most countries also have some purely private schools but for a minority of students from wealthier families. In the Americas, both North and South, the share of private schools with private funding is usually between 10 and 20 percent and in Chile it is around 6–7 percent.

on the same principles of publicly funded private provision, but they usually account for a minority of enrollments.[3]

These are ideal types. In practice, most countries have a predominant tendency, but also at least some mix of public and private providers, and centralized and decentralized administration. In some cases, some levels of schools may be centralized (e.g., secondary schools) while other levels are decentralized. And, some dimensions of school administration may be centralized (curriculum especially is often national) while other aspects are left to local authorities. Lastly, financing of decentralized systems is often a mix of local and central funding. However, it is still useful to distinguish among these ideal types, and empirical cases that approximate them, because the stakeholders and challenges of education can vary substantially across the three types. We turn first to the stakeholders.[4]

Government ministries. Most policy change in education starts with the executive branch of government, especially the Ministry of Education or decentralized equivalents such as provincial or municipal education departments. Ministry preferences can range across the goals of quantity, quality, and equality, depending on the incumbents. However, if electoral benefits are important, then ministry goals will tend toward quantity and equality and away from quality, because the political returns are higher in the former and political costs higher in the latter. For the same reason, ministries will tend to implement nonconflictive policies, such as those that increase educational inputs, instead of conflictive policies, such as those that affect specific actors (e.g., teacher evaluations) (see Stein et al. 2005). The interests of some ministry personnel may also be less programmatic and more clientelist. With their large budgets, even in more decentralized systems education agencies often attract politicians seeking appointments to top positions. Within the executive, the Ministry of Finance is usually involved in any major educational policies because education is a significant portion of total spending. The interests of officials in the Ministry of Finance are easier to predict: to keep spending under control.

Parties and politicians. Despite regular debate in electoral campaigns, political parties are often not major initiators of policy change, though they are crucial actors if policies have to be passed into law in Congress or parliament. Individual politicians may have especially close connections to, and dependence on, education either from strong ties to teachers' unions or from meddling in education spending for clientelist purposes (Kaufman and Nelson

---

3. See Patrinos, Barrera-Osorio, and Guáqueta (2009) for an extended discussion of the full range of public-private partnerships in education.

4. Kaufman and Nelson (2004b) provide a similar list though with special reference to reform politics.

2004b). In Chile, prominent think tanks affiliated with the two major party alliances enhance more sustained engagement by parties in partisan debates about education while also infusing more technical arguments into political contention.

Teachers' unions.[5] Teachers in all three models tend to be better organized than many workers in other sectors of the economy, and are usually pivotal, sometimes determinant, actors in policy change. Beyond their significant labor market strength and capacity for very disruptive strikes, teachers' unions usually have leverage in party and electoral politics because of their large numbers, wide geographic distribution, and embeddedness in local communities. Teachers' unions have strong preferences in most policy areas, but they are most intense when the policy affects salaries, employment stability, working conditions, and labor relations.

School directors or principals. Although rarely organized as a group to negotiate salaries or lobby, they are central stakeholders. They represent local management and can be crucial intermediaries among parents, teachers, and governments. Their interests are difficult to specify because they vary with the context, but generally school directors seek to maintain autonomy and discretion, and may therefore resist policies that seek to centralize information or control over teacher incentives.

Parents. Families are the major consumers of education. Although they are rarely organized in large groups, they may be significant actors in decentralized school systems. Their interests are mostly in easy access to education and, for smaller groups of parents, higher quality and greater equality. Despite the fact that parents should have the most intense interests in education policy, there are several reasons to expect little involvement in Latin America (Grindle 2004, 198). Besides the generic problems of collective action among such a large, diverse, and dispersed group, parents in Latin America also profess high satisfaction with their education systems (Lora 2008), even if they regularly come out poorly ranked in international testing, and are therefore less likely to mobilize to press for change. When active, parents can exert influence through elections (the long route of accountability [World Bank 2004b]) or directly on teachers, school directors, and local administrators (the short route of accountability).

Students. Students of course have the biggest stake in the educational system, yet they are rarely politically active in secondary school because they

---

5. There is a large literature on teachers' unions in Latin America. See, for example, Vaillant (2005) and Grindle (2004).

are young and dispersed. Chile witnessed a major exception in 2006 with the revolt of the "penguins" (students wear dark uniforms with white shirts). Secondary students took to the streets and shut down schools demanding, among other things, improvements in the quality of education. University students led the massive demonstrations of 2011 that focused largely on tertiary education, but secondary students joined the demonstrations and occupied schools with their own set of grievances and demands.

Private school owners. Private schools are prominent stakeholders in nearly all school systems. Although they usually account for a small minority of total enrollments, several factors boost their political weight. Collective action is usually easier because their numbers are small and their interests relatively homogeneous. Moreover, they cater to the political and economic elite and can usually count on influential people among their families and alumni networks. Lastly, private schools are often backed by religious authorities, mainly the Catholic Church in Latin America. In Chile, in addition to these factors, private schools now account for more than half of enrollments. The core interests of school owners, like most businesses, are in autonomy, regulatory stability, and more resources.[6] As potential additional veto players, private school associations can slow change and become a force for continuity.

Policy networks are also often crucial to education policymaking, especially for innovative and reform policies. These networks do not qualify as stakeholders because they lack formal organization, ideological coherence, and consensus, and a real stake in the education system. However, the origins of many policies can be traced back to these networks and their sometimes obscure or neglected commissions and committees.[7] In Chile, the policy network includes numerous economists and social scientists who combine careers that include stints as academics, think tank researchers, government officials, party advisers, and general public intellectuals.

Other actors, such as other NGOs, other government ministries, independent think tanks, the press, or local community groups, may occasionally appear in the mix of education policymaking.[8] However, these groups are not as central or as regular participants as those listed above. One surprising omission from the list is business (outside the education sector). In fact in some other regions business does mobilize to participate in education policy, as one would

6. Interview with Rodrigo Bosch; see appendix B for further information.
7. See Grindle 2004, chap. 4 on "design teams."
8. The Presidential Advisory Council on the Quality of Education in 2006 gives a sense of the broad range of stakeholders in Chilean education. The Council included parents' associations (2 members), other NGOs and think tanks (7), teachers' unions and other unions (9), municipal government (6), central government (2), Congress (2), student associations (15), academics (16), university rectors (10), private education providers (7), religious institutions (4), and indigenous peoples (3).

expect given that it depends on the education system for a supply of skilled workers. However, in Latin America business has rarely been a conspicuous actor in education policymaking (Kaufman and Nelson 2004b; Schneider and Soskice 2009; and interview with José Pablo Arellano).

All education systems face some common challenges and dilemmas in education policy, including the overall mix of results they promote (achievement and equality), mechanisms for managing information and motivating teachers, instruments for policy intervention (regulation and incentives), reconciling empirical mixes of market, hierarchy, and decentralization, and coordinating the politics of the major stakeholders. Among overall goals, policymakers balance quantity, quality, and equality. When education is not widely available, increasing quantity is often a top priority as well as being politically congenial and positive-sum, as all major stakeholders gain from building schools, hiring teachers, and giving families more access to education. Promoting quality and equality are more complicated, contentious, and therefore politically costly, goals.

Once goals are fixed, policymakers confront other challenges, especially the interrelated problems of information asymmetry, principal-agent dilemmas, and systemic coherence. As large, society-wide organizations with thousands or millions of dispersed providers and consumers, education systems always present severe problems of information asymmetry, because it is difficult for any of the multiple principals (government, families, and directors) to know exactly what transpires with their agents (teachers) in the classroom. Centralized systems may have the hardest time getting reliable information from dispersed agents to central policymakers, though they may also compensate by developing the most bureaucratic capacity to gather information. Market systems rely more on competition to generate information on quality. In principle, the exit of students from schools should be sufficient to signal to policymakers where problem schools are. Many recent educational reforms in both developed and developing countries have created systems for evaluating school and teacher performance, which becomes a huge exercise in generating new information about what happens in the classroom as well as the staff and agencies to process it.

For a competitive voucher system to encourage quality, parents first need to be fully informed about school quality (Patrinos, Barrera-Osorio, and Guáqueta. 2009, 51–53). Well-informed parents can exercise greater control over schooling decisions, demand quality from the schools, or, if the school does not respond, eventually transfer their children to different schools. In this sense, information on the quality of educational institutions may be considered a public good. To be effective, this information should be comparable across institutions, easy to understand, timely, and accurate. With a greater proportion of well-informed education consumers, the education market will function more efficiently. Indeed, the success of market-based education reforms depends on whether this information exists, and the extent to which parents use the information and make informed decisions over the range of school options that are available.

General principal-agent problems complicate educational policies in all models because the delivery of education depends on thousands of dispersed staff and teachers. Even decentralized systems have principal-agent issues because policies start with local authorities but are implemented by administrators, school directors, and teachers. A core policy issue in all educational systems is designing careers and pay schemes to align the interests of teachers with policy goals.

Overall incentive structures can be relatively clear in pure hierarchical or market models, but in practice most existing educational systems combine some elements of each system. Schools in the United States are mostly decentralized to the municipal levels but get important resources from the state and federal governments. Chile has a mostly market-oriented model financed by vouchers, but the national government controls curriculum and teacher salaries in public schools. So, within hybrid or mixed systems another policy challenge is to find measures that make systems and incentives within them more coherent.

Once policymakers have decided on goals, they also have to select the most appropriate policy instruments, in particular to choose between more hierarchical regulation (what is permitted and not permitted) and more market-like incentives (resources to reward particular behaviors), or both carrots and sticks. Lastly, although this may in fact be the starting point for many reform discussions, policymakers consider the reactions expected from various stakeholders, and may adjust policies accordingly. Compared to other policy areas, the stakeholders in education are more numerous and therefore electorally consequential, and some are well organized and vocal, so anticipated reactions may figure more centrally when policymakers weigh policy options.

Regulating Vouchers and Market-Decentralized Education in Chile

The Origins of the Voucher System

Beginning in the early 1980s, in a context of widespread neoliberal reforms undertaken by the military government that came to power in 1973, the Chilean government implemented a universal voucher mechanism and transferred public school management from the central government to municipal governments. The most important component of the reform was a new financing mechanism for public and private schools through a nationwide per-student subsidy (voucher), which allowed families to select the school, private or public, of their choice. Prior to 1980, the administration of the school system had been fully centralized in the Ministry of Education. The Ministry of Education established the curricula for the whole educational system and directly administered public schools, appointing school teachers and principals, as well as setting and paying their salaries.

After the 1981 reform, a large number of new private schools willing to take the new vouchers were created, and a massive migration ensued from the public sector to this new type of private school. In 1985 there were 2,643 private voucher schools in Chile, a number that has grown to more than five thousand in recent years. By the late 2000s, private-voucher schools reached almost 50 percent of the enrollment, at the expense of the public sector, where enrollment dropped from 78 percent in 1981 to less than 50 percent. Enrollment in private, nonvoucher schools has been largely unaffected by the reform; they consistently account for around 7 percent of total enrollment. The privately provided sector (voucher and fee-paying) includes both secular and religious schools, the latter supported by the Catholic Church or some other religious group. Fee-paying private schools are generally for profit, whereas private voucher schools may or may not be. Nonprofit private schools include church schools and those dependent on foundations or private corporations, some of which are linked to sectors of industry.

The Dynamics of the Chilean Voucher System

The Center-Left democratic Concertación coalition (Concertación de Partidos por la Democracia), which was in power from 1990 until 2010, maintained the same voucher system. Nonetheless, reformers in Concertación governments were very active and creative in implementing a range of policies designed to tackle nearly all the goals and challenges identified earlier. Among these a few stand out as especially central in regulating Chile's decentralized private model: information, equality, teacher incentives, and coherence and tensions among policies. These were areas that drew policymakers' attention and generated heated public debate. These are also areas that raise questions for theoretical and comparative analysis of how private decentralized systems function and how they shift patterns of policymaking.

Information on schools' performance is essential to the basic functioning of decentralized market systems. Yet despite the pivotal role of information in voucher systems, Chilean parents actually had access to very limited information through the first fifteen years the system was in place. Nationwide student testing began in 1988 with SIMCE (Sistema de Mediación de la Calidad de la Educación, Educational Quality Measurement System), but the government did not make the test results publicly available. It was only in 1995, in response to pressure by educational researchers (part of the policy network) and the right-wing opposition coalition in Congress, that the government started publishing SIMCE results for schools. Parents and families were surprisingly absent in pressuring the government for information.

However, some research suggests that parents do not make much use of even the minimal information available.[9] Elacqua, Schneider, and Buckley (2006) use a survey about school search behavior of parents in the Metropolitan Region of Santiago of the country and conclude that parents are not well informed, and they choose schools mostly for practical reasons such as how far from home the school is. These authors also find that the quality of the information sources and networks are related more to parental socioeconomic background than to the institutional factors of the education system. In contrast, Gallego and Hernando (2008) working with data for 2002 on fourth graders in the Metropolitan Region of Santiago find that the variables that have the greatest impact on parents' choices are student performance in standardized achievement tests and school proximity. However, they find significant heterogeneity in parents' preferences; richer parents place greater value on schools' academic results and tend to travel more kilometers to the school. Moreover, Mizala and Urquiola (2013) do not find systematic evidence that the information on school effectiveness (which may or may not be correlated with absolute measures of their standardized achievement test) has an impact on schools' market outcomes.

Overall, the Chilean experience with information on school quality demonstrates a range of market failures both in generating and disseminating information and, on the parent side, in using the information available. For advocates of quasi markets in education it is clearly not enough to create a voucher system and walk away. In Chile, the government had to intervene, under outside pressure, to improve the collection and dissemination of information. Thus the central information costs in a decentralized market system remain high, probably as high as in centralized systems (though without the additional cost of disseminating information to families).

The fact that parents do not seem to be investing much in collecting and using data on school performance is a serious problem in Chile, and a major challenge to theoretical arguments on the benefits of quasi markets in social services. It is also another indicator of the general absence of parents as important stakeholders and protagonists in the Chilean educational system. There are few parents' associations, and they are not active in national debates. In one region-wide survey, 23 percent of Chilean parents said they participated in school meetings, which put Chile in the lower half of the rankings for all the countries of Latin America (Cruz 2009, 1). In general, parents seem to be happy with their children's schools, though they have a more negative view of the educational system overall. In a 2010 survey in Chile, 83 percent of parents

---

9. Despite efforts to get more information into the public domain, the information available to parents in the late 2000s was still minimal and insufficient. The main information on quality is each school's average scores on the SIMCE tests. However, these averages mask important differences among schools. Moreover, school quality is more than student performance on standardized national assessments, and for this reason other information, such as the proportion of students who go on to pursue further studies, would provide crucial additional information for parents.

thought their children's schools were good, and another 12 percent said they were average (*"regular"*). However, only 46 percent of parents deemed the overall educational system as good, 36 percent said average, and 18 percent bad (Consultora Mori Survey on the Educational System, January 2010). This decentralized complacency and passivity may be reinforced by the continuing centralization of curriculum and, in public schools, of pay and personnel policies, which means there is little local parent associations could do to impact schools. At the same time, the greater dissatisfaction with the education system overall likely plays into strategies of parties and electoral candidates to invest in promoting new educational reforms.

Despite some initial optimism that a voucher system might help poor students by allowing them to switch to better schools, subsequent research has made clear that markets alone do not overcome deep-rooted inequalities. Standardized test scores vary widely across socioeconomic groups; students from low socioeconomic backgrounds have substantially lower test scores than do students from more privileged backgrounds (see table 10.1).

Poorer students require additional resources and attention to achieve better educational outcomes. Yet, through 2008 in Chile the amount of the student-based subsidy or voucher was equal for all students, regardless of the student's socioeconomic status. The problem is that a flat voucher led to significant differences in educational results and encouraged schools to select their student body by discriminating against poorer students.[10]

With the purpose of solving this design problem of the voucher system, in 2008 the Chilean Congress approved a law that created a differentiated, "preferential" voucher for students from poorer families in order to allocate more resources to those schools that educate low-income students. For students from the poorest families attending elementary schools (prekindergarten through eighth grade of basic education), the preferential voucher is worth 1.5 times the standard voucher. This differentiated voucher is also designed to discourage discrimination against low income students and help them to move to better schools, thus contributing to greater social integration and allowing access to potentially positive peer effects (see Hoxby 2000). The law also establishes certain regulatory conditions (accountability) for schools in order to accept students with preferential vouchers. Most important among the conditions, schools have to commit not to discriminate in selecting students.

The debates on this law in Congress highlighted the wide diversity of contending political views among different actors and stakeholders, as well as the threats stakeholders perceived with respect to the new law. One position, which we can consider pro voucher, shared by many in government and the

---

10. See Epple and Romano (2008). Countries such as the Netherlands and Colombia introduced differential vouchers to compensate for socioeconomic inequalities among students. In addition, government regulators of voucher systems in the Netherlands and Sweden expressly prohibit student selection by schools: Kloprogge (2003) and Levin and Belfield (2003).

TABLE 10.1.
SIMCE test results by type of school and students' socioeconomic status in Chile

Socioeconomic Groups	4th grade elementary education, 2008			8th grade elementary education, 2007			10th grade secondary education, 2008		
	Municipal/Public	Private-Voucher	Private Paid	Municipal/Public	Private-Voucher	Private Paid	Municipal/Public	Private-Voucher	Private Paid
Language test									
Low	242*	234	–	233*	225	–	224	225	–
Medium low	242	243	–	235	238	–	236	243*	–
Medium	255	263*	–	246	258*	–	271*	262	–
Medium high	276	282*	–	292*	277	–	314*	285	–
High	–	295	304*	–	299	301	–	306	307
Total	247	267	304	241	260	299	242	258	306
Math test									
Low	222*	209	–	234*	224	–	209	212	–
Medium low	226	226	–	236	240	–	223	235*	–
Medium	241	249*	–	248	260*	–	267*	259	–
Medium high	266	273*	–	299*	281	–	330*	292	–
High	–	289	302*	–	308	314*	–	320	325*
Total	231	254	301	242	263	312	231	254	323

Source: Education Ministry.
*This school type obtains a SIMCE score higher than the other school types in the same socioeconomic group.

policy network, favored keeping the voucher system but reforming it by correcting the original design flaw and adding an explicit equity component. Another position, pushed most strongly by the Colegio de Profesores, the national teachers' union, and supporters on the left, argued that the voucher system itself was the main source of educational inequities and social segmentation of the country. Therefore, they proposed an alternative policy that would provide more resources directly to schools attended by low-income students, most of which were public, instead of increasing the value of the voucher for poor students. This position implied a significant change of policy from a demand-side subsidy (through the voucher) to a supply-side subsidy (directly to the school).

A different line of criticism came from Libertad y Desarrollo, a think tank linked with the right-wing party Unión Demócrata Independiente, and the associations of private schools, CONACEP and FIDE.[11] Although some in this group supported the general idea of differentiated vouchers, they all criticized the law because it introduced accountability into the educational system and excessive intervention into the schools, and generally undermined school autonomy, the main principle defended by these associations.[12] Despite these criticisms the government of Michelle Bachelet (who served from 2006 to 2010) was able to pass the law creating the preferential voucher, but the debate revealed how far apart the policy preferences were among the major stakeholders, even at this late date in the evolution of Chile's voucher system.

In principle, a decentralized, market system leaves issues of the hiring, training, salaries, incentives, and working conditions of teachers up to markets and leaves decisions largely to school directors. This is mostly the case in private schools in Chile. However, the delicate politics of the transition to democracy in 1990 produced legislation that recentralized labor relations in public municipal schools. More specifically, the Colegio de Profesores pressed the newly elected Center-Left Concertación government to reverse the decentralized system created during the Pinochet dictatorship and return teachers to the civil service status they enjoyed before the dictatorship. The Concertación government did not reverse decentralization or the voucher system, but it did try to accommodate some other demands through a new Teacher Statute that, among other things, granted public school teachers tenure and centralized wage negotiations. This episode is a good example of how political mobilization by

---

11. CONACEP (Colegios Particulares de Chile) is a newer organization established in 1983 primarily for private voucher schools. Its 840 affiliated schools account for a quarter of private enrollment (http://www.conacep.cl/). CONACEP is mostly secular, but around 25 percent of its members are religious and some of them also belong to FIDE (interview Rodrigo Bosch). FIDE (Federación de Instituciones de Educación Particular) was founded earlier in 1948 as an association of Catholic schools. In the 1960s FIDE opened its membership to non-Catholic schools. It now has 731 member schools of which 497 are Catholic, 230 secular, and four from other religions (interview Carlos Veas). FIDE has additional influence in policy circles due to the implicit backing of the Church (interviews with Carlos Veas and Mariana Alywin).

12. Interviews with Rodrigo Bosch and Carlos Veas.

powerful stakeholders can introduce complications into purer models, in this instance centralized labor relations in a decentralized voucher system. Once the Teacher Statute was enacted, however, subsequent governments pursued reforms to make it less rigid and to introduce teacher's incentives that were more market compatible. We return to general problems of institutional coherence at the end of this section.

In part to make the Teacher Statute less rigid, subsequent Concertación governments made important reforms to teacher incentives by introducing first collective and then individual evaluations and bonuses (see appendix A). The first collective incentive was the SNED enacted in 1996 (Sistema Nacional de Evaluación del Desempeño de los Establecimientos Educacionales, or National System for Schools' Performance Evaluation). Its aim was to reward teachers' performance and to improve their motivation. Schools with excellent performance are chosen every two years and receive a collective bonus as an incentive. In the 2000s governments introduced additional individual incentive schemes that further differentiated salaries.

All these salary innovations linking pay to teachers' performance have been agreed on in the context of salary negotiations between the Ministry of Education (subject to approval by the Ministry of Finance) and the Colegio de Profesores. As is common in most countries, the teachers' union in Chile initially opposed incentives each time that government reformers introduced them. In principle, of course, differentiated incentives reduce the ability of a union to bargain effectively, and ultimately can lead to member defections as unions lose relevance relative to incentives in determining individual salaries. Nonetheless, two key factors facilitated the introduction of incentive pay over the objections of the teachers' union. First, at the beginning of the 1990s both sides entered negotiations expecting to come to an agreement in part because the political costs of lengthy strikes were very high for both sides, and over time because of the precedent of previous settlements. Second, salaries were increasing rapidly throughout this period (see figure 10.1), so union leaders could get members large increases in base salaries and acquiesce to government demands to add incentive payments (see Mizala and Schneider 2013).[13]

A final dimension of ongoing reform involves the quest for institutional coherence and the optimal balance between local control and centralized regulation, or between freedom of education and the right of access to a good education. In the current structure of the education system, the Ministry of

---

13. Figure 1 shows a steady real rise in teacher salaries at rates above average salary increases in the economy as a whole. However, it is important to remember that teacher salaries had fallen by a third in the 1980s and only recovered to the levels of 1981 by the mid-1990s. Moreover, by the late 2000s teacher salaries were still slightly below those of professional employees with equivalent education and other characteristics, and slightly below the OECD average of teacher salaries as a percent of GDP per capita (Mizala and Romaguera 2005b, Mizala and Schneider 2013).

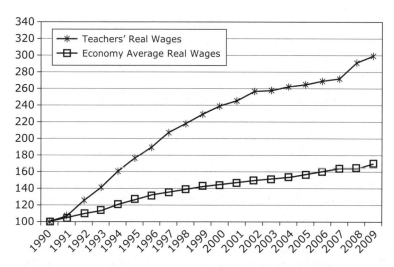

Figure 10.1. Evolution of teachers' salaries in Chile, 1990–2009 (1990 = 100). *Sources:* Ministry of Education, National Institute of Statistics, Central Bank of Chile. Teachers' remuneration includes Minimum Basic National Wage (RBMN) plus allowances (seniority: twenty years, responsibility, training, working in difficult conditions), professional improvement unit, taxable bonus, proportional bonus, performance in National System for Schools' Performance Evaluation (SNED), additional remuneration.

Education is in charge of technical-pedagogic issues (including the national curriculum) while the municipalities are responsible for administrative operations. In practice this division of responsibilities means that municipalities assume little responsibility for student learning while the Ministry of Education underestimates problems related to school management (see Traverso 2004). Moreover, in Chile, in spite of the decentralization and voucher reforms, there is relatively low parental participation in school-level decisions. In contrast, in several European and some Latin American countries, governments have transferred authority over school management to parents and communities; school governing boards—composed of a principal, parents, and other representatives of the community—manage publicly financed schools.[14] Chile is lacking one of the key elements of coherence—parental engagement—that is meant to emerge naturally in a decentralized system to improve its performance. Another area with problematic tensions between centralization and decentralization is salary negotiations and labor relations overall. As mentioned earlier, the Teacher Statute approved in 1991 recentralized decisions about contracts and salaries of teachers in public schools. Centralized agreements can raise teacher salaries

---

14. The case of the Netherlands, which since 1917 has had a school choice system similar to Chile, is relevant. The system is decentralized with each school having a school board in charge of complying with highly demanding state regulations (Karsten (1999).

without corresponding increases in enrollments, and therefore vouchers and revenues, creating chronic and structural financial disequilibrium in public municipal education.

The Consequences of Market-Decentralized Education in Chile

Many studies have focused on outcomes of the Chilean voucher system, mainly on issues of quality and equality (see, for example, Torche 2005; Hsie and Urquiola 2006; Mizala and Romaguera 2000; Lara, Mizala, and Repetto 2011; Mizala and Torche 2012). The general consensus is that the Chilean voucher system helped attain universal coverage, but it did not produce noticeably higher quality or equality of access to good-quality education. Moreover, tensions have flared up often in the 2000s between the right to have access to good quality education and freedom of education, understood largely in this instance as the right of the private sector to create schools and manage them as they see fit (in addition to the freedom of parents to choose schools). This debate is linked to the role of the state and the market in education. In fact, there has been a confrontation between those who seek a larger degree of regulation of the educational system and those who see any regulation as a threat to educational freedom.

Demonstrations by secondary students (the revolt of the "penguins") in 2006 generated an urgent need to debate these issues. With this aim President Bachelet established the Presidential Advisory Council on the Quality of Education in 2006. For the first time, all major stakeholders were in the same forum to debate their continuing large differences of opinion (see footnote 7 for a list of groups represented).[15] Since the 1990s, there has been a confrontation among three groups. On the left are those—mostly teachers, students, some members of Center-Left and left-wing political parties—who demand the elimination of the voucher system established under Pinochet and reversing the decentralization of public education; they argue that the outcome of this system is inequitable. In the center are those who agree with mixed (public-private) provision of compulsory education and with the decentralization of public education but advocate greater regulation to promote quality and equity. The composition of the second group is more diffuse, including some researchers in education, some policymakers, some Center and Center-Left politicians. On the right are the associations of private schools (FIDE and CONACEP), right-wing parties, and their think tanks that see more regulation as a threat to the freedom of education, complain about regulations and the cost of complying with them, and favor more markets and autonomy for private voucher schools.

---

15. Note: Alejandra Mizala was a member of this Council, so the analysis here comes from direct participant observation.

In addition to the disputes over trade-offs among freedom of education, regulation, and equality, many on the left flatly reject the idea of allowing for-profit institutions to receive subsidies from the state to provide a public service. This is an ethical position against introducing profits and capitalism into basic state functions. In contrast, the Center and Right groups accept public financing of for-profit schools and argue that for-profit schools expand the range of educational choices for families. For centrist groups, adequate regulation to assure quality and equality is more important than issues of ownership and profits.

These groups and stakeholders spent six months in the Presidential Advisory Council on the Quality of Education debating these and other issues. In the end, a majority agreed that there was an asymmetry between the right to a good quality education and freedom of education, in the sense that access to education was guaranteed but not its quality. This majority also felt that there was a national majority in favor of maintaining the basic market decentralized public-private provision of education. Thus, the Final Report of the Council recommended improving the overall regulation of the system, included a new general law to substitute for the one enacted by the military on its way out of power in 1990, but it contained no wholesale overhaul of the educational system. The lack of a proposal supporting a structural reform of the educational system implied that not all the members signed the report. In December 2006, the members of the "social bloc," which comprised students, teachers, and representatives of parents' associations, rejected the Council's final report. This group demanded, among other things, an end to decentralized education, a prohibition on selection by schools of students, a prohibition on for-profit schools, and greater financing for public over private schools. Overall, the Presidential Advisory Council on the Quality of Education played an important role in airing debate among all stakeholders and in forging a consensus among most groups, especially in the center and on the right on measures needed to improve the regulation of the educational system.

Following the recommendations in the final report, the Bachelet government presented a new General Education Law (Ley General de Educación). It includes many measures designed to regulate the effects of privatization, including the creation of a Quality Assurance Agency to oversee schools' academic performance and a Superintendency to monitor the spending of public resources by the schools. Other provisions of the law established new oversight bodies and set higher standards for persons wanting to open private voucher schools.

Outside government, political parties, students, and the policy network in education, the main political protagonists were the teachers in public schools and the owners of private schools. Both groups were very well organized, respectively, in the Colegio de Profesores and the two private sector associations FIDE and CONACEP. These two stakeholder groups are powerful in nearly all types of educational systems. In Chile, partisan politics and the extension of private, non-state provision shifted the leverage of these two groups. The steady movement of students from the public to the private sector increased both the market power of the private sector as well as the number of voters with children in private schools. However, for the most part private schools did not have to invest a lot in organizing or mobilizing supporters because they had good access to policymakers and strong defenders in the right-wing opposition in Congress. The shift in enrollments to private schools had the opposite impact on the Colegio de Profesores; they lost market power and the number of voters with children in public schools fell. They could, and did, still strike, but strikes were very costly in that they accelerated the movement of students to private schools. Moreover, given the steady increases in salaries, the Colegio de Profesores had a harder time getting parent support—which the union leaders thought essential—for teacher strikes.[16]

A new Chilean student movement began in May 2011 with marches and the occupation of high school and university buildings that lasted for six months. In contrast to the 2006 protest that was led by high school students (and later joined by university students), this time the protests were led by university students (although high school students also actively participated). The demands for reforms of the educational system covered both universities and high schools and included many of the positions of the Left noted in earlier debates. Among other things the demonstrators demanded free public education, quality education across all tiers of the system, the end of for-profit educational institutions, creation of a state agency to ensure quality and transparency in the use of state resources for higher education, and a more affordable and accessible university system as a whole. Overall, the students in the streets wanted to shift from a decentralized, market-driven model to a more centralized and state-financed education system. And, public opinion polls showed large majorities supporting the students.

The demonstrations in 2011 achieved far more than previous protests. In fact, the 2012 budget substantially increased funds for education in general, established new scholarship programs for the bottom 60 percent of the population, and increased funds for student loans to be offered at significantly lower interest rates than before. However, many student demands were not met, so contention and controversy over education policy and governance is unlikely to fade away.

The Chilean experience over the past two decades has been one of nearly constant reform (see appendix A) and continuous debate among most major stakeholders. As is increasingly common around the world, each new government in Chile promised significant reform, but unlike many other governments all four Concertación governments in fact delivered substantial reform. These

---

16. In order to gauge parental support, the Colegio de Profesores would ask parents to keep their children home in the days leading up to the proposed strike date (interview Jorge Pavez).

reform episodes revealed not only very active policymakers and policy networks but also active engagement with many of the core challenges noted at the outset: information asymmetry, equality, and teacher motivation. These reform episodes also revealed the often unexpected challenges of managing a decentralized market system. As with other quasi markets, stakeholders and policymakers worked to resolve problems of market failure (information), powerful centralized interest groups (especially the Colegio de Profesores and the associations of private schools), and regulatory complexity (as in teacher incentives and financing public schools).

Conclusion

One of the expectations of the decentralized, market model was that it would disperse stakeholders and allow them to pursue their interests individually through choice and exit, and thereby take pressure off the central state to provide policy direction. This dispersion and decentralization was clearly not the outcome in Chile, in part because changes after 1990 introduced more centralized elements, especially the regulation of teacher salaries, hiring, and firing in the public sector. Besides salaries and curriculum, the central government passed a long series of significant reforms, showing that overall policy also emanated from the center. So, despite the fact that most children are enrolled in privately owned schools, stakeholders continue to hold the central government responsible for educational outcomes. When students or teachers take to the streets, as they often do, the target of their protests is not their local school district but the national government.

Education has also remained a central political issue because politicians and governments at the national level made it a government or party priority. Moreover, public debate usually held the central government responsible for overall educational outcomes, especially as they related to general strategies to promote a knowledge economy. One of the surprising, and for some disappointing, outcomes was a lack of greater local political and community engagement in education policy. However, this is in part a reflection of the centralization of so many policies at a national level. This disjuncture between intense activity by the national government and national stakeholders versus local inaction also reflects the predominant views in public opinion surveys that show parents to be happy with their local schools but dissatisfied with the overall educational system.

Part of this centralization resulted from the politics of the transition to democracy and the goals of the Center-Left coalition that ruled Chile for two decades after the military left power in 1990. The Concertación acceded to the demands of the teachers' union to recentralize the teaching career and salary determinations. In addition, the Concertación had a goal of increasing teacher salaries and benefits, and expanding education spending overall, which it did in part through increasing the value of the voucher but also through other centralized resource transfers. Moreover, a policy to promote greater equality across regions and socioeconomic groups necessarily begins with centralized redistributive policies.

The combination of these centralizing tendencies with the overall decentralized framework of a voucher system with private providers greatly complicated the generic challenges of institutional coherence and related principal-agent dilemmas. Thus, for example, school directors (superintendants), the primary agents of both parents and the central government, often could not do much to respond to either principal (in the theoretical sense) because their hands were tied by centralized regulation. In more abstract terms, a voucher system is designed to strengthen the "short route" of accountability (from parents directly through schools) but most other elements of the Chilean education system shifted accountability to the long route from parents to politicians to education ministries to schools (see World Bank 2004b). At a minimum, families negotiate a complex mixture of the two routes.

Appendixes

Appendix A
Chronology of Major Policy Changes in Chilean Education

1981. Decentralization of public education to the municipal level. The Pinochet government establishes a voucher-type student-based subsidy that allows students to attend private schools with public funding.

1990. Ley Orgánica Constitucional de Enseñanza (Organic Constitutional Law on Teaching, or LOCE) announced by the Pinochet government on March 10, one day before the democratic government took office

1991. Teacher Statute (Estatuto Docente)

1996. National System for Schools' Performance Evaluation (Sistema Nacional de Evaluación del Desempeño de los Establecimientos Educacionales)

1997. Full Day School (Jornada Escolar Completa)

2000–2003. Teachers' Performance Evaluation and Individual Incentives

2006. Demonstrations by secondary students (Revolt of the "Penguins")

2008. Preferential Voucher established, grants larger subsidies for poorer students

2009. General Education Law (which substitutes for the 1990 LOCE)

2011. Six months of demonstrations, mostly by university students

Appendix B
Interviewees

José Pablo Arellano, budget director for national government, 1990–96, minister of education, 1996–2000; January 9, 2012

Mariana Aylwin, minister of education, 2000–2003, director of Corporación Aprender, 2003; March 16, 2007

Rodolfo Bonifaz, coordinator, Accreditation and Teacher Evaluation Program, Ministry of Education; November 17, 2009

Rodrigo Bosch, president of CONACEP; January 11, 2010

Pablo González, ex-director of Planning and Budget Division, Ministry of Education, 1994–96; November 17, 2009

Pedro Montt, subsecretary (vice minister) and other positions in Ministry of Education; January 8, 2010

Jorge Pavez, president of Colegio de Profesores, 1996–2007; director of Colegio de Profesores; January 11, 2010

Pilar Romaguera, subsecretary (vice minister), Ministry of Education, 2006–07; March 23, 2010

Carlos Veas, executive director, FIDE; March 22, 2010

11

"Spontaneous Privatization" and Its Political Consequences in Russia's Postcommunist Health Sector

Linda J. Cook

In Russia, as in other postcommunist states, non-state welfare providers emerged during the 1990s after decades of virtually complete state monopolization of social provision. Those decades produced a distinctive constellation of welfare institutions and providers, political interests and societal expectations. By the end of the Communist period most of the population had been incorporated into a basic internally stratified system of public social provision that included health, education, social insurance, and social subsidies. Some 15 percent of the late-Soviet labor force worked in the public sector, mainly in health care and education. Welfare was administered by an extensive state bureaucracy of central ministries and administrative bodies articulated down to regional and local levels. In 1991 the centralized political, economic, and allocational system in which the old welfare state was embedded collapsed, initiating a decade of economic decline and profound transformation of the social sector (Cook 2007a).

In this chapter I analyze the origins, dynamics, and consequences of non-state provision in Russia's health care sector since 1991. I argue that the historical role of the Soviet state shaped the origins of non-state provision. The centralized, bureaucratized Soviet health care system left a dense legacy of statist institutions and interests that resisted the privatizing initiatives of neoliberal

Thanks to the participants of the Conference on Non-State Provision, and especially Melani Cammett, Lauren MacLean, Scott Allard, Robert Kaufman, and two reviewers from Cornell University Press for comments on various drafts of this chapter.

reformers. Political struggles and economic pressures during the 1990s produced substantial "spontaneous privatization" and "shadow commercialization" that blurred the boundary between public and private provision. Doctors, nurses, and health sector administrators used their direct control over facilities and their existing skill sets to craft combinations of formal "cash register" and informal "shadow" payment requirements, becoming in effect informal brokers of citizens' access to medical care.

Spontaneous privatization and shadow commercialization began as a mix of survival strategies and opportunism on the part of social sector workers during the 1990s, when Russia's economy was undergoing a severe decade-long decline and the Yeltsin-era state was weak and ineffective. As later parts of the chapter will show, the economic decline forced down public spending and deeply depressed social sector wages, pushing official pay for the majority of health care workers below the subsistence level; sometimes even these wages were months in arrears. Beginning in 1999 Russia experienced a vigorous and sustained economic recovery that continued until 2008 and returned the economy to pretransition levels. During this period President Vladimir Putin stabilized the state, and social sector wages recovered and rose. The patterns of informal allocation and payment that had become entrenched during the 1990s nevertheless persisted. Despite successive state efforts to reform these practices, to reassert public control over medical services and payments, informal practices remained entrenched and pervasive. This sequence underscores the significance of path dependence for the Russian case; once these patterns became institutionalized, even informally, they proved extremely resistant to change.

Unlike most of the cases included in this volume, Russia is not part of the developing world; it is in most respects developmentally closer to advanced industrial (OECD) states, and has had an extensive state system of welfare provision since the 1930s. However, Russia does share key commonalities with developing countries in recent welfare state developments. In Russia as in the volume's other cases, non-state welfare provision has developed robustly in the past two decades, both replacing and supplementing the state. Welfare state change has been driven by the same IFI-promoted neoliberal ideologies of decentralization and efficiency. As in these other cases, non-state provision has not simply replaced inefficient state institutions with more effective and capable private providers. Rather it has had profound political consequences for distribution and equity, for the state's taxing and regulatory capacities, and for the ways in which citizens engage with their governments to meet basic needs.

The Russian case is, at the same time, in some ways distinctive. With a few marginal exceptions,[1] non-state welfare provision was virtually absent throughout the Communist decades. There was a modest, prerevolutionary

---

1. Dentistry, tutoring, and a few other types of private practice could be engaged in legally, but regulations and tax rates were prohibitive.

history of state, trade union, charitable, and religious social provision in Russia (and a much stronger Bismarckian inheritance in some East Central European states), but Communist regimes early on absorbed or closed down private and market-based social services (Inglot, 2008). Unlike in other cases, there was no (at least no legal) base of non-state provision on which to build. The establishment of non-state alternatives during the 1990s entailed an intense political struggle between entrenched interests in the state health sector and liberalizing domestic and IFI reformers. In the course of this struggle, many professionals and administrators from the state sector turned themselves into informal brokers of access to state-funded services. The structure of this informal brokerage relationship among providers, patients, and the state constitutes a subtype of non-state provision that is somewhat distinctive among the cases covered in this volume.[2] Informal brokers in Russia are typically employees of the state as well as trained medical professionals, whose brokerage role developed spontaneously from the historical-institutional context of the post-Soviet transition. Russian health care workers do have important features in common with the teachers and educational administrators who populate Mizala and Schneider's study (this volume); both studies demonstrate how privatized providers remain tied up with the state in complex ways that distort incentives.

Liberalization and spontaneous privatization have greatly affected distribution of social services in Russia, improving quality for some while producing serious obstacles to access, inequality, and corruption. Formal privatization has benefited mainly the wealthier, while informal payments remain widespread. The burden of household health expenditures is strongly regressive. Inequality of access across socioeconomic strata and regions has worsened over time, levels of exclusion and abstention from care have increased, and both objective and subjective assessments of the system's performance remain abysmal. The decline of access to health care contributed to (though by no means caused) a severe health and demographic crisis by the end of the 1990s.

Liberalizing and privatizing reforms have also had consequences for state capacity as well as accountability and state-citizenship linkages. The roles of informal brokers in controlling access and costs have become institutionalized, producing vested interests in informal rationing of care that resist the state's efforts to reregulate the health sector or increase equity. Informal payments and services, unaccountable and hidden from the state, have corrosive effects on its capacity to tax and allocate. Health sector informality affects the way citizens engage with their governments, potentially requiring them to engage with corrupt practices in order to meet basic needs.

In this chapter I track the development of non-state welfare provision in the Russian health care sector over the two postcommunist decades. The first part

---

2. Somewhat similar structures are present in other postcommunist states.

focuses on the political origins of non-state provision in inherited health sector interests and institutions and tracks the contentious politics of the 1990s. The second section analyzes the dynamics between the state and non-state providers, highlighting the path dependence of informality and resistance to the state's efforts at reversing it. The final part looks at the distributional and political consequences of spontaneous privatization and informal brokerage, particularly the effects on the population's access to health services, state capacity, and state-citizen linkages.

The Political Origins of Non-state Provision

In the Soviet period, the health care system was centralized, budget-financed, state-monopolized and planned, and managed by bureaucracies that were articulated down to regional and local levels. Access to basic care was nearly universal. Medical services were at the same time formally stratified, with the health care system legally divided into six distinct subsystems—departmental, elite, capital city, industrial, provincial city, and rural. Each subsystem served different population groups at differing levels of financing and standards of care.[3] Corruption and informal payments played a role, but had relatively less influence on access than the system's formal stratification. Pharmaceuticals were produced or imported and distributed exclusively by the state. The system was quite effective with broad public health measures such as controlling infectious diseases, vaccinating, and screening. It helped to bring adult life expectancy and infant mortality close to industrial nation norms temporarily in the 1970s. By the 1980s, however, it had become outdated and inefficient, and could not modernize to provide the more sophisticated treatments required for chronic diseases. The late Soviet health care system was deficient in comparative international terms, suffering from chronic shortages, especially of pharmaceuticals and advanced diagnostic technologies, relying on high rates of hospitalization and high provider-patient ratios, while utilizing low levels of medical technology and generally poor health facilities (Tragakes and Lessof 2003, 22–25; Preker and Feacham 1994, 288–300).

The extensive historical role of the Soviet state in health care left a legacy of statist institutions and interests that shaped the emergence of non-state provision. The new Russian state inherited dense networks of administrative organizations and health care personnel that had vested interests in the old system of state administration and financing. During the 1990s domestic and international neoliberal reformers promoted privatization and competition in an effort to transfer welfare responsibilities away from the state, increase the efficiency of service provision, and diversify sources of financing for the social sector.

---

3. In the 1980s less than half a percent of the population had access to the elite system, while about half were served in the lowest-quality, rural district system (Davis 1988).

The political struggles of that decade pitted liberalizing reformers against entrenched welfare state interests at federal, regional, and local levels that resisted, distorted, and co-opted privatization. Market reforms also confronted institutional deficits in Russia's weak new market and regulatory sectors. By the end of the decade political struggles over welfare reform, compounded by regulatory weaknesses, had produced a mixed, institutionally fragmented system of formal and informal, private and retained state provision.

Health Care Reform

Although most Russian health facilities were not formally privatized during the early 1990s, the Russian health care system underwent substantial structural change. New legislation legalized private outpatient practices, allowed the establishment of *de novo* private medical facilities and insurance, and privatized pharmacies and pharmaceutical and medical equipment production and distribution. Formal ("cash-register") payments for dental and some medical services, and charges for out-patient prescriptions, were introduced in state facilities (Davis 2001, 26–30). The inherited system of single-payer public budget financing was replaced by a new system of Mandatory Medical Insurance Funds that were supposed to be financed by a mix of payroll taxes and regional and local budget revenues. Newly established health insurance organizations were supposed to purchase medical care from providers according to a "competitive contracting" model. The system was decentralized, with devolution of responsibility for financing and policy to eighty-nine regional health committees. These reforms were initiated by executive and Finance Ministry officials with the support of global social policy elites from the World Bank and European states. The changes amounted to a radical departure from traditional lines of responsibility, an "overnight massive de-statization of medical care . . . extending 'shock therapy' into the health care system" (Twigg 1998, 586). A decentralized public-private mix replaced centralized state control, planning, and finance (Technical Assistance to the Commonwealth of Independent States 1999).

Reforms transferred much health care financing away from public, and especially federal, budget responsibility. Budget financing fell from 100 percent to about 50 percent during the 1990s, with insurance and household payments making up the difference. (See table 11.1.)

The proportion of household payments for medical services and pharmaceuticals increased from less than 3 percent to more than 30 percent. The average share of medical expenditures in household income grew steadily for the population as a whole from 1994 to 2003 (Blam and Kovalev 2006, 413). Payroll taxes became an important source of financing, and a small private medical services and health insurance industry emerged. These changes took place in the context of a severe decade-long economic decline that resulted in falling public sector and other wages, high inflation, declining public expenditure, and growing poverty among Russia's population.

TABLE 11.1.
Main sources of health care financing in the Russian Federation (% of total)

Source of finance	1992	1993	1994	1995	1996	1997	1998	1999
Federal budget	11.3	8.9	8.6	6.4	4.9	7.7	4.6	4.9
Regional health budgets*	88.7	75.3	64.7	60.6	58.6	53.1	47.1	44.7
Mandatory health insurance contributions for working population	–	–	15.6	14.7	15.7	14.5	16.0	15.9
Private contributions to voluntary health insurance	0	0.9	1.5	2.0	2.5	2.7	3.0	3.5
Household payments for medical services**	–	1.6	2.2	4.7	6.3	7.3	9.1	8.4
Household payments for pharmaceuticals	–	–	7.8	13.2	13.7	15.6	21.1	24.9
Corporate payments for medical services	–	–	1.1	0.3	0.7	1.7	2.1	1.2
TOTAL	100	100	100	100	100	100	100	100.7

Source: Tragakes and Lessof 2003.
*Including contributions to mandatory health insurance for nonworking population.
**Not including under-the-table payments.

Political Contention over Health Care Reforms

These reforms were contested by statist resisters who remained as the legacy of the Soviet period. The insurance reform threatened control by established state-administrative authorities at local, regional, and federal ministerial levels over medical institutions, personnel, and funds. Local health administrators fought to maintain control over budgets and facilities, in part by refusing to contribute to Mandatory Medical Insurance Funds for the 60 percent of the population (children, the elderly, unemployed people) that was not covered by wage taxes. The insurance mechanism was seriously underfinanced from the outset by their withholding of contributions.[4] Regional health committees also resisted the encroachment of health insurance organizations. By mid-decade fewer than half of Russia's eighty-nine regional governments allowed private insurance companies to operate, and lower-level governments were withdrawing licenses. Eventually many regional governments prohibited their operation (Blam and Kovalev 2006, 411).

Russia's Health Ministry also moved aggressively against the changes. According to a well-placed observer, "At first, people at the Ministry of Health didn't seem to understand how much of their power and authority were being

4. In 1996, for example, municipalities in half of Russia's regions made little or no insurance payments.

removed [by decentralization and the later introduction of insurance]. It fought against the plan. . . . Civil servants in the Ministry of Health at all levels are against [reforming] through insurance."[5] The Ministry of Health opposed privatization of medical services, seeking to maintain control over professional qualifications, appointments, and the setting of norms and standards. And while some activist doctors supported reforms, there was ideological resistance within the medical profession, with many providers believing that the state should continue to provide health care (Cook 2007a).

In sum, throughout the 1990s the system was caught up in continual bureaucratic and institutional infighting between reformers and inherited vested interests over responsibilities and control of resources (Twigg 1999, 337). Overall, the reform effort disorganized the health sector rather than making it more efficient, leaving multiple institutions—funds, insurance companies, private providers—unevenly distributed and poorly regulated (OECD 2001). In the end, public authorities maintained or reasserted control over two-thirds of health funds, which they used to keep existing facilities, personnel, and practices in place (Burger, Field, and Twigg 1998, 755–58; Russian Ministry of Health 1998).

With the exception of pharmaceuticals, levels of formal privatization in the health sector remained very limited. By the end of the 1990s 'only about 1 percent of all treatment facilities were classified as legally private, while private inpatient and outpatient facilities treated less than 5 percent of patients. Health insurance companies that engaged in "competitive contracting" for medical services developed in only a few major population centers; in fact, many local medical "markets" had only one source of service provision, the old polyclinic. The private insurance market remained miniscule. For most of the population, medical services continued to be delivered by public sector providers in public facilities. At the same time Russia's deep transitional recession pushed down real public health expenditures by an estimated one-third, and regions' holding back of Medical Insurance contributions worsened the decline in financing. The imbalance between declared state guaranteed medical services and funding led to persistent deficits at all levels of public health care financing, with estimates of the financing deficit varying widely, from 11–25 percent to 40–65 percent total health expenditure (Blam and Kovalev 2003; 2006, 410).

"Spontaneous Privatization" and "Shadow Commercialization"

As elite-level political conflict blocked development of legal private health care markets while deep deficits in public financing continued, the majority of health care providers' salaries fell below subsistence, and even these low

---

5. Interview with senior Russian health economist, conducted by Judyth Twigg, Moscow, Russia, May 21, 1997. Transcript provided to the author.

salaries were often in arrears (Government of Russia 2002). At the same time the supply of providers in some categories actually grew, with the numbers of medical doctors increasing from an already high 407 per 100,000 in 1990 to 426 in 2002. Most health care infrastructure remained in operation (WHO 2006). And, critically, the state continued to mandate free provision of a "Guaranteed Package" of health services (Blam and Kovalev 2003). Although legal charges or "cash register" payments were allowed for some services,[6] a substantial part of the Guaranteed Package was simply left unfunded. Public expenditures were too low to support existing networks of medical institutions and personnel, so new financing practices emerged spontaneously (Blam and Kovalev 2006). Health care providers and administrators turned to informal income-generating strategies, including "spontaneous privatization" and "shadow commercialization" (an "increasing tendency to spontaneous and unofficial replacement of free services with paid ones") (Feeley, Sheiman, and Shishkin, n.d.). Doctors, nurses, and health sector administrators used their control over access to facilities, and their existing skill sets, to craft combinations of formal cash register and informal shadow payment requirements, becoming, in effect, informal brokers of citizens' access to medical care.

By the mid-1990s payments played a significant role in access to health services, and people at all income levels were paying out of pocket. Survey data show that the proportion paying for medical services increased steadily, with most payments going to providers in public facilities (Shishkin, 2008b, 148). Figure 11.1 shows the growth in payments for various types of medical care from 1994 to 2004, with the sharpest increases for hospitalization and pharmaceuticals. By some estimates private spending equaled or exceeded public spending as a percentage of GDP by the mid-1990s, with a conservatively estimated half of private spending informal.[7]

There was also a steady increase in the role of private commercial pharmacies, and large-scale corruption emerged in the manufacture and distribution of pharmaceuticals. During the early 1990s transition, a nascent retail and wholesale pharmaceuticals market replaced the Soviet-era single state distributor. Small, loosely regulated private distributors and new privatized pharmacies developed rapidly at a time of great institutional and economic instability. Controls on wholesale and retail markups were ineffectively enforced. Research by Alexandra Vacroux (2004, 2005) shows that key positions in local regulatory apparatuses and regional health administrations were increasingly captured

6. Legal charges refer to payments that are authorized by the government and are not reimbursed.

7. A study by a group of Russian health experts estimated conservatively that the informal health care market in 1997 captured 0.86% of GDP, equal to about 25% of reported public health expenditures (Cook 2007a, 140).

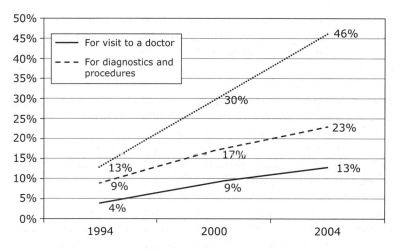

Figure 11.1. Proportion paying for various types of health care in Russia (various years). *Source:* Adapted from S. V. Shishkin, A. Ia. Burdiak, and E. V. Selezneva 2008b, 148, fig. 12. Used with permission.

by industry officials. Low salaries, underfunding, institutional flux, and poor regulation combined to create incentives and opportunities for corruption, which became pervasive in the production and distribution of pharmaceuticals throughout Russia's health sector.

Out-of-Pocket Payments and "Shadow Incomes"

Studies of out-of-pocket payments in Russia's health care system, based on interviews and public surveys, show that, by 2002, informal out-of-pocket payments to health professionals had become prevalent (Shishkin et al. 2003; Blam and Kovalev 2003). Norms and practices varied according to medical specialties, hospital departments, localities, patients' social and income group, inpatient and outpatient institutions, and arbitrarily. Hospitals relied on diverse and complex income-sharing practices to distribute informal payments among staff. Patients generally paid premiums for access to advanced diagnostic technologies and facilities, and for top specialists and surgeons. Collusion between doctors or hospitals and pharmaceutical companies over drug pricing and distribution was common. Besides insufficient public funding of state-guaranteed health benefits and low salaries among health workers, informal charges were driven by the fact that rank-and-file doctors and nurses benefit little from payments for legally chargeable services, which are mainly retained by administrators (Shishkin et al. 2003; Blam and Kovalev 2003).

The size of medical professionals' "shadow" incomes can only be estimated, but negotiable shadow price lists reportedly existed. Survey evidence indicates that surgeons may have exceeded their official incomes by five to ten times, hospital unit heads by three to four times, rank-and-file doctors in some specialties by two to three times, nurses and others by 1.5 to two times, with many considering what they got as fair reimbursement (Shishkin 2003, 24). Legal payments by patients did not provide them with protection against additional informal payments. There was little support for legalization among medical professionals. In pharmaceuticals, corruption also grew and became resistant to efforts at regulation and formalization. According to Vacroux's study, "An organization trying to generate rents to survive in an atmosphere of inconsistent funding can foster an internal corporate culture in which officials also exploit their personal authority for personal rents. The civil servant who has used reforms to carve out a profitable niche for himself and his organization has an incentive to block later reforms that eliminate this niche" (Vacroux 2004, 146). Experts concluded that these informal payment practices had become so deeply entrenched and broadly accepted among providers, health facility administrators, and patients that they could not be eliminated, and could perhaps be mitigated only by additional large increases in public expenditures on salaries and equipment.

To recap briefly, the historical role of the Russian state shaped the origins of non-state provision in health care. Non-state provision did not simply replace inefficient, overcentralized state institutions with a more efficient, capable, and politically neutral set of private providers, as envisioned in the neoliberal model. Rather, liberalizing reforms were contested by long-established statist interests in the health sector, and the financial and administrative weakening of the Russian state opened space for the emergence of spontaneously privatized and informally commercialized health services.

Dynamics: Reining in Non-state Providers?

Spontaneous privatization and informal brokerage in Russia's health sector emerged during the 1990s decade of continuous economic decline and political instability. With the return of high and sustained economic growth and a stronger state-political administration after 2000, the Russian state strengthened tax collection, regulation, and public expenditures, and focused on improving governance of the social sector (Cook 2007b; Popov 2008). Because health indicators had declined dramatically during the 1990s and excess mortality had created a demographic crisis in Russia, the health sector received high priority: the government increased its expenditures on health, raised official incomes for medical personnel, and mounted a campaign by the police and state prosecutors against shadow payments (Shishkin et al. 2008a). The Ministry of Health and Social Development accelerated its efforts to reclaim regulatory control over the health care system. The insurance reform was revived with more central control over regional Medical Insurance Funds competition and private insurance companies were again encouraged, and new regulations and price controls were put into place in the pharmaceutical sector. Indeed, of the five strategies recommended for dealing with informality by a 2007 OECD report—increasing official income levels, imposing sanctions against informal payments, formalizing additional payments, encouraging the private sector, and narrowing the range of guaranteed services—Russia's government adopted the first four and considered the fifth (Tompson 2007).

In 2005, the Russian government set the goal of raising access and quality of medical care for the whole population as its main policy task in the area of health care (Shishkin 2006). The National Priority Project on Health targeted federal funds to raise salaries for primary care doctors, establish fifteen new high-tech medical centers across the country to fill gaps in high-tech health infrastructure, instituted subsidies for maternity care, and increased federal subventions for children and pensioners (Cook 2010). A pilot program of "single-channel financing," designed to end the confusion and competition between regional health committees and Medical Insurance Funds, was launched in nineteen regions. The need to narrow the range of services in the Guaranteed Package and to develop means-tested medical assistance for the poor was recognized by federal political leaders. In sum, the revived Russian state sought to increase public resources, to regulate and expand the formal private sector, and to rein in "spontaneous privatization" and shadow payments and practices.

These efforts produced some, though ultimately limited, results. The state succeeded in recentralizing revenue collections, and average health sector wages rose above subsistence. But, with some exceptions, health care workers' wages stayed near the bottom of the urban wage scale, rising less than average, and, except for agriculture, the social sector continued to have the largest share of workers with below-subsistence wages economy-wide (Government of Russia 2002).

Incentives for informal payments were thus maintained; indeed, opportunities increased as society-wide incomes grew and some patients became more able to pay. Regional and local governments still resisted contributing to Medical Insurance Funds, sustaining the pattern of chronic underfinancing in most regions and a health care sector rife with deficits and unfunded mandates (World Bank 2005, 26). Formal privatization remained very limited, mostly concentrated in large urban centers and outpatient facilities with a few specialties. Though there was considerable regional variation, and a few cases of effectively reformed, well-managed regional health systems (e.g., Samara), overall the sector remained semireformed, institutionally fragmented, and poorly managed, with federal and regional government budgets continuing to administer about 60 percent of public health care expenditure (OECD 2006, 193).

Part of the problem rested with the continued limitations of the Russian state's capacities. Well-functioning privatized provision requires both well-functioning financial and social service markets and effective state regulation. In their absence, public insurance companies continued to operate as passive intermediaries, rather than active purchasers of health services (Popovich et al. 2011, 14). According to one analyst, by 2007 "a competitive, market-based insurance system had not emerged except in isolated instances. Insurance companies had not stimulated competition or cost-cutting among providers." The tiny private insurance industry—comprising fewer than four hundred companies—suffered from corruption, with employers often relying on "pocket" insurance companies that managers selected in exchange for kickbacks (Tompson 2007, 12). In 2006, an OECD report identified the poor contracting environment and weak state regulatory capacities as major challenges to growth of an effective insurance system in Russia (OECD 2006, 109; 206). Russian health care system expert Igor Sheiman reaffirmed that insurance worked poorly in most regions and concluded that "Russia is unlikely to be able to create a well-functioning competitive insurance system in the foreseeable future" (Sheiman 2005–06, cited in OECD 2006).

The Institutionalization of Informality

Instead of state-mandated costs and regulations, informal out-of-pocket payments became institutionalized and persistent in Russia's health care sector, as did the practice of medical providers acting as "informal brokers" that mediated the population's access to services. Private out-of-pocket spending on health care remained fairly steady from 2000 to 2006, at 35–40 percent of total health care spending (Popovich 2011). According to a major national survey on access to and usage of social services, the National Survey on Public Well-Being and Engagement with Social Programs (NOBUS) conducted in 2003, 50 percent to 69 percent of respondents across all income groups reported paying for medical services because there were no free providers or specialists available (World Bank 2005, 130–33). The largest share of household payments went to pharmaceuticals, with 80 percent of patients paying part of the cost for drugs. Informal cost-sharing remained pervasive in the hospital sector. The share of payments for legally chargeable services decreased steadily over time (OECD 2006, 195; Tompson 2007, 15). Unrecorded and unregulated work and monetary exchanges, as well as reliance on personal and social networks to access and provide services, remain pervasive in health care (Brown and Rusinova 2008).

   The most recent survey evidence on accessibility of health care in Russia shows that the practice of informal payments persisted through the period of economic growth and increasing state expenditure on the health sector. According to its author, the well-known expert Sergei Shishkin, "Despite the growth of state financing of health care and of state-guaranteed free services, informal payments seem to have increased. Forty-five percent of doctors surveyed said that "envelope" (i.e., informal and unrecorded) payments had increased in the past five years, forty-two percent that such payments had remained stable" (Shishkin et al. 2008a, 231). Although the proportional contribution of informal payments to doctors' incomes appears to have declined, there is evidence that the practice has taken on systematic, market-like features, responding to relative wages, degree of expertise, and quality of equipment. Payments depend on type of institutions and qualifications of doctors; they are higher in regional and urban hospitals, lower in *rayons*, or urban districts, and small cities. There is continuity in the concentration of payments in hospital departments doing planned surgeries with new medical technologies. Informal payments were found to be lower in polyclinics, and lower for those categories of doctors who received large wage increases under the National Priority Project on Health, or who have opportunities to earn in private practice. Pediatricians are least likely to take informal payments. There is some evidence of charges being adjusted according to patients' means, but payments do influence access and quality. Most respondents said that they received some free services, but the survey concluded that patients who do not pay when asked or given hints to do so risked not being admitted to a hospital or being admitted to a very crowded ward; not receiving current medications, but cheaper ones; having older technology used; having a less qualified surgeon; not receiving adequate attention from doctors and nurses; and so forth (Shishkin 2008a, 242–43).

In sum, by the early 2000s Russian health care administrators and providers had formed a vested interest against governmental efforts to formalize or reregulate the sector. According to prominent Russian social sector experts, writing in 2003,

> Central and local sociocultural authorities and the heads and employees of institutions resist privatization and any reorganization of their institutions, in part because they have already privatized most of the ownership rights. . . . Keeping the services free serves the interests of both the bureaucrats and the employees of service-providing institutions, for it provides the former with grounds to have public funds placed at their disposal and the latter with the opportunity to receive fees for their services directly from their customers. (Rozhdestvenskaya and Shishkin 2003, 606)

There is modest evidence that the private medical insurance market has been growing since 2005 (though it was hurt by the 2008–09 economic downturn); that the "best practices" of the most innovative regions are spreading, and that the single channel financing experiment is working (Tompson 2007, 13; Popovich 2011). However, there is little indication so far that any of these developments have mitigated the negative distributive consequences of the past two decades.

Distributional and Political Consequences

Formal and informal privatization of health care in Russia had, by 2008, contributed to large-scale inequities in access and quality as well as exclusion and abstention from care.[8] Access to the basic government Guaranteed Package of care varies with patients' ability to pay, and medical professionals act as informal brokers of access. Various studies indicate that the overall burden of out-of-pocket expenditure is income-regressive, and that those living in poorer regions are more likely to have to pay for specialists and diagnostic technologies than those living in wealthier regions. A significant part of Russia's population reports exclusion or abstention from at least some types of medical treatment because of inability to pay. Inequality in access to medical services exacerbates the deep income inequality across social and territorial groupings (Shishkin 2006). According to Russian researchers, "Steady growth of private expenditures on medical services has been associated with inequality of access among income groups. . . . Spontaneous commercialization has promoted de facto segregation of citizens on the basis of income, place of residence, and work" (Blam and Kovalev 2006, 407).

Stratification and benefits for higher-income people. Legally private, commercial health care is a luxury good available mainly to the wealthy. The small sector of legal private facilities is concentrated in Russia's largest cities and wealthiest regions. According to the Russian Longitudinal Monitoring Survey, with the growth of incomes since 1998, use of paid facilities has increased steadily among the top income quintile, rising to more than 20 percent in Moscow and St. Petersburg (Popovich 2011). At the same time, disparities in the use of formally paid services between the wealthiest quintile and all others grew with the recovery of incomes (Blam and Kovalev 2006, 413). Private outpatient treatment facilities served less than 4 percent of total patients federation-wide, while taking in one-third of total household outpatient expenditures. Those in the top income quintile sought help for a medical problem almost 40 percent more often that the bottom quintile. While households from the top quintile spent twice as much in absolute terms as households from the bottom quintile, in relative terms they spent ten times less as a share of income than the bottom quintile, and were much more likely to pay for all types of care in all types of facilities (Blam and Kovalev 2003).

Access and payment—getting the Guaranteed Package. Survey evidence shows that the bulk of both cash register and informal out-of-pocket payments go to the public sector, and that the burden of expenditure is income-regressive. Although the wealthy pay more and at higher rates, the highest burden of expenditure falls on the lowest-income quintile (Shishkin et al.

---

8. This section draws on the results of numerous national surveys, including the Russian Longitudinal Monitoring Survey, 1994–2000; National Survey on Public Well-Being and Engagement with Social Programs (NOBUS) in 2003; the Consumer Sentiment Index Survey carried out in March 2006, as well as regional surveys reported in Aarva et al. 2009; Blam and Kovalev 2006; Satarov 2001; and other sources.

2008b, 155). Arguably the most meaningful test of access is the Mandatory Medical Insurance standard, the government Guaranteed Package, which prescribes free-of-charge services to include consultation with a general practitioner or specialist and two or three lab or functional diagnostic procedures. In reality, access to this combination of services usually requires payment. In a three-city study of outpatient facilities, for example, only 20–30 percent of noncommercial patients received all guaranteed services, while the majority of commercial patients did so.

The study concludes, "For a large part of households, payment for treatment from their own resources has become a necessary condition for receiving medical help." More than 8 percent of households, including 5 percent of wealthy households (top quintile) and almost 10 percent of poor (bottom quintile) confront catastrophic medical expenditures, and spend more than 30 percent of their income on catastrophic illnesses (Shishkin et al 2008b, 146). Overall, the impact of Russia's health crisis is socially regressive, that is, with the likelihood of chronic illness and the probability that illness will lead to early retirement negatively correlated with income (Tompson 2007, 7).

Inequality across regions. There is also stark differentiation in access to and the quality of health care across regions. Russia's economic growth over the past decade has been characterized by a tendency to polarization of regions by level of economic development, contributing to different possibilities for financing health care (Shishkin 2006). The problem is exacerbated because lower proportions of the population are employed in poorer regions, and the informal share of wages is greater, so many employers undercontribute wage taxes because of informal or "gray" schemes for paying wages and salaries. Research has found an eightfold difference between the highest- and lowest-spending regions (Tompson 2007, 19). Regional comparisons show that those living in poorer, less-developed regions spend a higher share of their incomes for health care than those in wealthier regions. Patients living in more developed regions report paying to get a higher quality of care, while those in less-developed regions more often pay because of the absence of free specialists and diagnostic services (Blam and Kovalev 2003, V). A comparative study of out-of-pocket health care payment practices in the oil-wealthy Tymen region and the poorer Lipetsk region based on random sampling of populations, for example, found that formal payments were more common in Tyumen, and informal payments was more prevalent in Lipetsk, where specialists and diagnostic equipment were scarcer (Aarva et al. 2009).[9] A similar four-region study likewise concluded that the consequences of commercialization were

---

9. This study found that the probability of paying informally was higher among women, those with chronic diseases, pensioners, and those willing to pay, though various findings on these patterns of inequality have proven inconsistent.

more severe in the poorer provinces than in wealthier cities and regions (Blam and Kovalev 2006, 41; see also Davis 2001).

Exclusion and abstention. Although basic care in polyclinics remains broadly accessible to Russia's population, abstinence from medical care or failure to complete treatment regimes because of inability to pay has reached substantial proportions. Data from 1997 show that abstention from various types of medical treatment increased as income deciles fell, excluding 18–50 percent of those in the lowest income deciles from various types of care. A 2001 World Bank study found a "burgeoning underclass" without access to medical services (World Bank 2005, 26). The 2003 NOBUS survey found that 10–20 percent of patients could not get access to care or complete treatment regimes because of cost (World Bank 2005, 130–133; Manning and Tikhonova 2009). Lack of money was the reason most commonly cited in surveys for inability to obtain prescribed medications[10] (Thompson and Witter 2000, 178; Blam and Kovalev 2003). Two prominent investigators conclude that the commercialization of supply, along with heavy promotion of more expensive brand-name drugs, was the chief culprit in blocking access (Blam and Kovalev 2006, 417). Even for the new federal high-technology diagnostic centers, which were built under the auspices of the National Priority Project on Health to improve access, vague and unclear payment rules have been reported as a major factor deterring doctors' referrals and patients' use (Popovich et al. 2011).

Implications for State Capacity and Citizenship

The formal and spontaneous privatization of health care in Russia has had two critical types of political consequences or "feedback effects." First, the entrenched informal payment system and the vested interests it has created in the health care sector have had corrosive effects on the Russian state's capacity to tax, distribute expenditures, and implement policies that could improve equity and efficiency. Secondly, such "grassroots corruption" affects the way Russia's citizens engage with their government on a daily basis, forcing them to meet basic needs through insecure arrangements and "informal brokers," and thereby corrupting linkages between the state and its citizens.

Corrosive effects on state capacities. Although formal (cash register) payments create some accountability of health care providers to the state and to patients, informal payments and services are unaccountable, "hidden from the state, or not declared, for tax, social security, and labor law purposes" (Williams 2009). Informal payments in the health sector detract from the Russian

---

10. In 1994 nonavailability of the medication was the main reason cited for inability to obtain prescribed medications; after 1996 lack of money was consistently cited first by wide margins.

state's capacity to monitor or tax incomes, create perverse incentives for providers, and consolidate vested interests in public sector opacity and corruption, interests that resist reform, regulation, and efforts to enhance equity. Spontaneous privatization and informal commercialization undermine the state's regulatory competence, and generate opposition to reforms by governments of wealthier regions and administrators of public facilities who profit from their ability to ration services (Blam and Kovalev 2006, 422). Indeed, in Russia the state contributes substantial expenditures to the still mainly public health sector, while self-appointed "informal brokers" control and limit the population's access. In sum, "The entrenched informal payment system represents a failure to capture valuable revenue that could be targeted toward health policy objectives; . . . informal payments undermine the shift toward more transparency in governance and public services; and pose challenges to policy-makers seeking to cut inefficient activities and facilities, and to regulate health markets according to public health goals" (Thompson and Witter 2000, 183–86).

Consequences for state-citizen linkages. Health sector informality is damaging to state-citizen linkages. Widespread payment practices fundamentally violate the collectivist and inclusive norms articulated in the state's Guaranteed Package of medical care, norms to which much of the population still subscribes. Indeed, even formal privatization clashes with egalitarian values and broadly held ideas about the state's responsibility for social service provision that continue to be evidenced in opinion surveys. It should be recognized that there is considerable variation in the governance of health sectors across Russia's regions, and that equity and accountability ultimately depend on subregional political contexts. Access is generally more equal in regions and cities that have stronger tax bases to fund health services. Well-managed commercializing reforms have generated positive public responses in a few regions, most notably the reformist model in Samara (Konitzer 2005). Overall, though, a large majority of Russians are dissatisfied with the performance of the health care sector (Popovich et al. 2011).

I turn, finally, to the question of connections between health sector informality and trust in government. Here the work of the prominent Russian sociologist Georgi Satarov is relevant. Satarov argues that the health sector serves as an important source of "grassroots corruption," drawing and compelling citizens to comply with and engage in corrupt practices in order to meet basic daily needs. He calculates a "corruption risk" to citizens dealing with various public services, or the risk that they will be drawn into a corrupt relationship. Satarov's survey evidence shows that accessing health care in Russia presents a substantial corruption risk (though considerably lower than the risk posed by interactions with the traffic police or higher educational institutions). Widespread informality in the health sector, in other words, creates and perpetuates corruption. It has consequences for the way citizens engage with their governments on an everyday basis. Citizens cannot reliably access formal entitlements without the intermediation of informal brokers and the risk of corruption (Satarov 2001). One analyst has characterized similar practices in postcommunist Poland as a system of "welfare patronage," in which political authorities tolerate ubiquitous informal payments, and clients and providers collude to evade state regulation and taxation, a system that ultimately undermines the state's capacity to provide public services and potentially has negative ramifications for citizens' experiences of the state (O'Dwyer 2006, 239).

Conclusion

This chapter has analyzed the origins, dynamics, and consequences of nonstate provision in the health care sector of the Russian Federation. It explains how the emergence of non-state providers was shaped by the historical role of the Russian state. The centralized, bureaucratized Soviet health care system left a dense legacy of statist institutions and interests that resisted the privatizing initiatives of neoliberal reformers. Political struggles and economic pressures during the 1990s produced a semireformed health care system characterized by limited formal privatization, along with substantial spontaneous privatization and shadow commercialization, which blurred the boundary between public and private. Informal, out-of-pocket payments became widespread, and health sector administrators and providers came to serve as informal brokers of access to many medical services. Efforts by the Putin administration to strengthen state regulation and equity have produced limited results.

Two more general and comparative points from this analysis should be highlighted. First, though the spontaneous privatization and shadow commercialization of Russia's health care sector were initially products of the postcommunist economic recession and a weak state during the 1990s, they became entrenched in a strongly path-dependent pattern. Even when the Russian state became wealthier and stronger after 2000, it did not succeed much in dislodging these patterns, or forcing changes in these practices. Secondly, as in the partially privatized Chilean education system discussed by Mizala and Schneider, neoliberal policies did not detach health care from the state, which continues to finance most facilities, nor did it demonstrably improve equity or efficiency. In both cases, the state continues to provide funding that produces distorted incentives, and officials and politicians continue to debate, reform, and rereform these sectors.

Although Russia is not classified as a developing country, as are most of the cases considered in this volume, it has also experienced the political effects of expanding non-state provision. Privatization and especially informalization have had large ramifications for equitable access to welfare, the state's accountability to citizens, and its capacity to govern. The old Soviet health care system was surely characterized by overcentralization, inefficiencies, inequalities, and poor accountability. However, evidence from the past two decades shows that non-state provision has largely failed to produce more equal access to health care or efficiency. In Russia, formal privatization has benefited the well-off most, while inequality of access among socioeconomic strata and regions has widened, levels of exclusion and abstention from medical care have grown, and both objective and subjective assessments of the system's performance remain abysmal. Spontaneous privatization has produced vested interests that undermine most of the state's efforts to improve equity and performance, it has hidden income flows. The state's accountability to its citizens for delivery of universal access to the constitutionally mandated basic package of care is frustrated. Its capacities to control corruption, implement public health policies, and the expenditure of public health finances are also weakened.

12

State Dollars, Non-state Provision

*Local Nonprofit Welfare Provision
in the United States*

Scott W. Allard

On first pass, it may seem an odd choice to include an American case in a volume focused primarily on non-state welfare provision in the developing world. Poverty is qualitatively different in the United States than in developing countries. Similarly, the American welfare state is more highly institutionalized and stable than others discussed in this volume. In fact, recent efforts to stimulate the economy, cope with high rates of unemployment, and the passage of health care reform legislation have led the American welfare state to commit billions in additional public spending to unemployment insurance, food assistance, housing assistance, and health care coverage. International nongovernmental organizations (INGOs), typically identified as non-state welfare providers in developing countries, often turn to the American government and to private philanthropy in the United States for support. For these and many other reasons, one might reasonably conclude the American experience has little relevance to an inquiry about the role of non-state actors in welfare provision across the globe.

Yet, other characteristics of the American case make it particularly relevant to the study of non-state welfare provision in comparative settings. Consistent with its historical reliance on non-state or nonprofit organizations for provision of safety net assistance, the American welfare state has driven substantial growth in the non-state sector over the past four decades through dramatic transformation in governmental antipoverty program expenditures. Today, rather than cash assistance, a much larger share of American welfare state expenditures are directed to social service programs that support work activity, address barriers to self-sufficiency, and provide for basic material needs. For every \$1 spent on cash assistance programs, the United States spends about \$1.50 in government-funded social service programs for low-income populations (Allard 2009; Allard 2010). These publicly funded social service programs often are delivered by non-state actors, most typically local charitable nonprofit organizations that contract with government agencies. Non-state provision of state-funded safety net assistance has become so commonplace that it is a routinized part of welfare provision in nearly every American city and town (Smith and Lipsky 1993; Smith 2012).

Mature state–non-state relationships surrounding delivery of safety net assistance make the American case a useful lens through which to view the institutional consequences of non-state welfare provision. Increased government funding has fostered the steady expansion of non-state welfare providers in the United States, but it has created codependency between state and non-state actors along the way. Government relies on the capacity of the non-state sector to stretch public dollars farther than if programs were delivered directly through public bureaucracies; many non-state providers are highly dependent on public funding to maintain operations. Funding from the state can change from year to year even in good economic times, however, which leads to temporal variability in levels of non-state provision. Like many developing countries around the world (e.g., India, Brazil, Indonesia), the United States is a federal system where subnational government bears major responsibility for the implementation of social welfare programs. Non-state welfare provision is an inherently local activity and the rise of non-state welfare provision in the United States has reinforced federal pressures to decentralize delivery of safety net assistance.

The U.S. case also highlights the structural consequences of policy choices that favor non-state welfare provision. Non-state welfare provision tends to reflect local preferences about which types of assistance are available and to which populations they are available. Such autonomy leads to significant qualitative variation in non-state social welfare provision across communities. Rather than channeling program resources to the neighborhoods and communities where they are most needed, the American case strongly suggests that non-state welfare provision can lead to inequalities in welfare provision that systematically disadvantage the most vulnerable communities. Institutional realities also lead to a private and fragmented politics that can make it difficult for the American safety net to respond to widespread shifts in need.

These shifting realities within the American welfare state elude much of our scholarly discussion for several reasons. First, the primacy of social service programs within the American welfare state is a relatively new development, with most of the growth in the sector occurring in the last three decades. No federal or central oversight body closely tracks funding trends, services available, patterns of service utilization, or program outcomes. In addition, many of the important decisions surrounding non-state provision of social services relate to somewhat obscure state and local government technical guidelines about contracting arrangements, eligibility determination, reporting or accounting matters, and reimbursement for services. Research focused only on national policy or institutions in the United States or other federal systems will simply miss most of what is happening within local safety nets.

To gain insight into the types of institutional outcomes that are more likely to occur when non-state providers play a primary role in welfare provision, I examine data from the Multi-City Survey of Social Service Providers (MSSSP) and the Rural Survey of Social Service Providers (RSSSP), which I completed with executives and managers of government, nonprofit, and for-profit social service agencies in three major metropolitan areas (Chicago, Los Angeles, and Washington, DC) and four multicounty rural sites (southeastern Kentucky, south-central Georgia, southeastern New Mexico, and the counties on the of Oregon-California border) between November 2004 and June 2006. Although these survey data are not a representative national sample, these seven sites are broadly reflective of the urban, rural, and suburban landscape in the United States. Each survey gathered detailed information about location, services provided, clients served, funding, and organizational characteristics from these non-state service providers. With response rates that exceed 60 percent in each site, these surveys contain some of the most unique, comprehensive, and geographically sensitive data currently available that captures non-state social service provision targeted at working-age adults.

In the analyses that follow, I specifically focus on telephone survey interviews completed with 1,298 executives of nonprofit and for-profit service organizations in these seven different communities. Organizations interviewed provided at least one of several social services to nondisabled working-age low-income adults: employment and job placement; adult education; outpatient mental health; outpatient substance abuse; emergency cash or food assistance. Respondents were asked over one hundred questions that gathered detailed information on location, services provided, clients served, funding, and organizational characteristics. Because the sampling frame was drawn from lists of registered nonprofits, service referral guides, and web searches, these data focus on the formal non-state welfare sector and do not capture many of the informal, small-scale non-state providers that operate in low-income communities. These data, however, do capture the organizations most likely to receive public funding for programs and to provide services to significant numbers of individuals.[1]

---

1. More information about these surveys can be found at http://scottwallard.com/outofreach.html. It is important to note that many local social service providers in the United States have a difficult time maintaining operations from year to year. There is very little data about social service organizations that cease operations, however, but the MSSSP provides some insight into volatility within the sector. When survey interviewers attempted to make initial contact with social service organizations listed in the most recent community service directories, a surprisingly large share of organizations contained in those directories were no longer operational. Roughly 10 percent of social service organizations in the Los Angeles and Washington, DC, directories and 20 percent of organizations in Chicago directories were no longer operational when contacted by a survey interviewer. See Allard (2009) for a longer discussion of attrition, sustainability, and stability among social service organizations. Also, for more detail about MSSSP and RSSSP survey data, please visit www.scottwallard.com.

A few additional points should be clarified at the outset. First, within the United States, welfare most often refers to cash assistance programs targeted at single mothers. At times, definitions of welfare may include income maintenance or health insurance programs, but scholars and the public alike typically conceive of welfare as a narrow range of cash assistance programs (Gilens 1999). I use the term welfare provision, as do others in this volume, to capture a broader array of antipoverty programs and assistance, specifically the social service elements of the American welfare state. Readers will note that I use the terms welfare provision and social service provision interchangeably throughout the chapter. Similarly, the term non-state actor also has a different meaning in the American context, where the most common non-state actors engaged in welfare provision are local nonprofit organizations that register as charitable organizations with the Internal Revenue Service (IRS).[2] In recent years, however, there has been expansion in the number of private *for-profit* organizations contracting with government agencies to provide social services for low-income populations (Smith 2012). When discussing the role of non-state actors or organizations in welfare provision, therefore, I include formal nonprofit and for-profit social service organizations, unless otherwise specified.

Non-state Welfare Provision in the United States

Non-state actors have been important components of the American welfare state throughout its history. In contrast to local private charity work of the nineteenth and early twentieth centuries, contemporary non-state actors play a central role in the delivery of public welfare. Expansion of non-state welfare provision in the past three decades has been driven by dramatic increases in public funding of social service programs that provide basic food and material assistance, employment services, education and literacy programs, housing assistance, youth development programs, child care, child welfare, care for the disabled or elderly, as well as mental health and substance abuse services (Allard 2009; Smith and Lipsky 1993). Public expenditures for social service programs have grown over the past thirty-five years to exceed $150 billion annually, with the vast majority of funds supporting provision of services through tens of thousands of local non-state actors (Allard 2009). Total annual social service expenditures are comparable to combined expenditures for key cash

---

2. Despite their formal autonomy from government, nonprofit service organizations are regulated by the federal tax code and the IRS. All but the smallest nonprofit organizations are required to register with the IRS as 501(c)(3) public charitable organizations exempt from taxation and able to receive private donations that are tax deductible for the donor. The tax code specifies that registered nonprofits cannot transfer earnings to private shareholders or individuals beyond appropriate wages for work and prohibits registered nonprofits from "attempting to influence legislation as a substantial part of its activities and it may not participate in any campaign activity for or against political candidates" (U.S. Department of the Treasury 2009).

assistance programs such as the Supplemental Nutrition Assistance Program, the Temporary Assistance for Needy Families program, and the Earned Income Tax Credit (Center on Budget and Policy Priorities 2010; Kneebone 2009; U.S. Department of Health and Human Services 2009).[3]

The expansion of public funding for non-state welfare provision has been somewhat piecemeal since the early 1970s, with thousands of social service programs accumulating over time. Much of the financing for non-state social service provision has come from federal government programs. For instance, Lyndon Johnson's War on Poverty, beginning in 1964, established a federal commitment to addressing poverty in part through the creation of many new job training, social service, education, and community renewal programs. Numerous federal social service programs have been enacted in the decades following the War on Poverty: Comprehensive Employment and Training Act; Job Training Partnership Act; Workforce Investment Act; Community Services Block Grant; Social Services Block Grant; and the Community Development Block Grant. Federal welfare reform of the late 1990s required cash assistance recipients to work and placed time limits on duration of receipt, which then led to expanded funding for social service programs intended to help low-income adults find and keep jobs. Complementing these federal efforts, state and local governments have developed their own programs or contracts to provide social services to low-income populations since the 1970s (Allard 2009; Smith and Lipsky 1993). Non-state welfare provision also receives critical support from philanthropy, as Americans privately donate about $30 billion to social service organizations each year (Giving USA 2008).

Greater government and private financing of social service programs has led non-state actors to play a central and highly formalized role in welfare provision. Whereas most social service programs are funded through government agencies, private non-state actors deliver most social service program assistance to low-income Americans (Allard 2009; Smith and Lipsky 1993). State agencies often enter into contracting arrangements with local non-state actors, typically local nonprofit service organizations, which then deliver an agreed set of services or assistance to specifically defined populations for a prearranged fee or amount (Smith and Lipsky 1993; Smith 2012). Formal nonprofit organizations in particular have become essential partners for government agencies and policymakers seeking to enact, administer, and improve social service programs intended to alleviate need.[4] The private nonprofit sector, in effect,

---

3. The Supplemental Nutrition Assistance Program provides food assistance to the poor, while Temporary Assistance to Needy Families delivers welfare cash assistance to low-income families, and the Earned Income Tax Credit increases the incomes of working poor families through the tax code.

4. Small informal nonprofit organizations that provide material assistance and basic counseling services to a small number of low-income individuals or families are not required to register with the IRS as tax-exempt organizations. Difficult to quantify, these informal sources of assistance are critical elements on non-state welfare provision in the United States (Smith 2012).

strengthens the public safety net without creating large government bureaucracies or agencies to deliver services at the street level.

Expansion of non-state welfare provision has been dramatic in recent years. One study finds the number of nonprofit human service organizations grew by 115 percent between 1977 and 1997, with total revenues for those organizations more than doubling during that time (Salamon 2002). Using more recent IRS data, Allard (2009) estimates that the number of nonprofit human service and job training service providers increased by more than 60 percent between 1990 and 2003 and total revenues for those organizations doubled during that time to reach roughly $90 billion.[5] Smith (2012) reports that the number of people employed in nonprofit social services increased from about 1.6 million in 1997 to a little more than 2.2 million in 2007.

Complementing the work of nonprofit organizations, for-profit organizations have entered the social service sector in greater numbers in recent years and have developed close partnerships with government agencies. For-profit organizations are involved in all types of social service programming, but most deliver employment services, health services, child day care, mental health, and substance abuse service provision. Smith (2012) finds that for-profit social service organizations employed nearly one million workers in 2007—about one-third of the entire non-state social service sector. Although they must comply with federal tax laws, for-profit service organizations face comparatively fewer restrictions on their financial arrangements and use of excess revenue compared to nonprofits.

The emergence of non-state welfare provision within the United States reflects a distinctly American view about the causes of poverty. This again is an instance where the American experience deviates from much of the developing world. Americans are less likely to identify structural inequalities or limited labor market opportunities as determinants of need. Instead, society is more likely to emphasize individual-level choices, pathologies, or barriers to self-sufficiency as the primary causes of poverty. The public also is most comfortable with providing help through community-based private non-state organizations. Safety net programs have evolved accordingly. Cash assistance and income maintenance programs have come under greater scrutiny and controversy. Place-based policies intended to create job growth, redevelop neighborhoods, and relocate poor families to better neighborhoods do not occupy a prominent space on today's policy agenda. The increased reliance of the safety net on non-state social service programs targeted at individual-level causes of

---

5. These figures likely understate the size of the non-state components of the American welfare state. While providing an impression of the dimensions of the nonprofit service sector in the aggregate, IRS data do not contain information on the tens of thousands of small nonprofit or religious organizations that are not required to file tax-exempt status, but provide assistance to hundreds of thousands of poor persons each year. See Grønbjerg and Smith (1999) for more detail.

poverty, however, is entirely consistent with societal views of why need exists and how we should provide help to the poor.

Apart from providing direct services, non-state actors play a critical role in building civic community and strengthening social capital in poor neighborhoods. Non-state actors often link poor persons to community institutions and public agencies. By improving the ties between the poor and the institutions around them, nonprofits can build civic community and increase political efficacy. Non-state actors strengthen other local institutions and community-based agencies through programmatic partnerships and collaboration. Moreover, non-state actors also have been important advocates for safety net and antipoverty program expansion at many critical junctions in history (Austin 2003; Boris 1999; Grønbjerg and Smith 1999; Hula and Jackson-Elmoore 2001; Smith and Lipsky 1993). Combined, these efforts improve the capacity of communities to care for those in need and promote greater well-being among residents.

The Contours of Non-state Welfare Provision in the United States

Data from the MSSSP and RSSSP offer insight into the composition and characteristics of local non-state welfare providers operating within the U.S. safety net. Nearly 70 percent of the local organizations delivering social services in these seven urban and rural communities are non-state providers (see top panel of first column in table 12.1). Only 31 percent of social service providers are government agencies. Most local non-state service organizations interviewed were formal nonprofits. Secular nonprofit organizations compose the largest share of non-state welfare providers (see bottom panel of first column in table 12.1). Religious nonprofits—mostly formal nonprofits registered with the IRS—compose about one-third of all providers.[6] Only a small share of social service organizations—about 6 percent of all non-state actors—self-identify as for-profit entities. Because the MSSSP and RSSSP only interviewed organizations primarily providing assistance to working-age nondisabled adults, this latter finding is consistent with evidence elsewhere that for-profit organizations more often work with youth, elderly, and disabled adult populations (Smith 2012).

Organization-level data from the MSSSP and RSSSP also underscore the recent emergence of non-state welfare providers operating within the social

---

6. Religious nonprofit organizations, often referred to as faith-based service organizations (FBOs), are those maintaining an administrative, cultural, or financial connection to faith communities, traditions, or places of worship. By law religious nonprofit cannot use public funds for worship or proselytizing activities, nor can they incorporate elements of faith into service programs that receive support from government funds or contracts.

TABLE 12.1.
Types of non-state welfare provision in urban and rural America

| Type of organization | Percentage of local non-state welfare organizations (N = 1,298) | | | |
	All organizations	Organizations established before 1930	Organizations established after 1965	Organizations established after 1980
Among all organizations:				
Government agencies	31.0	13.9	63.3	40.8
Non-state organizations	69.0	14.6	73.5	44.1
Among non-state organi- *zations:*				
Nonprofit	93.6	15.6	71.9	41.3
Secular nonprofit	61.4	9.3	77.8	40.2
Religious nonprofit	32.1	28.3	60.6	43.4
For-profit	6.4	1.2	96.3	82.9

Sources: Multi-City Survey of Social Service Providers and Rural Survey of Social Service Providers.
Note: Reported numbers are column percentages of all service organizations.

service sector. Consistent across each urban and rural location in my surveys, less than 15 percent of all non-state welfare providers operating today were established prior to 1930 (see top panel, second column of table 12.1). A larger percentage of religious nonprofits were created prior to 1930, however, which reflects the prominent role that religious charities played prior to the emergence of the modern American welfare state. More than two-thirds of all state and non-state welfare providers were founded after 1965 when public expenditures for social service programs began to substantially increase. Almost half of all non-state providers in these seven communities came into being after 1980. Indicative of the trend toward market-based privatization of social service provision in the past three decades, 83 percent of for-profit providers interviewed in these seven sites were established after 1980.

Non-state welfare providers in the United States are a diverse group. Some organizations are very small, providing temporary food or shelter to a few families each month. Many of these small programs may be located in religious congregations or small storefront community-based nonprofits. Other non-state organizations may provide a limited set of services to a few hundred people per month. In this tier of non-state welfare providers are larger faith-based and secular nonprofit food pantries or shelter programs, literacy or adult education programs, counseling, and housing assistance programs. Further along the spectrum are large complex nonprofit and for-profit organizations that provide dozens of highly professionalized social services to thousands of clients each year through bureaucratized administrative apparatus and often as part of a national network. Examples of such large non-state providers include organizations such as Catholic Charities, the Salvation Army, or the YMCA.

The varied missions and sizes of non-state welfare providers are reflected in table 12.2. Secular nonprofit organizations are more likely to provide employment, outpatient substance abuse, and outpatient mental health services than religious nonprofits. Support to meet the material and housing needs of the poor, however, is more prevalent among religious nonprofits in these seven communities than among secular nonprofit or for-profit organizations. It is worth noting, however, that a significant share of religious nonprofit organizations provide more highly professionalized employment, substance abuse,

TABLE 12.2.
Characteristics of non-state welfare providers in urban and rural America

	Percentage of local non-state welfare organizations			
	All organizations	Secular nonprofits	Religious nonprofits	For-profits
Type of assistance				
Basic needs assistance	56.7	50.9	78.0	6.2
Employment assistance	51.7	58.5	45.8	24.7
Substance abuse/mental health	45.7	49.1	30.8	81.5
Assistance with housing needs	51.0	52.3	57.5	11.1
Financial planning/tax assistance	33.4	39.0	27.3	13.6
Annual budget				
Greater than $1 million	37.5	47.4	22.7	15.2
$1 million–$200,000	31.5	31.8	28.1	43.9
$200,000–$50,000	17.9	13.5	25.5	25.8
Less than $50,000	13.1	7.3	23.8	15.2
Government grants and contracts received in previous 3 years	68.7	83.8	46.4	35.8
Dependent for +50% of budget	51.0	57.8	26.4	46.4
Nonprofit grants and support received in previous 3 years	62.0	68.2	62.5	12.4
Dependent for +50% of budget	14.5	12.0	19.6	0.0
Private giving and donations received in previous 3 years	70.8	67.7	91.6	8.6
Dependent for +50% of budget	18.7	5.9	37.1	0.0
N	1,298	770	403	82

Sources: Multi-City Survey of Social Service Providers and Rural Survey of Social Service Providers.
Note: Reported numbers are column percentages of all service organizations.

and mental health services. In contrast, for-profit organizations operating in these seven communities appear to be primarily focused on outpatient mental health and substance abuse services, areas where private insurance or fees from higher-income clients can be combined with government reimbursement for services delivered to low-income clients to create a sustainable business model.

Given variation in service missions by type of non-state provider, it is not surprising that secular nonprofits often are much larger than religious or for-profit providers (see second panel of table 12.2). Almost half of secular nonprofits in these seven communities report annual operating budgets over $1 million (47.4%) and nearly 80 percent have annual budgets over $200,000. By comparison, about one in two religious nonprofits report annual budgets under $200,000 a year (49.3%).

Public funding plays an essential role in supporting the non-state social service sector in these seven communities (see bottom panels of table 12.2). Approximately 70 percent of non-state actors report receiving government grants or contracts to support operations at some point in the previous three years. Slightly more than half of non-state actors receiving public funding are reliant on it for a majority of their operating budget (51.0%).[7] Secular nonprofits are the most likely to receive government support and to be reliant on that support, with 83.8 percent of secular nonprofits reporting recent receipt of government grants and contracts and nearly 60 percent of those were dependent on public funds for more than half their budget. Although nearly half of all religious nonprofits receive state funding, only about one quarter that do receive public funding are dependent on it for more than half their budget. Perhaps more surprising is that nearly half of all for-profit organizations—46.4 percent—receiving government grants and contracts for services are dependent on those revenues.

Other sources of revenue support the work of non-state welfare providers, but no other single source is as crucial to the sector as government funding. Most secular and religious nonprofits draw some funding from other charitable nonprofit organizations. Only a small fraction of those organizations, however, are dependent on those funds. Similarly, many secular and religious nonprofits report private giving and donations. Nearly 40 percent of religious nonprofits, often those running smaller programs to address basic material needs, are dependent on private giving for a significant share of their budgets. By contrast, secular nonprofits do not draw significant portions of their budgets from private giving. Few for-profit organizations receive charitable gifts or grants, instead relying more on private fees for services to complement public revenue streams.

---

7. The MSSSP and RSSSP asked respondents whether they receive funding from government grants or contracts, charitable foundations and nonprofits, or from private donations. In addition, organizations were asked how much of their total budget comes from each source. Organizations are defined as "dependent" on a specific source of funding if they receive more than 50 percent of total organizational revenues from that source.

The prevalence of state funding in the non-state sector is not simply a matter of accounting; rather, it has implications for how non-state actors provide assistance to the poor. State-funded programs place limits on the discretion that non-state actors have over program eligibility and access to program benefits. Generally it is believed that state funding forces non-state actors to treat clients more equitably and with less flexibility than would be the case for programs that are not reliant on state funding (Smith and Lipsky 1993). Government funding can nudge or entice non-state actors into service delivery areas that may not fit an organization's original mission. Such mission creep can pull non-state actors away from their core values and competencies, possibly realigning organizational priorities to reflect the requirements of public funding obligations. Finally, the proliferation of government-funded social service programs has drawn many non-state actors into the sector and created incentives for the creation of new organizations. Over time this has translated into more intense competition for increasingly finite public program resources, which has reduced the predictability and reliability of those public program resources.

The Consequences of Non-state Welfare Provision

Reliance of the American safety net on local non-state welfare providers has a number of important consequences for the availability and accessibility of social assistance. Non-state welfare provision in the United States is a highly localized activity, with organizational capacity varying by community and within communities. In the American case, local variation in non-state welfare provision often leads to underprovision of programs and services in the most impoverished communities, where need is greatest but resources are scarce. The American case also shows how rising public social service expenditures have not eliminated instability in program funding streams, which threatens the sustainability of non-state welfare provision. Finally, the politics surrounding local non-state welfare provision have a fragmented and hidden quality that biases participation in social service policymaking to favor only those non-state actors most familiar with the intricacies of program delivery and public funding streams.

Equity of Access to Non-state Welfare Providers

As a general rule in the United States, low-income working age adults have no entitlement to noncash social service programs that may help them address any number of needs, obstacles to well-being, or barriers to employment. Non-state welfare provision, therefore, does not function as a rights-based system. States and cities are not required or compelled by law in most instances to provide specific social service programs, nor are they required to make programs available to all who live below the federal poverty line. Individuals have no legal or formal claim that social services must be provided in their communities. Neither nonprofit nor for-profit service organizations can be compelled to provide a particular program of assistance or service for low-income individuals. This arrangement differs from cash assistance programs and Medicaid, where individuals meeting certain income eligibility standards are entitled to assistance or insurance coverage.

The availability of social service programs, therefore, is jointly determined by state government, local government, and local non-state actors. Discretion over social service provision leads to wide variation in the availability and characteristics of services. Social service programs, particularly those delivered through non-state actors, reflect local needs, public resources, private philanthropy, politics, and entrepreneurs (Allard 2009; Allard 2010; Hyra 2008). Provision of assistance also reflects local patterns of inequality and opportunity. Ironically, because local tax revenues and philanthropy are directly related to local wealth and economic growth, the resources available to social service programs for low-income populations may more closely reflect a community's affluence than a community's level of need (Allard and Roth 2010).

Moreover, the provision and accessibility of social service programs will vary within cities and towns dramatically, creating another layer of complexity and local variation. Cash assistance program benefit levels vary by state in the American safety net, but individuals within a given state all receive the same benefit regardless of where they live. Many times, cash benefits are mailed or electronically transferred directly to low-income program clients. Most social service programs, by comparison, cannot be delivered to a person's home. Instead, individuals receiving assistance through social service programs typically travel to the offices of a service organization to receive help or support. Where non-state service organizations choose to locate matters greatly in determining which neighborhoods and populations have access to programs of assistance. Some places will be home to more social service organizations, thus offering more programs and assistance than others. As a result, not all neighborhoods have adequate access to the range of services necessary to address the needs or barriers to employment experienced by low-income adults living in those neighborhoods.

Place-based variation in the provision of social services also is a function of factors that shape the location decisions of non-state service organizations. Many non-state providers locate in counties or municipalities where government service grants and contracts are available. Some agencies choose to be closer to concentrations of low-income individuals in order to achieve economies of scale for service delivery. Others may locate to be near potential private donors, clients who generate fee revenue, or partnering service organizations. Religious nonprofit service providers are thought to be more likely to operate in high-poverty neighborhoods than other types of non-state actors, making them more responsive to the needs of the most disadvantaged persons and distressed communities. Agencies may choose to locate in a particular

community because of staffing concerns and the need to access trained professionals. Programs that address sensitive needs or serve at-risk populations may
choose locations that prioritize protecting anonymity and confidentiality over
shorter commutes. Moreover, service providers may be bound to particular
neighborhoods due to a lack of adequate facilities in more preferred areas, insufficient funds to relocate, or ownership of property and facilities that limits
mobility.

Analyzing MSSSP survey data, I found that high-poverty neighborhoods
have lower levels of service accessibility than neighborhoods with lower poverty rates (Allard 2009). For example, controlling for supply of services and
potential demand across a variety of social service programs, high-poverty
neighborhoods (those with a poverty rate over 20%) in Chicago, Los Angeles,
and Washington, DC, have about one-third as much access to a variety of
social services as low-poverty neighborhoods (poverty rate less than 10%).
Neighborhoods with higher poverty rates, however, appear to have greater access than the typical neighborhood to religious nonprofits that integrate faith
and religious elements into program administration (Allard 2009). Similarly,
coauthor Jessica Cigna and I examined RSSSP survey data and concluded that
rural communities often have several sparsely populated high-poverty areas
that are distant from any safety net providers (Allard and Cigna 2008).

Race differences in access are particularly profound. Also examining service
access in the MSSSP study sites, I have found that predominately black Census
tracts have access to almost 40 percent fewer employment-related service opportunities than the average tract (Allard 2008). Predominately Hispanic tracts
have access to 20 percent fewer employment service providers than the average
tract. Census tracts where whites compose at least 75 percent of the population have access to 21 percent more employment service opportunities than
the typical tract. Similarly, predominately black neighborhoods were found to
have access to roughly 40 percent fewer emergency food and cash assistance
program opportunities than the average tract.

To a greater degree than we might expect from cash assistance programs,
non-state service provision varies significantly by the class and race composition of a neighborhood. Such gaps in access to social services reflect the discretion of non-state actors and the incentives of social service-oriented welfare
provision. Local government agencies cannot require organizations to locate
in particular areas and have little control over which types of non-state actors
emerge in communities. The autonomy and discretion of non-state actors allows them to make choices about location and facilities that may be in the best
interest of each particular organization, but which aggregate into patterns of
mismatch because the incentives for organizational survival may not lead non-
state actors to locate near poor populations. As a result, it is difficult to know
which state or non-state actors, or both, are responsible for the mismatches in
access to welfare state resources that may exist at the local level and even more
difficult to hold any one party accountable.

Sustainability of Non-state Welfare Provision

Even though funding has steadily expanded over the past few decades, social service funding for non-state providers is not countercyclical. Economic recessions reveal one of the most perverse features of a service-oriented welfare state dependent on non-state actors: funding for social service programs—public and private—contract right at the moment when demand for assistance increases (Allard 2009). Because they lack entitlement status, publicly funded social service programs often are the first items cut when governments confront budget deficits during economic downturns. Politicians can rationalize such cuts because social service programs often do not provide essential basic needs. Funds from charitable foundations and nonprofits, as well as private gifts and donations, also contract during downturns because endowments fall in value and private individuals have less money for philanthropy. We should expect, therefore, that non-state welfare provision will exhibit weaker levels of stability and sustainability than other types of safety net assistance (Grønbjerg 2001; Salamon 1999; and Smith et al. 2006).

The vulnerability of non-state service organizations to funding cuts is shown in the top row of table 12.3. Nearly 45 percent of non-state organizations report a decrease in a core revenue source in the previous three years. Looking at instability across different types of non-state actors, half of all secular organizations report funding losses (49.2%), which makes them slightly more vulnerable to funding cuts than religious organizations or for-profit providers (37.0% and 40.8%, respectively). Although these numbers are striking, they reflect the instability of funding during a period of economic growth during the mid-2000s. We should expect non-state actors to experience even more

TABLE 12.3.
Instability of non-state welfare providers in urban and rural America, 2004-06

| | Percentage of local non-state welfare organizations | | | |
	All organizations	Secular nonprofits	Religious nonprofits	For-profits
Decrease in at least one revenue source in previous 3 years	44.8	49.2	37.0	40.8
Response to funding decrease in previous year:				
Reduced staff	41.2	49.8	26.9	32.5
Reduced services	33.0	36.5	30.4	17.5
Reduced clients	27.0	29.6	25.2	13.8
N	1,298	770	403	82

Sources: Multi-City Survey of Social Service Providers and Rural Survey of Social Service Providers.
Note: Reported numbers are column percentages of all service organizations.

frequent funding losses during economic downturns, when program dollars are most vulnerable.

Non-state welfare providers unable to receive a consistent flow of revenue or program resources will be forced to cut staff, reduce available services, limit the number of people served, and possibly shut their doors altogether because of insufficient or inconsistent funding. Program revenues determine which services are made available, how many clients are served, how many staff members are hired, and where providers can locate. Unless an agency draws on a broad array of revenue sources, unanticipated changes in funding can force a non-state provider to reduce service delivery sharply, disrupt regular operations, and in the extreme can lead to closure of a facility.

The bottom panel of table 12.3 reports the frequency of specific programmatic responses to funding cuts. Slightly more than 40 percent of non-state organizations report cutting staff when facing funding decreases. About one-third of non-state providers reduced the services available in response to recent funding cuts. Twenty-seven percent reduced client caseloads in order to cope with funding cuts. Secular nonprofits are nearly twice as likely to cut staff in response to reductions in revenue as religious nonprofits and for-profit organizations (50% versus 27% and 33%, respectively). Secular nonprofits are also more likely to reduce services and client caseloads in the face of funding cuts than either religious nonprofit or for-profit providers. Compared to nonprofits, for-profit organizations are much less likely to reduce services or clients when encountering lower program revenues. For-profit organizations, possibly because of access to fee-based program revenue streams or commercial revenues that are typically less available to nonprofit organizations, appear better able to weather funding cuts than either secular or religious nonprofits.

Despite evidence that different non-state organizations draw on different combinations of funding and have different coping strategies for funding loss, it appears that funding volatility and instability in service delivery arrangements are more commonplace among non-state welfare providers. Apart from the immediate cuts to programs and client caseloads, however, it should be noted that volatility in social service program funds can have a subtle but powerful ripple effect throughout the non-state sector. Funding cuts lead to fewer service opportunities for low-income persons in the near term, but these cuts also reduce the long-term viability of non-state actors and destabilize the very foundations of the contemporary American welfare state. Thus, a cut today may not only make assistance less available to the poor next week or next month but also in the years to follow.

Institutional Fragmentation and the Private Politics of Non-state Welfare Provision

Apart from creating gaps, mismatches, and instabilities in access, the localness of non-state welfare provision and plurality of actors engaged in social service provision creates a highly decentralized and fragmented institutional structure. More responsive to local-level priorities and values than a centralized system of assistance, the institutional structure that emerges from the state-financed, non-state-administered American social service safety net inhibits efforts to coordinate programs. Federal and state agencies struggle to coordinate activities across local safety nets, which are composed of hundreds of local government entities. Program funding originates in thousands of different public and private sources, with few mechanisms for systematic coordination across communities or regions. Evaluating program impact and outcomes also is difficult in such a fragmented institutional environment, as it is not easy to track which actors are providing which benefits to which populations.

Fragmented and privatized service delivery settings create inertia in policy-making processes and result in greater institutional resistance to change (Hacker 2002). Government and non-state actors involved in local social service provision operate with their own priorities, motivations, and goals that often do not correspond to those held by others. Consensus and agreement about program or funding priorities, therefore, can be difficult to reach. With non-state actors placing a high priority on maintaining their access to existing resources or revenue streams over broader concerns of the system, we should expect local safety nets to trend toward the status quo or modest incremental change. Combined, these institutional features of local safety nets make it difficult to enact responses to sudden increases in need or programs that promote widespread change in service delivery.

Fragmentation can lead to intergovernmental competitive pressures that powerfully shape non-state welfare provision, but create a system unresponsive to shifts in need. The political economy of the American federal system creates incentives for state and local government to be no more generous with social welfare program benefits or offerings than neighboring states or communities. To be more generous than neighbors would risk retaining and attracting higher numbers of poor persons, which would increase public expenditures, force higher tax rates, and decrease economic competitiveness (Peterson 1981). These competitive forces may be particularly acute in metropolitan areas, where suburban communities have dedicated few resources to social service programs compared to their urban neighbors. The geography of poverty in U.S. metro areas has changed in recent years, however, and most suburban areas have experienced significant increases in poverty (Allard and Roth 2010; Berube and Kneebone 2006; Kneebone and Garr 2010). Despite rising need, suburban communities may remain unable or unwilling to expand social programs in hopes of not damaging their fiscal position or economic competitiveness.

A service-based welfare state reliant on non-state actors also lacks a public politics surrounding important policy decisions. Social services do not emanate from a singular program, an easily identified budget item, or a prominent federal initiative. The politics of non-state welfare provision, therefore, are "subterranean," with low levels of visibility and traceability (Hacker 2002). Politics emerge in this manner because thousands of local nonprofits, many unknown to residents of those communities, deliver weakly salient social service programs funded through a confusing mix of funding streams. Only those actors and interests most familiar with social service program delivery and financing should be expected to become involved in policymaking activity.

Given these circumstances, we might expect frequent interactions between non-state welfare providers, local government officials that administer grants or contracts, and administrative agency staff regulating program funding or delivery. Indeed, patterns of communication with local elected officials, agency administrators, and state legislators presented in the top panel of table 12.4 are consistent with these expectations. Reflecting the localness of social service provision, non-state actors are much more likely to report frequent communication with local elected officials than state legislators (36.2% versus 20.1%, respectively). Likewise, non-state providers are twice as likely to report frequent interactions with state and local administrative agency staff that oversee grants and contracts (39.2%) than with state legislators. Such communications are often about the routine daily politics of non-state welfare provision: clarifying implementation guidelines; communicating about reimbursement and funding issues; and discussing program clients or outcomes.

Outside of communications related to implementation activities, however, it is common for nonprofits to advocate for particular causes or policies. At

TABLE 12.4.
Political communication and advocacy activity of non-state welfare providers in urban and rural America

Type of activity	Percentage of local non-state welfare organizations			
	All organizations	Secular nonprofits	Religious nonprofits	For-profits
Report frequent communication with . . .				
Representatives of local government	36.2	43.2	26.4	21.0
State legislators[a]	20.1	25.7	11.0	15.4
Local or state administrators[b]	39.2	49.2	23.0	21.0
Advocate for programs on behalf of poor populations	59.1	65.5	52.2	34.2
Educate public about issues relevant to poor populations	75.4	81.8	68.6	54.4

Source: Multi-City Survey of Social Service Providers; Rural Survey of Social Service Providers.
Note: Column percentages are reported.
[a] In the rural sites, organizations were asked if they communicated with elected representatives in the "state legislature or in Congress."
[b] In the rural sites, organizations also were asked if they communicated with administrators of federal agencies.

times, political advocacy of this kind may seek to draw attention to unmet needs, emerging community problems, and insufficient resource allocations. At other times, advocacy may promote particular policy solutions and programmatic innovations. Political activities of non-state actors can shape social welfare policy agendas and the programs or regulations that emerge from legislative processes. Contact with elected officials is useful for communicating the needs of low-income populations in communities and legislative districts, as well as conveying the work of an agency within the community. Public education, policy advocacy, and political activism also can be critical to achieving important internal organizational obligations, goals, or priorities. Advocacy and civic involvement can help secure public and private funding. Communication with administrative agencies can help clarify needs in communities, challenges to implementing programs, and new ideas for interventions.

The bottom panel of table 12.4 shows that advocacy and education activity is quite common among non-state welfare providers in these seven urban and rural communities. For example, almost 60 percent of non-state actors participate in some kind of program or policy advocacy activity on behalf of the poor. Three-quarters of non-state actors in each survey participate in public education campaigns relevant to the interests of their clients. An equally large share of non-state organizations report providing assistance to clients engaged in the legal system.

There are many reasons why we may not observe more frequent political or advocacy activity among non-state actors. Agencies with a strong service mission may not see the need to become particularly active in state and local politics or policymaking activity. Community-based organizations may not have the capacity or resources for political activity, as many providers are modest in size and have few staff hours to devote to activities outside of service delivery (Boris 1999; Frumkin and Andre-Clark 2000). The tax code also places legal limitations on the extent to which registered nonprofit organizations can devote time and resources to lobbying or legislative advocacy. Under IRS rules, lobbying or political advocacy cannot be the primary activity of nonprofit service organizations or an activity that consumes a "substantial" amount of an agency's time or resources. Nonprofit organizations operating in the United States, therefore, must be careful that efforts to influence legislative or administrative processes do not compose a significant share of staff time or organizational resources.

Moreover, these data say little about the content of the political activity and communication reported by non-state actors. It is presumed that non-state, particularly nonprofit, service organizations would pursue activities that might enhance the voice of clients and link relatively disenfranchised populations to local political institutions. Non-state actors are critical to policy feedback loops that directly shape the formulation and implementation of safety net programs (Mettler 2002; Soss and Schram 2007). Yet, dependence on government funding may lead many non-state service organizations to also pursue advocacy activity that helps secure funding or more favorable service delivery arrangements apart from client needs. Such attachment to public funding may limit their interest or ability in challenging status quo policies and programs. If this were the case, the incorporation of non-state actors into public safety net programs may constrain the policy feedback and civic advocacy roles of those non-state actors.

Conclusion

Contrary to common perception, the American welfare state is composed of thousands of local safety nets, where non-state actors serve as mediators between public programs, private donors, and recipients of assistance. The American state plays the role as primary financier and regulator of antipoverty assistance, funding the service delivery capacity of local non-state organizations that serve as the conduit through which the poor connect to assistance. No single watershed policy or national initiative has led to these arrangements. Instead, the primacy of non-state welfare provision in the United States is the result of many different policy and programmatic decisions occurring across the levels of government over time.

It is important to be cautious in drawing analogies between the American welfare state and those found in developing countries, but non-state welfare provision in the United States creates incentives for and constraints on behavior that are endemic to the enterprise. Consequences of non-state welfare provision may be particularly salient or pronounced in the American context, but its lessons are relevant to the study of non-state actors in a wide range of settings. First, the primacy of non-state provision leads to a welfare state that is more varied geographically than might be anticipated otherwise. Local discretion over non-state service provision means the welfare state only reaches communities in which non-state are actively engaged. Such variability appears to disadvantage high-poverty and predominately minority communities the most, exacerbating historic patterns of economic, political, and social inequality. Second, financing arrangements of non-state welfare provision may favor efficiency over concerns about equity, sustainability, and predictability. Politically, non-state welfare provision may occur with little public discussion, debate, or reflection. Relationships between public funding and private provision will be far from clear to most community residents and many program clients may not realize they are being served by a non-state organization. Moreover, the fragmented institutional structures that emerge from non-state welfare provision make it difficult to plan for the future, respond to sudden changes in need or poverty, or assess the impact of current investments.

The new institutional realities of welfare provision in the United States and in other cases presented in this volume challenge us to rethink the research agenda for the study of poverty, social policy, and non-state welfare provision.

This volume engages the institutional origins of non-state welfare provision in a number of settings and broadly assesses the consequences of these arrangements. Findings presented in this chapter, like those elsewhere in this volume, strongly suggest that the study of non-state welfare provision should not be confined to the implementation or management fields within public administration and social work. Non-state welfare provision is inherently political and demands that scholars of political science integrate non-state social service organizations into discussions of the politics of the welfare state. Many open questions remain about the nature of public resource commitment to non-state social service programs, about the political factors that shape resource allocation, and about shifting institutional dynamics within the American welfare state and welfare states in other developed and developing nations.

To do such work, we must overcome one of the most frustrating challenges facing the study of non-state welfare provision: the lack of information about social service programs and the non-state actors that deliver such programs. The work presented here and throughout the volume takes a significant step forward by presenting data from a range of sources and settings to generate insight into the origins and dynamics of non-state welfare provision. Advancing our understanding of the many roles and functions of non-state actors through continued theoretical and empirical effort is critical if we are to understand the continued evolution of welfare states in the twenty-first century and if we are to learn from the lessons of non-state welfare provision in comparative settings.

Conclusion

Melani Cammett and Lauren M. MacLean

Throughout the developing world, public systems of social protection tend to be weak or nonexistent. Where state social programs do exist, they are often diluted by a lack of resources, low state capacity or clientelist practices that effectively limit or preclude access to social assistance for most individuals and families. As a result, citizens of countries in Asia, Africa, Latin America, and the Middle East are forced to rely on a variety of non-state providers to meet their basic health, educational, and other social needs (Gough et al. 2004). Non-state providers range widely in terms of their level of formality, proximity, profit motivation, and eligibility requirements. In this context, the assurance of a minimum degree of well-being is far from a universal social right (Marshall 1950), but rather becomes an individual privilege linked to socioeconomic status, insertion in the appropriate social or political networks, or the good fortune to live in a region or community well covered by social programs.

Non-state forms of social welfare are therefore the central analytical foci of this volume. The book's contributors all demonstrate the growing importance of diverse NSPs in developing countries around the world. In Africa, Asia, Latin America, and the Middle East, NSPs play critical roles in the provision of social welfare. Even in the industrialized countries, as two contributions in this volume show, non-state actors are vital to social service provision.

In most cases, NSPs are not completely new arrivals on the scene but instead have long histories in the social welfare arena. What is novel, however, is that NSPs have consolidated or significantly expanded their social welfare activities in recent decades. For example, while NGOs and community-based organizations have long been active in Kenya, their numbers have exploded over the past two decades. And, even as the Indian state attempts to expand social services, the ranks of informal *naya neta* brokers continue to increase. Non-state providers are vital sources of social support for a growing number of individuals, families, and communities in many developing countries. At the same time, our collective analysis of the different types of NSPs operating in developing countries around the world reveals how the boundaries between the state and non-state actors are often blurred, making it difficult for citizens to perceive who and what is supplied or funded by the state or non-state actors. Our collective approach thereby unsettles outdated presumptions of linear progress from traditional to modern cultures, or from informal to more formal institutions of social security (Lerner 1958; Rostow 1962; Polanyi 1944) to build on more recent scholarship that shows the coexistence and interaction of state and non-state welfare provision over time (Cammett 2014; MacLean 2010; Midgley 2012; Patel, Kaseke, and Midgley 2012).

Non-state providers are not only large in number but also in type. Collectively, this volume shows the tremendous diversity of NSPs operating in developing countries. Secular and faith-based NGOs continue to be important players in the provision of social welfare, but they are by no means alone. Additional types of NSPs include private sector firms in Azerbaijan, Argentina, and Chile; sectarian organizations in Lebanon; family networks in Ghana and Côte d'Ivoire; and informal brokers in India. Although the book's authors tend to concentrate on one or another dominant type of NSP in a particular context, the empirical analyses acknowledge the role of multiple NSPs in each case.

The NSPs showcased in the book are diverse along several different dimensions: formality of organizational structure; location of operations; profit motive or mission; and eligibility. First, the NSPs covered in the chapters range greatly in the formality of their organizational structure and size. The book not only recognizes the importance of such formally structured organizations as World Vision, an enormous, faith-based NGO with about forty thousand employees in over one hundred countries and total revenues of over $1 billion,[1] but also highlights the single individual that informally brokers a child's admission into a secondary school. Several of the chapters in the book show that some NSPs do not directly provide or deliver alternative social services but, rather, indirectly finance or mediate access to state-delivered services.

Second, in chapter 2, our typology of NSPs highlights the importance of the domestic versus international axis of operations. What the empirical chapters reveal, however, is that in many cases NSPs are more accurately conceived of as transnational organizations. Their network members or subsidiaries are based in multiple nation-states with financial and other linkages that cross national boundaries.

---

1. See www.worldvision.org.

Third, we show how NSPs have diverse motives. In chapter 2, we highlight the distinction between a not-for-profit motive versus one seeking to generate individual or corporate profit. The empirical chapters reveal additional motivations held by NSPs, including political power, spiritual growth, and humanitarian development.

Fourth, the book details how this range of motivations by NSPs links to varied sets of eligibility requirements. As a result, access and accountability are not simply mediated by whether an individual or household is rich or poor, but may be shaped by the nature and intensity of spiritual belief, political loyalty, kinship among family and friends, or residence in a certain geographic location.

Collectively, this book indicates that NSPs are on the rise both quantitatively and qualitatively, but what is at stake in these developments? What does the expansion of non-state provision mean for the ability of populations to access services and meet their basic needs? What are the consequences of non-state provision for how citizens seek accountability for social service delivery, or for larger structures of state capacity? In the next section, we assess the extent to which the contributions of the empirical chapters support the propositions presented in the introductory chapters of the volume.

What Have We Learned? The Political Consequences of Non-state Social Welfare

In chapter 2, we focus on the potential effects of non-state provision on three core outcomes, including access to welfare, accountability, and state capacity. Each of the empirical chapters in this volume addresses the impact of a particular type of NSP on one or more of these outcomes. Do the empirical findings support the propositions presented in chapter 2? Overall, we find far-reaching political consequences of this expansion of the non-state provision of social welfare. Of course, these consequences are neither uniformly negative nor wholly positive. Rather, new inequalities of access, complex mechanisms of accountability, and hybrid patterns of state capacity have emerged. The chapters explore the parameters of these political consequences, showing how they are profoundly shaped by the types of NSPs operating in a particular context on the ground.

New Inequalities of Access

Access to social welfare refers to the degree to which people are able to meet their needs for basic services such as medical care, education, and social assistance. The concept of access encompasses the equity of access, which in turn is shaped by both the quantity and quality of services received, and sustainability, or the degree to which services are consistently available to populations. In chapter 3, we argue that the equity and sustainability of access to social welfare through NSPs is uneven, creating new social inequalities or consolidating old differences. To explain varied patterns around the world, we theorize that the form of NSPs affects access to social welfare. More specifically, we propose that more formalized and locally rooted NSPs, which use broad eligibility criteria and do not operate on a for-profit basis, facilitate greater access to social welfare.

The chapters generally support all or most of the components of this proposition. The analyses of social service provision by NGOs in Kenya (Brass) and by faith-based organizations in Tanzania (Jennings) suggest that the activities of NSPs have expanded access to welfare. These types of NSPs in these two African countries exhibit all of the properties specified in our proposition: They are formally structured, locally rooted, generally feature inclusive eligibility criteria, and are not-for-profit organizations. In Kenya, Brass argues that NGOs complement the administrative objectives of governments through the joint implementation, decision making, and long-term planning of specific projects. The government may provide technical expertise, while locally managed NGOs provide funds, transportation, and logistical support, leading to a net expansion of services available to Kenyan citizens. In Tanzania, faith-based organizations are a vital component of social safety nets and have been for centuries. Although a small percentage adopts exclusionary criteria based on sectarian values, most faith-based organizations are broadly welcoming to community members. As Jennings observes, the most significant, potentially detrimental effect of faith-based welfare provision is on gender equity, which may decrease depending on the core principles of the faith-based organizations' affiliated religious institutions related to sex and family planning in health care provision.

Conversely, and in support of our first proposition, NSPs that are more informally structured seem to reduce access to social services and support, particularly for the poor. MacLean argues that poorer individuals are less able to tap into informal family networks in Ghana and Ivory Coast to receive social assistance. In a very different context, postcommunist Russia, Cook shows that informal demands for side payments by medical staff officially employed in the public health system reduce access to health care for those who cannot afford these extra fees.

The chapters also provide some evidence that locally rooted providers afford greater access to social welfare, particularly with respect to sustainability. For example, Post demonstrates that domestic firms with significant operations within the jurisdiction of their contract (provinces, in the case of Argentina) can negotiate more effectively with local governments than foreign firms or domestic firms without significant local operations. Jones Luong cautions that multinational firms may contribute to the communities where they operate but do not necessarily have a long-term commitment to these localities. Their operations are ultimately driven by profits and, when natural resources decline or contracts with host governments are not renewed, they will take their operations elsewhere. Locally rooted domestic firms are likely to establish longer-term and, hence, more stable operations than MNCs or domestic firms without local operations.

Some aspects of Jones Luong's arguments about multinational corporations in Central Asia, however, appear to contradict other components of our propositions. She shows that international and for-profit corporations sometimes provide relatively high quality goods and services without discrimination in the communities where they are based. Notably, Jones Luong highlights that it is the foreign oil companies that are genuinely committed to corporate social responsibility—and thus not running this component of their operations according to a pure profit motive—that expand access. Furthermore, despite their "good" intentions, these expanded social services are delivered only in circumscribed parts of the countries where the foreign oil companies operate, generating additional regional inequalities. Jones Luong's analysis therefore points to another axis of exclusion that may arise with non-state provision—geography—which is also highlighted in other chapters.

Geographic disparities in non-state provision underscore a central limitation of most NSPs, notably that they are not national in scope (Wood 1997). Under some conditions, nonprofits in the U.S. welfare state (Allard), private water providers in Argentina (Post), and even sectarian political parties in Lebanon (Cammett) may provide higher quality or quantities of services in some localities than would otherwise be the case; but they almost always lack the national territorial reach to provide relatively equitable access to their services. In some cases, there is no evidence that private providers actually offer higher quality services than public actors. As Mizala and Schneider note, recent studies, using new data on Chilean students and an adequate identification strategy, show that, discounting for socioeconomic background, student performance is no better in private schools than in public schools.

Of all the chapters in the volume, Krishna's study of the *naya netas* in India, or informal, for-profit brokers of public benefits, seems to contradict certain dimensions of our propositions most clearly. The fact that the *naya netas* do not have an official occupational status and ostensibly work on a for-profit basis opposes our claim that informal, profit-seeking NSPs are less likely to increase access to social services. Operating at the intersection of public welfare programs and individuals, however, the *naya netas* are an unusual case among NSPs. Unlike public sector health care professionals extorting side payments in Russia, the *naya netas* are bona fide non-state actors who are not officially employed in government agencies or facilities. Whereas a richer citizen would more likely garner the assistance of a local government politician, poor citizens actually seek out the *naya netas'* services in order to obtain their entitlement rights from the vast and seemingly distant Indian bureaucracy (Krishna and Schober 2012). Another critical source of difference from the Russian case is that competition among existing and aspiring *naya netas* in this thriving profession spurs them to work hard to ensure that their clients are successfully connected and do receive their rights from state agencies. Finally, as Krishna argues, they are not solely or even primarily motivated by the pursuit of profit and are genuinely concerned about assisting their clients.

In chapter 3, we also propose that more collaborative—or at least not competitive—relations between NSPs and the state may improve access to social welfare for citizens. This might seem counterintuitive because a competitive dynamic may drive enhanced provision by both parties. For example, some suggest that competition from Islamists who run social programs compelled the Egyptian state under Mubarak to improve public services in some neighborhoods (McDaniel 2012). To the extent that the state is the only actor with broad national territorial reach, however, NSPs are unlikely to improve access on a large scale. When states collaborate with NSPs, the prospects of extending service provision on the greatest geographic scale are increased.

Two chapters in this volume describe collaborative relationships of "delegation" from governments to private actors to supply services, notably private water companies in Argentina and nonprofits in the United States. In both cases, the evidence in support of our hypothesis seems mixed. Although these NSPs may extend provision beyond what might otherwise be possible, access for the poor is uneven. These findings point to the importance of the state's capacity to monitor and regulate the activities of non-state actors in welfare regimes. Below we discuss the mutually constitutive relationship between NSPs and state capacity in more detail.

Overall, the chapters support some or all aspects of our propositions regarding the impact of NSPs on access to welfare. With some exceptions, more formal, locally rooted, not-for-profit, and inclusive NSPs tend to increase aggregate access to social welfare. We also find, however, that the non-state provision of social welfare is inherently uneven. Access for whom? NSPs are not created to deliver or mediate universal access to all eligible citizens of a nation-state. Some citizens may have more access to social welfare as a result of non-state provision; but others may receive less, or receive nothing at all. In the worst cases, where the state is unable to deliver any services to anyone, non-state provision obviously improves absolute levels of access for the population as a whole. Still, the equity of access across different individuals or groups, or both, within the population is not necessarily increased.

This assessment does not imply that existing welfare states are necessarily more equitable or beneficial to populations than all kinds of NSPs. Most of the chapters demonstrate the generally poor state of public welfare systems in most developing countries and reveal substantial gaps in social welfare provision by even the largest bureaucracies with the most expansive entitlement rights. Rather, our main point is to question the rush to non-state provision as the solution for deficient welfare regimes. NSPs generate new forms of inequality and lack the same degree of territorial reach that national states possess in all but failed states. Although the state might not have historically provided equitable access to social welfare either, the critical difference here is that NSPs rarely ever incorporate equitable, universal access as an objective.

The recognition of this inherent unevenness of access to services provided by non-state actors has important implications for future policymaking. Non-state provision has positive outcomes for certain groups, but not for all. In some contexts, access to social welfare may be greater for individuals who belong to a certain age cohort, socioeconomic class, ethnicity, religion, partisan group, or region. In other places, gender is more salient, with women and men targeted differently for welfare programs, or included in divergent ways in informal networks. Hence, it is vital to document more systematically the experience of gaining access to social welfare through non-state providers—to see who is benefiting and how. The subnational and subgroup inequalities of access to non-state provision should be tracked and evaluated more systematically over time both by non-state providers themselves as well as the state and non-state watchdog organizations. The need for policymakers to monitor and evaluate significant differences in the equity and sustainability of access for different groups leads us to the discussion in the next section of the process of seeking accountability.

Complex Mechanisms of Accountability

Our second set of claims presented in chapter 3 addresses the impact of NSPs on the accountability of providers to beneficiaries. To what degree do NSPs enable people to seek accountability regarding the services they offer, and when do they take responsibility for the quality and outcomes of their programs and benefits? We propose that more formal and locally organized NSPs with clear eligibility criteria are more likely to be accountable to citizens. With respect to profit orientation, the impact of non-state provision is more ambiguous. The accountability mechanisms of for-profit entities operate through market mechanisms. On the one hand, for-profit organizations may be more motivated to serve their clients, who are an important source of their revenue stream and may have other choices of providers in the marketplace. On the other hand, when the poor are able to access services from for-profit, private providers they are likely to be in a subordinate relationship vis-à-vis the NSP staff, who may regard them as charity cases with very few alternative options. As a result, for-profit providers may be less concerned with or responsive to needier beneficiaries. By virtue of the fact that only people with means can afford for-profit services in most welfare regimes, market-based accountability only applies to a circumscribed social stratum.

The empirical chapters generally support this set of claims. As predicted, informality generally reduces provider accountability to stakeholders. In post-communist Russia, the "spontaneous privatization" of medical care, which compels patients to pay informal side payments to clinicians just to receive services that are technically entitlements, is virtually devoid of accountability mechanisms. In this system, individuals can only exercise "exit" rather than "voice" options (Hirschman 1970) when they receive unsatisfactory care, placing great burdens on the poor in particular. Similarly, those who seek assistance through family and friendship networks in West Africa (MacLean) or access to public services via brokers in India (Krishna) have few if any alternatives, confining them to exit options rather than genuine opportunities to seek redress for unresponsive mediation or poor services. In Lebanon, providers linked to sectarian parties may be more formally organized, but beneficiaries, who tend to be lower income, have little leverage vis-à-vis these organizations and generally lack alternative options. Given these realities and the clientelist logic of distribution, accountability is low, even if intergroup competition and faith-based commitments compel them to offer quality services.

Low levels of accountability with informal non-state provision should not suggest that formally structured providers are automatically accountable to citizens, however. As Allard emphasizes, nonprofits in the U.S. welfare state are formal, local, and tend to articulate clear eligibility criteria, but accountability mechanisms are still complex due to fragmentation in the field of suppliers. The multiplicity of delivery and funding streams of social services has made it difficult for citizens to hold providers, funders, and the government accountable for service provision. Brass notes a similar dynamic in Kenya where boundaries are so blurred between the state and NGOs that citizens may not recognize or be fully aware of which actor is financing, delivering, or then supposed to be held accountable for services. The general institutional fragmentation of the federal system in American politics, which features multiple veto points, may make it difficult for citizens to identify a single or small number of actors to hold responsible for the nature and quality of the services they receive.

In Chile, too, the diversity of private providers in the education sector has complicated accountability processes. Although voucher systems are designed to strengthen the direct accountability of schools to parents through individual choice and exit, Mizala and Schneider find that the broader structure of the Chilean education system compelled parents to direct demands for accountability to state politicians, even though most children are enrolled in private rather than public schools. On net, privatization has merely added a new pathway of accountability, making it more complex for parents to navigate. They argue, "A voucher system is designed to strengthen the 'short route' of accountability (from parents directly through schools) but most other elements of the Chilean education system shifted accountability to the 'long route' from parents to politicians to education ministries to schools. . . . At a minimum, families negotiate a complex mixture of the two routes." To make sense of this paradoxical finding, Mizala and Schneider focus on the political context in which the reforms played out. First, under pressure from the teachers' union, the center-left Concertacion government recentralized teaching career and salary decisions. Second, the government's policy of promoting greater equality across regions and socioeconomic groups entailed centralized redistributive policies, ensuring that the state remained highly involved in educational planning. The examples of nonprofit providers in the United States and of educational reform in Chile point to the importance of political context and of state capacity in shaping the consequences of increased non-state provision.

The empirical findings also reinforce the idea that domestic NSPs exhibit greater accountability to citizens. Jennings suggests that faith leaders of FBOs, even if not democratically elected, may be more accountable to citizens because they are embedded in local communities. As Jones Luong's account of corporate social responsibility in Central Asia and Post's analysis of water privatization in Argentina show, the politics of accountability became more "volatile" and difficult to negotiate when providers were rooted internationally rather than locally. Furthermore, in the two Latin American countries examined in this volume—Argentina and Chile—private provision did not necessarily remove politicians from debates about the provision of basic services, nor did it reduce citizens' perceptions of state responsibility for public goods provision. In Argentina, the privatization of water delivery spurred politicians to blame private providers for poor delivery outcomes. In addition, privatization increased citizen expectations about their access to safe, reliable water sources, compelling them to mobilize more intensively to demand their rights. As Post shows, domestic private sector providers were able to manage these local politics more successfully than foreign firms. Mizala and Schneider emphasize that privatization ironically did not deter Chilean citizens from holding the public sector accountable for the quality of education. Nonetheless, the privatization of education did not necessarily increase the accountability of providers to the families of school-age children. Ironically, one of the major reasons why privatization did not induce greater accountability was the lack of demand-side catalysts: contrary to the expectations of privatization advocates, parents did not express much interest in collecting and using data on local school performance to push for better performance by private providers.

In chapter 2, we also propose that state capacity to monitor and sanction NSPs, whether in relationships of coproduction or domination, boosts NSP responsiveness to citizens. In particular, the case study of NSPs in Chile, which has relatively high state capacity to regulate welfare provision, appears to support this proposition when compared with NSPs in other countries covered in this volume. The Chilean state introduced specific measures to increase school accountability for performance and heretofore remains the focal point of citizen demands with respect to educational outcomes. Under Chilean law, schools must comply with certain regulatory conditions in order to receive students with preferential vouchers.

On net, non-state provision either reduces the accountability of providers to citizens or, at a minimum, renders accountability mechanisms more complex. These challenges imply that policymakers should expand the representative institutions of decision making for the non-state provision of social welfare. Not only should institutions be designed to facilitate more efficient *governance* of non-state provision, these institutions should be democratic. Opportunities to voice concerns and influence decisions should be included within the structures of the state, but also within the structures of the donors, NGOs, private firms, CBOs, and even informal networks. This conception of representation goes beyond the notions of voice and dialogue associated with existing paradigms of stakeholder consultation or participatory development by emphasizing the citizen's ability to influence substantive outcomes (Chambers 1984; Korten and Klauss 1984; U.S. Agency for International Development 1999; World Bank 1996).

State Capacity

Before assessing the effects of non-state provision on state capacity, it is vital to acknowledge that the causal arrow can also point in the opposite direction. The degree and substance of state capacity in a given country also shapes the political consequences of NSPs in the first place. The preceding discussions in the last two subsections have underscored the importance of state regulatory capacity in mediating the effects of non-state provision on access to welfare and accountability mechanisms. In order to avoid endogeneity problems in the analysis—the possibility of reverse or at least mutually constitutive causation—it is essential to study the relationship between non-state provision and state capacity *over time*. The comparative historical approaches employed in most chapters in this volume use this kind of longitudinal perspective to unpack the complex causal relationships between non-state provision and state capacity.

In our introductory chapters, we highlight two factors that affect the political consequences of non-state provision, including NSP characteristics related to the degree of formality in organizational structure, locus of operation, profit orientation, and eligibility criteria, as well as NSP-state relations. We do not articulate a specific set of propositions about the effects of NSP types on state capacity because we could not derive any obvious ex ante expectations about how the properties of a given NSP might affect state regulatory capacity or other core government functions. The chapters in this volume appear to support this analytical choice. Collectively, they do not suggest that particular qualities of NSPs are more or less associated with strong state capabilities. For example, the empirical findings regarding the degree of formality yield contradictory effects on the state. According to Jones Luong, multinational oil companies in Central Asia may improve social and economic development outcomes but actually undermine the state's long-term capacity for political development. The social service activities of equally formal NSPs, however, appear to boost state capacity in Kenya. As Brass argues, welfare provision by NGOs operating in Kenya—whether domestic or foreign—increased state legitimacy and capacity by expanding the overall supply of social services and public access to resources. In Argentina, Post contends that the privatization of the water sector "transformed rather than enfeebled" state capacity as local regulatory agencies began to monitor private contractors. In his chapter on Tanzania, Jennings speculates that, given their historically deep roots in the fabric of Tanzanian society, faith-based organizations are likely to have a less detrimental impact on state capacity than secular (and often international) NGOs, which have entered the domestic scene far more recently.

Based on evidence from the chapters, informality may be the only dimension of NSP characteristics that potentially undermines state capacity across the various countries covered in this volume, particularly when informal NSPs are profit-oriented. The system of spontaneous privatization in the Russian health sector clearly undercuts the functioning of the public health system, limiting the ability of state officials to monitor and assess the delivery of health care. This entrenched system of informal side payments also compels medical professionals to resist government efforts to reregulate health care and corrodes the state's ability to generate tax revenue. Similarly, in Lebanon, sectarian political organizations, which both operate their own health and educational facilities and broker access to public benefits, prefer to use the state as a source of patronage. In order to derive political gain from their own non-state welfare activities, sectarian providers therefore have an incentive not to empower the state. The Lebanese case is especially ironic because the very actors who resist efforts to strengthen state regulatory capacities often hold high-level positions in the government.

From a longer-term, demand-side perspective, MacLean argues that the rising importance of informal kinship networks in gaining access to social assistance undermines the constituency for public social welfare, thereby reducing state capacity. Similarly, in India, the reliance on informal mediators to gain access to social benefits may undermine state capacity by compelling citizens, and especially the poor, to bypass official government representatives in accessing social entitlements. Ultimately, a historical reading of these case studies exposes the interactive relationship between the state and NSPs: Low levels of state capacity facilitate the emergence of informal welfare provision in the first place, in turn further undermining public regulatory and other capabilities. Conversely, the Chilean state's investment in state capacity to regulate education by enhancing the Ministry of Education's ability to collect data and by expanding its personnel reflects the preexisting high levels of state capacity in that country (Soifer 2012).

Although we do not present ex ante expectations about the effects of NSP characteristics on state capacity, we do propose at the outset of the book that the relationship between NSPs and the state can affect the future development of state capacity. In particular, we suggest that a cooperative state-NSP relationship can enhance state capacity. In most developing countries, it is impossible for states to penetrate the full expanse of the national territory with the infrastructure and services central to welfare regimes. By working collaboratively with NSPs, states can effectively extend their reach and potentially claim at least some credit for service provision. In sub-Saharan Africa, both Brass and Jennings show that the Kenyan and Tanzanian governments expanded social programs as a result of their relatively collaborative relationships of "substitution" with NGOs and FBOs, respectively. In more ostensibly capable states, such as Argentina, Chile, and the United States, relationships of "coproduction" or "delegation" between states and NSPs enabled states to enlarge social welfare networks, notwithstanding some unevenness in the geographic spread and effectiveness of the goods and services provided. To the extent that citizens credit states with enhanced provision, these collaborative relationships between states and NSPs may increase overall state capacity.

Conversely, as the Russian and Lebanese cases of "appropriation" indicate, when providers have a vested interest in underdeveloped state regulatory capacity, they can block efforts to enhance state monitoring of their activities. Cook's chapter on Russia reveals how unstable or corrupt social service and insurance markets and pervasive informal exchanges have negative implications for the population's access to social services and their expectations of the state, which in turn affect the state's capacity to tax citizens and employers, distribute public goods, and construct and implement national welfare programs and policies. In a distinct context characterized by a far more "laissez faire" historical tradition, Cammett's analysis of the evolution of the Lebanese welfare regime shows how de facto control over social welfare and other policy domains by sectarian groups and local strongmen progressively weakens and even scuttles initiatives to build up public welfare capacity.

Overall, the complicated causal relationships between non-state provision and state capacity (and vice versa) have significant policy implications. The growing number and tremendous diversity of NSPs, as well as the informal structures of some of these actors, pose new regulatory challenges, particularly for the weaker states of the developing world. Some scholars worry that NSPs substitute for what were previously state-delivered services so completely that the state is left with little capacity or public constituency for continued involvement in the social welfare sector (Obiyan 2005; Wood 1997). The book's chapters have revealed, however, that NSPs do not simply crowd out the state's capacity (and, under some conditions, may even increase state capacity), but they can challenge the state's ability to regulate and to coordinate the overall welfare regime.

Thus, even where states (such as Kenya or Argentina) are content to contract out social services to NSPs, these states must still monitor and regulate the functioning of the NSPs. The sheer number of NSPs operating within any one country greatly challenges state regulatory capacities. Furthermore, the financing and operational authority for NSPs may originate from outside of the country in distant and disparate capitals. The chapters therefore suggest that the challenge to state capacity goes well beyond the regulation and monitoring of individual NSPs. Rather, the expansion of non-state provision requires increased *coordination* of activities among many different NSPs and the state.

Greater coordination of both state and non-state provision of social welfare would yield many potential benefits. First, the state and different NSPs would be able to identify where their respective activities duplicate each other's resources and expertise in particular places. This mapping of state and NSP service efforts would help to reduce waste and maximize the efficient allocation of scarce budgetary resources. For example, in many countries the lack of state regulation combines with a two-tiered health system, in which the wealthy seek care from high-cost, private providers, while the poor and uninsured receive more basic care through other channels. This type of dualistic system can lead to overinvestment in high-tech medical equipment, some of which could be shared among multiple facilities rather than purchased separately. Second, with enhanced information about NSP activities, the state and NSPs would be better poised to take advantage of potential economies of scale in service provision. These efficiencies are perhaps most apparent with respect to public health interventions such as vaccination or awareness campaigns, in which coordination between the state and NSPs would enable more communities to be covered with relatively low additional investment. Greater oversight of NSP social welfare activities could also enable public agencies to promote the replication of "best practices" across the national territory. Third, the coordination of state and non-state provision would enable an improved match between local citizen needs and preferences, on the one hand, and service availability, on the other hand. To the extent that NSPs are based in the community or employ staff from local areas, they are better positioned to discern and act on community goals and deficiencies with respect to social services. And, finally, the coordination across administrative boundaries might improve the equity of access to services overall, actually reducing some of the current and growing inequalities across national territories.

Of course, increased policy coordination requires significant capacity on the part of NSPs, local communities, and the state. To begin, one promising avenue for the regulation and coordination of non-state social welfare provision is for NSPs to develop improved methods of *self*-regulation and *self*-coordination. For example, an umbrella organization of NGOs may monitor and enforce certain standards of conduct among its members through "club accountability" mechanisms (Prakash and Gugarty 2010).

Another possibility for policy coordination is for individuals and communities to self-organize in order to regulate and coordinate the provision of social welfare. Over the past several decades, scholars have investigated "polycentric" modes of governance, in which overlapping and competing authorities enable individuals and communities to self-organize in order to coordinate and regulate the use of natural resources such as irrigation systems and forests (Ostrom 2009; Ostrom, Tiebout, and Warren 1961). More recently, analysts are exploring how communities might self-organize to regulate the provision of health care and other social welfare goods (McGinnis and Brink 2012). Self-regulation and self-coordination may be especially important in some developing countries where the state is so weak or close to collapse that public regulation and coordination is out of consideration for the near future.

Even though NSPs and communities can certainly play important roles in the self-regulation and coordination of non-state provision, these alternative strategies have their limits. Critics have highlighted that NSPs and communities are vulnerable to political cleavages (Agrawal and Gibson 1999; Lieberman 2009). For example, NSPs may resist sharing information about or coordinating their activities with other actors they view as rivals for shrinking resources. Furthermore, NSPs or communities might lack the information necessary to self-regulate effectively (Mizala and Schneider) or strategically reject any efforts to diminish their role in a particular sector. The book's chapters hence demonstrate the continued critical place of the state itself in regulating and coordinating non-state provision. NSPs may be here to stay; but so too are states. The problem is that most developing countries lack ideal-typical Weberian states with well-developed legal-rational bureaucracies. A broad implication of these conclusions, then, is the importance of investing in the capacity of the state itself.

Our emphasis on the effects of distinct state capacities on the political consequences of non-state provision complements recent efforts to disaggregate state capacities along different dimensions (Hanson and Sigman 2011; Soifer 2012). Rather than labeling states as "strong" versus "weak" in dichotomous terms (Acemoglu 2005), or focusing on a narrow conceptualization based on the state's ability to provide basic security within the internationally recognized territorial borders (Rotberg 2003a; Krasner and Pascual 2005), we emphasize the importance of a range of state capacities related to service delivery. These capacities include not only the state's ability to deliver and finance social services directly but also to gather information on community needs and welfare experiences; regulate, monitor, and enforce accountability by non-state actors; and coordinate activities among a multiplicity of NSPs and state actors at multiple levels across the national territory. Although we focus on social service delivery, non-state welfare provision likely also affects other roles of the state, such as the provision of security. For example, when NSPs substitute for the state in the realm of security, the state potentially loses control over its territory in even more tangible and fundamental ways and government accountability to citizens might decline or, at a minimum, become more circuitous. Since many NSPs have transnational linkages, state capacity—whether in social welfare or in other sectors—is not only affected by national political dynamics but is also shaped by the influences of donors, international organizations, and other global actors.

Furthermore, the chapters in this volume demonstrate the value of examining how state capacity is actually implemented over time and experienced on the ground on an everyday basis. A cross-national comparison of the ratio of direct taxes to total revenue or total taxes as a percentage of GDP is often used as a rough proxy for state capacity (Cheibub 1998; Levi 1989), but this does not adequately capture the informal exercise of state capacity and may actually obscure the unevenness of state capacity (Boone 2003). Cross-national snapshots of state capacity also miss the importance of history. The book's empirical chapters reveal that it is vital to analyze the history of state capacity in order to understand the mutually constitutive and iterative politics of non-state provision.

Beyond Middle-Income Countries in the Developing World?

The preceding sections summarize the key empirical findings and assess the extent to which they support or contradict the propositions presented in chapter 3. We focus on the middle-income countries that make up the bulk of developing countries around the world. At least two of the chapters in this volume—Allard's contribution on nonprofits in the U.S. welfare state and Cook's analysis of the health sector in postcommunist Russia—demonstrate the resonance of our main propositions beyond the core cases of middle-income, developing countries in Africa, Asia, Latin America, and the Middle East. In these more industrialized and developed economies, similar pockets of non-state social welfare provision exist even in places with relatively established welfare state bureaucracies.

On the one hand, these chapters reveal how segments of the population are forced to meet their basic needs through informal and insecure arrangements in more developed welfare states. On the other hand, they highlight the importance of NSP-state relations and, particularly, the state's capacity to regulate non-state providers in enhancing accountability to citizens and the quality of service provision. The chapters on the relatively high capacity Latin American countries covered in this volume, including Argentina and, especially, Chile, indicate that the findings are also applicable to major emerging markets around the world. At a minimum, probing the roles of NSPs in OECD countries underscores the critical importance of state regulatory capacity in shaping the politics of non-state provision.

In designing the scope of this volume, we purposefully exclude failed states, or countries where governments do not control their territories and fail to provide even basic security to their citizens. In part, this is due to the fact that they constitute a relatively small percentage of countries in the world, despite their widespread coverage in the global media. But our decision not to address the dynamics of non-state provision in failed states also stems from an analytical choice: when states are virtually absent in the lives of citizens, NSPs operate in a qualitatively distinct environment. Our core findings and propositions may not extend to these contexts, particularly given our emphasis on NSP-state relations in shaping the political consequences of non-state social welfare provision. In failed states, NSPs most likely provide greater access and accountability than would otherwise be the case. Furthermore, in these contexts some types of NSPs may not operate because a modicum of state capacity to provide a minimum of security and infrastructure (particularly roads) is necessary for certain non-state actors to intervene. For example, INGOs and MNCs do not operate in the most militarized or most unstable regions of the Democratic Republic of Congo and may even call for international military occupation to enable their operations, calling into question their alleged neutrality (de Waal 2009). In the absence of any kind of public social provision, informal kinship, tribal, ethnic, or religious networks would likely be the only sources of social solidarity. It is therefore impossible to construct a counterfactual benchmarking NSP provision against nonexistent public welfare programs and benefits. A distinct body of research documents the role of humanitarian NGOs and local organizations in areas with failed states (Autesserre 2010; Batley and Mcloughlin 2010; Ghani, Lockhart, and Carnahan 2005; Mertus and Sajjad 2005; Seay 2012, 2013; Zivetz 2006).

A Research Agenda

Non-state social welfare provision merits much more research given its significance throughout the world and especially in developing countries. At a minimum, further descriptive analyses are essential. The sheer lack of empirical data on the nature and extent of non-state provision calls for more cross-national and subnational data collection to develop quantitative measures of the numbers and activities of varied types of NSPs. Existing quantitative indicators that shed light on non-state provision of welfare emphasize national-level expenditures. This volume presents broad hypotheses and arguments about the consequences of non-state provision for important outcomes such as access to welfare, the accountability of providers to citizens, and state capacity. Our propositions and the empirical findings of the chapters point to several areas for future research.

The emergence and growth of non-state provision raises questions that are central to the functioning of states and welfare regimes and to experiences of citizenship in the twenty-first century. First, the sheer importance of non-state provision in welfare regimes calls for additional research analyzing the conditions under which NSPs provide social services and public goods effectively. Which types of NSPs are best equipped to engage in which types of social welfare activities? What types of public goods are best supplied by NSPs, and what is the nature of state-NSP relations in these circumstances? Carefully designed comparative projects—whether cross-national or subnational—examining state-NSP dynamics over time would help to illuminate the causal mechanisms behind improved or declining welfare provision by specific types of NSPs.

Second, virtually all welfare regimes create or reinforce inequities (Esping-Andersen 1990), and this is all the more true for NSPs whose mandates rarely stipulate universal access for all citizens in all regions of a given polity. Future research should therefore investigate what kinds of inequalities are established or strengthened by the non-state provision of social welfare. The specific cleavages accentuated by social provision are likely to vary across different types of non-state social welfare providers and political contexts. To take an obvious example, if an ethnic or sectarian provider explicitly claims to serve members of the in-group, then, by definition, out-group members will be excluded. Often, inequalities are more subtle and fall across gender, class, or regional lines, with overlapping and compounding stratifications.

It is also important to look beyond the concrete distributional differences to examine how ideology may shape the conceptualization of poverty and the social construction of inequality. The chapter by Cook shows how the ideological legacies of Soviet communism hindered the process of privatization in health care in Russia, which has subsequently spurred informal appropriation by the public sector health care workers themselves. In contrast, Allard reveals how, in the United States, neoliberal ideologies fostered the view of poverty as a problem of the individual, rather than a broader, structural problem that should be addressed by the central state, as is the view in many developing countries. These ideological differences significantly shape societal understandings of what inequalities are acceptable as well as the politics of responsibility for what should be done (Hochschild 1981; Kahl 2009; Schlesinger 2002).

A third set of issues that merits further research addresses the nature and mechanisms of accountability of NSPs to beneficiaries. When and how do citizens hold NSPs accountable for the type, quantity, or quality of services delivered? Are some types of NSPs necessarily more accountable to their beneficiaries? More likely, NSP accountability is less contingent on the type of NSP and more related to the nature of community mobilization or the ability of the state to regulate NSP activities. Further research should investigate the conditions under which NSPs and communities are able to self-organize for self-regulation and coordination of the non-state provision of social welfare.

Fourth, future research should focus on citizen perceptions of NSPs. How do individuals view the services they receive from NSPs and, more fundamentally, do they necessarily recognize the identity of and assign credit to the provider? In some instances, individuals may not understand which actors, whether public or private, actually finance and deliver social services and, as a result, they may attribute service provision inaccurately. Recognition of who provides services has important political implications. At a minimum, the failure to perceive the identity of the provider introduces new opportunities for credit-claiming—whether by states or non-state actors—which may take advantage of misperceptions to gain support among the population. This issue has become a central concern for policymakers and some scholars who fear that service provision is a means of gaining and maintaining recruits by Islamists and militant movements, which in the extreme may advocate and use violence against political authorities (Berman 2009; Levitt 2006; Alterman and von Hippel 2007).

A fifth set of questions raised by this volume centers on the effects of non-state provision on citizen perceptions of their political identities and on their political attitudes and behaviors. Under what conditions, if any, do NSP actions affect citizen views of their membership in different political communities as well as the rights and duties attendant with these categories of belonging? These questions raise methodological challenges because many factors shape political attitudes and behaviors, often interactively, and because attachment to national and other identities is difficult to capture through standardized measures. Nonetheless, it is important to understand whether and how non-state provision reconstructs the meanings and modalities of citizenship in the contemporary period. The varied experiences of citizens in gaining access to social welfare provision may fragment individual notions of political identity and citizenship. Although citizenship in the national community may not be entirely undermined, non-state provision may complicate experiences of citizenship when many different NSPs deliver what are frequently deemed the social rights of citizenship in the nation-state (Haggard and Kaufman 2008; MacLean 2010; Halisi, Kaiser, and Ndegwa 1988; Ndegwa 2001). A complicated sense of belonging combined with the fragmentation of NSPs and weak state capacity may make claims for accountability more difficult and burdensome for the average citizen.

A growing number and diversity of non-state providers mediate and provide access to social welfare around the world. Although non-state provision is not entirely new, the intensity and complexity of NSP roles has increased in recent decades. Understanding the politics of non-state provision is crucial because citizens in many developing countries continue to be extremely poor, struggling to meet their basic human needs, and non-state providers may be the main providers operating in their communities. The individual experience of poverty is not relative, but is often absolute, involving painful everyday choices about who may (or may not) receive schooling or health care in a family. Citizens in many developing countries face high-stakes challenges as they negotiate the rapidly evolving labyrinth of state and non-state providers.

NSPs provide access to critically needed social services across a variety of contexts. Although NSPs produce many positive outcomes for citizens and the state, we all—scholars, politicians, policymakers, practitioners, and citizens—need to reflect more systematically and critically on the political consequences of the non-state provision of social welfare. We cannot assume that NSPs will surpass the performance of weak, inefficient, and sometimes corrupt states. By investigating the conditions under which non-state provision works well (or does not work well), we may be able to improve the everyday well-being of individuals and families in many developing countries around the world.

References

Aarva, Paulina, Irina Ilchenko, Pavel Gorobets, and Anastasiya Rogacheva. 2009. "Formal and Informal Payments in Health Care Facilities in Two Russian Cities, Tyumen and Lipetsk." *Health Policy and Planning* 24:395–405.

Abouchedid, Kamal, and Ramzi Nasser. 2000. "The State of History Teaching in Private-Run Confessional Schools in Lebanon: Implications for National Integration." *Mediterranean Journal of Educational Studies* 5 (2): 57–82.

Abu Sharkh, Miriam, and Ian Gough. 2010. "Global Welfare Regimes: A Cluster Analysis." *Global Social Policy* 10 (1): 27–58.

Acemoglu, Daron. 2005. "Politics and Economics in Weak and Strong States." *Journal of Monetary Economics* 52 (7): 1199–1226.

Adams, Richard H. 1991. *The Effects of International Remittances on Poverty, Inequality, and Development in Rural Egypt*. Research Report, vol. 86. Washington, DC: International Food Policy Research Institute.

Adams, Terry. 1995. "Historical Beginnings: The AIOC–Azerbaijan International Operating Company." *Azerbaijan International* 3 (2): 33–38.

Aga Khan Foundation. 2006. *Annual Report 2006*. Available at http://www.akdn.org/publi cations/2006_akf_annual_report.pdf.

———. 2007. "Non-State Providers and Public-Private-Community Partnerships in Education." In *Education for All Global Monitoring Report 2008*. Geneva: United Nations Educational, Scientific and Cultural Organization.

Agrawal, Arun, and Clark Gibson. 1999. "Enchantment and Disenchantment: The Role of Community in Natural Resource Conservation." *World Development* 27 (4): 629–49.

Agrawal, Pradeep. 2008. "Economic Growth and Poverty Reduction: Evidence from Kazakhstan." *Asian Development Review* 24 (2): 90–115.

Aguas Argentinas. 2005. "Aguas Argentinas: 1993–2004." Buenos Aires: Aguas Argentinas.

Alderman, Harold, and Christina Paxson. 1992. "Do the Poor Insure? A Synthesis of the Literature on Risk and Consumption in Developing Countries." In *Agriculture and Rural Development Department Working Papers Series 1008*. Washington, DC: World Bank.

Alesina, Alberto, Reza Baqir, and William Easterly. 1999. "Public Goods and Ethnic Divisions." *Quarterly Journal of Economics* 114 (4): 1243–84.

Alesina, Alberto, Arnaud Devleeschauwer, William Easterly, Sergio Kurlat, and Romain Wacziarg. 2003. "Fractionalization." *Journal of Economic Growth* 8 (2): 155–94. doi: 10.1023/A:1024471506938.

Allard, Scott W. 2008. "Place, Race, and Access to the Safety Net." In *Colors of Poverty*, edited by Ann Chih Lin and David Harris. New York: Russell Sage Foundation.

———. 2009. *Out of Reach: Place, Poverty, and the New American Welfare State*. New Haven: Yale University Press.

———. 2010. "Nonprofit Helping Hands for the Working Poor: The New Realities of Today's Safety Net." In *Old Assumptions, New Realities*, edited by Robert D. Plotnick, Marcia K. Meyers, Jennifer Romich, and Stephen Rathgeb Smith. New York: Russell Sage Foundation.

Allard, Scott W., and Jessica Cigna. 2008. "Access to Social Services in Rural America." *Perspectives on Poverty, Policy, and Place*, vol. 5, RUPRI Rural Poverty Research Center. Available at http://www.rupri.org/Forms/PerspectivesWinter09.pdf.

Allard, Scott W., and Benjamin Roth. 2010. "Suburbs in Need: Rising Suburban Poverty and Challenges for the Safety Net." Washington, DC: Brookings Institution, Metropolitan Policy Program.

Alterman, Jon B., and Karin von Hippel, eds. 2007. *Understanding Islamic Charities*. Washington, DC: Center for Strategic and International Studies.

Amadi, Stella, Mekonnen Germiso, and Asle Henriksen. 2006. "Statoil in Nigeria: Transparency and Local Content. Report 1." Fredensborgveien, Oslo: Framtiden i vårehender.

Ammar, Walid. 2003. *Health System and Reform in Lebanon*. Beirut: World Health Organization, Eastern Mediterranean Regional Office.

———. 2009. *Health beyond Politics*. Beirut: World Health Organization, Eastern Mediterranean Regional Office.

Ammar, Walid, Hisham Fakha, Osmat Azzam, Rita Freiha Khoury, Charbel Mattar, Maher Halabi, Aoudat Douried, and Khaled Srour. 2000. *Lebanon National Health Accounts 1998*. Beirut: World Health Organization, Lebanese Ministry of Public Health, World Bank.

Amuzegar, Jahangir. 2001. *Managing the Oil Wealth: OPEC's Windfalls and Pitfalls*. London: I.B. Tauris.

Anand, Priyanka. 2009. "Indian Non-Governmental Organizations." Available at http://www.anand.to/india/ngo.html.

Ananthpur, Kripa. 2007. "Rivalry or Synergy? Formal and Informal Local Governance in Rural India." *Development and Change* 38 (3): 401–21.

Ananthpur, Kripa, and Mick Moore. 2007. "Ambiguous Institutions: Traditional Governance and Local Democracy in Rural India." *IDS Working Paper 282*. Brighton, UK: Institute of Development Studies.

Andersson, Kristen. 2004. "Who Talks with Whom? The Role of Repeated Interactions in Decentralized Forest Governance." *World Development* 32 (3): 233–49.

Andrés, Luis, J. Luís Guasch, Thomas Haven, and Vivien Foster. 2008. *The Impact of Private Sector Participation in Infrastructure: Lights, Shadows, and the Road Ahead*. Washington, DC: World Bank/Public-Private Infrastructure Advisory Facility (PPIAF).

Angrist, Joshua, Eric Bettinger, Erik Bloom, Elizabeth King, and Michael Kremer. 2002. "Vouchers for Private Schooling in Colombia: Evidence from a Randomized Natural Experiment." *American Economic Review* 92 (5): 1535–58.

Aquinas, St. Thomas. 1265–74. *Summa Theologiae*. New York: Oxford University Press.

Asiedu, Elizabeth. 2006. "Foreign Direct Investment in Africa: The Role of Natural Resources, Market Size, Government Policies, Institutions and Political Instability." *World Economy* 29 (1): 63–77.

Asociación de Entes Reguladores de Agua Potable y Saneamiento de América Latina (AD-ERASA). 2004. "Ejercicio Anual de Benchmarking." Asunción, Paraguay: ADERASA.

Atingdui, Lawrence. 1995. "Defining the Nonprofit Sector: Ghana." In *Working Papers of the Johns Hopkins Comparative Nonprofit Sector Project*, no. 14, edited by Lester M. Salamon and Helmut K. Anheier. Baltimore: Johns Hopkins University Institute for Policy Studies.

Attié, Caroline. 2004. *Struggle in the Levant*. London: I.B. Tauris.

Austin, Michael J. 2003. "The Changing Relationship between Nonprofit Organizations and Public Social Service Agencies in the Era of Welfare Reform." *Nonprofit and Voluntary Sector Quarterly* 32 (1): 97–114.

Autesserre, Séverine. 2010. *The Trouble with the Congo: Local Violence and the Failure of International Peacebuilding*. Cambridge: Cambridge University Press.

Auty, Richard M. 2006. "Optimistic and Pessimistic Energy Rent Deployment Scenarios for Azerbaijan and Kazakhstan." In *Energy, Wealth and Governance in the Caspian Sea Region*, edited by R. Auty and I. deSoysa, 57–76. London: Routledge.

Ayee, Joseph R. A. 1994. *An Anatomy of Public Policy Implementation: The Case of Decentralization Policies in Ghana*. Avebury, UK: Aldershot Press.

Azarya, Victor, and Naomi Chazan. 1987. "Disengagement from the State in Africa: Reflections on the Experience of Ghana and Guinea." *Comparative Studies in Society and History* 29 (1): 106–31.

Bagirov, Sabit. 2008. *Azerbaijani Oil: Revenues, Expenses, and Risks*. Baku, Azerbaijan: Yeni Nesil Publishing House.

Bailey, Frederick G. 1963. *Politics and Social Change: Orissa in 1959*. Berkeley: University of California Press.

Bakan, Joel. 2004. *The Corporation: The Pathological Pursuit of Profits and Power*. Toronto: Penguin Books.

Baker, Andy. 2009. *The Market and the Masses in Latin America: Policy Reform and Consumption in Liberalizing Economies*. New York: Cambridge University Press.

Balaa, Violette. 2005. "The Doors of Private Hospitals Will Be Open on Monday for Medical Care Requests." *Al-Nahar* 15.

Banerjee, Niloy. 2006. "A Note on Capabilities That Contribute to the Success of Non-Governmental Organisations." In *Discussion Paper 57P*. Maastricht: European Centre for Development Policy Management.

Bardhan, Pranab K., and Dilip Mookherjee. 2006. *Decentralization and Local Governance in Developing Countries: A Comparative Perspective*. Cambridge, MA: MIT Press.

Barkan, Joel D. 1975. *An African Dilemma: University Students, Development, and Politics in Ghana, Tanzania, and Uganda*. Nairobi: Oxford University Press.

Barnes, Jonathan. 1984. *Politics: The Complete Works of Aristotle*. Princeton: Princeton University Press.

Barr, Abigail, Marcel Fafchamps, and Trudy Owens. 2005. "The Governance of Non-Governmental Organizations in Uganda." *World Development* 33 (4): 657–79.

Barraclough, Geoffrey. 1982. *The Times Concise Atlas of World History*. London: Times Books.

Baru, Rama V. 2002. "Privatisation of Health Services in South Asia." Paper presented at the Globalism and Social Policy Program Seminar No. 5, "Emerging Global Markets in Social Protection and Health," Dubrovnik, September 26–28.

Baruti, Elias. 2008. "The Role of NGOs in the Delivery of Social Security." Presentation at the Thirty-Third Global Conference of the International Council on Social Welfare. Available at: www.icsw.org/doc/0011_2e_Barut_Eng.ppt.

Bashshour, Munir. 1988. "The Role of Education: A Mirror of a Fractured National Image." In *Toward a Viable Lebanon*, edited by H. Barakat. London: Croom Helm.

Bates, Robert H. 1981. *Markets and States in Tropical Africa: The Political Basis of Agricultural Policies*. Berkeley: University of California Press.

Bates, Robert H., and Amy Farmer Curry. 1992. "Community versus Market: A Note on Corporate Villages." *American Political Science Review* 86 (2): 457–63.

Batley, Richard. 2006. "Engaged or Divorced? Cross-Service Findings on Government Relations with Non-state Service Providers." *Public Administration and Development* 26 (3): 241–51.

Batley, Richard, and Claire Mcloughlin. 2010. "Engagement with Non-State Service Providers in Fragile States: Reconciling State-Building and Service Delivery." *Development Policy Review* 28 (2): 131–54.

Bayatly, T. 2003. "BP Current Developments." *Azerbaijan International* 11 (3): 78–79.

Bebbington, Anthony. 1997. "New States, New NGOs? Crises and Transitions among Rural Development NGOs in the Andean Region." *World Development* 25 (11): 1755–65.

Bebbington, Anthony, S. Hickey, and D. Mitlin. 2008. *Can NGOs Make a Difference? The Challenge of Development Alternatives*. London: Zed Books.

Behrman, J., and B. Wolfe. 1987. "How Does a Mother's Schooling Affect Family Health, Nutrition, Medical Care Usage and Household Sanitation?" *Journal of Econometrics* 36:185–204.

Belshaw, Deryke, Robert Calderisi, and Chris Sugden, eds. 2003. *Faith in Development: Partnership between the World Bank and the Churches in Africa*. Oxford: Regnum Books.

Bennett, Juliette. 2002. "Multinational Corporations, Social Responsibility, and Conflict." *Journal of International Affairs* 55 (2): 393–410.

Bennett, Sara, Barbara McPake, and Anne Mills, eds. 1997. *Private Health Providers in Developing Countries: Serving the Public Interest?* London: Zed Books.

Ben Romdhane, Mahmoud. 2006. "Social Policy and Development in Tunisia since Independence: A Political Perspective." In *Social Policy in the Middle East: Economic, Political, and Gender Dynamics*, edited by Massoud Karshenas and Valentine M. Moghadam. New York: Palgrave Macmillan.

Berendes, Sima, Heywood Peter, Sandy Oliver, and Paul Garner. 2011. "Quality of Private and Public Ambulatory Health Care in Low and Middle Income Countries: Systematic Review of Comparative Studies." *PLoS Medicine* 8 (4): e1000433.

Berman, Eli. 2009. *Radical, Religious, and Violent: The New Economics of Terrorism*. Cambridge, MA: MIT Press.

Berry, Sara. 1997. "Tomatoes, Land, and Hearsay: Property and History in Asante in the Time of Structural Adjustment." *World Development* 25 (8): 1225–41.

Berube, Alan, and Elizabeth Kneebone. 2006. *Two Steps Back: City and Suburban Poverty Trends, 1999–2005*. Washington, DC: Brookings Institution, Metropolitan Policy Program, Living Census Series.

Besley, Timothy, and Maitreesh Ghatak. 1999. "Public-Private Partnerships for the Provision of Public Goods: Theory and an Application to NGOs." *Development Economics Discussion Paper Series* 17. London: The Suntory and Toyota International Centres for Economics and Related Disciplines, London School of Economics and Political Science.

Bevan, Philippa. "Conceptualising In/Security Regimes." In *Insecurity and Welfare Regimes in Asia, Africa and Latin America: Social Policy in Developing Countries*, edited by Ian Gough, Geof Wood, Armando Barrientos, Philippa Bevan, Peter Davis, and Graham Room. Cambridge: Cambridge University Press.

Beyoghlou, Kamal A. 1989. "Lebanon's New Leaders: Militias in Politics." *Journal of South Asian and Middle Eastern Studies* 12 (3): 28–36.

Bindemann, Kirsten. 1999. "Production-Sharing Agreements: An Economic Analysis." WPM 25, Oxford Institute for Energy Studies. Oxford: Oxford University.

Blair, Harry. 2000. "Participation and Accountability at the Periphery: Democratic Local Governance in Six Countries." *World Development* 28 (1): 21–39.

Blam, Inna, and Sergey Kovalev. 2003. "Commercialization of Medical Care and Household Behavior in Transitional Russia." Draft paper prepared for Réseau universitaire international de Genève (RUIG) and the United Nations Research Institute for Social Development (UNRISD) Project on Globalization, Inequality, and Health. Geneva: UNRISD.

———. 2006. "Spontaneous Commercialization, Inequality, and the Contradictions of Compulsory Medical Insurance in Transitional Russia." *Journal of International Development* 18:407–23.

Bleck, Jaimie. 2011. "Schooling Citizens: Education, Citizenship, and Democracy in Mali." PhD diss., Cornell University.

———. 2013. "Do Francophone and Islamic Schooling Communities Participate Differently? Disaggregating Parents' Political Behaviour in Mali." *Journal of Modern African Studies* 51 (3): 377–408.

Blowfield, Michael, and Alan Murray. 2008. *Corporate Social Responsibility: A Critical Introduction.* Oxford: Oxford University Press.

Boaz, Taylor C., and Jordan Gans-Morse. 2009. "Neoliberalism: From New Liberal Philosophy to Anti-Market Slogan." *Studies in Comparative International Development* 44:137–61.

Boixadós, María Cristina. 2000. *Las tramas de una ciudad, Córdoba entre 1870 y 1895.* Córdoba, Argentina: Ferreyra Editorial.

Boone, Catherine. 2003. *Political Topographies of the African State.* Cambridge: Cambridge University Press.

Bordi de Ragucci, Olga. 1997. *El agua privada en Buenos Aires 1856–1892: Negocio y fracaso.* Buenos Aires: Editorial Vinciguerra S.R.L.

Boris, Elizabeth T. 1999. "The Nonprofit Sector in the 1990s." In *Philanthropy and the Nonprofit Sector in a Changing America*, edited by Charles T. Clotfelter and Thomas Ehrlich. Bloomington: Indiana University Press.

Bortei-Doku, Ellen, and Ernest Aryeetey. 1996. "Mobilizing Cash for Business: Women in Rotating Susu Clubs in Ghana." In *Money-go-rounds: The Importance of Rotating Savings and Credit Associations for Women*, edited by S. Ardener and S. Burman. Oxford: Berg Publishers.

Bowen, Howard R. 1953. *Social Responsibilities of the Businessman.* New York: Harper and Row.

Brass, Jennifer N. 2010. "Surrogates for Government? NGOs and the State in Kenya." PhD diss., University of California, Berkeley.

———. 2012a. "Blurring Boundaries: The Integration of NGOs into the Governance of Kenya." *Governance* 25 (2): 209–35.

———. 2012b. "Why Do NGOs Go Where They Go? Evidence from Kenya." *World Development* 40 (2): 387–401. doi:10.1016/j.worlddev.2011.07.017.

Bratton, Michael. 1989. "The Politics of Government-NGO Relations in Africa." *World Development* 17 (4): 569–87.

———. 1990. "NGOs in Africa: Can They Influence Public Policy?" *Development and Change* 21 (1): 87–118.

———. 1994. "Peasant-State Relations in Post-Colonial Africa: Patterns of Engagement and Disengagement." In *State Power and Social Forces: Domination and Transformation in the Third World*, edited by J.S. Migdal, A. Kohli, and V. Shue. New York: Cambridge University Press.

Brautigam, Deborah. 1994. "State, NGOs, and International Aid in The Gambia." In *The Changing Politics of Non-Governmental Organizations and African States*, edited by Eve Sandberg, 59–82. Westport, CT: Praeger.

Brinkerhoff, Derick W. 1999. "Exploring State-Civil Society Collaboration." *Nonprofit and Voluntary Sector Quarterly* 28:59–86.

———. 2002. "Government–Nonprofit Partners for Health Sector Reform in Central Asia: Family Group Practice Associations in Kazakhstan and Kyrgyzstan." *Public Administration and Development* 22 (1): 51–61.

———. 2007. *Governance in Post-Conflict Societies: Rebuilding Fragile States*. London: Routledge.

———. 2008. "The State and International Development Management: Shifting Tides, Changing Boundaries, and Future Directions." *Public Administration Review* 68 (6): 985–1001.

British Petroleum (BP). 2006. *BP in Azerbaijan Sustainability Report 2006*. Baku, Azerbaijan: BP Azerbaijan.

Brodhead, Tim. 1987. "NGOs: In One Year, Out the Other?" Supplement, *World Development* 15: 1–6.

Brooks, Sarah. 2009. *Social Protection and the Market: The Transformation of Social Security Institutions in Latin America*. Cambridge: Cambridge University Press.

Brown, David L. 1998. "Creating Social Capital: Nongovernmental Development Organizations and Intersectoral Problem Solving." In *Private Action and Public Goods*, edited by W. W. Powell and E. S. Clemens. New Haven: Yale University Press.

Brown, David L., and Archana Kalegaonkar. 2002. "Support Organizations and the Evolution of the NGO Sector." *Nonprofit and Voluntary Sector Quarterly* 31 (2): 231–58.

Brown, Julie, and Nina L. Rusinova. 2008. "Holding Up the Social Safety Net: Gender and the 'Hidden' Health Care System in Urban Russia." Paper presented at the Eighth Aleksanteri Conference, "Welfare, Gender and Agency in Russia and Eastern Europe," December 10–12.

Burger, Edward J., Mark Field, and Judyth Twigg. 1998. "From Assurance to Insurance in Russian Health Care: The Problematic Transition." *American Journal of Public Health* 88 (5): 755–58.

Butt, Riaza. 2010. "Your Equality Laws Are Unjust, Pope Tells UK before Visit." *Guardian*, February 2.

Cammett, Melani. 2011. "Partisan Activism and Access to Welfare in Lebanon." *Studies in Comparative International Development* 46 (1): 70–97.

———. 2014. *Compassionate Communalism: Welfare and Sectarianism in Lebanon*. Ithaca, NY: Cornell University Press.

Cammett, Melani, and Sukriti Issar. 2010. "Bricks and Mortar Clientelism: Sectarianism and the Logics of Welfare Allocation in Lebanon." *World Politics* 62 (3): 381–421.

Campbell, Will. 1996. "The Potential for Donor Mediation in NGO-State Relations: An Ethiopian Case Study." In *Working Papers 33*. Brighton, UK: Institute of Development Studies, University of Sussex.

Cannon, Christy. 2000. *NGOs and the State: A Case Study from Uganda*. In *Development, NGOs, and Civil Society*, edited by J. Pearce. Oxford: Oxfam.

Casanova, José. 1994. *Public Religions in the Modern World*. Chicago: University of Chicago Press.

Castles, Francis G., Stephan Leibfried, Jane Lewis, Herbert Obinger, and Christopher Pierson, eds. 2010. *The Oxford Handbook of the Welfare State*. Oxford: Oxford University Press.

Castles, Francis G., and Herbert Obinger. 2008. "Worlds, Families, Regimes: Country Clusters in European and OECD Area Public Policy." *West European Politics* 31 (1–2): 321–44.

Castro-Leal, F., J. Dayton, L. Demery, and K. Mehra. 2000. "Public Spending on Health Care in Africa: Do the Poor Benefit?" *Bulletin of the World Health Organization* 78 (1): 66–74.

Cebu Team. 1991. "Underlying and Proximate Determinants of Child Health: The Cebu Longitudinal Health and Nutrition Survey." *American Journal of Epidemiology* 33 (2): 185–201.

Center for Corporate Citizenship. 2011. *Corporate Citizenship Reporting Is Growing and Evolving at a Rapid Pace*. Boston: Center for Corporate Citizenship, Boston College.

Center on Budget and Policy Priorities. 2010. "Policy Basics: Introduction to the Food Stamp Program." Available at http://www.cbpp.org/files/policybasics-foodstamps.pdf.

Centro Nacional de Organizaciones de la Comunidad (CENOC). 2012. "Listado de Organizaciones inscriptas en nuestra Base de Datos." Government of Argentina: CENOC. Available at http://www.cenoc.gov.ar/busqueda.html.

Chambers, Robert. 1984. *Rural Development: Putting the Last First.* London: Longman.

Chandra, Kanchan. 2004. *Why Ethnic Parties Succeed: Patronage and Ethnic Head Counts in India.* Cambridge: Cambridge University Press.

———. 2006. "What Is Ethnic Identity and Does It Matter?" *Annual Review of Political Science* 9: 397–424.

Chatilla, Dona 2007. "National Security Fund: A Haven of Waste." *Daily Star*, August 13.

Chaudhry, Kiren Aziz. 1993. "The Myths of the Market and the Common History of Late Developers." *Politics & Society* 21 (3): 245–74.

Chazan, Naomi. 1988. "Patterns of State-Society Incorporation and Disengagement." In *The Precarious Balance: State and Society in Africa*, edited by D. Rothschild and N. Chazan. Boulder, CO: Westview Press.

———. 1994. "Engaging the State: Associational Life in Sub-Saharan Africa." In *State Power and Social Forces: Domination and Transformation in the Third World*, edited by J.S. Migdal, A. Kohli, and V. Shue. New York: Cambridge University Press.

Chege, Sam. 1999. "Donors Shift More Aid to NGOs." *Africa Recovery* 13 (1): 6.

Cheibub, Jose Antonio. 1998. "Political Regimes and the Extractive Capacity of Governments: Taxation in Democracies and Dictatorships." *World Politics* 50:349–76.

Chen, Yen-Ting, and Melani Cammett. 2012. "Informal Politics and Inequity of Access to Health Care in Lebanon." *International Journal for Equity in Health* 11 (23): 1–8.

Clark, John. 1991. *Democratizing Development: The Role of Voluntary Organizations.* West Hartford, CT: Kumarian Press.

———. 1992. "Democratising Development: NGOs and the State." *Development in Practice* 2 (3): 151–62.

———. 1995. "The State, Popular Participation and the Voluntary Sector." *World Development* 23 (4): 593–601.

Clarke, George, Katrina Kosec, and Scott Wallsten. 2004. "Has Private Participation in Water and Sewerage Improved Coverage? Empirical Evidence from Latin America." *World Bank Policy Research Paper 3445.* Washington, DC: World Bank.

Clarke, Gerard. 2006. "Faith Matters: Faith-Based Organisations, Civil Society and International Development." *Journal of International Development* 18:835–48.

———. 2008. "Faith-Based Organisations and International Development: An Overview." In *Development, Civil Society and Faith-Based Organisations: Bridging the Sacred and the Secular*, edited by Gerard Clarke and Michael Jennings, 17–45. Basingstoke, UK: Palgrave Macmillan.

Clifton, Judith, Francisco Comín, and Daniel Díaz-Fuentes. 2007. "Transforming Network Services in Europe and the Americas: From Ugly Ducklings to Swans?" In *Transforming Public Enterprise in Europe and North America: Networks, Integration, and Transnationalisation*, edited by Judith Clifton, Francisco Comín, and Daniel Díaz-Fuentes. Houndsmill, UK: Palgrave Macmillan.

Clignet, Remi, and Philip Foster. 1966. *The Fortunate Few: A Study of Secondary Schools and Students in the Ivory Coast.* Evanston, IL: Northwestern University Press.

Cnaan, Ram, John DeIulio Jr., and Paula Fass. 2002. *The Invisible Caring Hand: American Congregations and the Provision of Welfare.* New York: New York University Press.

Cochrane, Marisa. 2009. "The Fragmentation of the Sadrist Movement." *Iraq Report* no. 12, Institute for the Study of War. Washington, DC: Institute for the Study of War.

Cockburn, Patrick. 2008. *Muqtada al-Sadr and the Battle for the Future of Iraq.* New York: Scribner.

Collier, Paul, and Jan W. Gunning. 1999. "Why Has Africa Grown Slowly?" *Journal of Economic Perspectives* 13 (3): 3–22.

Connolly, Eileen. 2007. "Engagement with Civil Society in Tanzania: Perspectives of Tanzanian CSOs." Working Paper No. 4. Dublin: Centre for Development Studies, Dublin City University.

Consultora MORI. 2010. "Estudio demanda y cambios en el sistema educativo." Santiago, Chile: Pontificia Universidad Católica de Chile.

Contreras, Manuel E. 2004. *Corporate Social Responsibility in the Promotion of Social Development: Experiences from Asia and Latin America.* Washington, DC: Inter-American Development Bank.

Cook, Linda. 2000. "The Russian Welfare State: Obstacles to Restructuring." *Post-Soviet Affairs* 16 (4): 355–78.

———. 2007a. *Postcommunist Welfare States: Reform Politics in Russia and Eastern Europe.* Ithaca, NY: Cornell University Press.

———. 2007b. "Negotiating Welfare in Postcommunist States." *Comparative Politics* 40 (1): 41–62.

———. 2010. "Russia's Welfare Regime: The Shift toward Statism." In *Gazing at Welfare: Gender and Agency in Post-Socialist Countries,* edited by Maija Jappinen and Meri Kulmala. Cambridge: Cambridge Scholars Publishing.

Cooley, Alexander, and James Ron. 2002. "The NGO Scramble: Organizational Insecurity and the Political Economy of Transnational Action." *International Security* 27 (1): 5–39.

Corm, Georges. 1991. "Liban: Hégémonie milicienne et problème de rétablissement de l'état." *Maghreb-Machrek* 131:13–25.

Cornwall, Andrea, Henry Lucas, and Kath Pasteur. 2000. "Introduction: Accountability through Participation—Developing Workable Partnership Models in the Health Sector." *IDS Bulletin* 31 (1): 1–13.

Corrales, Javier. 1998. "Coalitions and Corporate Choices in Argentina, 1976–1994: The Recent Private Sector Support of Privatization." *Studies in Comparative International Development* 32 (4): 24–51.

Cox, Cristián, ed. 2003. *Políticas Educacionales en el Cambio de Siglo: La Reforma del Sistema Escolar de Chile.* Santiago: Editorial Universitaria.

Crook, Richard C., and James Manor. 1998. *Democracy and Decentralisation in South Asia and West Africa: Participation, Accountability and Performance.* New York: Cambridge University Press.

Cruz, José. 2009. "Social Capital in the Americas: Participation in Parents' Associations." *Americas Barometer Insights* 24: 1–6.

Cutler, David, and Grant Miller. 2005. "The Role of Public Health Improvements in Health Advances: The Twentieth-Century United States." *Demography* 42 (1): 1–22.

Dagher, Albert. 1995. *L'Etat et l'Economie au Liban: Action Gouvernementale et Finances Publiques de l'Independance a 1975.* Beirut: Centre d'Etudes et de Recherches sur le Moyen-Orient Contemporain.

Das, Jishnu. 2011. "The Quality of Medical Care in Low-Income Countries: From Providers to Markets." *PLoS Medicine* 8 (4):e1000432.

Das, Jishnu, Jeffrey Hammer, and Kenneth Leonard. 2008. "The Quality of Medical Advice in Low-Income Countries." *Journal of Economic Perspectives* 22 (2): 93–114.

Davies, Thomas. 2008. "The Rise and Fall of Transnational Civil Society: The Evolution of International Non-governmental Organizations since 1839." Report No. CUTP/003. London: City University Centre for International Politics.

Davis, Christopher. 1988. "The Organization and Performance of the Contemporary Soviet Health Care System." In *State and Welfare USA/USSR: Contemporary Policy and Practice,* edited by Gail W. Lapidus and Guy E. Swanson. Berkeley: University of California Press.

———. 2001. "Russia's Compulsory Medical Insurance Reform: Its Impact on Health Finance, Performance of the Medical System, and the Health of the Population." Project on "Improving Equity in Health Financing: Russia." Oxford: Oxford University, HLSP–Department for International Development (DFID).

Deaton, Angus. 1992. "Household Saving in LDCs: Credit Markets, Insurance and Welfare." *Scandinavian Journal of Economics* 94 (2): 253–73.

Dei, George J. Sefa. 1992. *Hardships and Survival in Rural West Africa: A Case Study of a Ghanaian Community*. Dakar, Senegal: Council for the Development of Social Science Research in Africa.

Department for International Development (DFID). 2000. *Realising Human Rights for Poor People*. London: DFID.

Dercon, Stefan. 2002. "Income Risk, Coping Strategies and Safety Nets." *World Bank Research Observer* 17:141–66.

———. 2003. "Poverty Traps and Development: The Equity-Efficiency Trade-Off Revisited." Paper prepared for the Conference on Growth, Inequality and Poverty, organised by the Agence française de développement and the European Development Research Network (EUDN).

de Soto, Hernando. 1989. *The Other Path*. New York: Harper and Row.

de Waal, Alex. 1997. *Famine Crimes: Politics and the Disaster Relief Industry in Africa*. Bloomington: Indiana University Press.

Diamond, L. 2008. "The Democratic Rollback: The Resurgence of the Predatory State." *Foreign Affairs* (March–April): 36–48.

Di Gropello, Emanuela, and Jeffrey Marshall. 2005. "Teacher Effort and Schooling Outcomes in Rural Honduras." In *Incentives to Improve Teaching*, edited by Emiliana Vargas. Washington, DC: World Bank.

Dillon, Nara. 2011. "Middlemen in the Chinese Welfare State: The Role of Philanthropists in Refugee Relief in Wartime Shanghai." *Studies in Comparative International Development* 46 (1): 22–45.

Domínguez, Jorge I. 1997. *Technopols: Freeing Politics and Markets in Latin America in the 1990s*. College Park: Pennsylvania State University Press.

Donahue, John D. 1989. *The Privatization Decision: Public Ends, Private Means*. New York: Basic Books.

Dror, David M., and Christian Jacquier. 1999. "Micro-Insurance: Extending Health Insurance to the Excluded." *International Social Security Review* 52 (1): 71–97.

Dunning, Thad. 2008. "Improving Causal Inference: Strengths and Limitations of Natural Experiments." *Political Research Quarterly* 61 (2): 282–93.

Easterly, William, and Ross Levine. 1997. "Africa's Growth Tragedy: Policies and Ethnic Divisions." *Quarterly Journal of Economics* 112 (4): 1203–50.

Economic Commission for Latin America and the Caribbean. 2010. "Public Social Spending in Latin America: General Trends and Investment in Developing the Skills of New Generations." In *Social Panorama of Latin America 2010*, edited by Economic Commission for Latin America and the Caribbean. Santiago, Chile: Economic Commission for Latin America and the Caribbean.

Economic Research Center (ERC). 2006. *Three Views on EITI Implementation in Azerbaijan*. Baku, Azerbaijan: ERC.

Economist Intelligence Unit (EIU). 2006. *Azerbaijan Country Profile*. London: EIU.

Edwards, Michael. 2000. *NGO Rights and Responsibilities: A New Deal for Global Governance*. London: Foreign Policy Centre.

Edwards, Michael, and David Hulme. 1996a. *Beyond the Magic Bullet: NGO Performance and Accountability in the Post–Cold War World*. West Hartford, CT: Kumarian Press.

———. 1996b. "Too Close for Comfort? The Impact of Official Aid on Nongovernmental Organizations." *World Development* 24 (6): 961–73.

Ekeh, Peter P. 1975. "Colonialism and the Two Publics in Africa: A Theoretical Statement." *Comparative Studies in Society and History* 17 (1): 91–112.

Elacqua, Gregory, Mark Schneider, and Jack Buckley. 2006. "School Choice in Chile: Is It Class or the Classroom?" *Journal of Policy Analysis and Management* 25 (3): 577–601.

El Khazen, Farid. 2000. *The Breakdown of the State in Lebanon, 1967–1976*. Cambridge: Harvard University Press.

Elkington, J. 2003. "Launch of AA1000 Conference." In *AA1000 Conference*. London: Accountability.org.uk.

Ellis, Stephen, and Gerrie Ter Haar. 2004. *Worlds of Power: Religious Thought and Political Practice in Africa*. London: Hurst.

Ente Nacional de Obras Hídricas de Saneamiento (ENOHSA) and Consejo Federal de Entidades de Servicios Sanitarias (COFES). 1999. *La cobrabilidad de los servicios sanitarios en Argentina*. Buenos Aires, Argentina: ENOHSA.

Epple, Dennis, and Richard Romano. 2008. "Educational Vouchers and Cream Skimming." *International Economic Review* 49 (4): 1395–1435.

Esping-Andersen, Gøsta. 1990. *The Three Worlds of Welfare Capitalism*. Princeton: Princeton University Press.

Esrey, S., J. Potash, L. Roberts, and C. Shiff. 1991. "Effects of Improved Water Supply and Sanitation on Ascariasis, Diarrhea, Dracunculiasis, Hookworm Infection, Schistosomiasis and Trachoma." *Bulletin of the World Health Organization* 69 (5): 609–21.

Estache, Antonio, Andres Gomez-Lobo, and Danny Leipziger. 2001. "Utilities Privatization and the Poor: Lessons and Evidence from Latin America." *World Development* 29 (7): 1179–98.

Estrada, Javier, Kristian Tangen, and Helge Ole Bergesen. 1997. *Manageable or Revolutionary? Environmental Challenges Confronting the Oil Industry*. London: Wiley & Sons.

Etzioni, Amitai. 1998. "A Moral Reawakening without Puritanism." In *The Essential Communitarian Reader*, edited by Amitai Etzioni, 41–46. New York: Rowman and Littlefield.

European Bank for Research and Development (EBRD). 1997. *Transition Report, 1997*. London: EBRD.

Evans, Peter. 1995. *Embedded Autonomy: States and Industrial Transformation*. Princeton: Princeton University Press.

Falleti, Tulia G. 2010. *Decentralization and Subnational Politics in Latin America*. New York: Cambridge University Press.

Fawaz, Leila Tarazi. 1994. *An Occasion for War: Mount Lebanon and Damascus in 1860*. Berkeley: University of California Press.

Feeley, G., I. M. Sheiman, and S. V. Shishkin. 1999. "Health Sector Informal Payments in Russia." Unpublished paper. Available at http://dcc2.bumc.bu.edu/RussianLegalHealth Reform/ProjectDocuments/n650.IIIB6.Article.pdf.

Flanigan, Shawn Teresa. 2008. "Nonprofit Service Provision by Insurgent Organizations: The Cases of Hizballah and the Tamil Tigers." *Studies in Conflict and Terrorism* 31 (6): 499–519.

Flounders, Sara. 2006. "450,000 NGOs in Russia." *Workers World*, February 6.

Foster, Vivien. 2005. "Ten Years of Water Service Reform in Latin America: Toward an Anglo-French Model." Water Supply and Sanitation Sector Board, Discussion Paper 3. Washington, DC: World Bank.

Fowler, Alan. 1991. "The Role of NGOs in Changing State-Society Relations: Perspectives from Eastern and Southern Africa." *Development Policy Review* 9 (1): 53–84.

———. 1995. "NGOs and the Globalization of Social Welfare: Perspectives from East Africa." In *Service Provision under Stress in East Africa*, edited by Joseph Semboja and Ole Therkildsen. Copenhagen: Centre for Development Research.

———. 1997. *Striking a Balance: A Guide to Enhancing the Effectiveness of Non-Governmental Organisations in International Development*. London: Earthscan Publications.

Fox, Jonathan A., ed. 1990. *The Challenge of Rural Democratization: Perspectives from Latin America and the Philippines.* London: Frank Cass.

Fox, Jonathan A., and David L. Brown. 1998. *The Struggle for Accountability: The World Bank, NGOs, and Grassroots Movements.* Cambridge, MA: MIT Press.

Frankel, Francine, and M. S. A. Rao, eds. 1989. *Dominance and State Power in India.* Delhi: Oxford University Press.

Freedom House. 2012. *Kenya 2012.* Available at http://www.freedomhouse.org/report/freedom-world/2011/kenya.

French National Archives. 1951–52. *Rapport Bi-Annuel sur la protection de la collectivite, de la famille, et de l'enfance.* Paris: Centre d'accueil et de recherche des Archives nationales (CARAN).

Fridenson, Patrick. 2007. "Transforming Public Enterprise in France." In *Transforming Public Enterprise in Europe and North America: Networks, Integration, and Transnationalisation,* edited by Judith Clifton, Francisco Comín, and Daniel Díaz-Fuentes. Houndsmill, UK: Palgrave Macmillan.

Frimpong-Ansah, A. 1991. *The Vampire State in Africa: The Political Economy of Decline in Ghana.* London: James Currey.

Frumkin, Peter, and Alice Andre-Clark. 2000. "When Missions, Markets, and Politics Collide: Values and Strategy in the Nonprofit Human Services." *Nonprofit and Voluntary Sector Quarterly* 29 (1): 141–63.

Frynas, Jedrzej George. 2000. *Oil in Nigeria: Conflict and Litigation between Oil Companies and Village Communities.* Hamburg: Lit Verlag Münster; New Brunswick, NJ: Transaction.

———. 2005. "The False Development Promise of Corporate Social Responsibility: Evidence from Multinational Oil Companies." *International Affairs* 81 (3): 581–98.

Fuller, C. J., and V. Benei, eds. 2000. *The Everyday State and Society in Modern India.* New Delhi: Social Science Press.

Fuller, C. J., and J. Harris. 2000. "Introduction: The Anthropology of the Indian State." In *The Everyday State and Society in Modern India,* edited by C. J. Fuller and V. Benei. New Delhi: Social Science Press.

Fung, Archon, and Erik Olin Wright. 2001. "Deepening Democracy: Innovations in Empowered Participatory Governance." *Politics and Society* 29 (1): 5–42.

Galiani, Sebastián, Paul Gertler, and Ernesto Schargrodsky. 2005. "Water for Life: The Impact of Privatization of Water Services on Child Mortality." *Journal of Political Economy* 113:83–120.

Gallego, Francisco, and Andrés Hernando. 2008. "School Choice in Chile: Looking at the Demand Side." Mimeo. Santiago, Chile: Economics Department, Universidad Católica de Chile.

Gariyo, Zie. 1995. "NGOs and Development in East Africa: A View from Below." In *Non-Governmental Organisations—Performance and Accountability: Beyond the Magic Bullet,* edited by M. Edwards and D. Hulme. London: Earthscan Publications.

Garner, Robert C. 2000. "Safe Sects: Dynamic Religion and AIDS in South Africa." *Journal of Modern African Studies* 38 (1): 41–69.

Garrison, J. 2000. *From Confrontation to Collaboration: Civil Society–Government–World Bank Relations in Brazil.* Washington, DC: World Bank.

Gary, Ian, and Terry Lynn Karl. 2003. *Bottom of the Barrel: Africa's Oil Boom and the Poor.* Baltimore, MD: Catholic Relief Services.

Gassner, Katharina, Alexander Popov, and Nataliya Pushak. 2008. "Does Private Sector Participation Improve Performance in Electricity and Water Distribution? An Empirical Assessment in Developing and Transition Countries." Public-Private Infrastructure Advisory Facility (PPIAF) Trends and Policy Series. Washington, DC: World Bank.

Gates, Carolyn L. 1998. *The Merchant Republic of Lebanon: Rise of an Open Economy.* London: I.B. Tauris.

Gaventa, John, and Andrea Cornwall. 2000. "From Users and Choosers to Makers and Shapers: Repositioning Participation in Social Policy." *IDS Bulletin* 31 (4): 50–62.

Gazley, Beth. 2011. "Co-optation, Coproduction or Competition? A Preliminary Empirical Look at Government-Supporting NPOs." Paper presented at the Annual Meeting of the International Society for Research on Public Management, Dublin, Ireland, April 11–13.

George, Betty Stein. 1976. *Education in Ghana.* Washington, DC: U.S. Department of Health, Education, and Welfare.

Gereffi, G., R. Garcia-Johnson, and E. Sasser. 2001. "The NGO-Industrial Complex." *Foreign Policy* 125 (July–August): 56–65.

Geschiere, Peter. 1993. "Chiefs and Colonial Rule in Cameroon: Inventing Chieftaincy, French and British Style." *Africa: Journal of the International African Institute* 63 (2): 151–75.

Ghani, Ashraf, Clare Lockhart, and Michael Carnahan. 2005. "Closing the Sovereignty Gap: An Approach to State-Building." London: Overseas Development Institute.

Gifford, Paul. 1994. "Some Recent Developments in African Christianity." *African Affairs* 93:513–34.

Gilbert, Alan. 1998 [1994]. *The Latin American City.* Nottingham, UK: Russell Press.

Gilens, Martin. 1999. *Why Americans Hate Welfare.* Chicago: University of Chicago Press.

Giving USA Foundation. 2008. *Giving USA 2008: The Annual Report on Philanthropy for the Year 2007.* Chicago, IL: Giving USA Foundation.

Global Witness. 2004. *Time for Transparency: Coming Clean on Oil, Mining and Gas Revenues.* Washington, DC: Global Witness.

Goldman Sachs. 2004. *Global Energy—Goldman Sachs Energy Environmental and Social Index.* London: Goldman Sachs.

Goldstone, Richard. 2006. *Imperial Nature: The World Bank and Struggles for Social Justice in the Age of Globalization.* New Haven: Yale University Press.

Gough, Ian. 2004. "Welfare Regimes in Development Contexts: A Global and Regional Analysis." In *Insecurity and Welfare Regimes in Asia, Africa and Latin America*, edited by I. Gough, G. D. Wood, A. Barrientos, P. Bevan, P. Davis, and G. Room, 15–48. Cambridge: Cambridge University Press.

Gough, Ian, and Goran Therborn. 2010. "The Global Future of Welfare States." In *The Oxford Handbook of the Welfare State*, edited by Francis G. Castles, Stephan Leibfried, Jane Lewis, Herbert Obinger, and Christopher Pierson. Oxford: Oxford University Press.

Gough, Ian, Geof Wood, Armando Barrientos, Philippa Bevan, Peter Davis, and Graham Room. 2004. *Insecurity and Welfare Regimes in Asia, Africa and Latin America: Social Policy in Development Contexts.* Cambridge: Cambridge University Press.

Government of Argentina. 1993. *Pacto Federal para el Empleo, la Producción y el Crecimiento.* August 12. Buenos Aires: República Argentina.

Government of India. 1998. *Indian Economic Survey 1997-98.* New Delhi: Ministry of Finance, Government of India.

———. 2009. "A Survey of Non-Profit Institutions in India: Some Findings." New Delhi: Central Statistical Organisation, Ministry of Statistics and Programme Implementation, Government of India.

Government of Kenya. 1992. Statute Law (Miscellaneous Amendments) Act.

———. 2002a. *Butere/Mumias: District Development Plan 2002–2008.* Edited by Ministry of Planning and National Development. Nairobi: Government Printer.

———. 2002b. *Kakamega: District Development Plan 2002–2008.* Edited by Ministry of Planning and National Development. Nairobi: Government Printer.

———. 2002c. *Kisii: District Development Plan 2002–2008.* Edited by Ministry of Planning and National Development. Nairobi: Government Printer.

———. 2002d. *Kuria: District Development Plan 2002–2008.* Edited by Ministry of Planning and National Development. Nairobi: Government Printer.

———. 2002e. *Makueni: District Development Plan 2002–2008.* Edited by Ministry of Planning and National Development. Nairobi: Government Printer.

———. 2002f. *Nyando: District Development Plan 2002–2008.* Edited by Ministry of Planning and National Development. Nairobi: Government Printer.

———. 2002g. *Rachuonyo: District Development Plan 2002–2008.* Edited by Ministry of Planning and National Development. Nairobi: Government Printer.

———. 2002h. *West Pokot: District Development Plan 2002–2008.* Edited by Ministry of Planning and National Development. Nairobi: Government Printer.

———. 2006. *Registry of NGOs.* Nairobi: Government of Kenya, NGO Bureau, NGO Coordination Board.

———. 2007. *Vision 2030: The Popular Version.* Nairobi: Government Press.

———. 2008a. "Kenya Public Service Week." Brochure. Nairobi: Government Press.

———. 2008b. *Service Charter.* Nairobi: Ministry of Livestock Development.

———. 2012a. "Summary of Regulatory System for NGOs in Kenya." Nairobi: Government of Kenya, NGO Bureau, NGOs Coordination Board. Available at www.ngoregnet.org/Library/SUMMARY_OF_REGULATORY_SYSTEM_FOR_NGOS_IN_KENYA.doc.

———. 2012b. Online Database Search. Nairobi: Government of Kenya, NGO Bureau, NGO Coordination Board. Available at http://www.ngobureau.or.ke/search_by_name_by_objective.aspx.

Government of Russia. 2000. *Russia in Figures.* Moscow: Goskomstat.

———. 2002. *Sotsial'noe Polozhenie i Urovenzhiznina Seleniia Rossii 2002: Statistichiskii Sbornik* [Social conditions and standard of living of Russia's population: Statistical yearbook]. Moscow: Goskomstat.

Government of Tanganyika. 1962. *Annual Health Report 1961.* Dar es Salaam: Government Printer.

Government of Tanzania. 1995. "The Directory of NGOs in Tanzania by 31st December 1994." Dar es Salaam: Government Printer.

Gray, Peter B. 2004. "HIV and Islam: Is HIV Prevalence Lower among Muslims?" *Social Science and Medicine* 58:1751–55.

Green, Colin. 2003. *Handbook of Water Economics: Principles and Practice.* Chichester, UK: John Wiley & Sons.

Grindle, Merilee. 2004. *Despite the Odds: The Contentious Politics of Education Reform.* Princeton: Princeton University Press.

———. 2007. *Going Local: Decentralization and the Promise of Good Governance.* Princeton: Princeton University Press.

Grønbjerg, Kirsten A. 2001. "The U.S. Nonprofit Human Service Sector: A Creeping Revolution." *Nonprofit and Voluntary Sector Quarterly* 30 (2): 276–97.

Grønbjerg, Kirsten A., and Steven R. Smith. 1999. "Nonprofit Organizations and Public Policies in the Delivery of Human Services." In *Philanthropy and the Nonprofit Sector in a Changing America,* edited by Charles T. Clotfelter and Thomas Ehrlich. Bloomington: Indiana University Press.

Guasch, J. Luis. 2004. *Granting and Renegotiating Infrastructure Concessions: Doing It Right.* Washington, DC: World Bank Institute.

Gugerty, Mary Kay, and Aseem Prakash. 2010. *Voluntary Regulation of NGOs and Nonprofits: An Accountability Club Framework.* Cambridge: Cambridge University Press.

Guillén, Mauro. 2005. *The Rise of Spanish Multinationals: European Business in the Global Economy.* Cambridge: Cambridge University Press.

Gulbrandsen, L. H., and A. Moe. 2005. "Oil Company CSR Collaboration in 'New' Petro-States." *Journal of Corporate Citizenship* 20:53–64.

Guyer, Jane, LaRay Denzer, and Adigun Agbaje, eds. 2002. *Money Struggles and City Life: Devaluation in Ibadan and Other Urban Centers in Southern Nigeria, 1986–1996.* Portsmouth, NH: Heinemann Publishers.

Gvosdev, Nikolas. 2005. "Russia's NGOs: It's Not So Simple." *New York Times*, December 8.

Habyarimana, James, Macartan Humphreys, Daniel N. Posner, and Jeremy M. Weinstein. 2007. "Why Does Ethnic Diversity Undermine Public Goods Provision?" *American Political Science Review* 101 (4): 709–25.

———. 2009. *Coethnicity: Diversity and the Dilemmas of Collective Action*. New York: Russell Sage Foundation.

Hacker, Jacob S. 2002. *The Divided Welfare State: The Battle over Public and Private Social Benefits in the United States*. New York: Cambridge University Press.

Haggard, Stephan, and Robert R. Kaufman. 2008. *Development, Democracy, and Welfare States: Latin America, East Asia, and Eastern Europe*. Princeton: Princeton University Press.

Halisi, C. R. D., Paul J. Kaiser, and Stephen N. Ndegwa. 1988. "The Multiple Meanings of Citizenship: Rights, Identity, and Social Justice in Africa." *Africa Today* 45 (3–4): 337–49.

Hanf, Theodor. 1993. *Coexistence in Wartime Lebanon: Decline of a State and Rise of a Nation*. London: Centre for Lebanese Studies in association with I.B. Tauris.

Hanson, Jonathan K., and Rachel Sigman. 2011. "Measuring State Capacity: Assessing and Testing the Options." Paper presented at the Annual Meeting of the American Political Science Association. Seattle, September 1–4.

Hanson, Kara, and Peter Berman. 1998. "Private Health Care Provision in Developing Countries: A Preliminary Analysis of Levels and Composition." *Health Policy and Planning* 13 (3): 195–211.

Hanssen, Jens. 2005. *Fin de Siècle Beirut: The Making of an Ottoman Provincial Capital*. Oxford: Oxford University Press.

Hardoy, Jorge. 1998. "Práctica surbanísticas europeas en América Latina." In *Repensando la Ciudad en América Latina*, edited by Jorge Ardió and Richard Morse. Buenos Aires: Grupo Editor Latinoamericano.

Harik, Judith Palmer. 1994. *The Public and Social Services of the Lebanese Militias*. Oxford: Centre for Lebanese Studies, Oxford University.

Hartshorn, J. E. 1967. *Oil Companies and Governments: An Account of the International Oil Industry in Its Political Environment*. London: Faber and Faber.

Haufler, V. 2006. "Corporate Transparency: International Diffusion of a Policy Idea?" Paper prepared for the IR Field Workshop, University of Maryland, April. Available at http://www.gvpt.umd.edu/irworkshop/previous.html.

Hazlewood, Arthur. 1979. *The Economy of Kenya: The Kenyatta Era*. New York: Oxford University Press.

Hearn, Julie. 2007. "African NGOs: The New Compradors?" *Development and Change* 38 (6): 1095–1110.

Hefferan, Tara. 2009. "Encouraging Development 'Alternatives': Grassroots Church Partnering in the US and Haiti." In *Bridging the Gaps: Faith-Based Organizations, Neoliberalism, and Development in Latin America and the Caribbean*, edited by Tara Hefferan, Julie Adkins, and Laurie Occhipinti. Lanham, MD: Lexington Books.

Hefner, Robert W. 2000. *Civil Islam: Muslims and Democratization in Indonesia*. Princeton: Princeton University Press.

———. 2005. *Remaking Muslim Politics: Pluralism, Contestation, Democratization*. Princeton: Princeton University Press.

Heins, Volker. 2008. *Nongovernmental Organizations in International Society: Struggles over Recognition*. New York: Palgrave Macmillan.

Heller, Patrick. 2001. "Moving the State: The Politics of Democratic Decentralization in Kerala, South Africa, and Porto Alegre." *Politics and Society* 29 (1): 131–63.

Henisz, Witold, Mauro Guillén, and Bennet Zelner. 2005. "The Worldwide Diffusion of Market-Oriented Infrastructure Reform, 1977–1999." *American Sociological Review* 70:871–97.

Henry, Alain, Guy-Honore Tchente, and Philippe Guillerme-Dieumegard. 1991. *Tontines et banques au Cameroun: Les principes de la societe des amis*. Paris: Karthala.

Hess, David, Nikolai Rogovsky, and Thomas W. Dunfee. 2002. "The Next Wave of Corporate Community Involvement: Corporate Social Initiatives." *California Management Review* 44 (2): 110–25.

Hill, Lori Diane, Jean Baxen, Anne T. Craig, and Halima Namakula. 2012. "Citizenship, Social Justice, and Evolving Conceptions of Access to Education in South Africa: Implications for Research." *Review of Research in Education* 36:239–60.

Hirschman, Albert O. 1970. *Exit, Voice, and Loyalty: Responses to Decline in Firms, Organizations, and States*. Cambridge: Harvard University Press.

Hirtz, Frank. 1995. *Managing Insecurity: State Social Policy and Family Networks in the Rural Philippines*. Saarbrucken: Verlag fur Entwicklungspolitik Breitenbach.

Hochschild, Jennifer L. 1981. *What's Fair? American Beliefs about Distributive Justice*. Cambridge: Harvard University Press.

Honey, Rex, and Stanley I. Okafor. 1998. *Hometown Associations: Indigenous Knowledge and Development in Nigeria*. London: Intermediate Technology Publications.

Horowitz, Donald. 2000 [1985]. *Ethnic Groups in Conflict*. Berkeley: University of California Press.

Horwitz, J. R. 2005. "Making Profits and Providing Care: Comparing Nonprofit, For-Profit, and Government Hospitals." *Health Affairs* 24 (3): 790–801.

Hovland, Ingie. 2008. "Who's Afraid of Religion? Tensions between 'Mission' and 'Development' in the Norwegian Mission Society." In *Development, Civil Society and Faith-Based Organisations: Bridging the Sacred and the Secular*, edited by Gerard Clarke and Michael Jennings, 171–86. Basingstoke, UK: Palgrave Macmillan.

Hoxby, Caroline. 2000. "Peer Effects in the Classroom: Learning from Gender and Race Variation." NBER Working Paper 7867. Cambridge, MA: National Bureau of Economic Research.

———. 2001. "Ideal Vouchers." Working Paper, Department of Economics. Cambridge: Harvard University.

Hsieh, Chang-Tai, and Miguel Urquiola. 2006. "The Effect of Generalized School Choice on Achievement and Stratification: Evidence from Chile's School Voucher Program." *Journal of Public Economics* 90: 1477–1503.

Huber, Evelyne. 1996. "Options for Social Policy in Latin America: Neoliberal versus Social Democratic Models." In *Welfare States in Transition: National Adaptations in Global Economies*, edited by Gøsta Esping-Anderson. London: Sage Publications.

Huber, Evelyne, and John D. Stephens. 2001. *Development and the Crisis of the Welfare State: Parties and Policies in Global Markets*. Chicago: University of Chicago Press.

Hudson, Michael C. 1968. *The Precarious Republic: Political Modernization in Lebanon*. New York: Random House.

Hula, Richard C., and Cynthia Jackson-Elmoore. 2001. "Governing Nonprofits and Local Political Processes." *Urban Affairs Review* 36 (3): 324–58.

Huntington, Samuel P. 1968. *Political Order in Changing Societies*. New Haven: Yale University Press.

———. 1993. "The Clash of Civilizations." *Foreign Affairs* 72 (3): 22–49.

———. 1996. *The Clash of Civilizations and the Remaking of the World Order*. New York: Simon and Schuster.

Huyse, Huib, Nadia Molenaers, Geert Phlix, Jean Bossuyt, and Bénédicte Fonteneau. 2012. "Evaluating NGO–Capacity Development Interventions: Enhancing Frameworks, Fitting the (Belgian) Context." *Evaluation* 18 (3): 129–50.

Hyden, Goran. 1980. *Beyond Ujamaa in Tanzania: Underdevelopment and an Uncaptured Peasantry*. Berkeley: University of California Press.

———. 1983. *No Short Cuts to Progress: African Development Management in Perspective*. Berkeley: University of California Press.

———. 1995. "Bringing Voluntarism Back In: Eastern Africa in Comparative Perspective." In *Service Provision under Stress in East Africa: The State, NGOs and People's Organizations in Kenya, Tanzania and Uganda*, edited by Joseph Semboja and Ole Therkildsen, 35–50. London: James Currey.

———. 2006. *African Politics in Comparative Perspective*. New York: Cambridge University Press.

Hyra, Derek. S. 2008. *The New Urban Renewal*. Chicago: University of Chicago Press.

Idelovitch, Emanuel, and Klas Ringskog. 1995. *Private Sector Participation in Water Supply and Sanitation in Latin America*. Washington, DC: World Bank.

Idemudia, U. 2009. "Oil Extraction and Poverty Reduction in the Niger Delta: A Critical Examination of Partnership Initiatives." *Journal of Business Ethics* 90 (1): 91–116.

———. 2010. "Rethinking the Role of Corporate Social Responsibility in the Nigerian Oil Conflict: The Limits of CSR." *Journal of International Development* 22 (7): 833–45.

Ikelegbe, A. 2001. "The Perverse Manifestation of Civil Society: Evidence from Nigeria." *Journal of Modern African Studies* 39 (1): 1–24.

Iliffe, John. 1979. *A Modern History of Tanganyika*. Cambridge: Cambridge University Press.

Inglot, Tomasz. 2008. *Welfare States in East-Central Europe 1919–2004*. New York: Cambridge University Press.

Instituto Nacional de Estadísticas y Censos (INDEC).1991. *Censo de Poblacion y Vivienda*. Series B. Buenos Aires: INDEC.

International Center for Not-for-Profit Law (ICNL). 1995. *Regulating Not-for-Profit Organizations*. Washington, DC: ICNL.

———. 2012. "NGO Law Monitor: Azerbaijan." International Center for Not-for-Profit Law. Available at http://www.icnl.org/research/monitor/azerbaijan.html.

International Crisis Group. 2007. *Central Asia's Energy Risks*. Asia Report No. 133. Brussels/Bishkek: International Crisis Group.

International Labor Organization (ILO). 2004. *Post-War Lebanon: Women and Other War-Affected Groups*. Geneva: ILO.

Iversen, Torben. 2005. *Capitalism, Democracy, and Welfare*. Cambridge Studies in Comparative Politics. Cambridge: Cambridge University Press.

Jackson, Robert, and Carl Rosberg. 1982. "Why Africa's Weak States Persist." *World Politics* 35, (1): 1–24.

Jalali, Ali. 2006. "The Future of Afghanistan." *Parameters* 26 (1): 4–19.

Jalan, J., and M. Ravallion. 2003. "Does Piped Water Reduce Diarrhea for Children in Rural India?" *Journal of Econometrics* 112 (1): 153–73.

James, Rick, and John Haily. 2007. *Capacity Building for NGOs: Making It Work*. London: International NGO Training and Research Centre (INTRAC).

Janin, Pierre. 1995. "Immuable, le changeant et l'imprevu: Les economies de plantation bamilieke et beti du Cameroun confrontees aux chocs exterieurs." PhD diss., Department of Geography, Université de Paris IV, Sorbonne, Paris.

Jeffrey, C., P. Jeffery, and R. Jeffery. 2008. *Degrees without Freedom: Education, Masculinities, and Unemployment in North India*. Stanford: Stanford University Press.

Jenkins, Heledd. 2004. "Corporate Social Responsibility and the Mining Industry: Conflicts and Constructs." *Corporate Social Responsibility and Environmental Management Journal* 11 (1): 23–34.

Jennings, Michael. 2006. "Missions and Maternal and Child Health Care in Colonial Tanganyika, 1919–1939." In *Healing Bodies, Saving Souls: Medical Missionaries in Asia and Africa*, edited by David Hardiman. Amsterdam: Rodopi.

———. 2008a. *Surrogates of the State: NGOs, Development and Ujamaa in Tanzania*. Bloomfield, CT: Kumarian Press.

———. 2008b. "The Spirit of Brotherhood: Christianity and Ujamaa in Tanzania." In *Development, Civil Society and Faith-Based Organisations: Bridging the Sacred and the*

Secular, edited by Gerard Clarke and Michael Jennings, 94–116. Basingstoke, UK: Palgrave Macmillan.

———. 2008c. "'Healing of Bodies, Salvation of Souls': Missionary Medicine in Colonial Tanganyika, 1870s–1939." *Journal of Religion in Africa* 38:27–56.

Johnson, Michael. 1977. "Political Bosses and Their Gangs: Zu'ama and Qabadayat in the Sunni Muslim Quarters of Beirut." In *Patrons and Clients in Mediterranean Societies*, edited by E. Gellner and J. Waterbury. London: Duckworth.

Johnston, Daniel. 1994. *International Petroleum Fiscal Systems and Production Sharing Contracts*. Tulsa, OK: PennWell Books.

Jones Luong, Pauline, and Erika Weinthal. 2010. *Oil Is Not a Curse: Ownership Structure and Institutions in Soviet Successor States*. Cambridge: Cambridge University Press.

Jordan, L., and P. Van Tuijl. 2000. "Political Responsibility in Transnational NGO Advocacy." *World Development* 28 (12): 2051–65.

Kahl, Sigrun. 2009. "Religious Doctrines and Poor Relief: A Different Causal Pathway." In *Religion, Class Coalitions, and Welfare States*, edited by P. Manow and K. van Kersbergen. Cambridge: Cambridge University Press.

Kaiser Family Foundation. 2011. "Snapshots: Health Care Spending the United States and Selected OECD Countries." April 12. http://kff.org/health-costs/issue-brief/snapshots-health-care-spending-in-the-united-states-selected-oecd-countries/.

Kajimbwa, Monsiapile. 2006. "NGOs and Their Role in the Global South." *International Journal of Non-Profit Law* 9 (1). Available at http://www.icnl.org/research/journal/vol9iss1/art_7.htm.

Kamat, Sangeeta. 2003. "The False Saviors of International Development." *Development and Modernization* 25 (1): 65–69.

Kameri-Mbote, Patricia. 2000. "The Operational Environment and Constraints for NGOs in Kenya: Strategies for Good Policy and Practice." In *IELC Working Paper* No. 2000–2. London: International Environmental Law Research Centre.

Kanyinga, Karuti. 1996. "The Politics of Development Space in Kenya." In *Service Provision under Stress in East Africa: State, NGOs and People's Organizations in Kenya, Tanzania and Uganda*, edited by Joseph Semboja and Ole Therkildsen. Copenhagen: Centre for Development Research.

———. 2004. "Civil Society Formations in Kenya: A Growing Role in Development and Democracy." In *Civil Society in the Third Republic*, edited by Duncan Okello. Nairobi: National Council of NGOs.

Kariuki, Mukami, and Jordan Schwartz. 2005. "Small-Scale Private Service Providers of Water and Electricity." World Bank Policy Research Working Paper 3727. Washington, DC: World Bank.

Karl, Terry L. 2000. "Crude Calculations: OPEC Lessons for the Caspian Region." In *Energy and Conflict in Central Asia and the Caucasus*, edited by R. Ebel and R. Menon. Lanham, MD: Rowman and Littlefield.

Karsten, Sjoerd. 1999. "Neoliberal Education Reform in the Netherlands." *Comparative Education* 35 (3): 303–17.

Kasparian, Chohig, and Walid Ammar. 2001. *National Health Utilization and Expenditure Survey*. Beirut: Ministry of Public Health, Government of Lebanon.

Katumanga, Musambayi. 2004. "Civil Society and the Government: Conflict or Cooperation?" In *Civil Society in the Third Republic*, edited by Duncan Okello. Nairobi: National Council of NGOs.

Kaufman, Robert R., and Joan M. Nelson. 2004a. *Crucial Needs, Weak Incentives: Social Sector Reform, Democratization, and Globalization in Latin America*. Baltimore: Johns Hopkins University Press.

———. 2004b. "The Politics of Education Sector Reform." In *Crucial Needs, Weak Incentives*, edited by Robert Kaufman and Joan Nelson. Baltimore: Johns Hopkins University Press.

Kaufman, Robert R., and Alex Segura-Ubiergo. 2001. "Globalization, Domestic Politics and Social Spending in Latin America: A Time Series Cross-Section Analysis, 1973–1997." *World Politics* 53 (4): 553–87.

Keese, James R., and Marco Freire Argudo. 2006. "Decentralisation and NGO–Municipal Government Collaboration in Ecuador." *Development in Practice* 16 (2): 114–27.

Kenworthy, Lane. 1999. "Do Social-Welfare Policies Reduce Poverty? A Cross-National Assessment." *Social Forces* 77 (3): 1119–39.

Kenya National Commission on Human Rights. 2009. KNCHR. Available at http://www.knchr.org/index.php?option=com_content&task=view&id=46&Itemid=89.

Keohane, R. O., and V. D. Ooms. 1972. "The Multinational Enterprise and World Political Economy." *International Organization* 26 (1): 84–120.

Khagram, Sanjeev, James Riker, and Kathryn Sikkink, eds. 2002. *Restructuring World Politics: Transnational Social Movements, Networks, and Norms.* Minneapolis: University of Minnesota Press.

Khan, Shahrukh Rafi. 1999. *Government, Communities and Non-Governmental Organisations in Social Sector Delivery: Collective Action in Rural Drinking Water Supply.* Aldershot, UK: Ashgate.

Kilby, Patrick. 2006. "Accountability for Empowerment: Dilemmas Facing Non-Governmental Organizations." *World Development* 34 (6): 951–63.

Klein, Michael U., Carl Aaron, and Bita Hadjimichael. 2001. "Foreign Direct Investment and Poverty Reduction." World Bank Policy Research Working Paper No. 2613. Washington, DC: World Bank.

Klein, Michael U., and Bita Hadjimichael. 2003. *The Private Sector in Development.* Washington, DC: World Bank.

Kloprogge, Jo. 2003. "Educational Policies and Equal Opportunities in the Netherlands." Mimeo. Utrecht, the Netherlands: Sardes Educational Services.

Kneebone, Elizabeth. 2009. "Economic Recovery and the EITC: Expanding the Earned Income Tax Credit to Benefit Families and Places." Washington, DC: Brookings Institution, Metropolitan Policy Program.

Kneebone, Elizabeth, and Emily Garr. 2010. "The Suburbanization of Poverty: Trends in Metropolitan America, 2000 to 2008." Washington, DC: Brookings Institution, Metropolitan Policy Program.

Kogut, Bruce, and J. Muir MacPherson. 2004. "The Decision to Privatize: Economists and the Construction of Ideas and Policies." In *The Global Diffusion of Markets and Democracy,* edited by Beth A. Simmons, Frank Dobbin, and Geoffrey Garrett. Cambridge: Cambridge University Press.

Kohli, Atul. 1987. *The State and Poverty in India: The Politics of Reform.* Cambridge: Cambridge University Press.

——. 1990. *Democracy and Discontent: India's Growing Crisis of Governability.* Cambridge: Cambridge University Press.

——. 2004. *State-Directed Development: Political Power and Industrialization in the Global Periphery.* New York: Cambridge University Press.

Konitzer, Andrew. 2005. "Popular Reactions to Social and Health Sector Reforms in Russia's Regions: Reform versus Retention in Samarskaia and Ul'ianovskaia Oblasts." In *Fighting Poverty and Reforming Social Security: What Can Post-Soviet States Learn from the New Democracies of Central Europe?,* edited by Michael Cain, Nida Gelazis, and Tomasz Inglot, 145–72. Washington, DC: Woodrow Wilson International Center for Scholars.

Koonings, Kees, and Dirk Kruijt. 2004. *Armed Actors: Organised Violence and State Failure in Latin America.* New York: Zed Books.

Kornai, Janos, Stephan Haggard, and Robert Kaufman. 2001. *Reforming the State: Fiscal and Welfare Reform in Post-Socialist Countries.* Cambridge: Cambridge University Press.

Korten, David C. 1990. *Getting to the 21st Century: Voluntary Action and the Global Agenda.* New York: Kumarian Press.

Korten, David, and Rudi Klauss, eds. 1984. *People-Centered Development*. West Hartford, CT: Kumarian Press.

Krasner, Stephen, and Carlos Pascual. 2005. "Addressing State Failure." *Foreign Affairs* (July–August): 153–63.

Kremer, M., N. Chaudhury, F. Rogers, K. Muralidharan, and J. Hammer. 2004. "Teacher Absence in India: A Snapshot." *Journal of the European Economic Association* 3 (2–3): 658–67.

Krishna, Anirudh. 2002. *Active Social Capital: Tracing the Roots of Development and Democracy*. New York: Columbia University Press.

———. 2003. "What Is Happening to Caste? A View from Some North Indian Villages." *Journal of Asian Studies* 62 (4): 1171–93.

———. 2004. "Escaping Poverty and Becoming Poor: Who Gains, Who Loses, and Why? People's Assessments of Stability and Change in 35 North Indian Villages." *World Development* 32 (1): 121–36.

———. 2006. "Pathways Out of and Into Poverty in 36 Villages of Andhra Pradesh, India." *World Development* 34 (2): 271–88.

———. 2007. "Politics in the Middle." In *Patrons, Clients, and Politics*, edited by Herbert Kitschelt and Steven Wilkinson, 141–58. Cambridge: Cambridge University Press.

———. 2010. "Dealing with a Distant State: The Evolving Nature of Local Politics in India." In *Oxford Companion to Politics in India*, edited by Niraja Gopal Jayal and Pratap Bhanu Mehta, 299–313. Oxford: Oxford University Press.

Krishna, Anirudh, and Gregory Schober. 2012. "The Gradient of Governance: Distance and Disenchantment in Indian Villages." Working Paper. Durham, NC: Sanford School of Public Policy, Duke University.

Kronfol, Nabil M. 2004. "Case Study: Lebanon." In *Long-Term Care in Developing Countries: Ten Case Studies*, edited by J. Brodsky, J. Habib, and M. Hirschfeld. Geneva: World Health Organization.

Lara, Bernardo, Alejandra Mizala, and Andrea Repetto 2011. "The Effectiveness of Private Voucher Education: Evidence from Structural School Switches." *Educational Evaluation and Policy Analysis* 33 (2): 119–37.

Latinobarómetro.1995, 1998, and 2008. Surveys. Santiago, Chile: Corporación Latinobarómetro.

Laurell, Asa Cristina, and Oliva López Arellano. 1996. "Market Commodities and Poor Relief: The World Bank Proposal for Health." *International Journal of Health Services* 26 (1): 1–18.

Lavy, V., J. Strauss, D. Thomas, and P. de Vreyer. 1996. "Quality of Health Care, Survival and Health Outcomes in Ghana." *Journal of Health Economics* 15:333–57.

Lee, Lung-Fei, Mark R. Rosenzweig, and Mark M. Pitt. 1997. "The Effects of Improved Nutrition, Sanitation, and Water Quality on Child Health in High-Mortality Populations." *Journal of Econometrics* 77:209–35.

Lee, Yih-Jiunn, and Yeun-wen Ku. 2007. "East Asian Welfare Regimes: Testing the Hypothesis of the Developmental Welfare State." *Social Policy & Administration* 41 (2):197–212.

Leonard, David K. 1977. *Reaching the Peasant Farmer: Organization Theory and Practice in Kenya*. Chicago: University of Chicago Press.

Lerner, Daniel. 1958. *The Passing of Traditional Society: Modernizing the Middle East*. Glencoe, IL: Free Press.

Levi, Margaret. 1989. *Of Rule and Revenue*. Berkeley: University of California Press.

Levin, Henry, and Clive R. Belfield. 2003. "The Marketplace in Education." *Review of Research in Education* 27 (1): 183–219.

Levitt, Matthew. 2006. *Hamas: Politics, Charity, and Terrorism in the Service of Jihad*. New Haven: Yale University Press; Washington, DC: Washington Institute for Near East Policy.

Levy, Brian, and Pablo Spiller. 1994. "The Institutional Foundations of Regulatory Commitment: A Comparative Analysis of the Telecommunications Sector." *Journal of Law, Economics, & Organization* 10 (2): 201–46.

Levy, Daniel C. 2006. "The Unanticipated Explosion: Private Higher Education's Global Surge." *Comparative Education Review* 50 (2): 217–40.

Lewis, David, and Nazneen Kanji. 2009. *Nongovernmental Organizations and Development.* London: Routledge.

Lewis, David, and Tina Wallace. 2003. *Development NGOs and the Challenge of Change.* Jaipur, India: Rawat Publishers.

Lieberman, Evan. 2003. *Race and Regionalism in the Politics of Taxation in Brazil and South Africa.* New York: Cambridge University Press.

———. 2009. *Boundaries of Contagion: How Ethnic Politics Have Shaped Government Responses to AIDS.* Princeton: Princeton University Press.

Linden, Ian. 2008. "The Language of Development: What Are International Development Agencies Talking About?" In *Development, Civil Society and Faith-Based Organisations: Bridging the Sacred and the Secular,* edited by Gerard Clarke and Michael Jennings, 72–93. London: Palgrave Macmillan.

Lipson, Charles. 1985. *Standing Guard: Protecting Foreign Capital in the Nineteenth and Twentieth Centuries.* Berkeley: University of California Press.

Liston, Vanessa. 2008. "NGOs and Spatial Dimensions of Poverty in Kenya." Paper presented at the meeting of the African Studies Association of the United Kingdom (ASAUK), University of Central Lancashire, Preston, Lancashire.

Lodge, George, and Craig Wilson. 2006. *A Corporate Solution to Global Poverty: How Multinationals Can Help the Poor and Invigorate Their Own Legitimacy.* Princeton: Princeton University Press.

Lora, Eduardo, ed. 2008. *Beyond Facts: Understanding Quality of Life.* Washington, DC: Inter-American Development Bank.

Lynch, Julia. 2006. *Age in the Welfare State: The Origins of Social Spending on Pensioners, Workers, and Children.* New York: Cambridge University Press.

Macassa, Gloria, Antonio Ponce de Leon, and Bo Buström. 2006. "The Impact of Water Supply and Sanitation on Area Differentials in the Decline of Diarrhoeal Disease Mortality among Infants in Stockholm, 1878–1925." *Scandinavian Journal of Public Health* 34 (5): 526–33.

MacLean, Lauren Morris. 2010. *Informal Institutions and Citizenship in Rural Africa: Risk and Reciprocity in Ghana and Côte d'Ivoire.* New York: Cambridge University Press.

———. 2011a. "Exclusion and Exhaustion in an African Village: The Non-state Social Welfare of Informal Reciprocity in Rural Ghana and Côte d'Ivoire." *Studies in Comparative International Development* 46:118–36.

———. 2011b. "State Retrenchment and the Exercise of Citizenship in Africa." *Comparative Political Studies* 44 (9): 1238–66.

Madeira, Ana. 2005. "Portuguese, French and British Discourses on Colonial Education: Church-State Relations, School Expansion and Missionary Competition in Africa, 1890–1930." *Paedagogica Historica* 41 (1–2): 31–60.

Madrid, Raúl. 2003. *Retiring the State: The Politics of Pension Privatization in Latin America and Beyond.* Stanford: Stanford University Press.

Mahmood, Saba. 2005. *Politics of Piety: The Islamic Revival and the Feminist Subject.* Princeton: Princeton University Press.

Mahoney, James. 2010. *Colonialism and Postcolonial Development: Spanish America in Comparative Perspective.* New York: Cambridge University Press.

Makdisi, Ussama. 2000. *The Culture of Sectarianism: Community, History, and Violence in Nineteenth-Century Ottoman Lebanon.* Berkeley: University of California Press.

Makhmutova, Meruert. 2005. "Implementation of Extractive Industries Transparency Initiative in Kazakhstan: Problems and Prospects." *Policy Studies* 5 (10).

Manning, Nick, and Nataliya Tikhonova. 2009. *Health and Health Care in the New Russia.* Burlington, VT: Ashgate.

Manor, J. 1999. *The Political Economy of Democratic Decentralization*. Washington, DC: World Bank.

———. 2000. "Small-Time Political Fixers in India's States." *Asian Survey* 40 (5): 816–35.

Manuh, Takyiwaa. 2006. *At Home in the World? International Migration and Development in Contemporary Ghana and West Africa*. Legon, Ghana: Sub-Saharan Publishers.

Mares, Isabela. 2003. *The Politics of Social Risk: Business and Welfare State Development*. Cambridge Studies in Comparative Politics. Cambridge: Cambridge University Press.

Mares, Isabela, and Matthew E. Carnes. 2009. "Social Policy in Developing Countries." *Annual Review of Political Science* 12:93–113.

Marin, Philippe. 2009. *Public Private Partnerships for Urban Water Utilities: A Review of Experiences in Developing Countries*. Trends and Policy Options No. 8. Washington, DC: Public-Private Infrastructure Advisory Facility (PPIAF)–World Bank.

Marshall, T. H. 1950. "Citizenship and Social Class." In his *Sociology at the Crossroads and Other Essays*. London: Heinemann.

Martin, Jay. 2004." Can Magic Bullets Hurt You? NGOs and Governance in a Globalised Social Welfare World: A Case Study of Tajikistan." *Discussion Paper no. 92*. Canberra: Graduate Program in Public Policy, Australian National University.

Mathew, George. 1994. *Panchayati Raj: From Legislation to Movement*. New Delhi: Concept Publishers.

Matthews, Jessica T. 1997. "Power Shift." *Foreign Affairs* 76 (1): 52–53.

Mayaram, Shail. 1998. *Panchayats and Women: A Study of the Processes Initiated before and after the 73rd Amendment in Rajasthan*. Mimeo. Jaipur: Institute of Development Studies.

Mayer, A. 1997. "Caste in an Indian Village: Change and Continuity 1954–1992." In *Caste Today*, edited by C. J. Fuller. New Delhi: Oxford University Press.

McDaniel, Charles. 2012. "The Role of Human Security in the Contest between the Egyptian Government and Muslim Brotherhood, 1980–2010." In *Religion and Human Security: A Global Perspective*, edited by J. Wellman, K. James, and C. Lombardi. Oxford: Oxford University Press.

McGann, James, and Mary Johnstone. 2006. "The Power Shift and the NGO Credibility Crisis." *International Journal of Not-for-Profit Law* 8 (2): 65–77.

McGinnis, Michael D., and Claudia A. Brink. 2012. "Shared Stewardship of a Health Commons: Examples and Opportunities from Grand Junction, Colorado." Paper presented at the Workshop on Political Theory and Policy Analysis, Office of the Vice Provost for Research, Indiana University, Bloomington.

McGuire, James W. 2010. *Wealth, Health, and Democracy in East Asia and Latin America*. Cambridge: Cambridge University Press.

McKern, Bruce. 1996. "TNCs and the Exploitation of Natural Resources." In *Transnational Corporations and World Development*. Geneva: United Nations Conference on Trade and Development (UNCTAD).

McSherry, Brendan, and Jennifer N. Brass. 2008. "The Political Economy of Pro-Poor Livestock Policy Reform in Kenya." In *IGAD-LPI Working Paper No. 03-08*.Addis Ababa and Djibouti: Livestock Policy Initiative, Inter-Governmental Authority on Development (IGAD).

Mehio-Sibai, Abla, and Katsuri Sen. 2006. "Can Lebanon Conjure a Public Health Phoenix from the Ashes?" *BMJ* (333): 848–49.

Mendoza, Ronald U., and Nina Thelen. 2008. "Innovations to Make Markets More Inclusive for the Poor." *Development Policy Review* 26 (5): 427–58.

Meo, Leila M. T. 1965. *Lebanon: Improbable Nation*. Bloomington: Indiana University Press.

Mercer, Claire. 1999. "Reconceptualizing State-Society Relations: Are NGOs 'Making a Difference'?" *Area* 31 (3): 247–58.

———. 2002. "NGOs, Civil Society and Democratization: A Critical Review of the Literature." *Progress in Development Studies* 2 (1): 5–22.

———. 2003. "Performing Partnership: Civil Society and the Illusions of Good Governance in Tanzania." *Political Geography* 22:741–63.

Mercer, Claire, B. Page, and M. Evans. 2008. *Development and the African Diaspora: Place and the Politics of Home Associations.* London: Zed Books.

Merrick, Thomas W. 1985. "The Effect of Piped Water on Early Childhood Mortality in Urban Brazil, 1970 to 1976." *Demography* 22 (1): 1–24.

Mertus, Julie, and Tazreena Sajjad. 2005. "When Civil Society Promotion Fails State-Building: The Inevitable Fault Lines in Post-Conflict Reconstruction." In *Subcontracting Peace: The Challenges of NGO Peacebuilding*, edited by R. Oliver and H. Carey. London: Ashgate.

Mettler, Suzanne. 2002. "Bringing the State Back In to Civic Engagement: Policy Feedback Effects of the G.I. Bill for World War II Veterans." *American Political Science Review* 96 (2): 351–65.

Meyer, Carrie. 1997. "The Political Economy of NGOs and Information." *World Development* 25 (7): 1127–40.

Midgley, James. 2012. "Social Protection and the Elderly in the Developing World: Mutual Aid, Microinsurance, and the State." *Journal of Comparative Social Welfare* 28 (2): 153–63.

Migdal, Joel S. 1988. *Strong Societies and Weak States.* Princeton: Princeton University Press.

Miguel, Edward. 2009. *Africa's Turn?* Boston: MIT Press.

Miles, William F. S. 1994. *Hausaland Divided: Colonialism and Independence in Nigeria and Niger.* Ithaca, NY: Cornell University Press.

Milward, H. Brinton. 1996. "Symposium on the Hollow State." *Journal of Public Administration Research and Theory* 6 (April): 193–95.

Ministry of Public Health (MOPH), Government of Lebanon. 2006. "List of Clinics and Dispensaries in Lebanon." Beirut: MOPH.

Mitra, S. 1991. "Room to Maneuver in the Middle: Local Elites, Political Action, and the State in India." *World Politics* 43 (April): 390–413.

Mizala, Alejandra. 2007. "La Economía Política de la Reforma Educacional en Chile." Serie Estudios Socio / Económicos 36. Santiago: Cieplan.

Mizala, Alejandra, and Hugo Ñopo. 2011. "Teachers' Salaries in Latin America. How Much Are They (under or over) Paid?" Working Paper 282. Santiago: Center for Applied Economics, Universidad de Chile.

Mizala, Alejandra, and Pilar Romaguera. 2000. "School Performance and Choice: The Chilean Experience." *Journal of Human Resources* 35 (2): 392–417.

———. 2005a. "Calidad de la educación chilena: El Desafío de la próxima década." In *La Paradoja Aparente. Equidad y Eficiencia: Resolviendo el dilemma*, edited by P. Meller. Santiago: Aguilar Chilena Ediciones.

———. 2005b. "Teachers' Salary Structure and Incentives in Chile." In *Incentives to Improve Teaching*, edited by E. Vegas. Washington, DC: World Bank.

Mizala, Alejandra, and Ben Schneider. 2013. "Negotiating Education Reform: Teacher Evaluations and Incentives in Chile (1990–2010)." *Governance* (forthcoming). doi:10.1111/gove.12020.

Mizala, Alejandra, and Florencia Torche. 2012. "Bringing the Schools Back In: The Stratification of Educational Achievement in the Chilean Voucher System." *International Journal of Educational Development* 32:132–44.

Mizala, Alejandra, and M Urquiola. 2013. "School Markets: The Impact of Information Approximating Schools' Effectiveness." *Journal of Development Economics* 103:313–35.

Molyneux, M., and S. Razavi. 2006. *Beijing Plus 10: An Ambivalent Record on Gender Justice.* UNRISD Occasional Paper 15. Geneva: United Nations Research Institute for Social Development.

Mommer, Bernard. 2002. *Global Oil and the Nation State*. Oxford: Oxford Institute for Energy Studies.

Moran, Dominique, and Richard Batley. 2004. "Literature Review of Non-state Provision of Basic Services: Private and NGO Provision of Health, Education, Water and Sanitation. What Do We Know?" Birmingham: International Development Department, University of Birmingham.

Morse, Edward. 1999. "A New Political Economy of Oil?" *Journal of International Affairs* 53 (1): 1–29.

Murillo, María Victoria. 2009. *Political Competition, Partisanship, and Policy Making in Latin American Utilities*. Cambridge: Cambridge University Press.

Muslim Aid. 2007. "Trustees' Report and Financial Statements for the Year Ended 31 December 2007." Available at http://www.muslimaid.org/images/stories/pdfs/financial_summary_2007.pdf.

Najam, Adil. 1996. "Understanding the Third Sector: Revisiting the Prince, the Merchant, and the Citizen." *Nonprofit Management and Leadership* 7 (2): 203–19.

Najman, B., R. Pomfret, and G. Raballand. 2008. *The Economics and Politics of Oil in the Caspian Basin: The Redistribution of Oil Revenues in Azerbaijan and Central Asia*. New York: Routledge.

Narayan, Deepa. 2000. *Voices of the Poor: Can Anyone Hear Us?* Oxford: Oxford University Press.

National Council of NGOs. 2005. *The National Council of NGOs 2005*. Available at http://www.ngocouncil.org/index.asp.

National Council of NGOs of Kenya. 2005. *Directory of NGOs in Kenya*. Nairobi: National Council of NGOs.

Ndegwa, Stephen N. 1994. "Civil Society and Political Change in Africa: The Case of Nongovernmental Organizations in Kenya." *International Journal of Comparative Sociology* 35 (1–2): 19–36.

———. 2001. "A Decade of Democracy in Africa." In *A Decade of Democracy*, edited by S. Ndegwa. Leiden, Netherlands: Brill.

Nwankwo, Emeka, Nelson Phillips, and Paul Tracey. 2007. "Social Investment through Community Enterprise: The Case of Multinational Corporations' Involvement in the Development of Nigerian Water Resources." *Journal of Business Ethics* 73 (1): 91–101.

Obiyan, A. Sat. 2005. "A Critical Examination of the State versus Non-Governmental Organizations (NGOs) in the Policy Sphere in the Global South: Will the State Die as NGOs Thrive in Sub-Saharan Africa and Asia?" *Journal of Asian and African Studies* 4 (3): 301–27.

Odell, Peter R. 1968. "The Significance of Oil." *Journal of Contemporary History* 3 (3): 93–110.

O'Dwyer, Conor. 2006. *Runaway State-Building: Patronage Politics and Democratic Development*. Baltimore: Johns Hopkins University Press.

OECD (Organization for Economic Cooperation and Development). 2001. *Social Crisis in the Russian Federation*. Paris: OECD.

———. 2005. *Private Sector Development: A Guide to Donor Support*. Paris: OECD.

———. 2006. *Economic Survey, Russian Federation*. Paris: OECD.

OECD-DAC (Organization for Economic Cooperation and Development—Development Assistance Committee). *Aid Statistics*. Available at http://www.oecd.org/dac/stats/ids online.htm.

Olson, Willy H. 2002. *Petroleum Revenue Management—an Industry Perspective*. Presentation to the Oil, Gas, Mining and Chemicals Department of the World Bank Group (WBG) and Energy Sector Management Assistance Program (ESMAP), "Workshop on Petroleum Revenue Management," Washington, DC, October 23–24.

Open Society Institute. 2010. *Glossary 2010*. Available at http://www.osi.hu/partnerships/glossary.html.

Ordoqui Urcelay, María Begoña. 2007. "Servicios de agua potable y alcantarillado en la Ciudad de Buenos Aires, Argentina: Factores determinantes de la sustenabilidad y el desempeño." Serie Recursos Naturales y Infraestructura 126. Santiago, Chile: Comisión Económica para América Latina—Deutsche Gesellschaft für Internationale Zusammenarbeit GmbH (CEPAL–GTZ).

Ostrom, Elinor. 2009. "Beyond Markets and States: Polycentric Governance of Complex Economic Systems." Paper read at Nobel Lecture, at Oslo, Norway.

Ostrom, Vincent, Charles M. Tiebout, and Robert Warren. 1961. "The Organization of Government in Metropolitan Areas: A Theoretical Inquiry." *American Political Science Review* 55 (4): 831–42.

Owiti, Jeremiah, Otieno Aluoka, and Adams G. R. Oloo. 2004. "Civil Society in the New Dispensation: Prospects and Challenges." In *Civil Society in the Third Republic*, edited by Duncan Okello. Nairobi: National Council of NGOs.

Oxfam. 2009. "Blind Optimism: Challenging the Myths about Private Health Care in Poor Countries." In *Oxfam Briefing Paper No. 125*. Oxford: Oxfam International.

Paes de Barros, Ricardo, Francisco H. G. Ferreira, José R. Molinas Vega, and Jaime Saavedra Chanduvi. 2009. *Measuring Inequality of Opportunities in Latin America and the Caribbean*. Washington, DC: Palgrave Macmillan and World Bank.

Patel, Leila, Edwell Kaseke, and James Midgley. 2012. "Indigenous Welfare and Community-Based Social Development: Lessons from African Innovations." *Journal of Community Practice* 20 (1–2): 12–31.

Patrinos, Harry, Felipe Barrera-Osorio, and Juliana Guáqueta. 2009. *The Role and Impact of Public-Private Partnerships in Education*. Washington, DC: World Bank.

Pellow, Deborah, and Naomi Chazan. 1986. *Ghana: Coping with Uncertainty*. Boulder, CO: Westview Press.

Peters, B. Guy, and John Pierre. 1998. "Governance without Government? Rethinking Public Administration." *Journal of Public Administration Research and Theory* 8 (2): 223–43.

Petersen, C. E., and N. Budina. 2002. *Governance Framework of Oil Funds: The Case of Azerbaijan and Kazakhstan*. Washington, DC: World Bank.

Peterson, Paul E. 1981. *City Limits*. Chicago: University of Chicago Press.

Petras, James F., and Henry Veltmeyer. 2007. *Multinationals on Trial: Foreign Investment Matters*. Burlington, VT: Ashgate.

Pierson, Paul. 1994. *Dismantling the Welfare State? Reagan, Thatcher, and the Politics of Retrenchment*. New York: Cambridge University Press.

Polanyi, Karl. 1944. *The Great Transformation: The Political and Economic Origins of Our Time*. Boston: Beacon Press.

Popkin, Samuel L. 1979. *The Rational Peasant: The Political Economy of Rural Society in Vietnam*. Berkeley: University of California Press.

Popov, Vladimir. 2008. "After 10 Years of Growth, Russian Economy May Be Losing Steam." *Russian Economic Digest* 48:15–20.

Popovich, L., E. Potapchik, S. Shishkin, E. Richardson, A. Vacroux, and B. Mathivet. 2011. "Russian Federation: Health System Review." *Health Systems in Transition* 13 (7): 1–190.

Posner, Daniel N. 2005. *Institutions and Ethnic Politics in Africa*. New York: Cambridge University Press.

Post, Alison. 2008. "Liquid Assets and Fluid Contracts: Explaining the Uneven Effects of Water and Sanitation Privatization." PhD diss., Harvard University.

———. 2009. "The Paradoxical Politics of Water Metering in Argentina." *Poverty in Focus* 18: 16–18.

PPIAF (Public-Private Infrastructure Advisory Facility)–World Bank. 2007–08. *Private Participation in Infrastructure Database*. ppi.worldbank.org.

Prager, Jonas. 1994. "Contracting Out Government Services: Lessons from the Private Sector." *Public Administration Review* 54 (2): 176–84.

Prattini, Chris. 2007. President, Indonesian Petroleum Association, "31st IPA Convention Opening Speech," paper presented at the IEA Review meeting, June 29.

Prakash, Aseem, and Mary Kay Gugarty, eds. 2010. *Advocacy Organizations and Collective Action*. Cambridge: Cambridge University Press.

Preker, A. S., and R. G. Feachem. 1994. "Health and Health Care." In *Labour Markets and Social Policy in Central and Eastern Europe*, edited by Nicholas Barr. *CASE-CEU Working Papers* Series 28-P. Oxford: Oxford University Press.

Prewitt, Kenneth. 1971. *Education and Political Values: An East African Case Study*. Nairobi: East African Publishing House.

Pritchett, Lant. 2004. "Access to Education." In *Global Crises, Global Solutions*, edited by Bjørn Lomborg. Cambridge: Cambridge University Press.

Probe Team. 1999. *Public Report on Basic Education in India*. New Delhi: Oxford University Press.

Provincia de Santa Fe, Argentina. 1994. "Pliego de Bases y Condiciones Generales y Particulares para la Concesión del Servicio Público de Agua Potable y Desagües Cloacales en el Ámbito de la Dirección Provincial de Obras Sanitarias." Santa Fe, Argentina: Provincia de Santa Fe.

Putnam, Robert D., Robert Leonard, and Raffaella Nanetti. 1993. *Making Democracy Work: Civic Traditions in Modern Italy*. Princeton: Princeton University Press.

Quadagno, Jill, and Deana Rohlinger. 2009. "Religious Conservatives in U.S. Welfare State Politics." In *The Western Welfare State and Its Religious Roots*, edited by K. Van Kersbergen and P. Manow. New York: Cambridge University Press.

Radon, J. 2007. "How to Negotiate an Oil Agreement." In *Escaping the Resource Curse*, edited by M. Humphreys, J. D. Sachs, and J. E. Stiglitz. New York: Columbia University Press.

Ramamurthy, S., and Elvind Tandberg. 2002. *Treasury Reform in Kazakhstan: Lessons for Other Countries*. IMF Working Paper No. 02/129, Washington, DC: IMF.

Rawls, John. 1971. *A Theory of Justice*. Cambridge: Belknap Press of Harvard University Press.

Reddy, G. R., and G. Haragopal. 1985. "The Pyraveerkar: The Fixer in Rural India." *Asian Survey* 25 (11): 1147–62.

Reilly, Charles, ed. 1995. *New Paths to Democratic Development in Latin America: The Rise of NGO-Municipal Collaboration*. Boulder, CO: Lynne Rienner.

Rhodes, Sybil. 2006. *Social Movements and Free-Market Capitalism in Latin America: Telecommunications Privatization and the Rise of Consumer Protest*. Albany: State University of New York Press.

Rice, Susan E., and Stewart Patrick. 2008. *Index of State Weakness in the Developing World*. Washington, DC: Brookings Institution.

Rose, Pauline. 2006. "Collaborating in Education for All? Experiences of Government Support for Non-state Provision of Basic Education in South Asia and Sub-Saharan Africa." *Public Administration and Development* 26:219–29.

———, ed. 2010. *Achieving Education for All through Public-Private Partnerships? Non-State Provision of Education in Developing Countries*. London: Routledge.

Rostow, W. W. 1962. *The Stages of Economic Growth*. New York: Cambridge University Press.

Rotberg, Robert. 2003a. *State Failure and State Weakness in a Time of Terror*. Washington, DC: Brookings Institution.

———. 2003b. "Failed States, Collapsed States, Weak States: Causes and Indicators." In *State Failure and State Weakness in a Time of Terror*, edited by Robert Rotberg. Washington, DC: Brookings Institution Press.

Rozhdestvenskaya, Irina, and Sergei Shishkin. 2003. "Institutional Reforms in the Social-Cultural Sphere." In *The Economics of Transition*, edited by Yegor Gaidar, 584–615. Cambridge, MA: MIT Press.

Rubin, Barnett. 2002. *The Fragmentation of Afghanistan: State Formation and Collapse in the International System*. New Haven: Yale University Press.

Rudra, Nita. 2002. "Globalization and the Decline of the Welfare State in Less-Developed Countries." *International Organization* 56 (2): 411–45.

———. 2007. "Welfare States in Developing Countries: Unique or Universal?" *Journal of Politics* 69 (2): 378–96.

Rueschemeyer, D., E.H. Stephens, and J.D. Stephens. 1992. *Capitalist Development and Democracy*. Cambridge: Cambridge University Press.

Russian Ministry of Health. 1998. "Interview with Judyth Twigg, Head of Dept. of Organization and Control of Medical Care for the Population, Trip Report (transcript)." Moscow, Russia, June 23–24.

Ryan, Michael. 1992. "Russia Report: Doctors and Health Service Reform." *British Medical Journal* 304 (January 11): 101–3.

Sacks, Audrey, and Marco Larizza. 2012. "Why Quality Matters: Rebuilding Trustworthy Local Government in Post-Conflict Sierra Leone." In *Policy Research Working Paper 6021*. Washington, DC: World Bank.

Sagheb, N., and M. Javadi. 1994. "Azerbaijan's 'Contract of the Century' Finally Signed with Western Oil Consortium." *Azerbaijan International* 2 (4).

Salamon, Lester M. 1994. "The Rise of the Nonprofit Sector." *Foreign Affairs* 73 (4): 109–22.

———. 1999. *America's Nonprofit Sector*. New York: Foundation Center.

———. 2002. "The Resilient Sector: The State of Nonprofit America." In *The State of Nonprofit America*, edited by L.M. Salamon. Washington, DC: Brookings Institution Press.

Salamon, Lester M., and Helmut K. Anheier. 1992. "In Search of the Non-Profit Sector." *Voluntas: International Society for Third-Sector Research* 3 (2): 125–51.

Salamon, Lester M., and S. Wojciech Sokolowski. 1999. *Global Civil Society: Dimensions of the Nonprofit Sector*. Baltimore: Johns Hopkins University, Center for Civil Society Studies.

Salibi, Kamal. 1966. "Lebanon under Fuad Chehab, 1958–1964." *Middle Eastern Studies* 2 (3): 211–26.

———. 1976. *Crossroads to a Civil War: Lebanon, 1958–1976*. Delmar, NY: Caravan.

Salti, Nisreen, Jad Chaaban, and Firas Raad. 2010. "Health Equity in Lebanon: A Microeconomic Analysis." *International Journal for Equity in Health* 9 (11): 1–28.

Saltman, Richard B., and Odile Ferroussier-Davis. 2000. "The Concept of Stewardship in Health Policy." *Bulletin of the World Health Organization* 78 (6): 732–39.

Sandberg, E. 1994. *The Changing Politics of Non-governmental Organizations and African States*. Westport, CT: Praeger.

Sanyal, Bishwapriya. 1994. "Co-operative Autonomy: The Dialectic of State-NGOs Relationship in Developing Countries." In *International Institute for Labour Studies Research Series 100*. Geneva: International Institute for Labour Studies, International Labour Organization.

Sarker, Profulla, and Gareth Davey. 2009. "Exclusion of Indigenous Children from Primary Education in the Rajshahi Division of Northwestern Bangladesh." *International Journal of Inclusive Education* 13 (1): 1–11.

Satarov, Georgi, ed. 2001. *Russian Anticorruption Diagnostics: Sociological Analysis*. Moscow: Information Science for Democracy (INDEM).

Satterthwaite, D. 2006. "The Role of Federations Formed by the Urban Poor in Communal Asset Accumulation." Paper presented at the Brookings Institution/Ford Foundation Workshop on Asset-Based Approaches to Poverty Reduction in a Globalized Context, Washington DC, June 27–28.

Savedoff, William, and Pablo Spiller. 1999. *Spilled Water: Institutional Commitment in the Provision of Water Services*. Washington, DC: Inter-American Development Bank.

Save the Children. 2005. *Beyond Rhetoric, Measuring Revenue Transparency: Company Performance in the Oil and Gas Industries*. London: Save the Children.

Sawyer, S. 2004. *Crude Chronicles: Indigenous Politics, Multinational Oil, and Neoliberalism in Ecuador*. Durham, NC: Duke University Press.

Sbaiti, Nadya Jeanne. 2008. "Lessons in History: Education and the Formation of National Society in Beirut, Lebanon, 1920–1960s." PhD diss., Georgetown University.

Schatzberg, Michael. 2001. *Political Legitimacy in Middle Africa: Father, Family, Food*. Bloomington: Indiana University Press.

Schlesinger, Mark. 2002. "On Values and Democratic Policymaking: The Fragile Consensus around Market-Oriented Medical Care." *Journal of Health Care Politics, Policy, and Law* 27 (6): 889–926.

Schneider, Ben Ross, and David Soskice. 2009. "Inequality in Developed Countries and Latin America: Coordinated, Liberal, and Hierarchical Systems." *Economy and Society* 38 (1): 17–52.

Schönwälder, G. 1997. "New Democratic Spaces at the Grassroots? Popular Participation in Latin American Local Governments." *Development and Change* 28:753–70.

Sclar, Elliott D. 2000. *You Don't Always Get What You Pay For: The Economics of Privatization*. Ithaca: Cornell University Press.

Scott, James C. 1976. *The Moral Economy of the Peasant: Rebellion and Subsistence in Southeast Asia*. New Haven: Yale University Press.

Seay, Laura E. 2012. "Substituting for the State: Evaluating Community Responses to State Fragility in the Eastern D. R. Congo." Atlanta, GA: Dept. of Political Science, Morehouse College.

———. 2013. "Effective Responses: Protestants, Catholics, and the Provision of Health Care in the Post-war Kivus." *Review of African Political Economy* 40 (135): 83–97.

———. Forthcoming. "Post-Conflict Authority and State Reconstruction in the Eastern Democratic Republic of Congo." In *War and Peace in Africa: History, Nationalism and the State*, edited by Raphael C. Njoku. Trenton, NJ: Africa World Press.

Seekings, Jeremy. 2008. "Welfare Regimes and Redistribution in the South." In *Divide and Deal: The Politics of Distribution in Democracies*, edited by Ian Shapiro, Peter A. Swenson, and Daniela Donno, 19–42. New York: New York University Press.

———. 2009. *Building Welfare States in the Global South: The Origins of Divergent Welfare Regimes*. Cape Town: University of Cape Town.

Segura-Ubiergo, Alex. 2007. *The Political Economy of the Welfare State in Latin America*. Cambridge: Cambridge University Press.

Selznick, Philip. 1949. *TVA and the Grass Roots*. Berkeley: University of California Press.

Sen, Amartya. 2000. *Development as Freedom*. New York: Anchor Press.

———. 2006. *Identity and Violence: The Illusion of Destiny*. London: Allen Lane.

Shadid, Anthony. 2002. *Legacy of the Prophet: Despots, Democrats, and the New Politics of Islam*. Boulder, CO: Westview.

Shamir, Ronen. 2004. "The De-Radicalization of Corporate Social Responsibility." *Critical Sociology* 30 (3): 669–89.

Shishkin, S. V., ed. 2006. *Zdravookhranenie Regionakh Rossiiskoi Federatsii: Mekhanismy Financirovaniia I Upravleniia* [Health care in the regions of the Russian Federation: Mechanisms of financing and administration]. Moscow: Nezavisimii Institut Sotsial'noi Politiki.

Shishkin, S. V., T. V. Bogatova, Y. G. Potapchik, V. A. Chernets, A. Y. Chirikova, and L. S. Shilova. 2003. *Informal Out-of-Pocket Payments for Health Care in Russia*. Moscow: Moscow Public Science Foundation.

Shishkin, S. V., N. V. Bondarenko, A. Ia. Burdiak, K. M. Kel'manzon, M. D. Krasil'nikova, L. D. Popovich, S. V. Svetlichnaia, E. V. Selezneva, I. M. Sheiman, and V. I. Shevskii. 2008a. *Rossiiskoe Zdravookhraninie: Motivatsiia Vrachei I obshchestvennaia Dostupnost'* [Russian health care: Motivations of doctors and social accessibility]. Moscow: Nezavisimii Institut Sotsial'noi Politiki.

Shishkin, S. V., A. Ia. Burdiak, and E. V. Selezneva. 2008b. "Razlichiia v dostupnosti medit-sinskio pomoshchi dlia naseleniia Rossii" [Variation in access to medical care for Russia's population]. *Spero* 8:135–58. Available at http://spero.socpol.ru/docs/N8_2008-135-158.pdf.

Sikkink, Kathryn, and Jackie Smith. 2002. "Infrastructures for Change: Transnational Organizations, 1953–1993." In *Restructuring World Politics: The Power of Transnational Agency and Norms*, edited by S. Khagram, J. Riker, and K. Sikkink, 24–44. Minneapolis: University of Minnesota Press.

Singer, Amy. 2008. *Charity in Islamic Societies*. Themes in Islamic History. Cambridge: Cambridge University Press.

Skavdal, Terje. 2003. "NGO Networking and Cooperation towards Total Disaster Risk Management in Asia." Presentation at the International Conference on Total Disaster Risk Management, Asian Disaster Reduction Centre, Kobe, Japan, December 2–4.

Skjaerseth, Jon Birger, Kristian Tangen, Philip Swanson, Atle Christer Christiansen, Arild Moe, and Leiv Lunde. 2004. *Limits to Corporate Social Responsibility: A Comparative Study of Four Major Oil Companies*. Fridtjof Nansen Institute Report 7. Lysaker, Norway: Fridtjof Nansen Institute.

Skocpol, Theda. 1992. *Protecting Soldiers and Mothers: The Political Origins of Social Policy in the United States*. Cambridge: Belknap Press of Harvard University Press.

———. 2003. *Diminished Democracy: From Membership to Management in American Civic Life*. Norman: University of Oklahoma Press.

Smith, B. C. 1985. *Decentralization*. London: George Allen & Unwin.

Smith, E. E., and J. S. Dzienkowski. 1989. *A Fifty-Year Perspective on World Petroleum Arrangements*. Austin: University of Texas at Austin School of Law Publications.

Smith, Steven R. 2012. "Social Services." In *The State of Nonprofit America*, edited by L. M. Salamon. Washington, DC: Brookings Institution Press.

Smith, Steven R., and Michael Lipsky. 1993. *Non-profits for Hire: The Welfare State in the Age of Contracting*. Cambridge: Harvard University Press.

Smith, Steven R., Michael R. Sosin, Lucy Jordan, and Tim Hilton. 2006. "State Fiscal Crises and Social Services." Paper presented at the meeting of the Association for Public Policy Analysis and Management Conference, Madison, WI, November 2–4.

Smith, David N., and Louis T. Wells Jr. 1975. *Negotiating Third-World Mineral Agreements: Promises as Prologue*. Cambridge, MA: Ballinger Publishing.

Smoke, Paul, and Blaine D. Lewis. 1996. "Fiscal Decentralization in Indonesia: A New Approach to an Old Idea." *World Development* 24 (8): 1281–99.

Snider, Lewis W. 1984. "The Lebanese Forces: Their Origins and Role in Lebanon's Politics." *Middle East Journal* 38 (1): 1–33.

Society for Participatory Research in Asia (PRIA). 2002. *Invisible, Yet Widespread: The Non-Profit Sector in India*. New Delhi: PRIA.

Soifer, Hillel. 2012. "Measuring State Capacity in Contemporary Latin America." Paper presented at the annual meeting of the American Political Science Association, New Orleans, LA, August 30–September 2.

———. 2013. "State Power and the Economic Origins of Democracy." *Studies in Comparative International Development* 48 (1): 1–22.

Soss, Joe, and Sanford F. Schram. 2007. "A Public Transformed? Welfare Reform as Policy Feedback." *American Political Science Review* 101 (1): 111–27.

Sparr, Pamela. 1994. "Feminist Critiques of Structural Adjustment." In *Mortgaging Women's Lives: Feminist Critiques of Structural Adjustment*, edited by Pamela Sparr. London: Zed Books.

Stallings, Barbara. 1992. "International Influence on Economic Policy: Debt, Stabilization, and Structural Reform." In *The Politics of Economic Adjustment: International Constraints, Distributive Conflicts, and the State*, edited by Stephan Haggard and Robert Kaufman. Princeton: Princeton University Press.

Stein, Ernesto, Mariano Tommasi, Koldo Echebarria, Eduardo Lora, and Mark Payne. 2005. *The Politics of Policies.* Washington, DC: Inter-American Development Bank.

Steketee, Amy M. 2004. "For-Profit Education Service Providers in Primary and Secondary Schooling: The Drive for and Consequences of Global Expansion." *Indiana Journal of Global Legal Studies* 11 (2): 171–203.

Stiglitz, Joseph E. 2005. "Rational Peasants, Efficient Institutions, and a Theory of Rural Organization: Methodological Remarks for Development Economics." In *New Institutions for Agrarian Change,* edited by Pranab Bardhan. Cambridge, MA: MIT Press.

———. 2007. "What Is the Role of the State?" In *Escaping the Resource Curse,* edited by M. Humphreys, J. D. Sachs, and J. E. Stiglitz. New York: Columbia University Press.

Stryker, J. Dirck. 1990. *Trade, Exchange Rate and Agricultural Pricing Policies in Ghana.* Washington, DC: World Bank.

Tabbarah, Riad. 2000. *The Health Sector in Lebanon.* Beirut: Center for Development Studies and Projects (MADMA).

Takyi, B. K. 2003. "Religion and Women's Health in Ghana: Insights into HIV/AIDS Preventive and Protective Behavior." *Social Science and Medicine 56.*

Tandon, Rajesh, and Kaustuv Kanti Bandyopadhyay. 2003. *Capacity Building of Southern NGOs: Lessons from International Forum on Capacity Building.* New Delhi: Society for Participatory Research in Asia.

Tanzer, M. 1969. *The Political Economy of International Oil and the Underdeveloped Countries.* Boston: Beacon Press.

Teamey, Kelly. 2007. *Whose Public Action? Analysing Inter-Sectoral Collaboration for Service Delivery: Literature Review on Relationships between Government and Non-State Providers of Services.* Birmingham, UK: International Development Department, School of Public Policy, University of Birmingham.

Technical Assistance to the Commonwealth of Independent States (TACIS). 1999. *Public-Private Mix in the Health Care and Health Insurance System: Current Situation, Problems, Perspectives.* TACIS Project No. EDRUS 9605. Moscow: TACIS.

Teichman, Judith. 2001. *The Politics of Freeing Markets in Latin America.* Chapel Hill: University of North Carolina Press.

Tendler, Judith. 1997. *Good Government in the Tropics.* Baltimore: Johns Hopkins University Press.

Thachil, Tariq. Forthcoming. *Recruiting the Poor, Retaining the Rich: Social Services as Electoral Strategy in India.* New York: Cambridge University Press.

Therborn, Goran. 1992. "The Right to Vote and the Four World Routes to/through Modernity." In *State Theory and State History,* edited by R. Thorstendahl. London: Sage.

Thompson, Robin, and Sophie Witter. 2000. "Informal Payments in Transitional Economies: Implications for Health Sector Reform." *International Journal of Health Planning and Management* 15:169–87.

Tompson, William. 2007. "Healthcare Reform in Russia: Problems and Prospects." Economics Dept. Working Papers No. 538. Paris: Organization for Economic Cooperation and Development.

Torche, Florencia. 2005. "Privatization Reform and Inequality of Educational Opportunity: The Case of Chile." *Sociology of Education* 78:316–43.

Townsend, Douglass. 2002. "Azerbaijan Country Update." *ITIC Bulletin* (April 19).

Traboulsi, Fawwaz. 2007. *A History of Modern Lebanon.* London: Pluto.

Tragakes, E., and S. Lessof. 2003. "Health Care Systems in Transition: Russian Federation." In *Health Care Systems in Transition,* edited by E. Tragakes. Copenhagen: European Observatory on Health Systems and Policies.

Traverso, Alejandro. 2004. "Las nuevas reformas que la reforma engendra." *En Foco* 26, expansiva.

Treakle, Kay. 1998. "Ecuador: Structural Adjustment and Indigenous and Environmental Resistance." In *The Struggle for Accountability,* edited by J. A. Fox and L. D. Brown, 219–64. Cambridge, MA: MIT Press.

Tripp, Aili Mari. 1997. *Changing the Rules: The Politics of Liberalization and the Informal Economy in Tanzania*. Berkeley: University of California Press.

———. 2001. "The Politics of Autonomy and Cooptation in Africa: The Case of the Ugandan Women's Movement." *Journal of Modern African Studies* 39 (1): 101–28.

Tsai, Lily. 2011. "Friends or Foes? Nonstate Public Goods Providers and Local State Authorities in Nondemocratic and Transitional Systems." *Studies in Comparative International Development* 46 (1): 46–69.

Twigg, Judyth.1998. "Balancing State and Market: Russia's Adoption of Obligatory Medical Insurance." *Europe-Asia Studies* 50 (4): 586.

———. 1999. "Obligatory Medical Insurance in Russia: The Participants' Perspective." *Social Science and Medicine* 49:377.

United Nations. 2012. *UN Global Compact*. Available at http://www.unglobalcompact.org.

United Nations Development Program. 2005. *The Great Generation of Kazakhstan: Insight into the Future*. National Human Development Report. Almaty, Kazakhstan: UNDP.

U.N.-Habitat 2001. *Cities in a Globalizing World: Global Report on Human Settlements*. London: Earthscan; New York: United Nations.

United Republic of Tanzania. 2001. *The National Policy on Non-Governmental Organizations (NGOs)*. Dar es Salaam: Vice President's Office. Available at http://www.tnnc.go.tz/onlinedocuments/NGO_Policy_2002_English.pdf.

U.S. Agency for International Development (USAID). 1999. *Participation at USAID: Stories, Lessons, and Challenges*, USAID Participation Forum Summaries. Washington, DC: USAID.

———. 2000. *2000 NGO Sustainability Index for Central and Eastern Europe and Eurasia*. Washington, DC: USAID.

———. 2011. *2011 NGO Sustainability Index for Sub-Saharan Africa*. Washington, DC: USAID.

———. 2011. *2011 CSO Sustainability Index for Central and Eastern Europe and Eurasia*. Washington, DC: USAID.

U.S. Department of Health and Human Services. 2009. "TANF Financial Data." Available at http://www.acf.hhs.gov/programs/ofs/data/index.html.

U.S. Department of State. 1998. *Kenya Report on Human Rights Practices for 1997*. Washington, DC: Bureau of Democracy, Human Rights, and Labor.

U.S. Department of the Treasury, Internal Revenue Service. 2009. "Exempt Requirements." Available at http://www.irs.gov/charities/charitable/article/0,,id=96099,00.html.

Uvin, Peter. 1998. *Aiding Violence: The Development Enterprise in Rwanda*. West Hartford, CT: Kumarian Press.

Vacroux, Alexandra. 2004. "Regulation and Corruption in Transition: The Case of the Russian Pharmaceutical Markets." In *Building a Trustworthy State in Post-Socialist Transition*, edited by Janos Kornai and Susan Rose-Ackerman. New York: Palgrave Macmillan.

———. 2005. "Formal and Informal Institutional Change: The Evolution of Pharmaceutical Regulation in Russia, 1991–2004." PhD diss., Harvard University.

———. 2006. "Decentralization Was Bad, but Will Recentralization Be Worse? What Failed Health Care Reforms Tell Us about the Russian State." Prepared for SSRC Training Seminar for Policy Research, "Public Health, Social Welfare Systems, and HIV/AIDS in Eurasia," New York and Washington, DC, June 6–9.

Vaillant, Denise. 2005. *Education Reforms and Teachers' Unions*. Paris: United Nations Educational, Scientific and Cultural Organization (UNESCO).

van de Walle, Nicolas 2001. *African Economies and the Politics of Permanent Crisis, 1979–1999: Political Economy of Institutions and Decisions*. New York: Cambridge University Press.

van Kersbergen, K., and P. Manow, eds. (2009). *The Western Welfare State and Its Religious Roots*. New York: Cambridge University Press.

Varshney, Ashutosh. 2001. "Ethnic Conflict and Civil Society: India and Beyond." *World Politics* 53:362–98.

Vernon, Raymond. 1971. *Sovereignty at Bay*. New York: Basic Books.

Vilas, C. M. 1997. "Participation, Inequality and the Whereabouts of Democracy." In *The New Politics of Inequality in Latin America*, edited by D. Chalmers, C. Vilas, K. Hite, S. Martin, K. Piester, and M. Segarra, 3–42. Oxford: Oxford University Press.

Vogel, David. 2005. *The Market for Virtue: The Potential and Limits of Corporate Social Responsibility*. Washington, DC: Brookings Institution.

von Benda Beckmann, Franz, Keebet von Benda Beckmann, E. Casiño, F. Hirtz, G. R. Woodman, and H. Zacher. 1988. *Between Kinship and the State: Social Security and Law in Developing Countries*. Dordrecht, Netherlands: Foris Publications.

von Benda Beckmann, Franz, and Renate Kirsch. 1999. "Informal Security Systems in Southern Africa and Approaches to Strengthen Them through Policy Measures." *Journal of Social Development in Africa* 14 (2): 21–38.

Watters, K. 2000. "Environment and the Development of Civil Society in the Caspian Region: The Role of NGOs." In *The Caspian Sea: A Quest for Environmental Security*, edited by W. Ascher and N. Mirovitskaya. Dordrecht, Netherlands: Kluwer.

Weber, Max. 1946. "Politics as a Vocation." In *From Max Weber: Essays in Sociology*, edited by H. H. Gerth and C. W. Mills. New York: Oxford University Press.

Weiner, M. 1963. *Political Change in South Asia*. Calcutta: K. L. Mukhopadhyaya.

———. 1989. *The Indian Paradox: Essays in Indian Politics*. New Delhi: Sage Publications.

Weinstein, Jeremy M. 2007. *Inside Rebellion: The Politics of Insurgent Violence*. Cambridge Studies in Comparative Politics. Cambridge: Cambridge University Press.

Wells, D. A. 1971. "Aramco: The Evolution of an Oil Concession." In *Foreign Investment in the Petroleum and Mineral Industries: Case Studies of Investor–Host Country Relations*, edited by R. F. Mikesell. Baltimore: Johns Hopkins University Press.

Wells, Louis, and Rafiq Ahmed. 2006. *Making Foreign Investment Safe: Property Rights and National Sovereignty*. Oxford: Oxford University Press.

Weyland, Kurt. 2005. "Theories of Policy Diffusion: Lessons from Latin American Pension Reform." *World Politics* 57:262–95.

Whaites, Alan. 1998. "NGOs, Civil Society, and the State: Avoiding Theoretical Extremes in Real World Issues." *Development in Practice* 8 (3): 343–49.

Wilkins, M. 1974. "Multinational Oil Companies in South America in the 1920s: Argentina, Bolivia, Brazil, Chile, Colombia, Ecuador, and Peru." *Business History Review* 48 (3): 414–46.

Williams, Colin C. 2009. "The Hidden Economy in East-Central Europe: Lessons from a Ten-Nation Survey." *Problems of Post-Communism* 56 (4): 15–28.

Wood, Geoffrey D. 1997. "States without Citizens: The Problem of the Franchise State." In *NGOs, States and Donors: Too Close for Comfort?*, edited by D. Hulme and M. Edwards, 79–92. London: Macmillan.

———. 2004. "Informal Security Regimes: The Strength of Relationships." In *Insecurity and Welfare Regimes in Asia, Africa and Latin America*, edited by I. Gough, G. Wood, A. Barrientos, P. Bevan, P. Davis, and G. Room, 49–87. Cambridge: Cambridge University Press.

Wood, Geoffrey, and Ian Gough. 2006. "A Comparative Welfare Regimes Approach to Global Social Policy." *World Development* 34 (10): 1696–1712.

Woods, Dwayne. 1994. "Elites, Ethnicity, and 'Home Town' Associations in the Côte d'Ivoire: An Historical Analysis of State-Society Links." *Africa: Journal of the International African Institute* 64 (4): 465–83.

Woodward, D. 2002. Interview on Azadliq radio. August 20. Available at http://www.azadliq.org.

World Bank. 1981. *Accelerated Development in Sub-Saharan Africa: An Agenda for Action*. Washington, DC: World Bank.

———. 1993. *World Development Report 1993: Investing in Health*. Oxford: Oxford University Press.

———. 1994. *Averting the Old Age Crisis: Policies to Protect the Old and Promote Growth.* New York: Oxford University Press.

———. 1996. *The World Bank Participation Sourcebook.* Washington, DC: World Bank.

———. 1997. *World Development Report: The State in a Changing World.* Washington, DC: World Bank.

———. 2000. *Health Sector in Lebanon: Issues and Prospects.* Washington, DC: Human Development Group, Middle East and North Africa.

———. 2001–02. *World Development Report: Attacking Poverty.* Washington, DC: World Bank.

———. 2004a. *Extractive Industries Review.* Washington, DC: World Bank.

———. 2004b. *World Development Report 2004: Making Services Work for the Poor.* Washington, DC: World Bank.

———. 2005. *Russian Federation: Reducing Poverty through Growth and Social Policy Reform.* Report No. 28923-RU. Washington, DC: World Bank.

———. 2006. *World Development Report 2006: Equity and Development.* Washington, DC: World Bank.

———. 2007. *World Development Report 2007: Development and the Next Generation.* Washington, DC: World Bank.

———. 2011. *Civil Society 2011.* Available at http://go.worldbank.org/19WRCK3AY0.

World Business Council for Sustainable Development (WBCSD). 2005. *The Akassa Community Development Project in Nigeria.* Geneva: WBCSD.

World Development Indicators. World Bank. Available at http://data.worldbank.org/data-catalog/world-development-indicators.

World Health Organization (WHO). 2000. *World Health Report 2000: Health Systems: Improving Performance.* Geneva: WHO.

———. 2006. "European HFA Database, 2006." Geneva: WHO.

World Health Organization Statistical Information System (WHOSIS). Available at http://www.who.int/whosis/en/.

World Health Organization and United Nations Children's Fund Joint Monitoring Programme for Water Supply and Sanitation (JMP). 2008. *Progress on Drinking Water and Sanitation: Special Focus on Sanitation.* New York: United Nation's Children's Fund (UNICEF); Geneva: World Health Organization (WHO).

World Vision International. *2009 Review.* Middlesex, UK: World Vision International.

Wrong, Michela. 2009. *It's Our Turn to Eat: The Story of a Kenyan Whistleblower.* New York: HarperCollins.

Wuthnow, Robert. 2004. *Saving America? Faith-Based Services and the Future of Civil Society.* Princeton: Princeton University Press.

Yadav, Yogendra. 1999. "Electoral Politics in the Time of Change: India's Third Electoral System, 1989–99." *Bombay: Economic and Political Weekly* (August 21): 2391–99.

———. 2000. "Understanding the Second Democratic Upsurge: Trends of Bahujan Participation in Electoral Politics in the 1990s." In *Transforming India: Social and Political Dynamics of Democracy*, edited by Francine Frankel, Zoya Hasan, Rajeev Bhargava, and Balveer Arora, 120–45. Oxford: Oxford University Press.

Yang, Lijing, Liying Rong, and Feng Deng. 2008. *China Migrant Schools in the Last Two Decades: Emergence, Policy Changes, Teaching and Learning, and Policy Recommendations.* Ann Arbor: School of Education, University of Michigan.

Yessenova, Saulesh. 2008. "Tengiz Crude: A View from Below." In *The Economics and Politics of Oil in the Caspian Basin: The Redistribution of Oil Revenues in Azerbaijan and Central Asia*, edited by B. Najman, R. Pomfret, and G. Raballand, 176–98. New York: Routledge.

Young, Crawford. 1988. "The Colonial State and Its Political Legacy." In *The Precarious Balance: State and Society in Africa*, edited by Donald Rothchild and Naomi Chazan, 59–62. Boulder, CO: Westview.

Young Men's Christian Association (YMCA)–Lebanon. 2006. "List of Clinics and Dispensaries in the MOPH Chronic Disease Medications Program." Beirut: YMCA.

Yudaeva, Ksenia, and Maria Gorban. 1999. "Health and Health Care." *Russian Economic Trends* 8 (2): 27–35.

Zivetz, Laurie. 2006. "Health Service Delivery in Early Recovery Fragile States: Lessons from Afghanistan, Cambodia, Mozambique, and Timor Leste." In *Basic Support for Institutionalizing Child Survival (BASICS) Final Report.* Arlington, VA: U.S. Agency for International Development.

Contributors

Scott W. Allard is an Associate Professor in the School of Social Service Administration at the University of Chicago and a Research Associate of the Population Research Center at NORC and the University of Chicago.

Jennifer N. Brass is an Assistant Professor at the School of Public and Environmental Affairs at Indiana University.

Melani Cammett is an Associate Professor of Political Science at Brown University.

Linda J. Cook is a Professor of Political Science and Chesler-Mallow Senior Research Fellow, Pembroke Center at Brown University.

Ian Gough is a Visiting Professor in the Center for the Analysis of Social Exclusion and an Associate at the Grantham Research Institute on Climate Change and the Environment at the London School of Economics. Gough is Professor Emeritus of Social Policy at the University of Bath.

Michael Jennings is a Senior Lecturer in the Department of Development Studies and Chair of the Centre of African Studies at the School of Oriental and African Studies.

Anirudh Krishna is a Professor of Public Policy and Political Science and Associate Dean for International Academic Programs at the Sanford School of Public Policy at Duke University.

Pauline Jones Luong is a Professor of Political Science and Director of the Islamic Studies Program at the University of Michigan.

Lauren M. MacLean is an Associate Professor of Political Science at Indiana University.

Alejandra Mizala is a Professor at the University of Chile with the Centro de Economía Aplicada in the Department of Industrial Engineering. She is the Director of the Department of Industrial Engineering at the University of Chile and also the Academic Director of the Center for Advanced Research in Education at the University of Chile.

Alison E. Post is an Assistant Professor of Political Science and Global Metropolitan Studies at the University of California at Berkeley.

Ben Ross Schneider is the Ford International Professor of Political Science and Director of the Brazil Program at the Massachusetts Institute of Technology.

Index

accountability
  to citizens of non-state provision, 3, 36–38
  in education system, 207, 214
  and measure of, 263–66
  and naya netas, 175
  and nongovernmental organization role in, 100–101, 114
  and non-state provider type, 33
  and privatization, 85–89, 219
advanced industrialized country, 4, 42, 52. *See also* United States
advocacy
  and citizen, 210–12
  and international nongovernmental organization, 85–86, 131
  and nongovernmental organization, 112–13
  and nonprofit, 243, 253–55
appropriation
  definition of, 29, 51, 161
  example of, 52–53, 148–52, 175–77, 219, 224, 268
  See also informal broker
Argentina
  domestic firm role in privatization, 28, 44, 81–83, 87–91, 94–95
  politics of provision, 85–87, 92–93, 96
  state role, 84–85, 88, 94, 265, 267–68
  water and sanitation system management, 9, 78–80, 84
  See also privatization
Azerbaijan
  corporate social responsibility (CSR), 43, 63–65, 70–71, 74

foreign oil company (FOC), current role, 27, 68–72
  government accountability, 58, 75
  local development, 43, 65, 71, 74
authoritarianism, 53, 105, 195
autonomy
  and education provision, 199–200, 207
  of faith-based organization, 132
  and NGO–state relations, 100–101, 105–8
  of non-state welfare provision, 238, 249

Bismarck, Otto von, 2, 219
brokerage system
  and appropriation, 29
  and health care access, 138, 148, 153, 219
  and informal institution, 157, 161
  and naya netas, 175–77
  See also informal broker

Catholic Church, 47–48, 121–22, 125–28, 131. *See also* religion
Chile
  accountability, 196, 200, 204, 209, 212, 265
  non-state role in education, 195, 207, 211, 213–14, 265
  state role in education, 197, 202, 205, 207–11, 213, 267
  voucher system, 195, 197, 203–14
Christians, 121–28, 131–34, 138, 143–44. *See also* faith-based organization; missionary